THE MARXIST AND THE MOVIES

SCREEN CLASSICS

Screen Classics is a series of critical biographies, film histories, and analytical studies focusing on neglected filmmakers and important screen artists and subjects, from the era of silent cinema to the golden age of Hollywood to the international generation of today. Books in the Screen Classics series are intended for scholars and general readers alike. The contributing authors are established figures in their respective fields. This series also serves the purpose of advancing scholarship on film personalities and themes with ties to Kentucky.

Series Editor
Patrick McGilligan

THE MARXIST AND THE MOVIES

A BIOGRAPHY OF PAUL JARRICO

LARRY CEPLAIR

THE UNIVERSITY PRESS OF KENTUCKY

Publication of this volume was made possible in part by a grant from the National Endowment for the Humanities.

Scholarly publisher for the Commonwealth,
serving Bellarmine University, Berea College, Centre College of Kentucky, Eastern Kentucky University, The Filson Historical Society, Georgetown College, Kentucky Historical Society, Kentucky State University, Morehead State University, Murray State University, Northern Kentucky University, Transylvania University, University of Kentucky, University of Louisville, and Western Kentucky University.

Editorial and Sales Offices: The University Press of Kentucky
663 South Limestone Street, Lexington, Kentucky 40508-4008
www.kentuckypress.com

11 10 09 08 07 5 4 3 2 1

Library of Congress Cataloging-in-Publication Data
Ceplair, Larry.
The Marxist and the movies : a biography of Paul Jarrico / Larry Ceplair.
p. cm. — (Screen classics)
Includes bibliographical references and index.
ISBN 978-0-8131-2453-7 (acid-free paper)
1. Jarrico, Paul. 2. Screenwriters—United States—Biography. 3. Motion picture industry—United States. 4. Blacklisting of entertainers—United States. 5. Communism and motion pictures—United States. 6. Hollywood (Los Angeles, Calif.)—History. 7. United States. Congress. House. Committee on Un-American Activities. I. Title.
PS3519.A89Z63 2007
808.2'3092—dc22
[B]
2007019777

This book is printed on acid-free recycled paper meeting the requirements of the American National Standard for Permanence in Paper for Printed Library Materials.

Manufactured in the United States of America.

Member of the Association of
American University Presses

CONTENTS

PREFACE

> I've had a rich political life, a rich professional life, and a rich personal life. They've intersected each other in kaleidoscopic ways. I'm almost ready to try to capture its richness in some memoirs. . . . There will be no false modesty. I did some good things; also some foolish things. Ego is as fundamental as sex, and is expressed in as many curious ways.
>
> —*Paul Jarrico, 1984*

When one thinks of the motion picture blacklist, one of the first names that should come to mind is Paul Jarrico. No individual fought against it on so many fronts and for so long. And yet his name does not resonate with this generation. But to the more than one thousand people who gathered at the Samuel Goldwyn Theater at the headquarters of the Academy of Motion Picture Arts and Sciences on the night of October 27, 1997, Jarrico represented an era of American history. That night, on the fiftieth anniversary of the House Committee on Un-American Activities hearings that engendered the blacklist, the Screen Actors Guild, the Screen Directors Guild, the Writers Guild of America, west, and the American Federation of Television and Radio Artists sponsored the program "Hollywood Remembers the Blacklist." It culminated with the current presidents of the four guilds delivering speeches of apology for their organizations' complicity with the blacklist mechanism. Ring Lardner Jr., the last surviving member of the Hollywood Ten, and Jarrico came onto the stage to accept the apologies. Following a lengthy standing ovation, Jarrico told the audience that patriotism had a contradictory history in the United States: "Our brutal history defines patriotism as 'My country right or wrong.' Our noble history defines it as 'My country: Right the wrong.' Right the wrong. It may take another 50 years, but we shall overcome. The good guys will win."[1]

Though Jarrico was, from 1937 to 1951, a successful screenwriter, with many credits and a high weekly salary, he was not on the A list of blacklisted screenwriters. And when the blacklist began to weaken, Jarrico found himself stuck in Europe, unable to regain the footing he had lost in Hollywood. But Jarrico's life, thoroughly documented by the huge archive he so carefully amassed, offers an excellent lens through which to view the radical and mainstream political cultures of the United States during the twentieth century and, in particular, the relationship between a dedicated Marxist and the Hollywood motion picture industry. Though one may disagree with his political ideas and his interpretations of world events, one will not find in his long career of political activism an evil or immoral act.

Two of the people who knew him best, Sylvia Gussin Jarrico (his first wife) and Lia Benedetti Jarrico (his third wife), have been invaluable resources. Sylvia Jarrico has been a constant source of information for twenty-five years, and Lia Jarrico gave me full access to Jarrico's archive and has spoken to me at length about him. I dedicate this book to them and to my wife, Christine Holmgren, who read the entire manuscript, provided a host of helpful suggestions and comments, and made my life away from the word processor an ongoing joy.

Becca Wilson, Jarrico's niece, provided me with a treasure trove of documents that her father (and Jarrico's brother-in-law), screenwriter Michael Wilson, and others wrote for Hollywood Communist Party discussions. These documents illustrate some of the key cultural concerns of Hollywood Marxists.

I would also like to express my appreciation for the assistance provided to me by several archivists and librarians. First and foremost, I am deeply grateful to the staff at the Margaret Herrick Library, Academy of Motion Picture Arts and Sciences, Beverly Hills, California. They have been consistently helpful and courteous. I am especially grateful to Howard Prouty, Jennie Romero, and Barbara Hall. In addition, I wish to thank Ned Comstock (Cinema-

Television Library, University of Southern California, Los Angeles), Lauren Buisson (Arts Library Special Collections, University of California, Los Angeles), Susan Berry (Silver City Museum, Silver City, New Mexico), Pat Leonard (Miller Library Special Collections, Western New Mexico University, Silver City), and Dorinda Hartmann (Film and Photo Archive, Wisconsin Center for Film and Theater Research, State Historical Society of Wisconsin, Madison).

I also wish to thank the staff of the UCLA Oral History Program; Department of Special Collections, Charles E. Young Research Library; and the regents of the University of California for permission to reprint significant excerpts from Jarrico's oral history.

Finally, I am deeply grateful to Julie Popkin, my agent, for her efforts to place this manuscript, to William McKay and Leila Salisbury of the University Press of Kentucky, and to Anna Laura Bennett for her superb copyediting.

ABBREVIATIONS

AFL	American Federation of Labor
ASP	Council of the Arts, Sciences and Professions
CIO	Congress of Industrial Organizations
CPA	Communist Political Association
CPUSA	Communist Party of the United States of America
CPUSSR	Communist Party of the Union of Soviet Socialist Republics
CSU	Conference of Studio Unions
HWM	Hollywood Writers Mobilization
IATSE	International Alliance of Theatrical Stage Employees
IPC	Independent Productions Corporation
IUMMSW	International Union of Mine, Mill and Smelter Workers
MPA	Motion Picture Alliance for the Preservation of American Ideals

MPIC	Motion Picture Industry Council
NSL	National Student League
OWI	Office of War Information
PCA	Progressive Citizens of America
SACLA	Special agent in charge, Los Angeles (FBI)
SAG	Screen Actors Guild
SWG	Screen Writers Guild
WGAw	Writers Guild of America, west
YCL	Young Communist League

PART 1

SCREENWRITING

1

The Early Years, 1915–36

When I was younger it was my belief that egotism was the first principle of life. I felt that all human behavior, however complex, whether evil or noble, could be traced to the single motive of vanity. Was a man generous? It was for esteem. Did he keep his generosity secret? It was for self-esteem. Did he laugh? Only because he felt superior. Did he love? He loved himself. Friendship was flattery, art exhibitionism, religion fear of extinction. It was wonderful. Self-exaltation explained everything.

—*Paul Jarrico, 1943*

The Shapiros

The cultural and political basis of the style and work of Paul Jarrico rested on Russian Jewish socialism as mediated by his father, Aaron, and his uncle Chaim. Their father, Israel Gildenberg, was the younger of two sons. To save him from being drafted into the Russian army, his parents sent him to a family named Shapiro, and he took its name.[1] Israel Shapiro became a well-to-do merchant in Kremenchug, a city on the Kremenchug River in Ukraine. His first wife bore three daughters and died giving birth to the third. His second wife, Pesia, gave birth to four children: Aaron (born August 18, 1883), Chaim, Abram, and Kalia.

They, along with the vast bulk of Russia's Jews, lived in the Pale of Settlement, the restricted area designated by Empress Catherine II in 1794. It stretched from Kovno province in the north to Bessarabia and Taurida in the south. Its boundaries were explicitly defined in 1835 by Tsar Nicholas I, and the status of its inhabitants was systematically reduced by hundreds of ensuing decrees. When Alexander II (1855–81) eased many of the restrictions, especially those pertaining to educational opportunities, a small number of Jews rose to affluence. Jewish prosperity, however, enraged many Russians, anti-Semitic attitudes festered, and the first modern pogrom exploded in Odessa in 1871. Matters worsened after the assassination of Alexander II and the accession of Alexander III (1881–94). Six weeks after the assassination, a series of pogroms erupted in the area where the Shapiros lived. New laws, the so-called Temporary Rules (1882), struck hard at Jewish life, causing a general economic collapse in the Pale. Thousands began to leave for the United States. A small number began to think about immigrating to Palestine. A smaller number became radicalized, and a Jewish working-class movement began to form.

This movement took two main forms: social-democratic and Zionist-socialist. The social democrats created a central organization, the General Jewish Workers' League in Russia and Poland, in October 1897. It was popularly known as *Der Bund* (the league or alliance). Other socialist-minded Jews, more attuned to Jewish philosophical and messianic traditions and more attracted by the budding concept of Jewish nationalism, organized the Zionist-Socialist Party, Jewish Socialist Workers' Party, and Poale Zion Party.[2] Aaron and Chaim Shapiro became Zionist-Socialists.

As a youth growing up in Kremenchug, Aaron loved to fight the gangs of young Russians who bullied Jewish people. He was, his only son, Israel (henceforth Jarrico), later wrote, "certain he could beat up the whole world. One at a time. This certainty never left him."[3] In Minsk, where he went in 1896 to study at the yeshiva, Aaron became involved with Zionists and organized youth circles for the study of Jewish literature. The following year, he moved to Kharkov and became more militantly Zionist. He helped organize the first workers' Zionist group and a Jewish self-defense corps, purchased a gun, and, he told his son, allowed no one to belittle a Jew in his presence. Though Aaron continued his studies in Kharkov, he no longer considered himself a religious Jew, and he began preparing himself for entrance into the university. His political record, however, kept him from being admitted. Aaron was sentenced to prison as a "dangerous character" in 1902 or 1903. While he was in prison, in April 1903, one of the worst of the pogroms occurred in Kishinev (250 miles southwest of Kremenchug). Forty-five Jews were killed, nearly six hundred were wounded, and massive amounts of property were destroyed. When Aaron escaped from his imprisonment in November 1904, he decided that it was futile to continue to fight anti-Semitism in Russia, and he immigrated to the United States. The following year, his father died and his brother, Chaim, was arrested for political activity. In November 1906, after Chaim's six-month prison term, Chaim and Abram also immigrated to the United States.[4]

The brothers lived in New York City, where Aaron attended night school and supported himself by selling newspapers. In 1908, he met and "flipped over" Jennie Kraus, a married woman, who was eight years older. She was born on April 15, 1875, in Uzda, a village about twenty miles south of Minsk (Belorussia). She immigrated to the United States, married a man named Morris Kraus (né Krachinsky), and bore two children, Rose and Edward. When Jennie and her husband, who was suffering from tuberculosis, moved to Denver, Aaron boarded the same train. "My father," Jarrico later wrote, "stole my mother from a dying man."[5] Following her husband's death, Jennie moved to Los Angeles. Aaron again boarded the same train and moved into a house with her. She bought a grocery store and horse and wagon, and Aaron delivered for her, reading poetry while the horse led the way, and studied law at night.

Jennie was "very cute: beautiful black eyes, little turned-up nose." She was hard working and principled, and she believed that people should be responsible for one another. Lillian Blake, Kalia Shapiro's daughter, remembered that Jennie wrote poetry and had a great sense of humor. But Jennie was an unhappy person. She had diabetes, which occasionally made her irritable and confused, and she believed that the men in her life regularly misunderstood her.[6]

"My mother," Jarrico later said, "was educated in Yiddish and read quite widely in it, but she never quite learned English sufficiently. I remember her working hard to learn how to leave a properly written note to the milkman and so on." In a composition book, she wrote rough drafts of notes and letters. In one, she wrote, "When I was rearing my children I was too busy to pay attention to my education."[7] Her address book was written in English, Yiddish, and Russian. Most of her letters to her son were in Yiddish or were written in English for her, and all the surviving letters addressed to her are in Yiddish.

Aaron was well educated. He had a speaking, reading, and writing knowledge of Russian, Yiddish, Hebrew, and English. He frequently recited, from memory, large portions of the poetry of Aleksandr Pushkin, but he never lost his Russian Jewish accent, and his English poetry was not, in Jarrico's estimation, particularly good poetry. He was a passionate man who could swear in several languages and get along with anyone. Lillian Blake said that he was "the warmest, most loving and dear person I had ever known. He was very family oriented."[8]

The rest of the family followed Aaron to Los Angeles, part of a surge of eastern European Jewish immigration that began in 1904. About one-third of them would reside in Boyle Heights, on the east side of the city. As in most other cities, the new arrivals worked as shopkeepers, laborers, artisans, and clerks, while many of their children entered the professions. (Some of the new arrivals created and dominated the Hollywood motion picture industry.) There was also a noticeable divide between the earlier, assimilated Jewish settlers and the new arrivals. They did not worship in the same synagogues or belong to the same organizations.[9]

Chaim attended law school at the University of Southern California from 1911 to 1913, and he passed the bar in 1912. He was a member of the Law Lyceum (an oratory and debate club) and president of the Socialist Club (a twelve-member chapter of the Intercollegiate Socialist Society). When Jarrico later asked his uncle why he was a Socialist, Chaim replied, "Because I think every person should have enough money and leisure to be able to enjoy God's great outdoors. I think every person should have the time and education to enjoy good literature, art, and music. It is my belief that through Socialism, this can be accomplished."[10]

Aaron also attended the USC School of Law, from 1914 to 1916, but he did not receive a degree. In those days, one could take and pass the bar without a law degree, so Aaron probably apprenticed with Chaim and then passed the bar in 1916. Abram, younger and lacking the armed-defense experience of his brothers, had a different outlook.

He went to work in a lemon-packing plant, bought a saddle horse at a time when most Jews thought that horses should be used only to pull carts, moved out of Boyle Heights, and started a successful produce business. He did not become a part of organized Jewish life in Los Angeles, nor was he political.

Aaron and Chaim established the law firm of Shapiro and Shapiro to defend the poor, trade unionists, and immigrants threatened with expulsion and deportation. "They were," Jarrico remembered, "left-wing lawyers and people's lawyers. Didn't make much money, but again were very pleased with their function. I mean, they were really good people." Though Aaron and Chaim were Socialists and left-wing Zionists, Jarrico believed that their socialism supervened on their Jewishness. He described Aaron as "a Jew not simply politically but culturally." Aaron helped organize Poale Zion groups in New York and Los Angeles. He was district chairman of the Workmen's Circle and a delegate to the Jewish People's National Workers' conferences in New York City (1915 and 1920). He was one of four men appointed by the nascent Jewish Congress movement, in 1917, to organize a nominating convention, and he was one of the four nominated for president. (He finished a distant fourth.) He was also the first chairman of the Los Angeles Histadrut, founded in 1920 to organize the economic activities of Jewish workers. On the occasion of his fiftieth birthday, at a celebration sponsored by the Workmen's Circle and Poale Zion, the gatherers were told that Aaron was one of the pioneer Jewish organizers in Los Angeles, who "devoted his life, time and energies to make the Jewish life organized and representative."[11]

Aaron and Jennie actively campaigned for Socialist Party candidates and worked especially hard to elect Job Harriman as mayor of Los Angeles.[12] Eugene V. Debs, the founder of the Socialist Party and its perennial candidate for president of the United States (five times between 1900 and 1920), was one of their heroes. When Debs spoke in Los Angeles, shortly after his 1921 release from prison, Aaron took his son and held him up to shake hands with Debs. In 1932, Aaron spoke at a Debs memorial meeting and Socialist rally.

Chaim was state chairman of the California Socialist Party. He ran as a candidate for lieutenant governor with Upton Sinclair in 1930 and for mayor of Los Angeles in 1933. Aaron made many speeches supporting his brother's campaign for mayor. In one, he said, "Chaim Shapiro believes in the right to work, and that it is our most solemn duty to combine our efforts and to do away with unemployment. That we, the citizens of Los Angeles, with our great population can *if we will* bend our efforts and use our credit and put tens of thousands to work *immediately*. . . . We need better streets. We need more playgrounds. We need city-owned auditoriums and other places of amusement and education. . . . We believe in social justice. We believe in free speech and assembly." Chaim received only 4,702 votes out of 330,803. He lost, his nephew speculated, because he had "offered a definite plan to relieve unemployment, instead of making vague promises of a 'new deal.' Planning is still a little too civilized for idiots. They cannot comprehend."[13]

According to his birth certificate, Aaron and Jennie's only child, Israel Payssah Shapiro, was born on January 8, 1915, at the Hospital of the Osteopathic College of Physicians and Surgeons. (His parents later told him that the certificate date was erroneous; he was actually born on January 12.) The family moved several times, from near downtown Los Angeles to Sierra Madre (a foothill community about fifteen miles away) and, when Jarrico was five, to Boyle Heights. He later said that most of his memories of being young "have to do with Boyle Heights. . . . My father really wanted to be there, because he felt himself very much a part of the community and in fact was a spokesman for the community, a leader of the community." Their house, Jarrico said, was filled with "political and cultural discussion and a good deal of good feeling: laughter, jokes, songs, a lot of friends. It was a good environment for me. . . . I was really very fortunate."[14]

Aaron and his son were extremely close, and Aaron was Jarrico's role model. In his oral history, Jarrico said,

> [My father] was open, he was active, he was a very good-natured person, he was—I grew up thinking that everybody's father went to meetings every night. I mean, it took a while to understand that he was really unique. No, the sense of social values, of social conscience, came directly from him and to a lesser extent from my mother, [who was, in her younger days,] a follower or at least an

> admirer of Emma Goldman, and it's interesting to me that the highest praise my mother had for anyone was to say, "Er iz ah radikahler mensch," meaning, "He is a radical person." That for her was not sectarian at all. That covered any kind of radicalism.

Aaron gave his son pamphlets on the Tom Mooney case and the executions of Sacco and Vanzetti.[15]

Because Aaron had divorced his devotion to Jewish culture from Jewish worship and had become, in Jarrico's words, a "card-carrying atheist," he did not enroll his son in Hebrew school. In fact, Jarrico entered a synagogue only when he accompanied his father, who himself went only to make political appeals. Aaron did expose his son to Jewish culture and politics and educated him to be proud of his religion and its traditions. Jarrico was a member of the Workmen's Circle Culture Club, and he attended for a short time the Workmen's Circle's Yiddish *volkshule* (school for children). He was expelled, he later said, "for not being sufficiently disciplined, which was a kind of minor scandal," since his father had founded the school. He went most summers to a Workmen's Circle camp in Brea.[16]

Jarrico quarreled constantly with his mother and acquired a love-hate relationship with her. Though Aaron regularly counseled his son to be patient with his mother, Aaron and Jennie had a problem that affected the three of them. Jennie disliked sex and Aaron had a vigorous sexual appetite. Jennie regularly became hysterical about Aaron's infidelities, and once she sent Jarrico as an emissary to complain to Aaron about one of his affairs. Aaron became angry and lied to his son about the affair. In a note he scribbled for his autobiography, Jarrico wrote, "My father had two extramarital affairs that I know of, both of them extremely painful for my mother. I was three years old at the time of the first one, and took very much my mother's side. I was seventeen the second time, and pro-father."[17]

In a letter to her son from her first marriage, Ed Kraus, probably from the late 1930s, Jennie wrote, "Israel is not a very good writer yet and is not a devoted son as usual. Anyway I didn't have very much success with my children. Perhaps I did not deserve it or I have a very bad muzzle [*mazel* (fortune)?]. . . . And I have given up the idea that I ever had any children, and must try to be contented."[18]

Schooling

Jarrico attended Sheridan Street Elementary School (to 1927) and Hollenbeck Junior High School (1927–29). In junior high he began to write, mainly New Year's resolutions, poems, and odes to Aaron. When he was thirteen, he wrote his first surviving social-minded essay, a critique of smoking. One year later, he tried to organize a Young Zionists Club. Each member was to pay five-cent dues, half of which would go to Poale Zion and the other half to buying books and bringing lecturers to the club. "Every meeting," he wrote, "some of the children will acquaint us with how Zionism stands then, will tell us stories about Palestine and different things. We will be enjoying ourselves and at the same time help others." He also wrote a short report about the labor organizer Mother Jones, whom he described as "one of the most forceful and picturesque figures of the American labor movement," and a polished five-page essay based on war novels he had been reading. When his homeroom teacher read the antiwar story to the class, the teacher "choked up, close to tears." It was Jarrico's "first realization of the power of the written word," and it helped to shape his ambition to be a writer.[19]

At Roosevelt High School, debate and public speaking captured Jarrico's interest because his father wanted him to follow in his footsteps and become a lawyer. After losing in two oratorical contests, in which he argued about the moral delinquency of youth and the scholastic performance of athletes, he made his first political argument in the constitutional contest at his high school in 1931. He advocated universal education as the only solution to the bane of ignorance (and its effects, poverty, disorder, and suffering) that was "tearing down the very soul of the Constitution [of the United States]."[20] He won the Roosevelt contest, and he made the semifinals of the *Los Angeles Times*' sixth International Oratorical Contest and the eighth annual National Oratorical Contest. Beginning in January 1931, Jarrico wrote regularly for the *Rough Rider*: articles on the writer James Russell Lowell and the Notre Dame football coach Knute Rockne, detective stories, and several humor columns. He was elected literary editor of the *Rough Rider* and editor in chief of the yearbook. In April, he was appointed to the editorial staff of the National Boys' Week edition of the *Los Angeles Times*.

On July 3, 1931, Jarrico met and fell for Sylvia Gussin (b. October 2, 1915), whose father had also come from Russia, also loved Yiddish culture, and was also a Socialist. She and her younger sister, Zelma, lived with their mother in Santa Paula, where Rose Gussin owned a dry goods store. Sylvia and Zelma spent the summer of 1931 in Santa Monica, and Sylvia became the secretary-treasurer for the Young People's Jewish Culture Club. One night, after hearing her read the minutes, Jarrico told her that he was impressed by her sense of humor. She remembered that he "was kind of cute. He was sixteen; he had acne; he didn't know how to comb his hair. So I didn't think he was attractive, but I thought he was fascinating," lively, enthusiastic, and "full of hopeful ideas about the world and his place in it. Something wonderful always seemed to be happening to him." Even at that young age, he seemed to her to be "a serious person" with whom she could have a serious relationship.[21]

Although Jarrico dated his "radicalization" to his college years, he was clearly inclined toward socialism while in high school. In a letter to Sylvia, recounting a Socialist meeting at his house, he wrote, "My uncle [Chaim] filled me with family pride. But William Busick made me want to go out and swing chairs at the American Legion fascists—the rats! Anyway, I have been shown that the capitalistic system is on its last legs. In fact, it is already crashing down around us!"[22] Jarrico attended a youth antiwar meeting to hear Upton Sinclair speak, and he participated in the state convention of the Socialist Party.

During his senior year at Roosevelt (1931–32), Jarrico's socialist ideas altered, and instead of education as the solution to unemployment, war, and crime, he now advocated massive relief by the government, reduction of armaments in the world, and a campaign against crime. And, as did many future Communists, he found inspiration in the writings of Thomas Paine. In an essay, Jarrico extolled the "voice that blared forth like some tremendous clarion," a voice that was needed today, when the country was again faced with a great crisis. He also began what would become a lifelong effort to understand the nature of humor. In early 1932, he wrote, "The humorist must find the illogical, the absurd, the unusual, the extreme, and the contrasting, and point it out to us." In that way, the humorist could fulfill his or her social function, which was to goad people into living and acting normally.[23]

But aside from Sylvia and his public writing and speaking, Jarrico found his daily life boring. "I am not very good in school," he wrote his mother, who was visiting family in New York, "as my interests do not interest me in the least." As a result, his high school grades were just sufficient to gain him admission to the University of Southern California, where he intended to major in journalism. Even though he would continue to live at home, his attending college was, he remembered, "a financial sacrifice on my father's part." But the prospect of college, he wrote Sylvia, "thrills me."[24] Sylvia enrolled at UCLA as a premed student.

College

In his first year at USC, Jarrico earned a B average and was admitted to Pi Epsilon Theta, the honorary philosophy fraternity. Still, although he was eager about ideas and enthusiastic about new experiences, he was unhappy and could not focus. In a letter to a friend, he confessed that he found college mostly boring. "Aside from some newly formed friendships and one brain-stirring professor [his philosophy professor, Heinrich Gomperz] I have found only disappointment. I continually feel that my uninteresting subjects are usurping time which could be better spent." Though he was on the college newspaper staff and the freshman debate squad, he found himself feeling "usually unhappy," because "my personal failures far outweigh my superficial successes." One month later, he wrote that his "unhappiness is just a question of ego. When one finds that one's aspirations are higher than one's possibilities, one can not help but be disappointed. Can one?" He also admitted that he saw opportunities in college, "but I haven't learned yet how to take advantage of them. The real trouble is that I haven't learned how to concentrate."[25]

This intellectual restlessness, this questing for the ultimate creative experience, and the malaise that ensued reappeared periodically throughout his adult life. In a journal he was assigned to maintain in his English class, Jarrico declared himself "an incurable introvert, destined to fester in and upon myself forever. My pure extrovert experiences . . . are rare. More usual is the condition wherein I attempt to direct my attention outside myself, only to fall back immediately into introspection."[26] Jarrico regularly bluffed a certainty he did not feel; he consciously and carefully "packaged" himself to appear secure. During his freshman year in college, he made a study of suicide as a remedy for ennui.

Politically, Jarrico was moving away from the socialism of his family. He later recalled, "As I reached the age of eighteen or so, in 1933, it seemed to me that the socialists weren't militant enough and that the communists were the ones who were leading the hunger marches and trying to organize the unorganized workers and leading demonstrations for relief, for welfare, and so on. I was increasingly drawn to the communist side of this issue." He was, for example, persuaded, after reading Calvin B. Hoover's book *Germany Enters the Third Reich*, that the German Socialists were more culpable than the German Communists for Hitler's accession to power. In a rambling letter to Sylvia in February 1933, Jarrico mused about going to Palestine. There, he wrote, "men and women work in communistic societies—work hard and are very happy. Schools, libraries and lecture courses dispense culture to the workers there. The culture is deep, and free."[27]

In the spring, he continued to write for the campus humor magazine, but he dropped debating entirely. For one of his English classes, he wrote an essay in which he blamed the machine age for the huge number of unemployed and the threat of world war; it had made an economic system as "stupid as it is wasteful. With the result that the machine is master of man." Though he hoped for a world in which human social intelligence equaled its mechanical genius, he did not offer a means of raising the former.[28] His writings and musings indicate that he was searching for some standard beyond that of individual experience and opinion.

At the end of his freshman year, a restless Jarrico drove across the United States in a 1928 Ford he and his college friend Ralph Benkaim had purchased. They were accompanied by two other students and Jarrico's mother, who was going to visit friends in Detroit. He spent several weeks in Scranton with the Benkaim family, and he began what would be a constant in his life: flirting with women and having affairs with some of them. He told Sylvia about some (Muriel, Esther, and Diana on this trip); others he kept to himself. He convinced himself that he was not being unfaithful, that he simply loved women and enjoyed responding to being loved by them. He wrote Sylvia from New York that he had been "captured by Diana [Bricks]," that "I am filled delightfully with Diana." He claimed that his writing about Diana to Sylvia "was the greatest proof I could give you of the complete love I hold for you." When Sylvia responded with a letter full of hurt, Jarrico wrote perhaps his most impassioned letter.

> Can't you see, didn't I make it clear, that my writing "the Diana experience" to you was the greatest proof I could give you of the complete love I hold for you. Didn't you hear me say, "We are brother," we are one; only to you do I give myself entirely, do I show my weaknesses and my strength unashamed; only before you do I disrobe, because I want you to know me, your lover, because I want you to understand? . . .
>
> Don't you know—Diana does—that to me you are the deepest, the most intense, the wisest, the most complete, the most perfect person there is? Diana is charming, Diana is intriguing, but Sylvia—the passion, the adoration I feel, I have felt for you is completely above any attraction Diana may have had for me, that a comparison is as insulting as it is ridiculous.

Jarrico then shifted his tone and began blaming Sylvia for his dalliances, because, he wrote, she did not reciprocate his effort to relate everything she felt or thought, thereby making their relationship a one-way arrangement. "I do not seek to justify my behavior but I seek to explain when I say, 'Had you written, had you shown any interest, had you given me just a little, it would have been different.'"[29]

In Scranton, Jarrico also formed what would be a longstanding friendship with Cyril Endfield, a boyhood friend of Ralph Benkaim's. At the end of July, Jarrico went to Philadelphia to see his cousin Eleanor and her two Communist half-brothers. "Communism and class struggle were my intellectual pabulum for the week," he wrote Sylvia. He accompanied his relatives to party headquarters, a party meeting ("12 Jews and 4 Chinamen"), a factory-gate meeting, and a Communist picnic "where Negroes and Jews laughed and laughed to see the man hit the heads off dummy Hitler, dummy Mussolini, and dummy [J. P.] Morgan with 3 balls for a ticket." They had numerous discussions about politics, and his cousins reproached him about his "bourgeois ideology" and raised doubts in his mind about socialism.

Jarrico wrote Aaron, "Their superior knowledge almost allowed them to defeat my militant socialistic ideas, but I stood firm—and resolved to study more. I can see the possibility of a shift of camp in the near future. But I shall not do it before finding out for myself—from less biased sources."[30]

Jarrico returned to Los Angeles on August 21 and enrolled at UCLA. He continued to live at home, and Sylvia lived with her aunt. As his radicalizing process continued, he became impatient with what he called "the gradualism of socialists" on the subject of unemployment and social reality. He wrote Endfield in early November, "My Marxian interests are being revived by an intended term paper, 'Economic Determiners of English Literature.'" This leaning toward communism, he recalled, "led to conflicts between me and my father. They were not bitter conflicts, but they were sometimes noisy conflicts. I mean, we argued. He was amused and a bit scornful about the beginning of my illusions about Russia, because he would tell me that the good communists had been wiped out not simply by the rise of Stalin but long before that—I mean by Lenin. . . . And he was really very much the defender of the socialist line as against the communist line." The entire family was at odds with Jarrico's tropism toward communism. There were bitter arguments, but no breaks in relations. At one point, Abram shouted at Jarrico, "Du bist ein nar!" (You are a fool!)[31]

Dissatisfied with college and jealous of the attention Sylvia was receiving from, and giving to, two other men, Jarrico contemplated leaving UCLA, hitchhiking to New York City, and becoming a writer. In a journal entry at the end of December, he wrote, "School has been futility, mostly, the moments of interest coming seldom. Intellectual advancement this semester, as far as scholastic stimulus is concerned seems to be nil."[32]

However, Jarrico's daydream about New York was altered by his father's sudden death. Suffering from a gallbladder problem, Aaron had been admitted to Santa Barbara Cottage Hospital in December. He died of uremia on December 31. Jarrico wrote to Endfield, "He was the major force in the formation of Israel [Shapiro]; a brilliant man, idealist, egotist, humorist, poet. I loved him very much, and he more than returned. . . . Strength—courage—was his ideal. A Jew first, socialist next, the only true democrat I've ever known: believing honestly that no one surpassed him in intellectual prowess, he was a personal *friend*, always, to the mass, the workers. And the 2000 or so people who came to his funeral were mostly poor. Someday I'll write his biography." In a letter to another friend, Jarrico called Aaron "my best friend, my greatest admirer, and completest ideal." To most observers, though, Jarrico seemed unaffected by Aaron's death. "He went on," Sylvia Jarrico recalled, "being the same person." He did not cry at Aaron's funeral, but three months later, he reexperienced a childhood memory of Aaron coming home, kissing him, and saying "Zun tyerer" (dearest son). Then Jarrico cried.[33]

Jarrico wrote Diana Bricks at the end of February 1934 that his future plans were uncertain but he would try to get to New York that summer and maybe to Europe. "My father," he wrote, "left some insurance, besides two brothers who are most generous."[34] Though he said he was again considering a legal career, he began to focus most of his time and energy on political activity and to insert political comments into the humor column he wrote for the campus newspaper, the *Daily Bruin*. He joined the National Student League (NSL), the most successful radical student organization in the country's history, and helped organize its protests against the "compulsory and militaristic" Reserve Officers Training Corps (ROTC).[35]

In April, the NSL and the Socialist Student League for Industrial Democracy planned the first nationwide student strike against war. Students were asked to walk out of their classrooms between eleven and twelve o'clock and pledge "not to bear arms except in cases of invasion of the mainland of the United States, and to work actively for the organization of the world on a peace basis." Jarrico chaired the publicity committee for the Southern California district, and in his column four days before the strike, he quoted the antiwar poet Siegfried Sassoon to the effect that war is hell and warmakers are criminals.[36] On April 13, two thousand students packed Royce Hall and enthusiastically applauded the antiwar speeches. Jarrico, wearing his ROTC uniform, carried a funeral wreath and led the chanting of the pledge with his left fist held high.

Jarrico was also becoming more sympathetic to communism and to labor strikes, and he participated in one of the most impressive and bloodiest strikes of the mid-1930s: the West Coast maritime strike of May–July 1934, which extended from San Diego to Canada and involved more than fourteen thousand maritime workers.[37] It also involved hundreds of university students, some as strikebreakers for the employers and some as picketers for the workers. Jarrico and Sylvia felt a strong tie to the longshoremen; they believed that the workers had a good understanding of economic and social conditions. Union recruiters Jarrico had met at the Shapiro and Shapiro law office invited him to speak at one of their meetings. "Much radicalism," he wrote to Diana Bricks: "I spoke the other night to 2000 striking longshoremen." During the strike, Jarrico's newspaper column was "suspended indefinitely for obscenity (ha!) and, perhaps, redishness." After the strike, UCLA seemed to him "deadeningly dreadful, dreadfully deadening."[38]

Jarrico wrote his mother, who had gone to Russia and Palestine for several months, "I have been quite active with the Communists here in Los Angeles. I spoke the other day at a mass meeting at the Plaza to 5000 people, and was very well received. I wore my ROTC uniform, and spoke against war, particularly capitalist, or imperialist war." He had told the crowd, "Today we see capitalism crumbling about us. We see the putrid remains of what had once been a proud and arrogant system." Such was its state, he continued, that "only one thing can make it possible for the system of exploitation to continue its blood-sucking way. That thing is war. Only through the accelerated destruction of humanity and the things which humanity has produced can the profit system be saved." But, he warned, "Slowly the inert mass which is the American student body is awakening. . . . *Slowly* we are seeing that the words 'Patriotism,' 'Courage,' 'Sacrifice' are delusions, are pretty screens to cover up the real reason for mass murder—Profits!" He urged those students who had not yet taken an interest in the struggle against war to "Join the National Student League, Help us to fight the ROTC, with its jingoistic attempt to screen the real nature and causes of imperialist war with phrases about 'Defense of Home.'"[39]

"I have become convinced," he wrote to his mother, "that you cannot bring about a change through voting, because the capitalists control the State. The family is very shocked by my swing to the Left, but they will get used to it." The family members who had come from Russia, however, could not understand how Jarrico could embrace communism. Jarrico's cousin Violet Gershenson said, "My father [Chaim] was anti-Communist, but he loved Israel [Jarrico]," and he thought he could talk him out of becoming a Communist.[40]

That summer, Jarrico and some friends drove east. He spent three weeks in New York City, attended an NSL convention, and worked on the Student Review, the NSL paper. But he found New York to be "hard, uncomfortable, and unsubtle, contact with it is grinding. The city is afflicted with an acquisitive perversion," and he missed Sylvia. He wrote her that he could not live without her, and he suggested that they transfer to the University of California at Berkeley and live together. He promised that he would finish college, begin submitting stories for publication in magazines, and, if he could not make a living as a writer, go to work for his uncle Abram.[41]

Jarrico hitchhiked and rode freight trains back to California. "The freights," he remembered, "were absolutely covered with unemployed people getting from here to there, there to here, and being rousted, chased off the train, and sneaking past the cops and catching the train again as it left whatever town had given us trouble. This was obviously rich experience for a kid, especially a socially conscious kid." Back in California, he wrote a story called "Superior Boy Goes Traveling." In it, he tried to combine realism (the look of the country, his conversation with an unemployed older man) and poetry (a stream-of-thought interior monologue about consciousness, social issues, and writing). The story ends with the boy asking the older man about Franklin Roosevelt. "'What about him?' 'What do you think of him?' And the man replied: 'Boy . . . you are trying to make talk.'"[42]

Jarrico was accompanied on this trip by Hal Smith, a new friend who was, Sylvia Jarrico recalled, "a fast guy" who smoked, drank, and flirted with women. Jarrico described him as "one of nature's noblemen, with humor, with sincerity, with brains which don't spill all over the place but are ready and creative and sure." In September 1934, the three of them enrolled at the University of California at Berkeley, and Jarrico and Sylvia joined a Berkeley unit of the Young Communist League (YCL). He wrote Endfield, "Radicaling occupies most of my time. Especially writing for *The University*

Communist, the bulletin issued fortnightly by the U.C. Unit of the Young Communist League. Which information is for your private consumption, the Pacific Coast terror being what it is . . . and let me tell you, felleh, it is."[43] In November, Jarrico helped organize a student strike to protest the suspension of five NSL members at UCLA. Five thousand students participated, and they were attacked by fraternity members and the football team.[44] Jarrico, one of the speakers, was pelted with eggs by hecklers.

At the start of the spring semester, Jarrico curtailed his radical activity "to develop myself and my grades. . . . I'm working hard and enjoying it." In fact, he wrote several people that he was now loving college. He continued to read Marxist literature, particularly John Strachey's *Literature and Dialectical Materialism* and Granville Hicks's *Great Tradition*, and he had come to the conclusion that dialectical materialism lent purpose to one's thinking. Though he found "dissatisfaction in Stalinism" and recognized the validity of some criticisms of it, he had become convinced that if the United States and the rest of the world were to be saved, "it will be done, if not by the Communist Parties, by communist thinking." He became involved in a student strike against war, scheduled for April, and he was among twenty-two protesters arrested for violating a municipal ordinance that prohibited distributing leaflets on street corners. Released on his own recognizance, he spoke at a mass meeting supporting the strike and opposing the arrests. When the charges were dismissed, Jarrico wrote Endfield, "Public pressure did it too, by Lenin. They crowded the chambers of the city council, and the politicians immediately changed the law so that it could not possibly cover us. But tomorrow [April 12] is the strike. Professors are dismissing classes (*some* professors), and we seem to have quite a bit of support, plus a promise from the Berkeley police that they will protect us from vigilantism. And an amplifying system!"[45]

Jarrico was also writing more regularly, mainly short stories for his writing class, and he was contemplating a play about a group of Hungarian miners who threaten suicide during a strike. "There are," he wrote André Marrin, "too damned many personal short-story writers and personal novel writers and personal poets, and not enough—say 'proletarian' though that's beginning to be a lousy literary word—playwrights." He also began an autobiographical novel that, he later noted, talked "in a scarcely veiled way about my relations with my father and my mother."[46]

During the summer of 1935, Jarrico wrote to Hal Smith that he had put aside his autobiographical novel because it would require him to spend hours on a single paragraph, to make a "literary effort." He thought it would be best if he learned "facility."

> So I am writing another novel, designed to sell as a sex novel. Jack Woodford's "Trial and Error" is the basis of this ambition. Whatever you do, if you ever expect to write for money, read this book. No crap—straight, intelligent, and clever advice. Anyway, I have been reading books like "Impatient Virgin," by Clarke, and I have planned a book which should not take me over three weeks to write—and may take me much less, if I get into swing. Get this though: I am *not* making the book deliberately bad. It is a sex novel, because I think I'll be able to sell it; but I'm going to write as well as I can at a very rapid pace. The material for the first six chapters I take from your life—with your permission.

Jarrico included in the letter a chapter outline, but apparently Smith did not approve, or else he did not send the required information, because no more was heard of this story.[47]

Jarrico went back to work on the autobiographical novel, but he was still struggling with it. He wrote Endfield,

> When I pretend a style I am dissatisfied. When I want to say something and I say it I am satisfied and I know that anyone looking for what anyone calls style will find it. It has been very seldom that this has happened. Usually I don't know what I want to say or I do know and I haven't the literary guts to say it. There is a lot more to this literary guts business than writing shit in a novel. Beyond the obvious exhibitionism of all writing there is self-revelation which is unbearable. The problem becomes how one is to reach the glorious honesty which is the core of great writing without sacrificing the secrecy which molds a compact personality, the secrecy without which all men are fools. I shall solve the problem, I think.[48]

Jarrico completed and dispatched five stories to *Woman's Home Companion*, *Story*, *Esquire*, *Scribner's*, and *Vanity Fair*, but none were accepted.

While trying to become a popular writer, Jarrico decided again to pursue a law degree. In September, he and Sylvia enrolled at USC, which allowed students to enter law school in their senior year and earn a bachelor of arts degree at the end of the first year of legal study. (Sylvia, whose grades had slumped at Berkeley, switched from premed to psychology.) They did not transfer to a YCL unit in the Los Angeles area, but Jarrico did participate in some NSL activities. He also voiced some criticism of Soviet tactics. He wrote Endfield, "All my red friends, most of whom I painted red, are attacking me. . . . But I've read the resolutions of the 7th Congress, and it seems pretty clear to me that isolation is the worst of the revolutionary evils."[49]

Though he wrote Smith that nothing interested him "as much as communism," Jarrico admitted that he could not force himself into activity even on its behalf. In early October, he dropped out of law school because it required more time than he thought the study of law was worth. In particular, it left him too little time to write. Eager to complete his senior year as quickly as possible, he enrolled in the easiest courses he could find, which were, it turned out, in the cinematography department. He enrolled in motion picture production and planned to take motion picture story and continuity in the spring. He remarked, "Film studies were in the hands back then of a squat Russian emigré who may have known something about movie making but nothing he was able to communicate. He not only dispensed with articles, as Russians will, he was sparing of prepositions and verbs as well, and said 'mnieh' rather than 'uh' while searching, usually in vain, for the right word. 'Today mnieh lecture light. Film mnieh sensitive mnieh light. Light mnieh necessary mnieh film image.'"[50]

Jarrico began seriously to plan for a movie career early the next year, following his and Sylvia's decision to wed. After the January 8 ceremony, he wrote Endfield,

> My present ambition is to work in the studios and *learn* [cinematography] completely, technically—lights, film and camera, sound—as well as theoretically (though I am afraid I consider myself beyond the pedagogical influence of Hollywood in that respect), and then go

> to Russia, perhaps to enroll in the Institute of Cinematography in Moscow, perhaps already prepared to contribute to production. Not that I've given up the emphasis on writing. I'm convinced more and more that the script is the basis of all movie work. But I know that only the technically trained are welcome in the land of plenty.

In the meantime, wanting to earn some money from his current writing, Jarrico decided to submit his autobiographical novel as a candidate for a James D. Phelan Award in Literature and Arts. He told Endfield, "I'm returning to my novel, for the while. If I win, it will give me a year's freedom to do as I like. Which is just what I need. To get away from school, home, and financial responsibility. This past month has been one of creative stagnation. But since I decided on the novel (that is, since yesterday), I've been having that delightful pain in the stomach once more. It will not be 'I' alone. It will be rather two 'I's . . . my father's and my own." He borrowed the title, "A Young Man Must Not Sleep," from Robinson Jeffers's poem "Promise of Peace."[51]

But Jarrico could not overcome what he called his "creative stagnation," and he submitted only one chapter to the Phelan competition. That chapter was written as an internal monologue, combining realistic description with flights of flamboyant imagery. Transparently autobiographical, it narrates a day in the life of David, a first-year student at USC. Feeling his world closing in on him, David tells his father, "I'm a smart guy, papa. I think smart things. . . . But I'm crazy. I watch my mind—and it isn't sane. For no reason at all it goes blank. For no reason at all! It changes—first I'm excited, talking and thinking, and then, in a minute, I'm completely morbid, and my brain is empty. Sometimes I think about suicide—but it's just a mental game, intellectual calisthenics, and I know it. But suddenly I become completely indifferent, and when I think about suicide, it's not a game anymore, it's—it's a determination." David's father assures him that those moods will pass; it is just a matter of adjusting to maturity. "You want to appreciate and create—and your mind has gotten a little ahead of your emotional development. But it will catch up."[52]

It is difficult to see, from the outline and the completed chapter, whether this novel was going to be a bildungsroman or an extended plaint. In their rejection letter, the Phelan judges told Jarrico that his plan for a proposed book was "somewhat vaguely stated" and that they considered the manuscript he had submitted "as entirely inadequate for a satisfactory judgment." Nevertheless, the letter continued, "the Committee thought so well of your work from the little evidence which they did have before them that they regarded it as important that you be encouraged to apply again next year with a more clear cut plan and much more evidence of your actual power as a creative writer."[53] Jarrico did not appear too disappointed with this rejection.

Like many young, would-be artists, Jarrico was casting about for a style and a content. He was also struggling with discipline and genre. He never considered writing easy work, even after he had become a successful screenwriter. And he believed strongly that rewriting was the essence of good writing. Much later, he would say, "I would rather rewrite than be President."[54]

The day before he was graduated, Jarrico assessed his four years in college. He computed his overall grade-point average, 1.55 (on a 3-point scale), and concluded, "That is one way to evaluate. That means my grades were between good and fair, a trifle closer to good. But this has no meaning. What I must do is find what I am and what I know today." None of the best books he had read had been assigned in his courses. From what was assigned, he could, with several months' solitary application, have gained much more knowledge than he did. But his college years had provided him with leisure and freedom. "I have learned what workers' solidarity means because I was at a meeting of striking longshoremen in May, 1934. And I was at that meeting because I belonged to the National Student League. And I would not have belonged to that organization if I were not attending a University." But he could discover no direct and obvious causality between a university education and his present self. "My impulse is to credit it with nothing. Barrenness and futility—these are the words I associate with the college life."[55]

On June 6, 1936, at a ceremony at the Los Angeles Coliseum, Sylvia Rina Gussin and Israel Paul Shapiro were awarded bachelor of arts degrees.

2

Screenwriting and Communism, 1936–39

> I believe in comedies, in their social efficacy, in their value as entertainment. And I believe in compromise. . . . I believe that half a truth is better than none, that it is better to get some good stuff in a picture rather than a perfect script on a shelf.
>
> —*Paul Jarrico, 1944*

The newly married couple lived in a studio apartment on $100 a month provided by their mothers. Sylvia was taking psychology courses in preparation for her admission to the graduate program at UCLA. Jarrico was looking for a job. Fate intervened in the forms of Edwin Knopf, head of the MGM writers' department (and brother of publisher Alfred A. Knopf); Rufus Von Kleinsmid, president of USC; and Frank Baxter, Jarrico's favorite English professor. Knopf had asked Von Kleinsmid to send to him the names of graduating seniors with literary potential. Von Kleinsmid turned the assignment over to Baxter, and Baxter gave him four names, including that of Israel Shapiro. Jarrico was nervous about the approaching interview, especially when he learned that Knopf had been curt and almost insulting when he had interviewed Hal Smith, Jarrico's college friend, just two days earlier. After the interview, Jarrico wrote, "I had thought that I was beginning to acquire a little poise, after all these awkward years—but I was nervous during that interview! With his secretary taking down my stuttered words in shorthand." But Knopf was affable and friendly. He boasted about the uniqueness of MGM's program (a long-term apprenticeship with an established writer) and asked Jarrico to send the studio some samples of his writing. The job paid $35 a week.[1]

In early August, Knopf wrote Jarrico that the junior writers' department would not be making any further appointments. But, bitten by the screenwriting bug, Jarrico sent stories to Warner Brothers and RKO. He received rejections from both studios. In November, Knopf wrote again, saying Jarrico would have a job in the next week or so. Then, four weeks later, he wrote, "There seems to be little chance we can take you on." Frustrated by what he considered a "stall," Jarrico decided on a policy of "Hollywood or bust." His vow was enormously aided when Hal Smith introduced him to Dore Schary. Schary, who had just been hired by MGM, had accumulated more than one dozen screenwriting credits from several major studios. He was also a politically active left liberal: he worked for the Anti-Defamation League and had campaigned for the reelection of President Roosevelt. Schary advised Jarrico to write an original script, because the studios would not employ him on "faith, hope, or charity." Jarrico took the advice seriously, and he wrote Endfield, "I have been brooding about a detective story involving a professor of oriental civilization, and a chinese revolutionist, and a newspaper man taking graduate work in chinese and chinese civilization. Not being a detective story fan, I bogged down. Not knowing new ways to kill, I got stuck." But he was forcing himself to write every day, which made writing easier, if not better. "Too often have I begun, only to quit because I was not in good form, or had nothing to say at the moment, or thought of something else to do. And every time I excused myself from writing, I became a worse writer. It is important to me that I keep this resolution, that I keep this pledge, no matter how disappointed I am in what I am writing."[2]

Schary's interest in Jarrico grew. He was, wrote Jarrico, "plugging me and the [manuscript], advising, correcting, telephoning, getting me appointments, and punching me in the ribs with the joke that says—I'm your pal. . . . I'm a little awed at Dore's good fellowship. And if nothing came of it, I would still be thankful that guys like Dore are around." The manuscript in question was a satire of the escape-to-the-south-seas dream, which Jarrico had developed into what he called "a fairly fresh comedy romance." Schary arranged appointments for Jarrico with RKO, Columbia, and Warner Brothers and put him in touch with Nat Goldstone, Schary's agent. Al Lewis, a producer at RKO, asked Jarrico to come to the studio for an interview. Jarrico wrote Hal Smith,

> Before the appointment Dore pulled wires and found what the offer would be, coached me in the right answers. So when Lewis said "I like the idea of your story, and I want you to make some changes, and we'll work together, and then if it shapes up right we'll buy it—" I knew that I wasn't supposed to say yes, but that I was to offer him an option and say I would work on it, if they put me on salary while I worked. Surprisingly though he thought that was rather a good idea. He'd suggest it to the other bosses. Goldstone got busy, doubled the wage Dore had advised me ask, and is going to try to close the deal Monday. $200 a week, for four weeks, the $800 to apply on the purchase price of $2000 at the end of that time, if they are satisfied with the story then.[3]

Goldstone also advised him that Israel Payssah Shapiro was "too Jewish" a name. So, to accommodate his agent, Israel Shapiro created the name Paul Jarrico. He later said, "I thought that was a name that was distinctive. I wanted it to sound biblical, I think, because I didn't want people to think I had changed my name to avoid being known as Jewish. I spelled it peculiarly: I used the vowels of the name Shapiro in the same order, and I also spelled it peculiarly so it wouldn't seem to be a made-up name."[4]

When RKO decided not to pay him $200 a week, Jarrico wrote Endfield, "I'm a scenario writer, . . . hanging by a thread over the pit of employment. . . . Any minute now my agent, Nat (Dionysus) Goldstone, will snap the thread and I will fall, a ripe and willing plum, into the maw of Hollywood exploitation."[5] But interviews at Republic and Monogram proved fruitless, and by the end of the year he was in a depressed frame of mind.[6]

Nevertheless, Jarrico had begun to study movies seriously. He attended them regularly, read books about them, and discussed them with Sylvia and his friends. Jarrico recalled,

> I was very taken, not as a serious student of films but as an audience, with the romantic comedies that were really the high point of the

> thirties. [*It Happened One Night*, *My Man Godfrey*, *Easy Living*, *The Devil and Miss Jones*, and *Man's Castle*] were the ones that not only impressed me the most but also influenced me the most. That is to say, my natural bent as a writer was romantic comedy at the time, partly because those were the films I admired most. Those were the films I enjoyed most. The idea that I could maybe write something like that was pleasing to me, exciting to me.[7]

He wrote seven original treatments (summaries of plots and main characters), some of which contained social and political criticism, and he and Sam Rudnick cowrote several more, including a satire on war movies intended for the Marx brothers.

In May 1937, still without a job in the studios, Jarrico took a job selling canned beer for Pioneer Jobbers. When Endfield wrote that he too now aspired to be an artist, Jarrico responded, "Artist. Shit. What I want is a job. The height of my aesthetic ambition is $800 per week at MGM. And some day I'm going to get it. . . . I haven't given up battering my head against the stone wall of Hollywood. I've got a mighty hard head. And something tells me the stone wall is paper mache." But the beer job lasted only a few days, and Jarrico wrote Hal Smith that he was in line to be a social worker, maybe, or he would find some other sort of work. But, Jarrico swore, "I am going to break into the movie business, god damn you and god damn it—not because I want a swimming pool and a deep leather couch, but because that is the work I'm interested in, and trained for, and able to do—and because somebody is going to run this superb culture-art-education mechanism when it finally belongs to the masses."[8]

Schary, who had dutifully continued to send Jarrico's manuscripts to various studios, finally succeeded in arranging an appointment for him with Nat Perrin at Columbia Pictures. That studio, one of the minor majors, was known for two things at the time Jarrico interviewed there: the studio boss, Harry Cohn, who ran it like a police state and kept a close watch on his writers, and the studio's productions, which were "smart, usually astringent, and finally moral comedies."[9] Jarrico met with Perrin ("a swell guy, young, Jewish, sympathetic, shrewd") on August 3. As Jarrico later related, Perrin was having trouble with a script, "and I suggested an angle," and "he put me on for a week to develop my angle. So they're using my angle, it looks like, and he's asked the studio to keep me on."[10] Jarrico was also assigned to come up with a new angle on another troubled script, then to write a treatment for it. Columbia agreed to pay him $100 a week.

Even though Perrin suspected that Jarrico knew nothing about screenwriting, he assigned him as sole writer on the first story Jarrico had read for him, an adaptation of Paul Gallico's "'Twas the Night before Christmas," which had been published in the *Saturday Evening Post*. After reading the screenplays that Perrin had rejected, Jarrico decided to adhere more closely to the Gallico story but alter the romantic interest. In Jarrico's version, two newspaper reporters who are on their way to get married are ordered by their editor to find goats to pull the wagon he has bought for his son as a Christmas present. In the scavenger hunt–type plot, the reporters and an accompanying photographer stumble across a kidnapped heiress and become involved in a series of mixups with various women. And, of course, everything gets sorted out in the end. Jarrico completed a fourth draft on October 5, and the movie, *No Time to Marry*, featuring Richard Arlen, Mary Astor, and Lionel Stander, opened the following March, to pallid reviews. There were no kind remarks about the script. Jarrico himself thought it was "pretty lousy" and later wrote, "As it turned out, [Perrin's] faith in me was misplaced, the picture lost money, and Nat lost his job as a producer. Just as well, too. The experience made him [Perrin] a much more successful writer, and a much less naive man."[11]

Despite the film's financial failure, Columbia executives were sufficiently impressed with Jarrico's work to give him a seven-year contract calling for $150 a week the first year, $200 a week the second year, at the studio's option, and peaking at $900 if he lasted the full seven years. In a letter to Schary, Jarrico described the events leading up to his signing:

> So last week Mr. [William] Perlberg wants you in his office please right away. So "Paul, we're very satisfied with your work. We're giving you a raise—to one fifty—and a contract. Step right through the door to Mr. [Benjamin] Kahane's office and settle the details." I'm no dope. I run quick to my office and call up Goldstone. "Nat!" I gasp. "I'm dying. They're rushing me into a contract. Come quick!"

> So Nat comes and he spars with them a little. "What kind of business is this? Shteitsh! Why should it go up to two hundred at the end of a year? Why not at the end of six months?" So they say they'll think it over. I'm saved.
>
> The next day I talk to Perrin. "Idiot," he says. "What are you arguing? A contract is the best thing that could happen to you. You think you're set already? You'll go out and get better money on the strength of 'Night Before Christmas'? And if it stinks? Don't let Goldstone ruin it for you. I'm telling you. They'll get mad, and you'll be out on your behind. They're doing you a favor. They change their minds quick around here."
>
> So I begin dying again. Oi. I'll lose my contract. So I call up Nat. "Nat! Don't argue with them!" "Who's arguing?" "Nat . . . please . . ."

Jarrico signed the contract. Soon after, he underwent his first baptism of fire with the studio rewrite process. He wrote Schary, "I wouldn't have believed it if I hadn't seen it with my own eyes. 'Take out the riot between the gobs and the marines. Censorable.' The next week—after I sweat from 7 a.m. to 11 p.m. to make the tissues knit: 'Take out the whole Navy Yard sequence.' . . . Lionel Stander won't go in a [lion's] cage. . . . 'We'll have to double Stander.' 'Why not double the lion?' I'm dying. I love it."[12]

Jarrico's next assignment was to write a script for Edward G. Robinson based on the racket-busting efforts of Thomas E. Dewey in New York. Jarrico was told to "keep it from being another gangster picture," to make it an "epic," a "saga," "David and Goliath." He worked for Sidney Buchman, whom Jarrico termed "a brilliant guy" from whom he was "learning much."[13] Jarrico researched the problem of political corruption, composed for himself a seven-page essay on the subject, and then wrote three treatments. None of them satisfied the head of the story department, and Jarrico received a layoff notice on December 16. (Writers' contracts contained a clause allowing the studio to lay them off, without compensation, for twelve weeks during every twelve-month period.) He did not receive a screen credit for the finished film, *I Am the Law*.

When the layoff ended, Columbia, which did not have an assignment for him, loaned him to Samuel Goldwyn to work on *The Duchess of Broadway*, intended as a vehicle for Carole Lombard. Jarrico wrote Hal Smith, "The way it happened was that they put a lot of money into it, and a $2,000 a week writer failed and Goldwyn got disgusted and said shelve it, and Garson Kanin, who has just been made an associate producer said why not put on a low-priced writer instead of shelving it, and the idea happened to hit Goldwyn right, so for the second or third time in history Goldwyn hired a low-priced writer. So even if I don't come thru on this story, the prestige is something terrible, and my stock at Columbia has gone up."[14]

The story involved a nightclub singer who meets and befriends a millionaire with an unfaithful wife. He is killed, and he leaves his entire estate to the singer. She convinces his corporate board to invest in slum clearance projects and housing for the poor, but the evil widow and her lover connive to obstruct those plans. Jarrico wrote a series of treatments and outlines during his six weeks at Goldwyn. He wrote to a friend, "I wish it was in me to describe the mores of Hollywood and try to analyze the relationship between the Artist and Commerce and Stuff, but you will have to be satisfied with a simple assertion that I'm happy, like the work, find little frustration in contriving entertainment for the millions and no difficulty in reconciling this with either my respect for the aesthetic or my social consciousness."[15] But after six weeks' work, Goldwyn decided not to make the movie.

Back at Columbia, Jarrico turned down two assignments and was punished for what he called "his naive independence" by being assigned to the action unit, where he was told to do a story about policewomen. When the studio abandoned that project, he was given the choice of a layoff or writing a serial for a Wild Bill Hickock project. He chose the latter but hated it so much that he refused to continue. He was then reassigned to a script based on the comic strip *Blondie*, but, after one week's work on it, was put on layoff.

Jarrico believed that he had learned much about story construction, but he remained concerned about mastery of "personal efficiency—how not to waste time, how to finish whatever I start." He believed that he had the qualities that made a successful screenwriter. "I know a little about an awful lot of things, and I've got a feeling for surface logic in character and construction, and above all I'm eclectic as all get-out."[16]

In May 1938, he went back to work to write a script titled *The Little Adventuress*. It involved an orphaned girl, a horse, an uncle who does not like horses, the uncle's fiancée who does not like the girl, and a smart, independent female racehorse owner. The original story had gaps, in his appraisal, but he apparently was unable to fill them in his treatment. He was removed from the project, but he received a co–original screen story credit for the finished movie. He was then reassigned to *The Duchess of Broadway*, which Columbia had purchased from Goldwyn. He turned out another treatment, was put on layoff, and then was loaned to RKO.

Jarrico worked at RKO for two months on *Beauty for the Asking*, a story about a heel who dumps a beautiful but poor beauty operator for a homely heiress. When the beauty operator makes a great cosmetic discovery and builds a successful company, financially backed by the heiress (who does not know she loves her husband), the heel woos the beauty operator. The beauty operator and the heiress become friends, and ultimately both dump the heel. Jarrico hoped to use the story to expose what he called "the beauty racket." He researched the industry and developed a critical list of various beauty products: "Sulfide depilatories all bad. Hair treatments stink. Shampoo okay. Hand lotions needless expense. Cold cream ok. Lipsticks—bromo acid, an indelible dye."[17] The resulting movie, starring Lucille Ball, has elements of screwball comedy but is not very funny or dramatic, and it contains none of Jarrico's research. Its only clear message is that beauty depends on health. It was panned by the reviewer for the *Hollywood Reporter* as a minor mistake, "a trite and clumsy triangle story hung on the so-called beauty racket. . . . There are a lot of writers connected with this story and evidently no two of them saw the story eye to eye. With any number of possibilities for laughs, they chose to make it a problem." The reviewer for *Variety*, however, termed it an "intriguing story of conflicting loves laid against [a] beauty parlor background," offering "a potent bid for feminine trade." In any event, Jarrico had earned his third screen credit (as co–screenplay writer) in less than a year. He considered it a "comparatively extra-ordinary achievement. . . . On no absolute basis can this be called Accomplishment, but very few screenwriters have a first year's record to equal it."[18]

Back at Columbia, Jarrico was put to work on an untitled story involving another romantic triangle, this one set in the fast-growing commercial airline industry. However, his treatment did not satisfy the studio bosses, who put him on layoff and then let his contract lapse. He was not surprised. "In the next few months my agent should be able to get me a job someplace, and I'm not worried—but the fact remains I'm one of two hundred small time writers. . . . Luckier than the two thousand writers trying to get in (I mean here in Hollywood—there must be two million in the country)—not yet as lucky as the two hundred bigger time writers."[19]

In September, Jarrico started what he referred to as "a journal of intellectual growth." It represented both a plan to organize his life and work more efficiently and an effort to study movies more seriously. He called this new venture a scenarist's notebook, and he divided it into ten sections. Four years later, reflecting on the blank pages, Jarrico wrote, "I found—fortunately, I guess—that whatever knowledge I acquired about screenwriting went into the writing of my scripts, and not into my Notebook."[20]

In October, Jarrico signed a week-to-week contract with Nat Levine, who had once headed Republic Pictures but was now producing at Selznick International Pictures. He was, Jarrico noted, a caricature of a New Yorker. He wanted Jarrico to work with Jimmy Gruen on a story called *Frank Morgan for Senator*, but Levine told them he did not want any politics in it. Jarrico later described what it was like working for Levine: "We were explaining a set up one day in which Morgan was a frustrated radio comic, who wanted to be a public figure. Levine didn't understand what 'frustration' meant. 'Look,' said my collaborator, by way of illustration. 'A man works hard all day. But he dreams of sailing the seven seas, of taking a sail-boat to Pago Pago. . . . ' 'That's good,' said Levine. 'Put a boat in it.' We did. So help me."[21] The film was not made.

Following Jarrico's assignment with Levine, Republic Pictures hired him on a flat-rate basis ($350) to polish a treatment titled *Probation Nurse*, a story about a woman who takes refuge in a hospital to escape the mob, only to find herself assigned to nurse the mob boss. Jarrico tried to improve it by tinkering with the story line, but he did not think he had succeeded. When the studio tried to get him to write a third treatment for free, he walked off the lot. He was out of work for two months.

In March 1939, Jarrico signed a $150-a-week contract with Universal Pictures to write an original movie about logging. He carefully researched the topic, and in his research notes he commented on the efforts of Presidents Theodore and Franklin D. Roosevelt to conserve the national forests. He also concluded that here, as in other areas of the economy, private interest must give way to public welfare. Jarrico's story pits a forester for the U.S. Forest Service, who argues that devastation of timberlands causes erosion and flooding, against a group of lumber barons who practice clear cutting. Jarrico set the story in a Civilian Conservation Corps frame so it would also function as propaganda for the New Deal. His script was rewritten, but when it was issued as *Men of the Timberland*, featuring Richard Arlen and Andy Devine, Jarrico received an original story credit.

Even though he had switched agents in May, he was unemployed for two and a half months.[22] Sylvia Jarrico, meanwhile, had been hired to assist Leo C. Rosten on his sociological study of Hollywood (*Hollywood: The Movie Colony, the Movie Makers*), and she was preparing material for a doctoral thesis on film content. One night, she mentioned to Jarrico that many of the films she was seeing propagated the success story or the Cinderella myth. For fun, they elaborated on the concept, and Jarrico had what he later termed "the smart-ass notion that I would attack" the myths. Jarrico told Garson Kanin about the idea. Kanin liked it and told it to the RKO producer Pandro Berman, who also liked it. Berman signed Jarrico to another $150-a-week contract, to develop an original screen story, *Star Light Star Bright*. But in August, just as Jarrico was completing the original story, the studio suspended Kanin for refusing an assignment. Jarrico was also suspended.

After being out of work for a month, Jarrico was hired by Monogram Studios, which he described as "the smaller, cheapest independent in town." He was paid $200 a week to write a script about Rip Van Winkle. It was not made, but it remained one of his favorite scripts. Rip awakens in the midst of the debate over ratification of the Constitution and learns that it does not contain any guarantees of the rights the people had fought for during the War for Independence. Rip meets with many of the founding fathers and tells them, "The heart and marrow [of liberty is] *the right to be wrong.*

That's what liberty really means—*the right to criticize*, even if you're mistaken. . . . [I]f you haven't the right to disagree, you're nothing." He demands that they add a bill of rights to the Constitution. They concur. Rip's final words are words Jarrico recited regularly for the rest of his life: "And if we love our country, it's not enough to say 'My country, right or wrong.' What a true patriot says is 'My country, right the wrong! Right the wrong!'" He finished the script at the end of November 1939, but he was laid off when the studio decided not to film it. In December, he began what would be a five-year collaboration with Richard Collins, who had worked at 20th Century-Fox as a junior writer and had just received his first screen credit, *Rulers of the Sea* (Paramount).[23]

Looking back on his early days in the motion picture industry, Jarrico remembered that, as a screenwriter, one encountered "a lot of stupidity on the part of the people one was working for." He liked the challenge of writing, but he discovered that he needed a sense of humor to deal with producers: "I must have worked for . . . twenty producers or more, and perhaps five of them were really bright. Usually they were writers who had become producers." Jarrico himself was becoming a skilled script architect. He took his craft seriously, and he worked hard at it. He was very good at structure and spotting script problems. He was fair at dialogue. He regularly counseled himself (and others) about the need for dramatic tension, conflict, and character development, but he did not regularly accomplish them. Content, for him, was the most important element of screenwriting. But though he was capable of writing on a wide variety of subjects, he mainly stayed within the genre of the romantic comedy triangle. He did not consider himself a modernist. Rarely did he experiment with style. Michael Wilson, who would marry Sylvia Jarrico's sister, Zelma, remembered that Jarrico had a matter-of-fact attitude about screenwriting: "He didn't try to sell me on the fact that movies were a great art form."[24] Nor did Richard Collins challenge Jarrico or their partnership to attempt something different. Theirs was a conventional writing partnership, and Jarrico was the dominant force. When they taught Screenwriting III: An Advanced Course in the Screen Original at the League of American Writers–sponsored School for Writers in fall 1941, they focused solely on comedy writing.

Nevertheless, Jarrico, Collins, and Wilson, all members of the Communist Party of the United States of America (CPUSA), believed that a politically conscious screenwriter could, by paying close attention to content and character development, create better scripts and movies. By the time they joined the party, however, it was less concerned with changing the quality of Hollywood movies and more concerned with enrolling intellectuals, writers, and artists. To increase that flow, CPUSA leaders, on May 1, 1935, issued a call for an American Writers Congress to be held in New York City. Several Hollywood screenwriters (including John Howard Lawson, Samuel Ornitz, and Guy Endore) signed the call. Party leader Earl Browder told the assembled writers that the party had no intention of telling them how to write and that there was no fixed party line dividing one type of art from another. The League of American Writers was established to fight war and fascism, persecution of and discrimination against minorities, the influence of bourgeois ideas, and the imprisonment of revolutionary writers and artists. The writers pledged to defend the Soviet Union and colonial peoples in their struggle for freedom.[25]

But the Russian party leaders wanted access to a much wider public. The foundation for that gateway, what became known as the Popular Front, was laid at the seventh congress of the Communist International, which opened on July 25. There, Comintern head Georgi Dimitrov proposed a proletarian united front consisting of the "*class bodies of the united front chosen irrespective of party, at the factories, among the unemployed, in the working class districts, among the small townsfolk and in the villages.*" And, alongside it, he proposed a people's front, composed of local action committees, to recruit the unorganized, working masses (peasants and urban petite bourgeoisie). These two fronts, he continued, "are interwoven, the one passing into the other in the process of the practical struggle against fascism. . . . For it cannot be seriously supposed that it is possible to establish a genuine anti-fascist People's Front without securing the unity of the working class itself. . . . At the same time, the further development of the united proletarian front depends, to a considerable degree, upon its transformation into a People's Front against fascism."[26]

During the next four years, a variety of left-wing front groups (variously designated as united, people's, popular, or democratic front groups) were created, and CPUSA enrollment grew steadily, from 41,000 to 75,000. At the height of the Popular Front era, August 1937–August 1939, the American Left would be more unified and influential than at any other time in its history. Communists both pushed and rode the cresting waves of antifascism and industrial unionism. They and their allies would elect dozens of candidates to state and local offices, and they would launch the first significant civil rights efforts. Flush with the success of the Popular Front, Earl Browder declared in May 1938 that the CPUSA was "continuing the great American tradition, we are carrying on the work of Jefferson, Paine, [Andrew] Jackson, and Lincoln," and he proclaimed a new party slogan: "Communism is twentieth-century Americanism."[27]

As the party gravitated toward the Popular Front, party culture critics developed a more liberalized attitude toward mass-oriented entertainment. There were already a variety of Marxist-oriented groups in place, but party officials in Southern California had shown little interest in organizing the members of these groups into a Communist Party branch. Then, in the spring of 1935, party headquarters in New York sent a directive to all units in the Los Angeles section calling for "an intense concentration on Hollywood and the motion picture industry." It sent Stanley Lawrence to recruit movie writers, actors, and directors. He established a series of studio study clubs. According to Lester Cole, club meetings "were held twice a month, rotating from one member's home to the next. . . . We took turns giving 'educationals,' which for us were mainly on literature and art. In my branch, made up mostly of film people, we discussed how to increase membership and how we could support, both in activities and financially, the organizations fighting Fascism."[28] A motion picture subsection of the Los Angeles County section was formed in the summer of 1935.

In 1936, the CPUSA's national office replaced Lawrence with V. J. Jerome. Jerome separated the motion picture industry Communists from all connections with party district no. 13 and placed them directly under the supervision of party headquarters in New York City. In June, forty actors, writers, directors, and their spouses met at screenwriter Martin Berkeley's house to form the Hollywood section, which was then divided into fifteen-member groups. According to Berkeley, the more famous members, Donald Ogden Stewart, Dorothy Parker, Dashiell Hammett, and Lillian Hellman, were assigned to be party members at large. When Jerome was reassigned in 1937, the party leadership selected John Howard Lawson to replace him.[29]

In early 1937, Jarrico was approached by an acquaintance who was a Communist activist. She put him in touch with a group of young Communists working in the industry, who invited him to lunch at the Hillcrest Country Club. "It was," he remembered, "rather peculiar. . . . [I]t felt rather strange to be sitting in this den of capitalist iniquity with two sons of film executives [Maurice Rapf and Budd Schulberg], and another screenwriter, asking me to join the club."[30] As was the norm, Sylvia Jarrico was also invited to join. She recalled,

> Paul was more eager than I. [He said,] "This is the most effective way to fight fascism, and that is why we should join." I was not that intrigued by organizational politics, and I was shy of self-appointed leaders who told one what to do. But the Marxist critique and the Party's antifascism were irresistible magnets. [And] I thought it was an organization of people who really wished to make a better world, who knew ways of organizing people to get things done that they wanted to get done. I thought that they were doing the best work that I knew about in trying to respond to current issues.[31]

In those early years, Jarrico harbored few doubts about the party or any of its activities. In a letter to Cyril Endfield in late 1937, Jarrico wrote, "I want it clearly understood that I am a Communist." A few months later, in another letter to Endfield, he wrote, "So real is the revolution for me that I would—and probably will—die for it. I, molded every move by the matrix of Marxism, which was molded by the matrix of history, have begun to think socially. My ego becomes more centripetal, my thought forms and processes more collective. And what is involved is societal life, not individual life."[32]

Jarrico believed, for example, that the Soviet Union and the world's Communists were playing a necessary and positive role in Spain, despite reports he had heard that the Communists there were eliminating other *frente popular* groups. He later said,

> I felt that the only ones that Communists were interfering with were people who were trying to disrupt the united front. If there were separatists or anarchists or Trotskyites in Barcelona, then they were people who were raising conflicts within the united front that should not be raised. I didn't really know what role the Communists were playing, except that of heroic defenders of the legitimate government of Spain, and the only ones who had rallied internationally when England and France and the United States . . . had joined in this nonintervention policy, which was designed to strangle the Spanish Government at the very same time that Italy and Germany were pouring help into Spain for Franco.[33]

Jarrico also did not question the rationale for the series of show trials that had commenced in the Soviet Union in August 1936. At the first such trial, sixteen Soviet leaders were accused of participating in a "Trotskyite-Zinovievite" terrorist conspiracy, and its two "leaders," Grigorii Zinoviev and Lev Kamenev, "confessed" and were executed. At the second trial, seventeen defendants "confessed" to plotting with Trotsky, Germany, and Japan to provoke a war against the Soviet Union. Jarrico later said, "I didn't know enough about the inner inside of the Soviet history. If Stalin said Trotsky was a traitor and Trotskyites were enemies of the socialist revolution, I accepted that." He admitted that he worked out "a really simplistic explanation of why they confessed, and it was that they confessed because they were guilty."[34]

In the spring of 1937, Jarrico did some sympathetic picketing at a strike at Douglas Aviation and attended the now-annual antiwar strike at UCLA. He also played a prominent role in the Screen Writers Guild's campaign to eliminate a company union, the Screen Playwrights, which had nearly destroyed the guild the previous year. Jarrico served on the committee that sought a certification election by the National Labor Relations Board, which would allow screenwriters to vote for the union they wanted to represent them in collective bargaining negotiations with the studios. Jarrico helped to prepare the petition that convinced the board to order the election on June 6, 1938. The guild won an overwhelming victory, sweeping every studio, with a 267–57 vote margin.[35] However, it would be another two years before the writers won a contract with the studio heads, well after the actors and directors guilds had done so.

Party membership involved a great deal of time and effort. According to writer Roland Kibbee, who joined at the same time the Jarricos did, "You were given a choice of inner party or extra party work." For the latter, one would attempt to utilize one's contacts and leverage in the Hollywood community on behalf of the party and its causes. "Inner party work was more of a theoretical matter. You read books. You read a lot of literature. You were expected to report to the unit that you belonged to on various pamphlets and books and novels and treatises and so on."[36] Members attended party-related events four or five nights a week.

A typical Hollywood branch meeting consisted of reports on current affairs, political affairs (concerning a subject selected by the national office for discussion), community affairs, and procedure and a discussion of an educational or cultural issue. The cultural discussions in the writers' branches usually provoked debates on the relationship between art and propaganda. Some argued that propaganda was artless; others argued that art was a weapon in the class struggle. According to Sylvia Jarrico, the writers regularly discussed what they called "the power of film," which they thought "was the most potent educational invention in history. They did not look to alternative film making. They believed that socially responsible writers belonged in the film industry, because feature films were the most significant way in which the people of the world were being educated. This media reached so far that any victory was important."[37]

The younger writers were preoccupied with finding ways to use the movie scripts they wrote as a force for change, but they did not aspire to be, in the Soviet jargon of the time, "social realists" or "engineers of human souls." Ring Lardner Jr. admitted that it was difficult to find much of a relationship between his politics and his screen assignments, but he did try to secure projects that had some potential for injecting more progressive content. Although Communist Party officials never forced writers to develop a script in a certain way, a party writers' clinic offered assistance to Communist writers in solving script problems and adding political content to them. Rapf remembered that script discussions at the clinic sometimes degenerated into an attack on the script's political correctness. Lardner did not think that the clinic helped many individuals with the technical aspects of scriptwriting, nor that its sessions made much impact on what reached the screen.[38]

Indeed, Communist screenwriters, like other screenwriters, had very little control over the final script. A classic example was John Howard Lawson's experience with *Blockade*. When Lawson, who was perhaps the dominant personality in the Hollywood party, wrote a script about the Spanish civil war, one of his most passionate causes, he had to disguise it as a spy melodrama, and the Production Code Administration did not allow him to identify the warring sides.[39] Jarrico thought the final product was a disappointment. "If you were here," he wrote Endfield, "I'd tell you something of the conditions under which it was written, the defects of the screenplay from a craft standpoint."[40]

As it happened, Jarrico and Lawson were on opposite sides of several ongoing cultural debates among Communist screenwriters. The so-called rightists (reformists, revisionists, idealists), like Jarrico and most of the other young writers, believed that compromises were necessary to achieve success, and that once a writer became successful, he or she could "sneak in" radical material. Jarrico later said, "Even if we were more or less forced to realize that we could never have anything really radical on the screen, we did think we could have a more human attitude toward human beings in general and as individuals—humanistic values." They thought they could depict women and members of minority groups with more fairness and represent them with greater dignity, and they hoped that, on occasion, they could introduce working-class characters into their scripts. They were not, however, deluded into thinking they could add revolutionary content. "For one thing," Jarrico said, "revolution was not our line during the period of our greatest strength and influence in Hollywood," and they did not believe that the producers would ever let such content reach the screen. Though they understood the limits of what they could write, they desired to express their ideas in some form. "We were unable to get anything more than the most moderate kinds of reform messages into our films. If we thought we got some women treated as human beings rather than as sex objects, we thought it was a great victory."[41] The rightists believed that the studios had produced some great movies (*All Quiet on the Western Front*, *Scarface*, *A Farewell to Arms*,

Arrowsmith, *Of Human Bondage*, *It Happened One Night*, *Modern Times*, *The Informer*, *The Grapes of Wrath*, and *Citizen Kane*) and could, in the future, produce others.

The so-called leftists (realists), comprising Lawson and the older writers, believed that Communists could not change screen content or the industry from within because the industry was too corrupt and the studio owners too ignorant. They believed that they had to work to change the economic base of the United States before its cultural superstructure could be altered. Lawson later said, "I didn't labor under the delusion that the writer could control his material. . . . But I did think that the writer should have more participation in production."[42] The leftists believed that lists of "great" films misled people about the true nature of the motion picture industry.

These debates regularly became heated because the participants were serious about the issues on which they disagreed, but Paul Jarrico later claimed that no one expressed feelings of open hostility or betrayal during them. Though he and others disliked the style of Lawson's leadership, Jarrico and Lawson remained friends until Lawson's death.[43]

Jarrico was not perceived as a leader, even of the younger set, nor as one of the leading explicators of Marxist theory. Ben Barzman derided him as "the boy Marxist," but Dorothy Healey, a veteran Los Angeles party leader with close connections to the Hollywood groups, thought he was "a serious and sober Marxist" with "a marvelous capacity for finding the funny side of Party issues." Jarrico read the classic Marxist and Leninist texts and popularizations of Marxism, but he later noted, "I didn't consider myself a leading theoretician in any way, but as somebody who was deeply interested in social science and thought that Marxism had a lot to contribute to an understanding of society and history and forces at work in history, and also philosophically." Sylvia Jarrico said that he knew the issues and felt "the need to do something about them." Jarrico deeply respected the party as an active agency. He himself was "always engaged in activity," Sylvia remembered. "He was in constant touch with other people. I don't remember him challenging Party positions. In his own eyes, he did not have that authority, nor did he assume it. He was a high-spirited collaborator."[44]

Jarrico considered himself a reformist Communist. He did not believe that a violent revolution was required to transform the United States from a capitalist to a socialist economic system. He did, however, believe that social transformation was "pretty far down the line" and that, when it came, it would be accompanied by a "very, very sharp conflict."[45]

Jarrico never felt that party membership placed him outside the mainstream of American politics. He did not feel like "some sort of foreign agent, not just in the conventional sense of some spy for Russia, but . . . in the sense of some man from Mars who was . . . not really in tune with what was happening in his own country."[46] He joined, among other groups, the Motion Picture Democratic Committee and the Hollywood Anti-Nazi League. He worked on the former's 1938 campaigns to elect progressive politicians, notably the gubernatorial candidate Culbert Olson, and he helped raise money for the John Steinbeck Committee to Aid Migratory Workers. For a mass meeting held at the Philharmonic Auditorium, Jarrico wrote lyrics to be set to the tune of "Old MacDonald Had a Farm":

Walter Chambers had a fright
CI, CIO
He woke up screaming in the night
CI, CIO
With a picket line here
And a picket line there
Here a picket, there a picket
Everywhere a picket picket
Walter Chambers had a fright
CI, CIO
He laid off workers left and right
CI, CIO[47]

Jarrico also renewed his interest in Jewish affairs, and here he took exception to some of the party's positions. For example, he disagreed with the Comintern's line that Zionism was a distraction from antifascism. He argued that Zionism was primarily a mass movement of Jewish workers and that, "whether we like it or not, a *Jewish* problem does exist, that in Germany and other fascist countries a large group of men and women are attacked as Jews, not as workers, or small capitalists, and that no matter how clearly these Jews realize that their salvation lies in a class attack, they must for the present defend themselves as Jews." He also criticized the Communist press for its continual attacks on Zionism. Those attacks, he said, undermined a possible united front between the many Jewish Socialists who were also Zionists and the CPUSA. He wrote to Hal Smith, "My Uncle Chaim, I am proud to say, is one of the strongest supporters and builders of this united front, despite his fervent Zionism. He was recently elected, by a popular vote of Los Angeles Jewry, to be a delegate—one of fifty from the United States, I think—to Biro Bidjan [the autonomous Jewish province in the USSR]."[48] Though Jarrico also expressed approval of the Zionists' goal to establish a Jewish state in Palestine, he did not think it the most important objective for Jewish radicals.

In May 1939, in an article on anti-Semitism he submitted to the literary magazine *Black and White*, Jarrico attacked the "Jews make the movies" charge. That accusation, he argued, was part of the campaign by reactionaries, using the canard of "Jewish influence" to condemn all of Hollywood's products. He called on people to "reiterate, answer, explain, refute! . . . [W]e who love democracy must post signs in every public place: Beware of the little mouse of anti-Semitism. On its back it carries a flea, and the flea bears a plague that will destroy mankind! And because Hollywood bears the brunt of the Jew-baiter's barrage, Hollywood must resist it most forcefully. Appeasement, as Europe has discovered is suicidal surrender. An uncompromising and united effort is victory."[49]

3

World War II, 1939–45

> And that, of course, is when we made our biggest and most stupid blunder, one that cost us most of the respect we had won.
>
> —*Paul Jarrico, 1997*

The Popular Front groups had effectively united liberals, Socialists, a few conservatives, and all Communists in a series of organizations to elect progressive candidates, organize unions, and fight against fascism and Nazism. But the fronts had been constructed on an unstable foundation: non-Communist adherents treated it as a permanent bloc; Soviet Communist leaders treated it as a tactical arrangement. At the height of its success, in late summer 1939, a seismic jolt radiating from a Soviet foreign policy decision razed the edifice.

Front groups had already come under attack from two newly formed liberal antifascist groups: the Committee for Cultural Freedom and the League for Cultural Freedom and Socialism. They conflated fascism, Nazism, and communism and branded them as totalitarian doctrines. They also questioned the commitment of Popular Front groups to the maintenance of peace. In reaction to this charge, four hundred "supporters of democracy and action" sent a letter to the *Daily Worker* on August 14, ridiculing the notion that Stalin would make a deal with Hitler and proclaiming the Soviet Union "a bulwark against war and aggression."[1]

Nine days later, German foreign minister Joachim von Ribbentrop flew to Moscow to sign a nonaggression treaty with the Soviet Union.

He and Soviet foreign minister Vyacheslav Molotov, "guided by their desire to strengthen the cause of peace" between the two countries, agreed "to refrain from any act of force, any aggressive act, or any attack against each other, either individually or in conjunction with other powers." Eight days later, Molotov told the Supreme Soviet that the treaty "served the cause of universal peace."[2] On September 1, the German army invaded Poland, and two days later Britain and France declared war on Germany.

In the weeks following the announcement of the nonaggression treaty, Communist Party leaders all over the world desperately tried to find a way to meld the collective security tactics of the antifascist fronts with the treaty and the start of a new European war. Finally, in October, the CPUSA Political Committee announced, "The present war is an imperialist war for which the bourgeoisie of all belligerent powers are equally guilty." It also stated that the world was no longer divided between the "camps of democracy and fascism." Rather, the main camps were now "the anti-imperialist, antiwar, anti-monopoly camp of the working class and its allies" and "the camp of the imperialist bourgeoisie of all capitalist countries."[3] Party leaders prepared a series of educational papers arguing that the Soviet workers' state had to protect itself from the warmongering conspiracies of other states. Party members were ordered to transform the antifascist and political organizations to which they belonged into institutions that would urge the United States to remain neutral. The National Committee declared in October that the main party task was to "keep America out of the imperialist war!"

The Communists succeeded in these transformations, but at a high cost: virtually all non-Communists resigned from the Popular Front organizations, and many Communists left the party. The Hollywood Anti-Nazi League was renamed the Hollywood Peace Forum, and the Motion Picture Democratic Committee was renamed the Hollywood League for Democratic Action. In his autobiography, Dore Schary wrote, "What irritated us [liberals] was that so many of our [Communist] associates touched their fingers together and spoke piously of peace," instead of admitting it was a temporary tactic.[4] Similar chasms opened within labor organizations.

The exodus from Popular Front groups fed the stream of anticommunism in the United States, which had weakened between 1925 and 1938, and a new red scare commenced. In a June 1940 *Fortune* magazine poll, 43 percent of respondents supported some form of "drastic action" against Communists in the United States. And polls during the next eighteen months showed that most Americans believed that Communists were the greatest single menace to the American way of life.[5] Echoing the Committee for Cultural Freedom and the League for Cultural Freedom and Socialism, one contributor to an academic symposium on totalitarianism labeled the Soviet Union, fascist Italy, and Nazi Germany as totalitarian states.[6] Eugene Lyons, in his lengthy polemic *The Red Decade: The Stalinist Penetration of America* (1941), included an indictment of Hollywood in which he provided a long list of "Communist" organizations and the names of people affiliated with them.[7]

The nonaggression treaty generated a strong anti-Communist surge in the newly formed Special Committee on Un-American Activities of the U.S. House of Representatives and sparked the creation of the Fact-Finding Committee on Un-American Activities in California, spearheaded by Senator Jack Tenney.[8] State and federal legislatures passed dozens of laws aimed against the Communist Party. The main one was the Alien Registration Act, an omnibus bill that Congress voted into law in May 1940. This act required the mandatory registration and fingerprinting of all resident aliens; facilitated the deportation of anyone who challenged the armed forces; and made it unlawful for any person "to knowingly or willfully advocate, abet, advise, or teach the duty, necessity, desirability, or propriety of overthrowing or destroying any government in the United States by force or violence," to prepare or distribute any printed or written matter advocating such an overthrow, or to organize or become associated with any society or group that taught, advocated, or encouraged such an overthrow. Congress also authorized the attorney general to prepare a list of subversive organizations. And the Federal Bureau of Investigation, given enhanced powers of investigation by the president and Congress, increased its staff of agents from 713 in 1939 to 7,442 in 1943 and its support staff from 1,199 to 7,442.[9]

Jarrico stalwartly defended the party and what remained of the Popular Front organizations, but he later said that the anti-interventionist line of October 1939 "was the one switch that did trouble me and troubled me a lot." Dorothy Healey recalled that Jarrico was outraged by it. On the one hand, Jarrico believed that the United States, Great Britain, and France were attempting to arrange a war between Germany and the Soviet Union and that Stalin had signed the nonaggression treaty both to prevent such a war and to buy time to build the country's defenses. On the other hand, he did not believe that France and Great Britain were acting in an imperialist, warlike manner. In his mind, the Communist leaders, by insisting on an anti-imperialist line and a "Yanks are not coming" slogan, placed U.S. Communists on the same side as the most reactionary isolationists. Jarrico was "embarrassed by it." Sylvia Jarrico was also troubled by the party rationale. Nevertheless, she recalled, most of the Hollywood Communists acquiesced and shifted to an anti-interventionist position. Though there were no serious defections from the Hollywood branches, there were no new recruits either. "One had to be very strong in one's beliefs," she said, "to remain in or join the Party during that period."[10]

The nonaggression treaty was the first experience most Hollywood Communists had with a sharp turn in Soviet-directed strategy, and they possessed few guidelines. Jarrico wrote to Hal Smith that he spent most of his nonwriting time "talking to people who think Stalin has betrayed them. I am thinking of opening a rest-home for liberals." Years later, Jarrico recalled that he would tell people who were appalled by this shift in the party line, "Don't worry! The day will come when the Soviet Union will save you yet." Haskell Shapiro, Jarrico's cousin, recalled that Jarrico's support of the nonaggression treaty produced a bitter reaction from the family. "I felt he had joined the Nazis. I was totally appalled by his failure to denounce the Soviet Union at that point." In an agenda book entry for October 18, Jarrico wrote, "Bet with Dore [Schary] on the USSR."[11]

Jarrico devoted most of his political energy to organizations, like the American Peace Mobilization and the Hollywood League for Democratic Action, that, in addition to their antiwar campaign, attempted to protect the civil liberties of those in the antiwar camp and combat anti-Semitism. Jarrico wrote to Hal Smith in July 1940, "We have a peace crusade in this neck of the woods which is really beginning to look like something."[12] When Ellis Patterson ran for Democratic nominee for governor of California at the head of an antiwar, anti–third term (for Roosevelt) slate and was attacked by Governor Culbert Olson, Jarrico accused Olson of red baiting.

In January 1940, Jarrico legally changed his name. One month later, the Jarricos' only child, William Aaron Jarrico, was born. Jarrico's delight with his new son was tempered by his discomfort with his on-again, off-again employment. He had been hired at Fox to work on *Pier 13*, which was, he said, "a very bad story. . . . It's a remake of an old Spencer Tracy picture called *Me and My Girl*, only now it's without Tracy and it's a B. I don't like Bs anymore. I do not know why, but I do not."[13] For reasons he did not disclose, Jarrico was suddenly fired by the studio.

In March, RKO rehired Jarrico to write the screenplay for *Star Light Star Bright*, which would be retitled *Tom, Dick and Harry*. He was to be paid $250 per week. By the time he completed the first draft, however, Garson Kanin, who had been brought back to direct, was shooting another film. Jarrico, placed on leave, revised scripts at two other studios. He returned to RKO in October, wrote two more drafts of the screenplay, and worked alongside Kanin while *Tom, Dick and Harry* was shot (February–May 1941). Jarrico and Sylvia often joked that when Bill grew older and someone asked him what his father did, Bill would reply, "He works on *Tom, Dick and Harry*."

The witticism was only partly humorous. Jarrico's work on that script had begun in July 1939, when he wrote an original story about a woman who possesses the qualities of "skeptical naivete and healthy *humorous* romanticism." She is looking for her prince charming among three eligible suitors: an ambitious automobile salesman, a rich man, and an auto mechanic. She finally chooses the mechanic because "he offers her dignity as a human being." In a memo to producer Pandro Berman, Jarrico explained his theme: "There have been so many Success Stories, so many Cinderella Stories. But actually there are as few rich men available to the millions of romantic girls as there are places at the top of the economic ladder for the millions of ambitious boys. These millions are in the theaters, they are the audience. This story glorifies *them*, the failures and the frustrated ones. It tells them that their lives too have importance and meaning. And I think this is well worth saying."[14]

But there were problems with the story. In his revision notes, Jarrico wrote that the main flaw was that "the characters were insufficiently understood and badly drawn." The woman was "two dimensional, a caricature of a dreamy romantic girl"; the salesman was too stereotyped; and the mechanic was "too damned namby pamby. . . . He should be tough, vital, a guy who works hard and knows how to laugh and likes a lot of people." He should also strongly assert cooperation over competition as a working-class value.[15]

In the final shooting script, telephone operator Janie becomes engaged to three men. During each engagement, she dreams about what her life would be like with the current fiancé. Though they are all decent men, only Harry, the mechanic, lives by a worthy credo. He tells Janie that it is all right to try to get ahead but that one must do so "without slugging all the time. I think that living with people is better than fighting with them. And I don't believe in every man for himself. I get lonesome." Though Janie at first chooses the millionaire because she has been dreaming about doing so her whole life, she changes her mind when she hears bells ring as she kisses Harry goodbye.

When Kanin began shooting the film in February 1941, he asked Jarrico to be on the set for each day's filming. Jarrico wrote Hal Smith, "I don't do much—make a few line changes on the set, work with Kanin nights on the stuff he's going to shoot the next day and it's all getting a little irritating, like too much ice cream. But it looks as though the picture will be good, just how good I don't know, but certainly not bad." In a letter to Diana Bricks, however, he admitted that he was fortunate to be allowed to follow the production all the way through and that he had learned a great deal.[16]

Tom, Dick and Harry, starring Ginger Rogers (Janie), George Murphy (salesman), Alan Marshal (rich man), and Burgess Meredith (Harry), opened on July 19. It was well received by the critics. The *Hollywood Reporter* critic wrote that "no brighter piece of satirical foolishness has emerged from Hollywood in many a day." The

Variety critic complimented Jarrico on the story and screenplay. All the Los Angeles and New York dailies printed glowing reviews, as did *Newsweek*, the *New Yorker*, and the *New Republic*. It was even selected as *Life* magazine's movie of the week. But when Otis Ferguson, in the *New Republic*, titled his review "Garson's Guard" and wrote that the flow of the movie "may be credited to the work of several writers and assistants," Jarrico wrote to him angrily, "Will you tell me what the fuck you meant by [that] sentence . . . ? If you meant everybody helped, okay. But the sentence, unfortunately, implies a couple of ghost writers. This makes a shit out of Jarrico. Out of Ferguson, too. So have the little colored boy [!] who writes your stuff be more careful in the future." Ferguson replied that he would apologize publicly and reiterated his belief that it was "a very smart bit of screenwriting." A few months later, Ferguson added the following paragraph to his column: "In reviewing 'Tom, Dick and Harry,' I used the term 'Garson's guard' in a loose and foolish way to designate the people who did some of the worrying on the stages and over the rushes. If this confused anybody about Paul Jarrico's true worth as the author of the screenplay except Jarrico (the rat), I'm mortified. It was a sweet little job."[17]

Even the Communist press ran positive reviews. Future screenwriter Alvah Bessie wrote in *New Masses* that the script "abounds in excellent comedy lines," though he found the "message" routine. The critic for the *Daily Worker* simply raved, "the screwiest and most delightful farce of the year"; "striking originality"; "an ingenious, witty film." One year later, however, Joy Davidman, writing in *New Masses*, singled out *Tom, Dick and Harry* for special criticism in an article that condemned the treatment of women in American films and criticized Hollywood for lagging behind the rest of the country in the emancipation of women. Though she complimented it as "an unusually original comedy, with much genuine wit and some genuine tenderness," she chastised the writer for commodifying sexuality and for depicting Janie's work as a mere stop-gap to her marriage. She also condemned Jarrico's romantic solution to Janie's dilemma. Having her marry the one whose kisses ring her bell the loudest was the "romantic" solution, wrote Davidman, but "'romance' is an indispensable adjunct of male chauvinism." The movie, she continued, "never made any suggestion that the heroine might have something to offer the world as an individual."[18]

Jarrico took the criticism seriously and composed a three-page outline of the article in which he listed what was "right," "partly right," and "wrong" with Davidman's criticisms. The gist of his response was that Davidman did not understand the movie industry and, though she had made some accurate points about movies involving women, she was blind to the exceptions and the positive trends. She had, he wrote, particularly failed to see that movies are a "people's culture," that films are responsible for providing entertainment to their audience, and that it was a "thrill" to write for a mass audience. He concluded, "She doesn't like or understand Hollywood. The affirmative truth of a people's culture." In a draft of a letter that he apparently never sent, he sarcastically congratulated her: "To have arrived at such correct conclusions on the basis of such miasmal reasoning seems to me a triumph of dialectical thought."[19]

At the time, Jarrico was pleased with his work on *Tom, Dick and Harry*. He wrote Kanin, "No writer . . . was ever treated more fairly or credited more fully and I know I have you to thank for that. Thank you." When Jarrico received an Academy Award nomination for best original screenplay, he wrote Kanin, "Dear Gar, I.O.U. 1 career." But his later reflections on the film echoed Davidson's criticisms. "Essentially, the girl marries the poor fellow not because his ideology is more persuasive, but because when they kiss they ring bells. So I found the picture propagating the very basic notions of love conquering all that I had set out, if not to subvert, at least to provide a substitute for. . . . But I don't blame myself for having tried."[20] In the end, *Tom, Dick and Harry* is a sweet movie lacking critical bite.

In the months between finishing the first draft of *Tom, Dick and Harry* and the commencement of filming, Jarrico cowrote (with Lester Koenig) a script titled *All Night Program* for Republic, for which he was paid $50 more a week than he received from RKO. He then received another $50-a-week raise from Columbia to do a polish job on *The Face behind the Mask*, which featured Peter Lorre. Jarrico received a co–screenplay credit for his work on this script about a hideously burned man who joins a robbery gang so he can pay a plastic surgeon to repair his face. The surgeon informs him that the damage is irreparable. The protagonist falls in love with a blind girl and leaves the gang; the gang members, thinking he has informed on them, kill the girl. He kills them and himself. The reviewer for the *New York Times* wrote, "Despite a certain pretentiousness toward things psychological, . . . [it] is just another bald melodramatic exercise," with "hackneyed dialogue and conventional plot manipulations." *The Weekly Variety* review complimented the story but complained that it included too much "stilted dialogue."[21] Still, it is the best movie Jarrico worked on. Now a cult favorite, it is an excellent protonoir with a clear story line, believable dialogue and motivations, and a powerful ending.

Jarrico and Richard Collins soon began writing, on speculation, a love story between a militant feminist and a male chauvinist editor who work for a big-game hunting magazine. MGM purchased *That Was No Lady* for $12,500 (though the film was not made because the producer assigned to it thought the heroine too militant). Buoyed by that success, Jarrico and Collins began work on another speculative story, based on Collins's experience selling vacuum cleaners, titled *Boy Wonder*. They intended it as a satire on the rise-from-the-bottom myth. A meek door-to-door salesman is tricked into believing he can read minds. He gains self-confidence, becomes a success, is promoted, and then is summoned to company headquarters, where he eventually democratizes a soulless corporate giant. Universal purchased the story for $15,000 and contracted with Jarrico and Collins to write the screenplay for another $15,000.

When they ran into difficulty melding the confidence-in-oneself theme with the guy-who-represents-the-people theme, they submitted the script to a party writers' clinic for comments. Herbert Biberman, John Howard Lawson, Michael Wilson, and Morton Grant read the script and pointed out four major problems: it lacked conflict, climax, structure, and a hero exercising free will. They wondered what Jarrico and Collins were trying to satirize. Though they agreed it might be commercially viable, they were concerned with what the script revealed about the writers' level of sophistication, particularly with respect to their skill at crafting a story supposedly focused on social problems. Lawson was scathing, calling it a bad, unfunny script that dealt with too abstract a problem (illusion versus reality). In his typed summary of the discussion, Jarrico noted that the participants had questioned whether the authors had accomplished their original goal of debunking the success story, "or is it (as stated forcefully by one person present) *a success story as it stands:* to be sure, there are some satirical trimmings, but basically it shows how you can get away with anything if you believe in yourself—which is the typical success story. It was further questioned whether the whole idea of the success story has any validity at the present time? It was a valid angle on American life a few years ago. But the crucial life-and-death fight going on to save the nation today makes the success story seem old-fashioned." Jarrico and Collins accepted the general criticism, but they doubted that the studio would allow them to undertake a complete rewrite. They decided that they would attempt to polish and strengthen the script along the lines indicated and to find a more effective climax.[22]

They also sent the script to Garson Kanin and Dore Schary, both of whom found it disappointing. A few months later, in a letter to Kanin, Jarrico admitted that he had still not figured out what the problem was, but, he continued, "I think it has something to do with an attempt to induce large social meanings from small dramatic potatoes. We wanted to satirize the folklore of capitalism and we wound up with cliché symbols (straight out of [Frank] Capra) for characters, and ideological differences (mysticism vs. Realism) for conflict, and a segment of the class struggle (the petty bourgeois vs. the finance capitalist) for a climax." In any event, their script was not put into production.[23]

While Jarrico and Collins were working on *Boy Wonder*, on June 21, the German armed forces invaded the Soviet Union, temporarily muting official anticommunism in the United States and resurrecting the Popular Front. The Communists became fervent supporters of the war against "fascist aggression." The American Peace Mobilization became the American People's Mobilization and drafted a new program: support all people fighting fascism, strengthen democracy at home, and struggle for a "people's democratic peace."[24]

The Communist Party subordinated everything to the goal of winning the war. Jarrico later said, "During the war, the CPUSA was more patriotic than anyone, so fucking patriotic in fact that we didn't protest the internment of the Japanese or the prosecution of the Trotskyites under the Smith Act. Yes, we were right in the mainstream."[25] The party also militantly supported a no-strike policy, which antagonized many workers. The Communists remained faithful to only two of their prewar positions: antifascism and antiracism.

Party front groups of intellectuals and artists were notably patriotic. When the CPUSA leaders decided to abolish the League of American Writers, its more than one hundred Communist members joined the Hollywood Writers Mobilization (HWM), the largest and most active wartime Popular Front organization in the movie capital. Created by and headquartered at the Screen Writers Guild (SWG), the HWM also represented several other associations, including the Radio Writers and Screen Cartoonists guilds. Its members drafted speeches for stars and studio executives who were selling war bonds or encouraging donations of blood. They also helped prepare theatrical material for troop entertainment and wrote pamphlets explaining rationing, price control, and conservation. The HWM's most significant effort was its cosponsorship (with UCLA) of a national writers' congress, which met in the fall of 1943. As a result of its activities, the HWM became a constant target of red baiters, notably California senator Jack Tenney.[26]

Jarrico and Collins served on the staff of *Communiqué*, the HWM's weekly bulletin. Jarrico wrote one of his friends, "Most of us are working very hard through the Hollywood Writers Mobilization, a triumph of unity and effectiveness. . . . Every dream we've ever had for the unity of anti-fascist writers is being realized through the Mobilization." According to Collins, the party altered its approach to non-Communist organizations such as the HWM. Instead of holding fraction meetings, where party members in a particular organization met separately to plan tactics, the Communists worked openly, in a "progressive caucus" of Communists and non-Communists. That is, the Communists began to operate on the theory "that there were no interests of the mass organizations that were in any way different from the Communists'." Hence, anything that could be discussed in a Communist meeting could be discussed outside it.[27]

Though many other Hollywood Communists tried to enlist in some branch of the armed services, Jarrico at first did not seem interested. He wanted the Communist screenwriters who remained in Hollywood to focus on the content of the feature-length films they wrote. He thought they could make their greatest impact on content if they convinced the studio executives to establish industry committees, in particular a coordination committee and a labor management production committee. The former would function "as a Censorship Board to stop the production of any and all stories, sequences, or dialogue harmful to the Allied War Effort and helpful to the Axis Propaganda Line." The latter would help solve labor problems, integrate the motion picture industry with the national economy, and advance labor unity in the industry. Neither committee would attempt to change the basic structure of the industry or the "basic control of product." In the section of his outline titled "Our Approach to Content of Pictures," Jarrico wrote,

> A. Content of motion pictures has always been designed to condition audiences to capitalist way of life. This is still the main responsibility of pictures.
>
> B. Pictures must reflect changes in American life as dictated by war necessity . . . and must pave the way for further changes in daily life which war is bringing about.
>
> C. This aim is a basic capitalist aim, and therefore nothing is being put over on producers.
>
> D. Must retain familiar forms and patterns, as these are acceptable to American audiences, developing new content within these forms as the people portrayed are faced with new problems. Gradual changes in forms possible with development of war.

He also argued that there should be "no separation of propaganda and escapism. Everything is propaganda. Problem is to help the war. We want it *all* to be entertainment—comedies, musicals, with content that helps win the war."[28]

As part of his effort to improve screen content, Jarrico served as secretary for the Hollywood party's writers' clinic, which met frequently between February 1 and August 9, 1942. During these meetings, the "script doctors" discussed thirty-three projects (including twelve written by members of the clinic). Jarrico noted that only one of the scripts "failed to be benefitted" and that "two were benefitted but unhappy."[29]

Though there was much discussion of structure, plot continuity, character development, and climax, the main focus of each discussion was the manner in which the writer integrated the war into the project. The doctors criticized the script *Story about a Judge* for failing to consider the impact of the war. They thought that a script for a radio program about rehabilitation of criminals should explain how the war was promoting a better understanding of unity, service to a bigger cause, and the values of a collectivist social outlook. A story about a European violinist who immigrated to the United States after the Munich conference offered the possibility "to show that not the fat people of the salons, but the organizations of the soldiers and people were emerging, like the U.S.O. and Red Cross, to give music to the people." Bernard Vorhaus, author of *China Story*, was told that if he could not tie his characters into "a conscious relation to the war," the movie made from his script would not be "as commercially successful."[30]

At the eighth session, on March 29, the script doctors posed the following questions for themselves:

> 1. When is a war story a war story?
> 2. Is it enough to have war as a background and talking about it without integrating story's plot in it? Can any story be the same or essentially the same in war or in peace?
> 3. Fifth columnist is melodramatic—can be corny—can be tremendously revealing.[31] Can we be superior to devices?
> 4. When one permits plot and characterization to be shallow is this an indication of lack of respect for Hollywood and pictures?
> 5. What is heroism? . . .
> 6. Can a full and satisfactory story of men be told with no attempt to integrate women into the story? Is love relationship central or just diverting and hence dispensable at will?[32]

Two scripts, one for a play titled *Winter Soldiers* and the other for a movie titled *A Tank Named John*, raised a theoretical question: "Can such an abstraction [as the story of a military offensive or the building of a tank] carry an audience forward with the same personal interest as they would feel in a play that develops one set of characters?" According to the notes of the discussion of *A Tank Named John*, the doctors split into two main camps. The "factory partisans" (probably led by Lawson) argued that "the key to the story lay in the tank factory itself and the production problems raised by the new factory and of the workers in it." The "human relations partisans" (Jarrico and Wilson among them) insisted that the story be told in human terms and "not in terms of production problems." The factory partisans "countered with the argument that human relationships apart from the factory are abstract." The human relations partisans responded that political values and social values would come naturally out of a well-written background story. The group also split over a story about the United Nations, this time into "historians" and "humanists."[33] The historians wanted the script's writer to analyze the backgrounds of the key characters, while the humanists wanted the focus to be on the current conflicts between them. The doctors tepidly reviewed the antifascist script by Donald Ogden Stewart that became the basis for the film *Keeper of the Flame* (MGM) and, as we have seen, responded equally unenthusiastically to Jarrico and Collins's *Boy Wonder*.[34]

For the last clinic discussion, Michael Wilson prepared a paper, "Notes on Change in Character," an "attempt to re-examine certain basic theses of the Marxist aesthetic." Marxist writers, he explained, tend "to confuse *development* in character with *transformation* and *metamorphosis* of character. There has been a feeling, expressed in many ways, that 'mere development' of character is not enough—that for a story to be intriguing, a character must undergo a complete *qualitative* change." He cited as an example, without naming it, *Thousands Cheer*, in which a jerk becomes a deserter becomes a hero. "This is 'change' with a vengeance, and with at least enough conflict to shake a stick at—but is it *development* of character? . . . I am getting a little weary of conversion pictures. . . . Usually they don't reveal American character—they only libel it. I'm tired of seeing the American people portrayed as knaves and fools who need a second-act climax to wake them up." Wilson cited two pictures, both written by non-Marxists, that demonstrated his point: *Joe Smith, American* (MGM, 1942) and *Mrs. Miniver* (MGM, 1942). In both movies, the main characters change in small, realistic ways; they are "in a constant process of becoming." To do otherwise, that is, to transform characters in "one fell swoop for purposes of artistic finality does not, as *Tass* [the Soviet news service] would say, correspond to reality." Indeed, it is often "a short-cut, a device that gives us an easy escape from character development by oversimplifying conflicts, by introducing a dramatic switch in a character's values, etc."[35]

In June 1942, Jarrico reported to the clinic that MGM was planning a biography of President Andrew Johnson that lionized Johnson, an outspoken white supremacist, and demonized Thaddeus Stevens, leader of the Radical Republicans' effort to provide rights and land to the freedmen. Four MGM writers (Donald Ogden Stewart, Hy Kraft, Richard Collins, and Ring Lardner Jr.) and director Jules Dassin had already registered a protest, to no avail. In the discussion that ensued, the writers' clinic doctors concluded that the script was "a deliberate and calculated effort" by studio reactionaries to distort "historical material to sell fascist ideas." They were sharply divided, however, on what to do if given the script. Jarrico's notes read,

> One said that inasmuch as the picture was based on a lie, there was absolutely nothing that could be done. That, should one of us be given this assignment an effort should be made to change entirely the point of the story, or turn down the job, if the writer could afford to. The second viewpoint was that many of the speeches, scenes and ideas could be watered down so that the picture would become innocuous.
>
> This last view was sharply attacked on the following lines: 1) There were limits to what the writer was expected to demand of himself as a craftsman; 2) That, in the political arena, there was a point at which we refused to go along with certain groups, and the same applied in the accepting of assignments of this sort.[36]

There was, however, no discussion of what the Hollywood Communists as a group could or should do about this movie. Someone on the MGM lot did send a copy of the synopsis to David Platt, the film critic of the *Daily Worker*, who in turn alerted the Office of War Information (OWI) and Walter White, the head of the National Association for the Advancement of Colored People. White sent a critical analysis to MGM and applied personal pressure on studio head Louis B. Mayer and Lowell Mellett of the OWI. Mellett wrote to Mayer, "The film, as currently planned, would be injurious to national war morale and especially that of the country's Negro population." Mayer, who blamed the "communist cell in [his] studio" for this problem, flew to Washington to discuss the protest with OWI officials and, in September, ordered a series of script revisions and retakes.[37] Thaddeus Stevens was now depicted as a sincere but misguided man, and Andrew Johnson remained a man of virtue.

When *Tennessee Johnson* was released in December, most reviewers termed it a fine, absorbing, and accurate biography.[38] Viewed today, it is a fabrication, a whitewash of a racist and a denigration of a sincere partisan of civil rights. It fails as history in that it neither associates Johnson with the rise of white supremacy in the postwar South nor demonstrates the effects of his policies on black people.

Jarrico's Screenwriting

Following the attack on Pearl Harbor, Jarrico and Collins were paid a flat fee to write an additional scene for Alfred Hitchcock's *Saboteur* (Universal, 1942). They then returned to Universal for two weeks to do more work on *Boy Wonder*. When a promised job from MGM producer Joe Pasternak did not materialize, they accepted an offer from Samuel Goldwyn to work on *Treasure Chest*, a screwball comedy about the inventor of rubber. Jarrico and Collins completed a step outline, but neither the producers nor Goldwyn liked it. Believing that they could not satisfy Goldwyn, they asked a producer at Universal for a job. At Universal, they were assigned to write the script for *Three Smart Girls Join Up*, a Deanna Durbin feature. Durbin's character, the youngest of three wealthy sisters, studies welding, gets a factory job, falls in love with another welder, overcomes family objections to her lover, and marries him. The producer, however, wanted the emphasis placed on the home relationship of the three sisters, while Jarrico and Collins insisted it should be on her relations with the other workers in the factory. They were replaced, and the studio did not give them a screen credit on the final product, *Hers to Hold*.

On April 13, Jarrico and Collins went to work at MGM, then considered to be the ideal studio in terms of stars and properties. Screenwriter Daniel Fuchs called it "the top, the Bank of England." It was also the most politically divided. Collins remembered that in the studio commissary there was "a left-wing table, a liberal table, and a right-wing table." When director Frank Tarloff went to work at MGM in 1942, he sat "at what was known as the 'Red Table,' with Dalton Trumbo, with Paul Jarrico, all the lefties."[39]

Jarrico and Collins were assigned to Joe Pasternak's unit. He asked them to write a musical story situated on an army base as a vehicle for Kathryn Grayson and Gene Kelly. Jarrico and Collins's story, based on a synopsis prepared by the head of the story department, Kenneth MacKenna, concerned an egotistical circus star (Kelly) who is bitter about having to join the army. He falls in love with the daughter (Grayson) of his commanding officer, and she eventually (in sixty minutes of screen time) teaches him that there is no contradiction between democracy and discipline, that people need to depend on one another, and that humility, love, and respect are human strengths. When the Kelly character proclaims that there are only two kinds of people in this world, big shots and little shots, and that "wars are made because big shots order 'em—and peace too," Grayson responds, "No. This is the war of the little shots—the common people control their own destiny—they're going to win the war and make the peace, and fix a world where there won't be any more war." Jarrico wrote Garson Kanin, "We have high hopes for its propaganda value and fair hopes for its cinematic value." But when he and Collins brought a copy of the script to the party writers' clinic in July, the doctors suggested that they make the Kelly character bitter about the army, not the war, and have him learn that the U.S. Army is democratic, not autocratic.[40]

Jarrico and Collins turned in a completed script at the end of October 1942. Eleven other writers made revisions and wrote retakes through the end of June 1943. Dorothy Kingsley, one of the studio's best musical writers, was brought in four times to rewrite or add skits and sketches for the closing big show. By the time the movie was released, in January 1944, MGM executives had become convinced that movie audiences were tiring of war movies, and so the movie's title was changed to *Thousands Cheer*. As we have seen, Michael Wilson faulted the film as an inadequate conversion picture; Jarrico himself considered it a banal story. But the reviewer for the *New York Times* wrote that the script "has a warmth not usually found in the boy-meets-girl formula," and the *Variety* reviewer noted that the writers "supplied a smooth story."[41] In addition, the movie was financially successful, and it raised Jarrico and Collins's status at the studio. Overall, however, the film is an unremarkable example of the Pasternak unit's output. The hero learns that the army is fair, that army officers are worthy of respect, and that discipline, teamwork, and cooperation are worthy goals, but the story does not get in the way of the many musical numbers parading MGM's arsenal of performing stars (Mickey Rooney, Judy Garland, et al.).

The Russian Connection

In the war's early years, it was considered patriotic to be pro–Soviet Union. A Gallup Poll published on July 13, 1941, found that 72 percent of the respondents favored a Soviet victory over the Germans. In November 1942, a group of distinguished New York City politicians and business leaders sponsored a Thanks to Russia month (from Thanksgiving to Christmas), inaugurated by a gala dinner for more than one thousand people at the Waldorf-Astoria Hotel. *Time* magazine named Stalin its man of the year for 1942, and *Life* magazine in 1943 devoted a special issue to the Soviet Union, with a picture of Joseph Stalin on the cover. Probably two dozen movies about the Soviet Union were made or distributed by the major studios, five of which were notable: *Mission to Moscow* (Warner Brothers), *The North Star* (Samuel Goldwyn), *Song of Russia* (MGM), *Three Russian Girls* (United Artists), and *Days of Glory* (RKO). Though the first three, after the war, were regularly cited by anti-Communists as evidence of Communist infiltration of the movie industry, at the time of their release only *Mission to Moscow* was so targeted.[42]

American Communist screenwriters were, of course, eager to write about the Soviet war effort. In early 1942, Nat Goldstone sent *Scorched Earth*, written by Leo Mittler, Victor Trivas, and Guy Endore, to Kenneth MacKenna at MGM. Goldstone summarized the story: "A settlement, dedicated to music in honor of Tchaikovsky who wrote his masterpieces here, prepares for war, despite elderly people's conviction that even Hitler would consider this world-shrine sacred. They soon find out how little regard the Nazis have for culture. A young American conductor [John], in love with a girl of the village [Nadya], tries to persuade her to come with him to safety, but she understands, as he later learns from experience with the Nazi atrocities, that nothing is important now but to crush fascism." The studio reader enthusiastically endorsed the story, describing it as unusual and exciting and praising it for emphasizing America's participation in the war. It would, he concluded, "make an interesting picture from this country's point of view." Louis B. Mayer, when questioned by the House Committee on Un-American Activities about the finished product, *Song of Russia*, in October 1947, related a different version of the movie's origin. He claimed that the idea for the project had originated with one of his producers, who wanted to make a movie using the music of Peter Ilyich Tchaikovsky. Since the story would have to be set in Russia, Mayer continued, *Scorched Earth* was "dug up as the premise on which we would be able to use that music."[43]

Mittler, Trivas, and Endore were hired to write the script, and they prepared two revised treatments. Dissatisfied with the results, MGM assigned two other writers, Guy Trosper and Irmegard Von Cube, to write another treatment. In July, Anna Louise Strong, a Communist labor organizer and journalist, was assigned to write the script. Two weeks after she turned in her version, Jarrico and Collins were given the assignment.[44]

For the first time, Jarrico later said, his politics and writing career "met in a very appropriate way, because I was being paid a lot of money to work on a film about the necessity for American-Soviet friendship during a period in which both America and the Soviet Union were fighting Nazism." Shortly after they completed the script, Collins wrote that they had felt handicapped by their lack of knowledge about the Soviet Union, especially how the people talked and what the countryside was like. Though they managed to get some "feeling of intimacy with this material" via newsreels and Soviet movies and novels, Collins continued, "we would have welcomed the opportunity to explore more deeply and fully the people in our story and to use this wonderfully fresh and alive material in a less conventional way."[45]

In their first outline, Jarrico and Collins stated their theme: "No sacrifice is too great to destroy fascism." They described one of the characters, Boris, the chairman of the collective farm, as "the new Russian man—dependable, open, loves art and fun, but loves the land and responsibility more." The first draft contained Stalin's "scorched earth" speech of July 3, 1941; Nadya dying while blowing up a power plant; and Nadya's father asking John to conduct the village musicians' playing of Tchaikovsky's "1812 Overture." At the end, John decides to stay in the Soviet Union to kill Nazis. He tells the villagers, "My country's going to have to fight this thing too. Every decent person in the world will fight it. I'm just lucky enough to be where I can start right now." The second draft (dated October 30) replaced that speech with a "guerrilla oath": "I, a citizen of the great Soviet Union, true son of the heroic Russian people, vow that I will not lay down my arms until the last Fascist reptile has been crushed." In this version, Nadya is killed by a German bomb, and John returns to the United States to raise funds for Russian aid. At the Carnegie Hall concert that concludes the film, John "hesitantly begins to speak. Simply but with difficulty he brings them Nadya's message of friendship, expresses our debt to the Soviet people and appeals for true understanding of their country. And then, as we move into a CLOSE SHOT, he looks directly into the CAMERA and tells America that friendship between America and Russia can banish war from the earth forever."

On December 1, the writers met with Pasternak, director Gregory Ratoff, executive producer Sam Katz, and Joseph Mankiewicz, the head of the story editing department. In a letter to Michael Wilson, Jarrico wrote that he and Collins were "tense," but grateful when Katz said "it was a fine screenplay" and Mankiewicz said "that it would allow the American people to identify themselves with the Russian people." They then trooped over to Mayer's office to confer with him and studio vice president Ben Thau. Jarrico wrote Wilson,

> Mayer started by saying he was a little worried by what Sam (Katz) had told him. He went on to state very explicitly that he did not want to make a pro-Soviet picture. The Russians were all right, but when you think of Germany you think of Nazism, when you think of Italy you think of Fascism and when you think of Russia you think of Communism. And everybody knows that after the war Communism is going to be our big problem.
>
> He didn't want to make any pictures that would subject him to protests. . . . People in Congress or the newspapers or somebody might raise hell. He wasn't going to have it. He made pictures so that the stockholders could make money—and not to sell Ideas.
>
> The fate of our script hung by a thread. And it was unraveling.
>
> Casually, but persuasively, Mankiewicz pointed out that the script was not political, that it was not about Communism, but about people. People like us. People you could like.

> Mayer wasn't convinced. Russians *aren't* like us. They're Communists. Americans aren't. Look at the results of the elections.
>
> Katz said there was nothing about Communism in the script at all. So, carefully did Pasternak. So did I. Mankiewicz spoke again, casually, persuasively, told him something about the story. Ratoff spoke, said it was a Great Love Story, "wid a Capital L." He started to tell it. Horribly. I hated him. He murdered it. But Mayer seemed to like it. "No Comrades in it?" No.
>
> Someone suggested that Mayer ought to read the script himself. He said no, you men are going to make it and I trust your judgment. I just wanted you to understand my position.[46]

Much later, however, Jarrico stated (as Collins would in his testimony to the House Committee on Un-American Activities) that the sole reason for the conference with Mayer was to discuss the possibility of borrowing Ingrid Bergman from David O. Selznick (Mayer's son-in-law and the head of Selznick International Pictures) to play the female lead. When they arrived at Mayer's office, they were told that Selznick had read the script and told Mayer that it was pure Communist propaganda. Mayer ordered the writers to remove the word "community," because it sounded too much like "communism." He also told them that none of the farms in the village could be depicted as collective farms.[47]

The second draft, under a new title, *Russia*, was sent to the Production Code Administration. Its head, Joseph Breen, wrote Mayer that though the script met the basic requirements of the Production Code, nine pieces of dialogue, containing sexual suggestiveness, drinking scenes, improper language, a description of a Molotov cocktail, and a priest firing a machine gun should be changed. On December 11, Ratoff informed Pasternak that the Soviet consul thought the script "perfectly wonderful in every respect." A few weeks later, the OWI wrote to Pasternak, "If accurately done, this picture can serve a splendid purpose in acquainting the world with one of our least known of the United Nations." The letter extolled the script's depiction of Russia as "a vast, industrial-agricultural community, not unlike our own"; its characterization of the Russians "as a peaceful and constructive people"; its emphasis on the "continuity of aims and interests of Americans and Russians"; and its characterization of the Nazi enemy as destroyers.

It concluded, "Russia can be of enormous value to the war program." The first secretary of the Soviet Embassy requested eight changes to ensure authenticity of names and behaviors.[48]

When *PM*, a leftist newspaper, published a story about the movie with the headline "Louis B. Mayer Manicures Russia for M-G-M," Jarrico and Collins wrote to the editor, calling the story "a distortion of the truth." They admitted that their screenplay probably would not "be worthy of its heroic subject" but said neither would it falsify aspects of Soviet life. The script would fulfill "the studio's original intention of making a picture completely sympathetic to the Russian people." They sent a copy to David Platt, film editor of the *Daily Worker*, who responded, "If 'Russia' is a good film we will be the first to say so."[49]

A much more positive story appeared in the *Los Angeles Daily News*. Jarrico and Collins had told the writer that *Song of Russia* was "the happiest assignment of their career." They said that they had endeavored to write a script that would correct a large amount of misinformation about the Soviet Union without becoming a propaganda vehicle, and they hoped the movie would contribute to a wider, more sympathetic understanding of the Soviet Union. The reporter thought they had succeeded. Jarrico and Collins, she wrote, "avoid the hammer blow technique to put over facts about the existence of religious freedom and try to correct misunderstandings about the once-existent Russian-German pact." She also praised their depiction of Soviet citizens as sympathetic people deeply devoted to the arts and to the soil.[50]

Robert Taylor, who was cast as John, did not like the script, and Pasternak assigned five other writers to make revisions. Finally, Pasternak brought in John Wexley, also a Communist, to make the changes Taylor and Mayer wanted. Wexley, who spent four weeks on the set, recalled, "I was trying to touch it up and was there as a mollifier or pacifier—a diplomat—toward Robert Taylor, who was a very strong reactionary. He hated anything that had to do with the Soviet Union, and they kept trying to tell him it was his contribution to the war effort. . . . Actually I changed very little. But the act of changing seemed to satisfy him." In fact, Wexley devised the ending that would be used. Instead of a speech by John, there is a speech by Boris, the head of the village resistance, telling John that he must return to the United States and that Nadya (who is allowed to live in this version) must accompany him. As he is speaking, there is a fade from the village to John conducting a New York concert in tribute to Russia. Boris asks John and Nadya to tell the Americans that "we are all soldiers in the same army, fighting to bring a new life to our children, for that great day of victory when the whole world will ring with a new song of freedom. You will be bringing our great countries closer together in this fight for all humanity."[51]

The reviews of *Song of Russia* were mainly positive. Most reviewers focused on the music and the love story, which is not surprising given that John and Nadya's romance and the musical numbers constitute the greater part of the film. The German invasion section is perhaps twenty minutes long, and a good portion of it focuses on John's attempt to return to Nadya's village. All the antifascist and pro-Stalin dialogue was scrubbed; when Nadya advocates a "scorched earth" strategy to the villagers, she refers not to Stalin but to "the commander in chief." Still, the *Los Angeles Times* reviewer thought it was "excellent propaganda," and the *Los Angeles Herald-Examiner* reviewer called it "a tribute to Stalin's people." The foreign commissar of the Soviet Writers Union extolled it, writing, "It is truthful in the main since it conveys the culture and the spirit of the people."[52] Indeed, it is basically a movie about Russians who love farming and music, and a paean to their courage in the face of the German invasion.

It was precisely those elements that provoked the movie's most negative appraisal, which came four years later, when Ayn Rand viewed it at the request of an investigator from the House Committee on Un-American Activities. She told the committee in October 1947 that the film was "Communist propaganda" because it "gives a good impression of Communism as a way of life." She did not accuse MGM of trying to make a Communist movie, but she did charge the studio with being careless with ideas, "not realizing that the mere presentation of that kind of happy existence in a country of slavery and horror is terrible because it is propaganda."[53]

Several years later, in 1951, Collins told the House Committee on Un-American Activities,

> In terms of what we said in the picture I doubt if it had anything to do with our being Communists except that we were pleased with it. We were pleased with the assignment. But at this time we . . . would have been pleased with a picture on the resistance movement in Europe. We would have been pleased with anything of that nature that we felt would help the war. And we certainly felt that this picture would. And also we believed, as I think many millions of people hoped, that the relations between the United States and Russia would be friendly and this couldn't hurt it.

Collins emphasized that he and Jarrico had not tried to sneak in any subversive material and that they had made all the changes Pasternak had instructed them to make.[54]

Robert Taylor would later tell the committee that the script contained Communist propaganda and that he did not think it should have been made, but that he had not been forced to appear in it. (A few months before his appearance, however, he had been quoted as saying that the studio had put pressure on him.) In response to Taylor's press statement, Mayer released a statement claiming that *Song of Russia* "is simply a love story. . . . The picture contains no Russian ideology to my knowledge. Instead of a Russian girl in Russia, the heroine could just as well have been an English girl and the locale England." He denied that the studio had made the movie because the Soviet Union was a U.S. ally in 1943.[55]

The movie did well at the box office, bringing more than $7 million to MGM's coffers, and the studio rewarded Jarrico and Collins with new contracts, which raised their salaries to $1,250 a week. Jarrico, however, thought that Collins had dragged his feet on the project. Jarrico later said, "I felt the faster we could get that picture out, the better. I felt it was a matter of real urgency, that I was making some real contribution to the war effort by working on that film. So I pushed ahead very hard and very fast. Collins, when we were finished, said, 'You've done 90 percent of the script. I don't really deserve credit.'" Although Jarrico replied that they were a team and that a team should share screen credit, he decided to end their collaboration. When he was told what Jarrico had said, Collins replied that Jarrico had woven "a fairy tale." Collins denied that he had contributed less than Jarrico and that he had invited Jarrico to take full credit. But he did not explain why their writing partnership dissolved.[56]

Jarrico's Political Activities and War Record

Jarrico remained active in a variety of groups and on behalf of a variety of causes. In July 1942, he met with representatives of the American Russian Institute who were attempting to establish a cultural exchange program between the United States and the Soviet Union. For a War Production Board radio broadcast, he coauthored a script (with John Wexley and Lester Cohen) dramatizing a factory and its workers, titled *Salt of the Earth* (a title he would later reuse). And he was elected to the board of the SWG. According to an investigator for the House Committee on Un-American Activities, he also met several times with visiting Communist leaders. On May 3, 1942, for example, he and some other writers met with Alexander Stevens (J. Peters) at the home of Herbert Biberman.[57] Sylvia Jarrico worked for the Commission for Care of Children in War Time, a branch of the War Manpower Commission.

But Jarrico was not satisfied. He believed that neither his political activities, extensive as they were, nor his film work constituted a significant contribution to winning the war. He yearned to become involved in the war itself. He wrote Kanin, "We're getting a little tired of telling ourselves that the greatest contribution to the war we can make is right at our desks. Even with a few odd jobs for the Writers Mobilization and some civilian defense work . . . , the tendons of conscience grow taut." When he expressed his frustration to Michael Wilson, who was then serving in the U.S. Marine Corps, Wilson replied,

> I am but little closer to the action than you are, but even the few steps I've taken brings the problem of the writer and the war into sharper focus. For chrissake, don't go off the deep end. . . . Your life is easy, but don't let that throw you. And in this life, the life of the line or the line officer, consciousness is almost inevitably reduced to a lower level; your effectiveness in terms of the group has definite limitations; your effectiveness as an individual, as a writer, is necessarily swamped under by a mass of other details. In short, under present conditions, you would commit a grievous error to become an officer of the line. Because you're in a position to choose your scripts, relatively speaking. And god knows we need them. We have movies at Quantico every night for those who want to go, and believe me, it is their *only* means of political education.

Jarrico replied that his desire to get out of Hollywood "is not an individual problem. It's the key to what's wrong with this town, and how to change it. The fact is that aside from a few exceptions like Scorched Earth (now called Russia), the motion picture is *not* a war product," and the movie industry had not converted to a war industry. In March 1943, Jarrico wrote a friend, "Private Miss Jones [*Thousands Cheer*] will be a big commercial pile of shit and should be out shortly. [*Song of*] Russia will be a diluted sentimental hodge-podge. . . . Metro has given us two big contracts at enormous salaries and I am working up the biggest sense of guilt you ever saw."[58]

In July 1943, after several months of soul searching, Jarrico, while sitting at his desk in the MGM writers' department, decided, "What I need is a *complete* change of environment, a *real* participation in the war." It occurred to him that he could do that most easily by enlisting in the merchant marine. "The merchant marine meant danger—but most ships were getting through. A good amount of danger, not too much, not too little. The merchant marine meant not only working with a group of the kind of men I wanted to know and understand—it meant living with them, day and night, eating and sleeping and relaxing with them." And it meant going to Europe, because he was more eager to fight Nazi aggression than Japanese imperialism.[59]

He consulted with John Howard Lawson, who had researched the merchant marine for his script for *Action in the North Atlantic* (Warner Brothers, 1942). Lawson suggested that Jarrico contact an officer in the National Maritime Union. Jarrico did so and was told that he could enlist in the merchant marine after he obtained papers from the National Maritime Union and a limited availability certificate from the War Manpower Commission, certifying that he was on a leave of absence from MGM, lest he get frozen in the merchant marine for the duration of the war. Jarrico then wrote letters to Leo Huberman, the labor editor at *PM* and the director of education and public relations for the National Maritime Union, and to Blackie Myers, a union official whom Jarrico had met in New York. He told Huberman, "I don't want to appear the romantic escapist in this. . . . I don't want to make a permanent change of work. I'd like to go out for three months or six months or so, and then resume screenwriting. I think it would make me a better writer and a better guy." Both

Huberman and Myers responded positively, and a seaman's certificate of identification was issued to Jarrico on August 6. He was rated an ordinary seaman and was assigned to the U.S.S. *Thomas W. Bickett*, a Liberty ship scheduled to stop in Oran and Naples. Jarrico would be on board for three and a half months. He asked for and was granted a leave of absence from MGM. He did not ask for permission or advice from the party, nor was any offered.[60]

At about the same time that Jarrico was boarding his ship, the first FBI report on him was completed. It noted that he had recently been referred to as one of the leading people in the northwest section of the Communist Party of Los Angeles. It listed the various organizations to which he belonged, stated that he had registered as a Democrat and that his gross income in 1940 was $9,844.99, and provided a physical description of him. A second report, three weeks later, noted that he would be serving in the merchant marine until December. In January 1944, FBI director J. Edgar Hoover informed the Los Angeles bureau that a security index card had been prepared on Jarrico at the bureau, captioned "NATIVE BORN, COMMUNIST."[61]

In a letter written to his mother from Norfolk, Jarrico wrote, "Just to be here, just to be contributing a little, just to meet and talk to the men who are giving up all they have, perhaps their lives, is an experience which fills me with pride and pleasure. . . . We have the most wonderful country in the world. I thank you for coming to live there, and for allowing me to be born there." His job required hard physical labor. He worked two shifts: one involved cargo handling, and the other included topping and lowering booms, securing boats, securing and rigging jumbo gear, stowing dunnage, hauling coal, and manning a gun. The ship, he wrote Michael Wilson,

> was a Liberty, slow cumbersome and capacious beyond belief. . . . [W]e carried tanks, trucks, heavy artillery, rations, and troops. . . . We got rid of the troops in North Africa and hung around awhile waiting for the Fifth Army to take Naples. . . . [T]he men were great, I got along very well with them, we saw some action, I was scared as hell, and fascinated, and happy with my reactions (which, of course, I analyzed like a regular Proust).
>
> The voyage was wonderful, everything I wanted, the smartest thing I ever did. We were out three and a half months, we delivered

> the goods under fire, I learned how to wash my own clothes and clean toilets and run a steam winch and take care of myself, I'm healthier than I have ever been before and I've read the first four volumes of [Proust's] Remembrance of Things Past.[62]

Jarrico landed in New York City on December 8 and returned to Los Angeles on December 17. He did not, however, want to return to MGM, and he was disappointed to learn that no other studio seemed eager to hire him. In addition, he learned that while he had been gone, his local draft board had sent a notice reclassifying him as 1-A (delinquent for leaving town without registering a forwarding address). Sylvia Jarrico had appealed on his behalf and been told by the draft board that MGM had not notified it that Jarrico had been granted a leave of absence to serve in the merchant marine. Though his agent and the studio claimed they had sent the required forms to the draft board, the board ordered Jarrico to report for a physical. His 1-A classification was affirmed, removing any basis for a successful appeal. He tried to join the Naval Photographic Science Laboratory (as a writer), the photographic section of the U.S. Marine Corps, the U.S. Coast Guard (as a combat correspondent), and the psychological warfare branch of the Office of Strategic Services. Unsuccessful in all these efforts, he agreed to be inducted into the navy.

Jarrico was allowed to complete his current assignment at MGM, which had put him back on the payroll to work on a project titled *A Woman's Place* (based on the play *Action in the Living Room*). Jarrico wanted to transform it into a comedy about women in industry and add a labor union angle. In one of his notes to himself, he wrote, "I want to tell the story of the development of a woman in war time. A charming, tempestuous woman to begin with, a fine actress, a wonderful hostess, she realizes that her relations with her husband are worsening, that other women are passing her by, and decides to go into industry." The central conflict would be, he decided, "male egotism versus female development."[63]

In Jarrico's script, the wife leaves her husband, goes to work in his factory, joins the union, and tries to organize a strike. The workers balk, telling her they want to win the war, not help her in her personal vendetta. Sobered by this experience, she reunites with her husband, leaves the factory, and volunteers for a win-the-war community project. But Jarrico became caught on the horns of a dilemma: his producer, Everett Riskin, thought that Jarrico's first draft was "too socially conscious" and war oriented, and Jarrico was unable to resolve the problems of marrying a screwball comedy to a sociological documentary. He wrote Michael Wilson, "Every conflict I've ever faced as a writer of pictures (every creative conflict, that is, putting aside the 'social' conflicts) is repeated and intensified by this assignment. This is compromise with a vengeance. A chance to say very honest things about Unions and Labor-management and the Child-care problem (hero and heroine have a seven year old kid) and the Woman Question, and the self-imposed necessity of making the picture so funny and so commercial that even Metro won't dare not make it."[64] Riskin concluded that Jarrico could not produce a satisfactory second draft and gave the script to another writer.

MGM then laid him off and loaned him to Columbia to write *I'll Be Seeing You* with his friend Lou Solomon. It involved a romantic triangle and a man reincarnated as a racehorse. "I'm having a good time of it," Jarrico wrote. "Not much social significance, except that any presentation of unimportant people as basically decent is significant."[65] The producer liked the story idea, but studio boss Harry Cohn did not.

Jarrico had become dissatisfied with almost every aspect of his life: his writing, his pending induction, the Communist Party—and his wife. He thought that instead of volunteering for the child care commission, Sylvia should get a job: "Sylvia's lack of organization was not a profound and complex fault, as she was inclined to view it, but rather a question of habit. That discipline was a habit, like brushing teeth, that it was something to be learned, that it couldn't be achieved by will power, that the failure to achieve it by strength of will resulted in feelings of guilt, and that that was bad, that it could be learned easily in a social situation which required it, that working for pay was such a situation." She did not agree. A few months later, Jarrico wrote, "Sylvia is more troubled, less integrated into an ambition every day. And I grow more impatient, and this hurts our relationship, and this makes for even less organization of her talent and will, and it's a vicious circle."[66]

During this time, his mother's declining health also weighed on Jarrico. She suffered a debilitating stroke in November 1944 and died two months later. He did not express any grief.

Jarrico seemed to be happy only with being a father to Bill, who grew up thinking that his father was an interesting person who held forth every night at the dinner table about politics. Political pamphlets were always lying around, and political meetings were regularly held at their house. Jarrico gave Bill a copy of Karl Marx's *Das Kapital* when he was eleven. Bill remembered that his father "couldn't understand it when I became discouraged." In his agenda book for 1954, Jarrico recorded what seemed to have been a recurring conversation with Sylvia regarding Bill:

> P: (whining) Sylvia!
> S: (businesslike; not looking at him) What's the matter, Paul?
> P: (with dignity) Nothing at all.
> S: (laughs)
> P: (laughs)
> S: (embracing him) I really don't mind at all because it shows our son a person can be a jerk and still be a very nice fellow.[67]

Politically, Jarrico was not thrilled with the leadership of party head Earl Browder. At a party gathering at Madison Square Garden in January 1944, Browder had announced that the CPUSA would continue its wartime Popular Front policies but would abandon its status as a political party and become the Communist Political Association (CPA). The newly named organization would not raise the issue of socialism in any form or manner that might endanger or weaken national unity; it would abandon the tactic of interclass violence; and it would seek to solve domestic issues in a peaceful manner.[68]

Browder's speech seems to have brought to the boiling point Jarrico's simmering dissatisfaction with party directives. He wrote in his journal,

> I made up a poem like this: "Oh the C.A. is for Unity, and Unity's for me. So hip hip hooray for the new C.A. and to hell with the old C.P." Which is a joke but doesn't really express my opinion. I think Browder's speech isn't a turn but a recognition of a turn that

> occurred a long time ago. A new change of form to match an old change of content. And what I say is that until they give up dialectics I maintain my unalterable opposition to the Communist Party, and they can call it an Association if they want to, that doesn't change my mind one bit.

Sylvia Jarrico also found Browder's proposal disturbing, because to her it represented a more significant "flip-flop" than the nonaggression treaty. Even though she agreed with the motivation behind the switch, she was "shocked and startled" at the speed with which the transformation occurred and the use of so-called scientific principles to rationalize it.[69]

During 1944, Jarrico contributed money to and wrote speeches for Helen Gahagan Douglas's campaign for the U.S. Senate. He also wrote a script for a campaign movie that actress Karen Morley was producing for the Hollywood Democratic Committee. At the conclusion of the Yalta conference in February 1945, Jarrico wrote a statement for the *People's World* extolling the unity he perceived between Roosevelt, Stalin, and Churchill and proclaiming that the "bell tolls for fascism everywhere." When Roosevelt died on April 12, Jarrico wrote to his wife, "When I think of it I feel like crying. But I think the foundation he laid is too solid for anyone to fuck up the final structure. Tell Billy for me that I want him to remember President Roosevelt, that he was a great man—the leader of the American people." Other Communists felt likewise. Adrian Scott told Ben Barzman, "[Roosevelt's death] is very bad for the world."[70]

During the war, the activity that seemed to engage Jarrico the most was his work for Jewish causes. He attended a Poale Zion meeting at his mother's house and promised himself that "the Jewish Question is one of the things I'm going to be studying and acting upon this year." In December 1941, he helped his uncle Chaim organize a seventy-fifth birthday celebration for Chaim Zhitlowsky, a Jewish writer and philosopher, the honorary chairman of the Yiddish Cultural Federation. In February 1943, Jarrico again helped his uncle, this time to organize an evening at the Shrine Auditorium featuring the writer Sholem Asch, president of Jewish Writers, Artists and Scientists. The goals of the organization (formed in November 1941 with Albert Einstein as its honorary president) were to support the Soviet Union in its struggle against Germany, to handle problems of Jewish unity, to promote closer relations with world Jewry, and to cooperate with the World Jewish Congress in Palestine. In June 1944, Jarrico became secretary of the Jewish Writers, Artists and Scientists Hollywood chapter. He drafted a call for membership that stressed the urgent needs to rescue the surviving Jews of Europe, to fight vigorously against anti-Semitism, and to achieve a just and lasting peace. To accomplish these goals, the Hollywood chapter would distribute *The Jewish Black Book* (a record of the German government's program of extermination) and help produce a movie on anti-Semitism. In a draft of the letter he wrote to recruit people to this cause, Jarrico criticized Hollywood's Jews for isolating themselves from world events and for trying to escape their responsibilities as Jews. He advised them that they could resist antifascism and anti-Semitism better if they saw themselves not simply as Americans but as Jewish Americans, people with a special responsibility.[71]

The major element of Jarrico's unhappiness was his writing, or what he perceived as his failure to develop as a writer. In his journal, he reflected on what his desultory attitude toward his script for *A Woman's Place* signified about him as a writer. He admitted that, as a screenwriter, he had been getting by on cleverness and that he had a long way to go to achieve "any real creation." He acknowledged that studio writing imposed severe limitations on creativity, and that his "quixotic idealistic approach will accomplish nothing, and this is something I face every day as a screenwriter, it is something all screenwriters face, and it is necessary to understand it."[72]

From May 24 through September 29, 1944, Jarrico was on layoff. During these seventeen weeks, he contemplated writing a novel about his experience in Naples and a play about life on a Liberty ship, reteamed with Richard Collins to write a utopian comedy, and worked on an original story about a returning soldier that he had begun to write while serving on the *Thomas Bickett*. Jarrico also attempted to collaborate with Sylvia on two writing projects. They worked together on an OWI documentary, *American Housewife*, and on a play dramatizing the problems, particularly fidelity, faced by married couples separated by the war.

On September 30, Jarrico went back to work at MGM. But he balked at writing the script for *Cabbages and Kings*, another Pasternak musical. Instead, Jarrico suggested that Pasternak purchase the *Rip Van Winkle* script from Monogram. When Pasternak said no, another producer, Al Lichtman, promised Jarrico a shot at directing if Jarrico would agree to write the sixth in a series of adventure movies about Maisie, a wisecracking dancer portrayed by Ann Sothern. For this episode, "Murder, Maisie, Murder," Jarrico has Maisie playing a magician's assistant who gets involved in a jewel heist–murder case. In November, however, the studio decided it did not want Maisie involved in a murder and loaned Jarrico to RKO.

At RKO, Jarrico was assigned to adapt Vincent McHugh's novel *I Am Thinking of My Darling*, a satire about a society in which people are allowed to do whatever they feel like doing. Jarrico adapted it in the form of "a modern psychological fairy tale," in which a woman married to a flirt is afflicted with a strange disease that makes her a flirt also. Their respective flirtations lead to a series of comic misadventures that reinstates their belief in marital fidelity. Before Jarrico could finish the final shooting script, he was ordered to report for duty.

On April 10, 1945, Jarrico entered active service as a seaman second class and was sent to San Diego for boot camp. He wrote Sylvia, "It's as healthy a routine as I've ever had. I'm in fine shape. . . . We're learning close-order drill and manual of arms to make us feel like a military outfit and build us up physically."[73] At the end of boot camp, Jarrico was assigned to the training center to survey motion pictures used for training purposes and to analyze recruit-training testing programs. He was able to return to Los Angeles every weekend.

During one of those trips, he renewed contact with Sanora Babb, a writer he had known from the League of American Writers, who asked him to read a novel she had written. After he had communicated his thoughts about the novel to her, she wrote that she would like to get to know him better, that "it seems to me that you are generous and warm, rather cautious and shy; that you are gentle and tender, that you have a quietness that has nothing to do with an uncertainty, that you are capable of simple gaiety, which is rare. . . . I like the way you behave with women—a kind of promiscuous and sincere attention which seems to contain no real promiscuity or emotion, but a fairly large liking for them." Jarrico was completely won over. "Do you know," he replied, "how long it's been since I've had a letter like yours, Sanora? Anything like yours at all, I mean, long and warm and with things to say and questions to ask?" He agreed with most of what she said about him, especially her remarks about him and women. He wrote, "I not only love women, I like them." But her description of his personality, he added, "as a whole would indicate that I have taken you in. For the things you note are the things I sell. They're part of me, all right—I don't pretend them—but they're the parts of me I like to believe are attractive. I am all those things, and I am also very aggressive, and very stubborn, and very quick to anger. I am a lot of other things too. Energetic, hard-working, clever, intelligent, well-informed, passionate and talented. I am also a romantic, a push-over, a fool, a fumbler, and bungler and a sucker for a compliment."[74]

Following his completion of basic training, Jarrico was permanently assigned to the entertainment office of the welfare division, located in the Naval Trading and Distribution Center, Treasure Island (San Francisco). Now a seaman third class, he arranged shows for naval personnel, including performances by such stars as Bob Hope, Jack Carson, and Eddie Bracken. He entertained those entertainers, lived at the Palace Hotel, and had his own car. On occasion, he put on his civilian clothes and attended meetings of the Communist fraction of the International Longshoremen's Association. When he was assigned the project of dedicating three theaters at the base, he saw an opportunity to make a political statement. He organized a contest to name them after navy heroes but rigged it so that one of them was named for Dorie Miller, a black navy steward who had died heroically at Pearl Harbor; the second for John Basilone, a marine gunnery sergeant killed on Iwo Jima; and the third for a much-decorated navy flyer, Lieutenant Commander Edward "Butch" O'Hare. Jarrico arranged for Jimmy Durante, Paul Whiteman, and Martha Tilton to perform at the dedication ceremony and for Orson Welles to broadcast it on his national radio program *Orson Welles Commentaries*.

To prepare for the dedication ceremony, Jarrico flew around the country, interviewing the families of the men being honored. He was most impressed with the sharecropper family of Dorie Miller.

Jarrico wanted Miller's father to say positive things about the war, but he wouldn't. "What he said was, 'If we had our druthers, we'd rather have our boy.' I said, 'But when black boys and white boys fight and die together, don't you think it makes for a change?' He said, 'Could be. I don't see no change yet,' and so on." Jarrico then asked him to make the same remarks to Welles on the broadcast. Welles liked the script Jarrico had written, but he asked, "What makes you think he'll answer this way?" Jarrico said that he had arranged for the station manager in Waco to rehearse with Miller. Welles replied, "You trust a southern station manager to coach this man to say these things?" Jarrico admitted that he did not, so he flew back to Waco and coached Miller up to and during the broadcast.[75]

At the end of January 1946, Jarrico was reassigned to temporary duty in Beverly Hills. He received his notice of separation from the navy on March 17. He later learned that his immediate superior at Treasure Island knew that he was a Communist, put that information on his record when he came on board, and had him followed all the time he was stationed there.[76]

Meanwhile, Jarrico's agent, Alan Miller, had negotiated an end to his contract with MGM and was negotiating a new one with RKO. Jarrico was definite about the terms of that new contract. He wanted, he wrote Miller,

> twenty-six consecutive weeks a year for five years, first two years at fifteen hundred, last three years at seventeen fifty. No options except after second year, when they may cancel for any reason and I may cancel if not directing. I to have complete freedom remaining six months a year to work anywhere at any price, with two provisions. First, if at the end of any twenty-six week term at RKO I am on an incomplete assignment, I will finish that assignment on week to week basis at same salary. Second, RKO has first crack at any original material I write during my own time. In principle, I will do one picture a year for RKO for five years at considerably less than my market value in return for a chance to direct. I want very much to work at RKO but will not compromise on desire for several months uninterrupted freedom every year.[77]

RKO agreed to Jarrico's terms.

PART 2

BLACKLIST

4

The Cold War in Hollywood, 1945–47

> In the coming struggle for power the middle-class intellectual will face a great moral crisis. He will have to choose between security (for himself and his family) and sacrifice. Since the security offered him will be illusory, his real choice will be between cowardice and heroism. . . . He will not serve fascism in America even if his refusal to do so is called treason.
>
> —*Paul Jarrico, 1946*

Well before World War II ended and the cold war between the United States and the Soviet Union commenced, anti-Communist organizations and government agencies began to position themselves for a full-scale offensive against communism and Communists in Hollywood, their liberal allies, and their front organizations.

J. Edgar Hoover, the director of the Federal Bureau of Investigation, led the attack. In September 1942, he sent to the bureau's Los Angeles office a memorandum and a copy of a pamphlet titled *Radical Artists—Writers—Actors—Musicians Demand a Second Front*, which had been provided to the bureau by an "unknown outside source."[1] Noting that 21 of the 116 signers of that pamphlet were from Hollywood, Hoover authorized a massive investigation of the industry under the code name COMPIC (Communist Infiltration—Motion Picture Industry). The following February, the special agent in charge of Los Angeles (SACLA) sent to Washington a 211-page report that stated that about one-half of the Hollywood unions were controlled by the Communist Party or closely followed the party line and that "quite a number of directors and executives are well-known Communists." The Hollywood Communists, it was alleged, "form part of a gigantic world-wide conspiracy of control which has its origin and direction in the Communist Party of the Soviet Union," and they are laying "the foundations for a future coup" to take control of all guilds and unions. The report listed a broad range of activities; analyzed every guild, union, cultural front organization, and publication; and identified the "Communist" participants.[2]

The SACLA followed with a series of reports concerning movies containing "Communist propaganda." In August, he sent to the bureau a complete breakdown of the branches, officers, and members of the Los Angeles party's northwest section. The report, based on the materials provided to the SACLA by a paid party organizer, Elizabeth Benson (a.k.a. Leach), listed the names of 347 members of the twenty Hollywood branches. In February 1944, the SACLA sent to FBI headquarters a history of the Communist Party in Hollywood, including a summary description of 319 members: 125 males, 194 females; 317 whites (200 of whom were Jewish), 2 blacks. The median age of the membership was thirty-five, and the median length of party membership was five years.[3]

In May, Hoover directed the SACLA to compile a list of all persons in the motion picture industry who were members of the party or its front groups, because "such a list will not only be of value to the Bureau but also to your office for reference purposes in future investigations to be conducted in this case." He asked that each name be followed by a "brief identifying paragraph," including activities in the industry and political groups and facts of party membership (section and branch). "If this is not known, a short sentence stating how the person is known to be a Communist Party member should be added." Hoover later sent summaries of these files to the U.S. attorney general and to President Truman's military aide.[4]

While the SACLA gathered his data, anti-Communists in Hollywood organized the Motion Picture Alliance for the Preservation of American Ideals (MPA). On the evening of February 4, 1944, seventy-five motion picture people gathered at the Beverly Wilshire Hotel to listen to anti-Communist speeches. Director Sam Wood was elected president and Walt Disney first vice president.[5]

Two months later, the MPA announced it was opening an active campaign against Communist groups' infiltration of the motion picture industry. Among the speakers at this meeting were Clark Gable, Lela Rogers (Ginger Rogers's mother), and several MGM writers who had led the fight against the SWG in the 1930s.[6] Barbara Stanwyck and Gary Cooper were among the two hundred in the audience.[7] Billy Wilkerson, owner-publisher of the *Hollywood Reporter*, and Hedda Hopper, gossip columnist of the *Los Angeles Times*, strongly supported the MPA's efforts.

At the same time, Congressman John Rankin (D-MS) was positioning the House Committee on Un-American Activities for another investigation of Hollywood. In January 1945, he had sponsored a successful motion to make the committee permanent.[8] Three months later, he announced that the committee was planning an investigation of communism in the motion picture industry. Rankin told the House of Representatives on July 9 that "appeals for an investigation are coming to us from the best people in California," and at a news conference a few days later, he stated that Hollywood was a "hotbed of Communism."[9] In August, Rankin sent Louis Russell, a former FBI agent, to California to begin the investigation. The SACLA kept close tabs on the investigation. He noted in September that the investigators had devoted most of their efforts to the "so-called cultural groups, writers, actors, and directors," and that they had concluded that "a serious situation exists within the Hollywood motion picture industry in respect to Communist infiltration and influence." Russell prepared a preliminary report, but he made only four copies of it. In fact, two years would pass before the committee found its way back to Hollywood.[10]

While Rankin was issuing his public pronouncements, Roy Brewer, who would soon become the most influential anti-Communist in Hollywood, quietly arrived. As the international representative of the International Alliance of Theatrical Stage Employees (IATSE), he was dispatched to Hollywood in March 1945 to defeat the challenge posed to IATSE domination of Hollywood craftspeople by the Conference of Studio Unions (CSU).[11] The CSU had just announced a strike against the studios because the studio heads refused to recognize its set decorators' local and continued to do business with the IATSE's set erectors. Although many individual Hollywood Communists joined the CSU picket line, the Communist Party itself opposed the strike because it violated its no-strike pledge, and the party's West Coast newspaper, *People's World*, proclaimed in a front-page editorial, "End the Movie Strike at Once!" Yet Brewer decided that the strike had been provoked by the Communists. He told IATSE president Richard Walsh, "It's either the Communists or us, you might as well make up your mind. And you'd better face it." He later said, "I was not Red baiting for the reason of an advantage, or for trying to prejudice people against somebody. I was fighting against the real thing."[12]

The strike ended before Jarrico returned to Hollywood. But he arrived just in time to become involved in an internal Communist Party conflict whose outcome would severely damage the party's reputation with intellectuals and writers. The "Maltz controversy" was an unexpected outgrowth of Soviet party leaders' belated rejection of Earl Browder's 1944 decision to replace the CPUSA with the CPA. The attack on "Browderism" began in April 1945 when an article attributed to Jacques Duclos, a leader of the Parti communiste français, appeared in *Cahiers du communisme*. It was translated and reprinted in the *Daily Worker* on May 24.[13] When Browder refused to repent and began to publish an independent newsletter, he was expelled from the party. New instructions were sent to all party groups, informing them that the CPUSA was once again the independent, vanguard party in the United States. Members were told that they must secure the complete destruction of fascism throughout the world, struggle against the aggressive circles of American imperialist reaction, and develop mass movements on behalf of the most pressing and immediate needs of workers, blacks, veterans, farmers, and the urban middle class.[14]

Some Hollywood Communists, like Michael Wilson, were pleased with the changes and readily accepted the new party line that American imperialism was the main enemy in the postwar world. Jarrico had believed that the United States and the Soviet Union would continue to cooperate during the postwar period, but he thought that Duclos had made a compelling argument against that position. By contrast, Abraham Polonsky thought that it was foolish for the party to have undertaken such a sudden and complete reversal.[15]

The debate over Browderism caught one of the party's most successful writers, Albert Maltz, directly in the crossfire. He had read and responded to an article by *New Masses* editor Isidor Schneider, inviting writers to discuss writers' problems. In his contribution "What Shall We Ask of Writers?" Maltz criticized the thinking of what he called the "literary left wing." He contended that the atmosphere they had created confused and restricted writers and turned them away from life because it propounded the vulgar theory that "art is a weapon." He himself had been forced to repudiate that slogan to write anything of value. To Maltz's surprise and shock, the party's biggest political and cultural guns turned on him. Polemical articles appeared in *New Masses*, including one by screenwriter Alvah Bessie (who, like Maltz, would be among the Hollywood Ten). A special meeting of the Hollywood Party branch met to discuss Maltz's article. Even though most of those who attended privately agreed with Maltz, few defended him. The majority publicly attacked him. Leopold Atlas described the meeting as a "nightmarish and shameful experience." At a second meeting, a week later, Atlas said, "they completely broke" Maltz. Shaken by the onslaught and unwilling to face expulsion, Maltz recanted two months later, in another *New Masses* article.[16]

Though this episode did not provoke many writers to leave the party, it strengthened the anti-Communist sentiment in Hollywood. Non-Communists were shocked not by the criticism per se (writers, in and out of the party, were always criticizing one another in public) but by the perceived ganglike savagery of the attack upon such a distinguished writer.

For his part, Jarrico agreed with Maltz's position and was somewhat upset when Maltz recanted.

> I participated in some of the meetings in which he was pressured to recant his position, though I wasn't among those who were pressuring him. I mean it was one thing to agree with the Duclos analysis. . . . It was another to agree with what I considered to be a vulgarization of the Marxist position about the role of literature. I could see where, under certain circumstances, art was a weapon and narrowly defined, defined in terms of its immediate utility for a struggle. On the other hand, there were plenty of quotations in the Marxist classics about art being something that was broader and deeper than simply an

> immediate propaganda weapon. So I thought Maltz's position was correct and that the position of those who pressured him to recant was incorrect.[17]

In terms of his own career as a Communist screenwriter, Jarrico, after some soul searching, decided to continue working in the studios. Although he thought that the quality of Hollywood movies remained low, he believed that film was potentially the greatest art form in history. He convinced himself that Communist writers should accept the challenge to improve the quality of Hollywood movies and lay the basis for a "people's art."[18]

Jarrico's first assignment at RKO was to adapt James Ramsey Ullman's novel *The White Tower*, which tells the story of an international collection of mountain climbers who attempt during World War II to climb the so-called White Tower in the Swiss Alps. Although the studio had contracted with Ullman to write the screenplay, it simultaneously assigned Jarrico to prepare a breakdown of the novel. He criticized the novel's focus on abstract virtues and its lack of clarity about the social, natural, and romantic "realities" of the situation, and he suggested that the plot be simplified. Jarrico set the story in the postwar period and reduced the main characters to three: a man who has become disillusioned and bitter after the war, believing that fascism is on the rise in his own country and that a third world war is pending; a woman whose father died trying to climb the White Tower; and "a fascist." The competition and conflicts between them cause the former antifascist to "regain his hatred of fascism . . . , his will to fight . . . , and his belief in life." He decides to return to the United States "to escape the third world war in the only way it can be escaped—by fighting American fascism *now*."[19]

The studio liked Jarrico's approach and assigned him to write the screenplay. A fellow Communist, Edward Dmytryk, would direct. In June 1947, Jarrico accompanied Dmytryk to Europe to scout locations. Jarrico intended to stay for only a few weeks, but the producer told him to stay in London until he finished writing the script. (Dmytryk was also there, shooting *So Well Remembered*.) Though Jarrico continued to read and discuss Marxist issues in London, he was not impressed by the British Communists he met, and he felt exiled from active political involvement. Most of his nonwriting time was spent defending the Soviet Union's foreign policy and unraveling "the Alice in Wonderland logic on which the whole anti-Soviet propaganda campaign is based."[20]

He was also at odds with Dmytryk, who wanted Jarrico to make *The White Tower* script "less pointedly political and take out the references to the Russians, just as a tactical maneuver of course." Jarrico wrote Sylvia, "Eddy says there is a big red scare in the Hollywood Reporter now and [head of RKO J. Peter] Rathvon . . . will not like my propaganda now but we will shoot it that way next summer, my way that is, only now we will water it down. This I will do and this gives me a psychological advantage over Eddy that I have needed."[21] At the end of August, Jarrico wrote Sylvia that he had finished the first draft. "I don't know how good it is yet, but I suspect it needs considerable work." A week later, Jarrico wrote that he had finally had some constructive conferences with Dmytryk and that Dmytryk was now making reasonable and moderate demands for changes.[22]

But the script did not please one of the studio executives, James Francis Crow, who told Rathvon that considerable rewriting would be necessary. Crow thought that Jarrico had reduced the antifascist character to a "flip, glib, thoroughly uncouth, and rather cheap" individual. By contrast, the fascist came across as strong, dignified, and gallant. Though Crow approved of the world peace message, he thought Jarrico's preachment was "not integrated with the script, but merely tacked on. It sounds forced and artificial to me." Six pages of specific criticisms followed.[23]

Toward the end of his sojourn in England, Jarrico had an idea for a play about the coming struggle between patriotism and peace. The main character was based on former head of the Manhattan Project J. Robert Oppenheimer, who, Jarrico wrote, "is faced with the choice of serving fascism in America or treason." He wrote Sylvia, "I think it's fissionable material, very dangerous, but if I can bring it off it will be both a literary and a political triumph. . . . Probably finish me in Hollywood, but so will fascism." When he returned to Los Angeles, he discussed the idea with his wife, Michael Wilson, Abe Polonsky, and actor Richard Carlson. In his notes about the play, he wrote, "What I am after primarily is *emotion*—political emotion perhaps, but not agit-prop and not intellectual debate. . . . The PURPOSE of the play is to *move* people, . . . to move them in a certain direction, to direct their emotions into activity against war and fascism." He wanted his hero to be "a *great* man . . . , a truly great man, a *human* man and a hero." Jarrico worked on this play off and on for the next twenty years, regularly changing the theme and characters and motivations, but he never decided if it should be a drama or a comedy, and he never made it work to his satisfaction.[24]

His outline of the play, however, provides insights into the political message he wanted to express. His villain was "monopoly capital," which aimed to impose fascism in the United States and U.S. hegemony over the entire world. Using red baiting as its chief weapon, monopoly capital was trying to destroy the labor movement and the antiwar movement and to eliminate all the democratic freedoms being used against it. It was going to destroy, "in the name of patriotism," those who opposed war and fascism. But monopoly capital would be defeated by the working class and the middle-class intellectuals, who would demonstrate "that it is they who are the true patriots, who really love and defend the interests of their country, and that it is the monopoly capitalists and their servants who are the real traitors, the betrayers of all our democratic traditions, the murderers of our sons."[25]

As part of his antiwar effort, Jarrico wrote, for the Southern California Committee to Win the Peace, a pamphlet criticizing U.S. support of Chiang Kai-shek and his "fascist" Kuomintang. He also wrote a dramatization for a Win the Peace mass meeting held at the Shrine Auditorium on December 10, 1946. In it, he indicted the governments of Korea, Japan, China, and the United States as suppressors of the people, especially workers.[26]

Sylvia Jarrico, meanwhile, had become assistant editor for *Hollywood Quarterly*, a copublishing venture of the Hollywood Writers Mobilization and the University of California. (Its first issue appeared in October 1945, with John Howard Lawson as one of five editors.) The SACLA reported that the magazine was "the product of a group whose sympathies with Communism and the Communist Party is beyond doubt." Sylvia had also begun, with Pauline Lauber Finn (who had been the executive secretary of the HWM), Polonsky (who would replace Lawson on the *Hollywood Quarterly* board in

January 1947), and Richard Carlson, to plan for another writers' congress involving writer-representatives from all the member countries of the United Nations.[27]

Jarrico returned to RKO from his guaranteed layoff in January 1947 to rewrite *The White Tower* script. Dore Schary, now vice president in charge of production, agreed to allow him to write and direct a movie featuring Harpo Marx, to be titled *Studio Ghost*. Harpo's character, who is living illegally at RKO studios as a janitor, provides a place there for a penniless young ballet dancer and her son. When he discovers them, the studio head (Dore Schary, playing himself) is torn between his duty as an executive and his duty as a human being but allows them to stay. Others at the studio find out, however, and Schary is fired. In the movie's last shot, Schary and Harpo walk together "down a lonely road." But Jarrico was not impressed with his own work. He thought that his story lacked a theme, real characterization, and effective satire. Nor was it funny enough. "Why," he asked himself, "didn't you do a real original? Open City [Italian neorealist film]? You wanted to do 'The Treasure of the Sierra Madre.' [John] Huston is doing it. Does that mean you have to do Harpo?" After listing sixteen ideas for a "real original," he decided to make the Harpo script a satire on contemporary films (the eternal romantic triangle) and society (homelessness and ambition).[28]

Finally, on April 8, Jarrico told Schary that he would like to cease working on the project because "the picture seems puny to me, and unimportant." He did not want to direct a B picture. He explained to Schary, "What I need is the kind of time and technical assistance that John Huston, Delmar Daves, Billy Wilder, and Clifford Odets got on their first cracks at directing. If I haven't reached that stage yet, why maybe I'd better recognize it and write another important picture or two. I'm in no hurry. And I'm not so anxious to direct that it's worth my taking a step backward."[29]

The next day, on a different subject, though still in the grip of his frustration over the Harpo script, he wrote a much angrier letter to Schary, in which he protested the studio's failure to inform him that John Paxton had been assigned to make some revisions on *The White Tower*. Jarrico wrote, "This is old stuff, Dore. This goes back to the writer as a commodity. . . . But I had thought things were changing in the industry. And I particularly thought that a guy like you would be last to indulge in this nonsense, and the first to grant that a writer had certain intellectual and moral rights in his picture, even though the contracts maintain the fiction that the studio is 'the author.'" Schary agreed that Jarrico's protest was valid, but he noted that Dmytryk claimed he had tried to inform Jarrico about Paxton's assignment. A calmer and repentant Jarrico wrote another letter to Schary, admitting that he should have simmered down before putting his concerns in writing. He pleaded with Schary to provide him with another opportunity to direct a movie: "I do want to direct. I think about it and think about it and I'm so positive I can do it well and I get so impatient jumping hurdles that I wind up saying 'To hell with it. I don't want it as a favor. Either he sees it as a commercial proposition or he doesn't.' . . . I think if you'll be patient with me just a little while longer and let me throw a few more properties at you, we'll find one that we agree on wholeheartedly." But Schary's patience with Jarrico had run out. Though he expressed his wish for Jarrico to be "happily organized," Schary told him that he was being paid too much money to simply look around for a suitable project, and that if he did not find one immediately, he would be laid off. Jarrico did submit several script ideas to Schary in the following weeks, but Schary found none compelling. On April 24, RKO laid Jarrico off. He claimed to be elated and said that he "ran all the way home" to resume work on his atomic scientist play.[30]

At the end of May, RKO agreed to loan Jarrico to Praesens-Film A.G., a Swiss company, to revise a screenplay for a movie about child war refugees titled *The Search*.[31] This assignment required Jarrico to spend four weeks in Switzerland, working with director Fred Zinnemann on a rewrite of a script by Richard Schweizer. Schweizer's script tells the parallel narratives of a lost Jewish refugee child, who is helped by a U.S. soldier, and the mother who is looking for him, who is helped by a United Nations Refugee Relief Administration officer. Jarrico thought that Schweizer's script failed to depict the real problems faced by refugee children. He wanted to broaden the film's focus to depict the harm done to all children by war and use the film to argue that the United States should take responsibility for refugee children in Europe. Zinnemann agreed with Jarrico's ideas, and Jarrico traveled to Germany to investigate the conditions of refugee children there. He returned to Switzerland full of new ideas, but the producer told him, "Nein nein nein nein, sie verstehen nicht [no no no no, you do not understand], your job is to translate Mr. Schweizer's dialogue into English." "And what dialogue!" Jarrico wrote to a friend. "When I got unhappier they granted me the additional right to cut the dialogue, to polish it, but not to change the dramatic content or structure of the scenes." Jarrico was, he said, "a glorified translator."[32]

But Zinnemann was more generous. He told one correspondent, "[Jarrico] saved my life by rewriting an impossibly over-written script we were about to start shooting." And he told another, "Paul's main contribution to *The Search* was the construction of a workable script and a basic foundation for each of the characters involved. Until his arrival, the script . . . had been rather nebulous, particularly in depicting the American characters."[33] But the final film contains no political commentary beyond a description of war orphans' plight in the opening narrative voice-over.

At the end of the assignment, Jarrico became concerned about his credit. He wrote to Praesens-Film, "The only possible credit I can at the moment conceive of my getting on your picture will be 'Additional Dialogue by,' and this will depend completely on how much of my material is used. For this and other reasons it is absolutely essential (and my legal right) that I have a typed copy of all the material I write. . . . I feel very strongly about this, and I am afraid that I can turn in no further pages until some arrangement on this question is made." The company agreed, and Jarrico received an additional dialogue screen credit. But when the movie won the Academy Award for best original story, Jarrico did not receive an Oscar because the Academy rules did not allow additional dialogue contributors to share in that award. (The producer's son, David Wechsler, who was credited with contributing to the story, did share the award.) Jarrico later said that he considered it one of his finest credits.[34] *The Search*, featuring Montgomery Clift, was the first postwar feature filmed in the U.S. zone of Germany. When it was released in March 1948, it received good reviews, mainly for Zinnemann's decision to shoot it in a semidocumentary fashion, which included casting actual refugee children.

After Jarrico completed his work on the script, Sylvia and Bill flew to Paris to meet him. They bought a Buick and spent three weeks driving through Italy and the French Riviera and then spent another three weeks in Paris. From Paris, he wrote a letter to Schary to attempt to smooth matters. He asked,

> Dore, when I come home, can I *talk* to you please? Just talk to you. At least! Sometimes, very selfishly, I wish you weren't my boss so I could go to you with my problems. "What kind of property do you think I ought to do, Dore? What do you think of this one? How about that one? I'm in a pretty good position over there, got a chance to direct, but I don't want to compromise too much, and that first one's awfully important, isn't it?" Stuff like that—and you'd give me clear headed advice, because you always have.[35]

But when the Jarricos returned to the United States by ship at the end of September, Schary was preparing to depart for Washington to testify before the House Committee on Un-American Activities.

The committee's plan to reopen its investigation of communism in the motion picture industry had been advanced in February 1947, during a session involving Gerhart Eisler, reputed to be the main liaison between the CPUSSR and the CPUSA. Following his citation for contempt, his sister and political enemy, Ruth Fischer, took the witness stand. Karl Mundt (R-SD) asked her whether she had another brother, Hanns, in Hollywood who was a Communist. She replied, "He is a composer of films and he is a Communist in a philosophical sense." She also testified that Hanns was close with Gerhart.[36] At the end of March, the committee held five days of hearings. California senator Jack Tenney testified that the newly formed Progressive Citizens of America (PCA) and the Hollywood chapter of the Independent Citizens Committee of the Arts, Sciences and Professions were the most significant Communist political fronts in Hollywood,[37] that the CSU strike had been dominated and directed by Communists, and that "many of the so-called stars in Hollywood had permitted their names to be used by Communist-front organizations." He specifically mentioned Edward G. Robinson, John Garfield, Charlie Chaplin, Frederic March, and Frank Sinatra. On March 26, FBI director Hoover testified that "Communist activity in Hollywood is effective and is furthered by Communists and sympathizers using the prestige of prominent persons to serve, often unwittingly, the Communist cause." He urged the committee to investigate "those fields which mold public opinion and in which Communists have been successful in effecting infiltration, such as the radio, the motion pictures." Eric Johnston, president of the Motion Picture Association of America, testified that "if the Communists set out to capture Hollywood, they have suffered an overwhelming defeat." He did not deny that there were Communists in the industry, but he denied that Communist propaganda ever reached the screen. When Congressman Richard Nixon (R-CA) asked what the industry was doing to stop the infiltration of Communists or to root out those already there, Johnston replied that only unions and the Department of Justice had the legal means to police Communist employment. Rankin said, "I am surprised at your attitude. I think you are going to have to change your position and join us in this crusade to save America from its enemies within our gates. And you can't wink at them in the moving picture industry. . . . You need a house cleaning, and you need it very badly."[38]

That cleaning process began on May 8, when three members of the House Committee on Un-American Activities (J. Parnell Thomas [R-NJ], John Wood [D-GA], and John McDowell [R-PA]) and two staff members (Robert Stripling and Louis Russell) came to Los Angeles to hold a ten-day inquiry. According to Stripling, their "primary task was to uncover and subpoena Hanns Eisler." The day before, Ronald Reagan, president of the Screen Actors Guild (SAG), had publicly stated that SAG was ready to cooperate with any legitimate congressional investigation. Reagan admitted that there were reds in SAG, but he claimed that he knew who they were. He denied that Hollywood was dominated by Communists, and he said that the industry was fighting them. (When Reagan and his then wife, Jane Wyman, were visited by FBI agents on April 10, they had named those members of SAG whom they suspected of "carrying out Communist party work.")[39]

J. Parnell Thomas told the press, "We know where to go and we know whom to see." Twelve witnesses appeared voluntarily, among them two studio executives, Jack Warner and Henry Ginsberg (Paramount). The other ten witnesses—Roy Brewer, Lela Rogers, four writers, three actors, and one director—were members of (or sympathetic to) the MPA. Thomas said that five of those who testified were "friendly witnesses" who provided the committee with the names of hundreds of Communists. Thomas advised Hollywood to "clean its own house of insidious Communist propaganda and not wait for Congress to spotlight the sorry spectacle." He announced that he would hold public hearings in Washington starting June 16. Hoover, meanwhile, had decided to provide selected dossiers and reports to House Committee on Un-American Activities investigators. In late August, Stripling asked the Washington FBI office for information on forty-one potential witnesses who were likely to be "unfriendly." The bureau agreed to prepare blind memoranda (without identifying headings) on the people on that list and, in mid-September, sent to committee investigators copies of twenty-five CPA membership cards.[40]

Jarrico, who was in Europe, was not among those subpoenaed on September 21. Sylvia Jarrico recalled that he was offended by his omission. "How hard do you have to work at being a Communist?" he asked in jest.[41] Jarrico returned to Los Angeles while eighteen of the "unfriendly" witnesses were meeting with lawyers to prepare for the hearings in Washington.[42] They wanted to pose a constitutional challenge to the committee while staying out of jail and keeping their jobs. Herbert Biberman later said that the eighteen decided not to invoke the Fifth Amendment as the basis for their refusal to answer, because if they had used it "there would be nothing in contention. We would not be challenging the Committee and could not take it to court." They decided instead to challenge the committee on First Amendment grounds. One of their attorneys, Robert Kenny, advised them not to refuse outright to answer the committee's questions but to say that they were answering the questions in their own way. The attorneys were certain that if the eighteen were convicted of contempt by the trial court, it would be reversed by the U.S. Supreme Court.[43]

Eleven of the unfriendly witnesses were called to testify during the October 1947 hearings. Ten were cited for contempt of Congress; the eleventh, Bertolt Brecht, was allowed to leave for Germany after he denied that he was a member of the Communist Party. Among the friendly witnesses, only Dore Schary was grilled by committee members. They questioned him sharply about RKO's employment of Hanns Eisler. When asked if he would rehire Eisler, Schary replied, "I would not hire anyone who is dedicated to the overthrow of the government by force." He continued, however, that although he was opposed to the Communist Party, he could not refuse employment to a man "purely because of his politics" and would not hesitate to rehire Eisler "if it was not proven he was a foreign agent." When asked what he was going to do about RKO employees Scott and Dmytryk, Schary replied that they were under contract. He told committee members that the Communist Party was not as great a danger as some seemed to think: Communists were defeated every time they tried to dominate an organization in Hollywood, and they had no influence on film content.[44]

Jarrico later commented that the so-called Hollywood Ten had made a mistake by pretending that they were answering the committee's questions and failing to identify themselves as Communists. But Jarrico was primed for the struggle. He was the coordinator of the November 5 welcome-home gathering for the unfriendly witnesses who flew back to Los Angeles. Two weeks later, he attended a PCA-sponsored rally at Gilmore Stadium, where approximately three thousand people gathered to sign petitions to Congress to protest Eisler's deportation and to demand the abolition of the House Committee on Un-American Activities and the dismissal of the contempt citations.[45]

On November 6, Jarrico checked back in at RKO to complete his second contract period. He was assigned to write a movie, *Joe Tanaka—American*, also known as *Honored Glory*, about the removal of Japanese Americans from their homes on the West Coast and their incarceration in "relocation centers" for the duration of the war. While he was researching, he sent a letter to Schary asking for a very short meeting, "not to protest, but to discuss some business."[46]

Schary, however, was too busy preparing for a trip to New York, where the top executives of the major movie companies were to convene at the Waldorf-Astoria Hotel on November 25 (the day after the House of Representatives voted to cite the Ten for contempt). After what Schary termed "a series of hysterical speeches," the executives decided to fire those of the Ten who were under contract (Dmytryk, Scott, Lardner, Trumbo, and Cole) and not to rehire "any of the ten until such time as he is acquitted or has purged himself of contempt and declares under oath that he is not a Communist." They announced this decision in the form of a publicity release that has come to be known as the Waldorf statement.[47]

As soon as they returned to Hollywood, the studio heads created a committee to sell the Waldorf statement to the guilds. The members of the producers' committee, headed by Schary, met with guild representatives on November 28 and December 3. Two weeks later, Schary and two others (Eddie Mannix of MGM and Walter Wanger, an independent producer) addressed a meeting of the SWG. Schary remembered that he told the writers that he "was not there to either condone or condemn certain parts of the statement in relationship to individual companies firing or not hiring communists. I think I mentioned that I, myself personally, was opposed to this part of the statement, that what I was there to discuss with them was their cooperation in the formation of a public relations organization that would, in some way, help create a different impact in the future for Hollywood in connection with attacks that might be leveled on it." Jarrico and other writers who were there said that Schary, in effect, told them, "This is not a blacklist. The five men were not dismissed because they were believed to be Communists, but because it was believed that they have impaired their usefulness to the industry by their actions. If you do not fight the Waldorf Statement and work with us, we might be able to prevent further dismissals."[48]

Shortly after that meeting, in a note to himself that he wrote at RKO while waiting for word on *Honored Glory*, Jarrico waxed cynical:

> My name is Paul Jarrico. I'm in cell block 79 [the rumored number of subpoenas waiting to be served]. At least I think I am. God knows I've worked hard enough in progressive organizations including the Guild for ten years, and if I'm not on the list of 79 it's rank discrimination. Probably because I'm Jewish. Anyway, we in cell block 79 are presumably being offered a reprieve now. All we have to do is keep our mouths shut and not protest too loudly against illegal execution of the men in cell block ten. It's very tempting. Personally, I've thought it over, and I say to hell with it. It's not that I don't trust the warden. Dore Schary is a very nice guy. He got me my first job in pictures ten years ago, and I guess it would only be poetic justice if he fires me from my last job now. Dore and the others say

> they hated to execute the ten, but the governor made them. If we'll be good they won't execute any more, honest. Well, it's not Dore I mistrust. It's the governor. Mr. J. Parnell Thomas. If we can learn anything from history it's that men like J. Parnell Thomas and John Rankin *cannot be appeased*. We are told that the Guild is weak, too weak to act effectively in this. I say that if [we] don't act effectively on this the Guild is not only weak, it's finished.

He had already begun thinking of using another name on his scripts. In his agenda book entry for November 20, he wrote, "William Gussin (pseudonym?)."[49]

Jarrico and fifty-nine other members of the SWG signed a petition to the board asking for a general membership meeting to vote on three resolutions: to reinstate the three fired screenwriters (Cole, Trumbo, and Lardner) and abolish "any blacklist whatsoever"; to provide legal assistance to the three writers in any action they might bring against the producers; and to unite the full resources of the guild "into a massive public relations organization to bring the SWG's case to the public in all parts of the world where American motion pictures are shown." The petitioners wanted "to use the moral, legal, and political strength of the SWG, and the great body of American opinion which will unite with us on these issues, against the indefensible and un-American positions of the producers, until such time as they abandon their collaboration with the Thomas-Rankin Committee, and its illegal and unconstitutional acts and procedures."[50]

To some Paris friends, Jarrico wrote, "The town is sick with fear and unemployment, and of all the guilds and unions only the Writers have begun to fight back. . . . As for my own situation, I don't know. Apparently I'm not on this over-all blacklist myself—yet—I seem to be in line for a couple of assignments at other studios after I finish here—but the kind of crap those of us who can still get jobs will be expected to turn out is not something I look forward to." In fact, the SACLA had recommended that Jarrico's name be removed from the "key figure list." It would, however, be reinstated on March 22, 1951, just about the time the House Committee on Un-American Activities opened a new investigation of communism in Hollywood.[51]

5

The Interregnum, 1948–50

> What we underestimated was the direct connection between the Cold War abroad and repression at home. . . . There was a logic to the reactionary position that we underestimated.
>
> —*Paul Jarrico, 1987*

As the Hollywood Ten began their three-year effort to stay out of prison, the nation descended further into the polar regions of the cold war. Relations between the Soviet Union and the United States steadily worsened, a nuclear arms race began, and, in two instances (the Berlin blockade of 1948 and the Korean War), the war turned hot. At home, the domestic version of the cold war also increased in intensity. The major event was the presidential campaign of Henry Wallace, who had been fired as secretary of commerce because of his public opposition to Truman's increasingly hard-line foreign policy. Some of those who opposed Truman's foreign policy wanted Wallace to challenge Truman for the Democratic nomination for president, while others pushed him to establish a third party. In California, for example, Robert Kenny established a Democrats for Wallace organization, while Hugh Bryson, president of Marine Cooks and Stewards, formed the Independent Progressive Party. When, in December 1947, the PCA endorsed the Independent Progressive Party, the CPUSA accepted it.

Many rank-and-file party members, like Jarrico, devoted a great deal of time and energy to the Wallace campaign. They did not consider it a quixotic cause but rather a potent means of protesting against the international and domestic cold war. Jarrico wrote two pamphlets and arranged the program for a Wallace speech at Gilmore Stadium. The first pamphlet, *Are You Intimidated?* stated, "The barrage of propaganda accusing Wallace of being a 'tool of the Communists,' a 'Soviet foreign agent,' etc. has been so tremendous that even a great many people who know it isn't true are afraid to speak out, for fear of being red-baited themselves." The second pamphlet, *Can Wallace Win?* argued that the more votes Wallace received, the better chance the country had of preserving peace. For the Gilmore event, Jarrico recruited Howard Da Silva, Dalton Trumbo, Charlotta Bass (publisher of the black newspaper *California Eagle*), and several labor and religious spokespeople.[1]

As Communists became more involved in the Wallace campaign, liberals began to leave the Independent Progressive Party, and Wallace, who had not sought Communist support, became increasingly antagonistic toward them.[2] But this disarray within was nothing compared to the red-baiting from without: from the Truman campaign, liberal organizations, and the CIO. In November 1947, Clark Clifford, one of Truman's advisors, counseled the president to make every effort "to identify him [Wallace] in the public mind with Communists" and to point out that the core of Wallace's supporters were "Communists and fellow-travelers." The liberal Americans for Democratic Action unreservedly condemned the Wallace campaign, and Philip Murray formally associated the CIO with that group.[3]

During the campaign, the Truman administration and Congress played politics with informers' testimonies. In June, former Communist Elizabeth Bentley revealed to a federal grand jury her participation in a Soviet spy ring and named its members. When she failed to produce any evidence to support her charges, the Department of Justice, to cover its embarrassment (and to avoid weakening Truman's reelection chances), decided to seek indictments of the top leadership of the CPUSA. On July 20, twelve CPUSA leaders were charged with violating the Alien Registration Act.[4]

In the election, Wallace garnered just over one million votes (2.4 percent), and Truman was narrowly reelected (with the full support of the AFL and the CIO). Although the Democrats regained numerical control of Congress, both houses were effectively controlled by a conservative, anti-Communist majority in the form of a Republican–southern Democratic bloc. The president was now even more firmly committed to prosecution of the cold war at home and abroad, the AFL and CIO had formally enlisted in the cold war, and the Communist Party had been severely damaged.[5]

Jarrico remained optimistic despite Wallace's poor showing at the polls, the pending defeat of the third CSU strike (which further weakened the progressive labor movement in Hollywood), and the incessant red baiting by the MPA, Roy Brewer, and Billy Wilkerson.[6] Though he acknowledged that "the forces of reaction" were attempting to remove "progressive content" from movies and make them "more and more openly a weapon of fascist propaganda," Jarrico was certain that Hollywood remained a progressive community and that "no Thomas Committee witchhunt" was going to destroy it or prevent the progressives from fighting against the "forces of reaction." In fact, he argued, a struggle for progressive content in movies offered Hollywood Communists the best means available to fight these forces.[7]

As chairman of the film division of the Council of the Arts, Sciences and Professions (ASP; formerly the Hollywood chapter of the Independent Citizens Committee of the Arts, Sciences and Professions), Jarrico planned a series of seminars and put out a bulletin that he hoped would stem the "shameful deterioration of the content of films" and demonstrate that the progressive creators and workers in Hollywood were "*not* prepared to surrender this industry to those who would make of it an open weapon of fascist and war propaganda." The film division's bulletin, *Hollywood Memo*, began publication in April. During its short life, it contained film reviews and various comments about the industry. *The Hollywood Reporter* said about it, "You might as well be getting the *Daily Worker*," whereas the *People's World* said that its content "is tops." The film seminars, which continued through June, included discussions of the growing popularity of television, the depiction of war in the movies, and types of screen humor. For an ASP fund raiser, Jarrico wrote a parody of *South Pacific* titled *North Atlantic*. Among the rewritten songs were "Bally Hoo" and "Some Subversive Evening."

Some subversive evening
You may see a stranger
You may see a stranger
From the FBI

And somehow you know
You know even then
That somewhere you'll see him
Again and again[8]

The Jarricos also helped plan an ASP-sponsored Hollywood peace conference, which would follow (and be organized along the lines of) the Cultural and Scientific Conference for World Peace scheduled to occur in New York City March 25–27, 1949. The New York conference, however, was ferociously red baited, and the Hollywood conference was a failure.[9] Jarrico wrote Abe Polonsky,

> There was our famous peace conference [April 9], about which you may already have heard, the big plans we made when we thought international guests were coming here, the diminution of our plans when we thought at least some big names from New York would come, the frantic dwindling of our plans as we saw we couldn't even get some medium size names from our own community, the twilight of the gods as Mike Wilson, Paul Jarrico and Betsy Blair (reading for Waldo Salt [one of the nineteen]) addressed the half-filled El Patio on various aspects of Motion Pictures and the Cold War. . . . [W]hat a sad flop it was, our peace conference.[10]

That failure, along with other events that year, presaged a worsening atmosphere for Communists and fellow-travelers in Hollywood. In March 1949, Judith Coplon, a Department of Justice employee, was arrested. She had in her possession FBI reports she had pilfered, documenting the bureau's surveillance of several actors, among them Frederic March and Edward G. Robinson. Adrian Scott learned that House Committee on Un-American Activities investigators were conducting secret interviews in Hollywood. And Carey McWilliams wrote that studio bosses had begun a "graylist," which included people suspected of left-wing political activities and movies containing subversive themes.[11]

The domestic cold war struck directly at the Jarrico home in the form of a non-Communist oath instituted by Sylvia Jarrico's employer, the University of California (publisher of *Hollywood Quarterly*). The oath approved by the regents required all faculty and staff to swear, "I am not a member of the Communist Party or under any oath, or a party to any agreement, or under any commitment that is in conflict with my obligation under this oath." University employees who refused to sign were told they would be fired. Although the faculty were overwhelmingly opposed, the vast majority of them signed. But 32 faculty members and 157 nonacademic employees refused, including Sylvia Jarrico, who recalled,

> I was told that these forms were being collected every day—that I would not be alone—that I would be surprised at the number of people who were signing. The man who made the request said: "I do not understand what you are doing. Just sign and that will be the end of it. The faculty will not support you, because in your case it is not a question of academic freedom. The magazine board will not support you for fear that it will lose its university funding." I resigned in the face of their silence. It was a horrible period. I couldn't eat. The pressure was so intense that if I had not been morally prepared the situation would have been absolutely unbearable. I was emotionally unprepared to be deserted by my friends and colleagues. I had a sense of being hunted, of being different from everyone else.[12]

Increasingly concerned by the effects that such oaths, blacklists, and graylists were having on U.S. culture, Jarrico became determined, in February 1950, to broaden the influence of ASP's film division. "We had," he wrote, "too little effect on the industry. We seldom mobilized for *action*. . . . The chief faults seems to have been *a failure to define our goals*—the lack of a coherent and unified program of action. We went off in all directions at once or stood still. We did too much or too little. We lacked long range plans." But now, he argued, the industry had reached a turning point: it had recognized that "fascist films have flopped without exception" and that the "few semi-progressive films have cleaned up." He proposed a three-point program to take advantage of what he termed an "area of contradiction" and the "room to struggle" opened by it. He wanted the film division

1. To mobilize Hollywood on the issue of peace, with particular reference to the hydrogen bomb, *at the same time* as we fight against war propaganda on the screen.

2. To wage a real fight on the issue of Negro discrimination in the motion picture industry—both in terms of jobs and content.

3. To redouble our efforts for the 10, relating it to the whole issue of censorship and a free screen.

This plan aroused the opposition of some of the members, who feared that Jarrico was trying to substitute by force a political program for a cultural one. Jarrico did not retreat. He told the committee, "We have always been political. We shall remain cultural."[13]

The members did agree to do more about the Hollywood Ten, two of whom, John Howard Lawson and Dalton Trumbo, had just been tried in a U.S. district court and convicted for contempt of Congress. (The others, to save time and money, had agreed to accept for themselves the outcome of those trials.) The U.S. court of appeals had upheld the convictions. The majority opinion stated, "So that there may be no mistakes or misunderstanding and because the point here involved has proven to be one of constant recurrence, we expressly hold herein that the House Committee on Un-American Activities, or a properly appointed subcommittee thereof, has the power to inquire whether a witness subpoenaed by it is or is not a member of the Communist Party or a believer in communism and that this power carries with [it] necessarily the power to effect criminal punishment for failure or refusal to answer that question." The U.S. Supreme Court refused to grant certiorari.[14] One judge sentenced eight of the men to one year in prison, and another judge sentenced two of them (Dmytryk and Biberman) to six months.

The ASP film division decided to make a film about the pending incarceration of the Ten to raise money for their legal fees and to warn the American public about the threat to civil liberties represented by the House Committee on Un-American Activities and the domestic cold war. Jarrico said that he "volunteered [to produce it], without being asked. In fact, it was my idea that such a film be made. . . . It was written by all ten men plus myself. . . . [B]ut I had general responsibility for the script."[15] The first half focuses on the individuals, their personal lives and writing achievements. The second half features them sitting at a long table, making a serial speech about their plight and its ramifications for the rights of others. Samuel Ornitz warns that the House Committee on Un-American Activities "is now free to operate, to drag before it a thousand people." Lester Cole calls the investigations "a form of legal lynching." Alvah Bessie speaks of "a developing nightmare of fear in our land, in which increasing numbers of citizens are forced to swear I am not this I am not that, I don't belong to anything, I don't believe in anything, and I don't criticize anything." They warn of a new form of government, one operated through the use of stool pigeons; of the cold war's becoming a pretext to undermine civil liberties; and of a pending world war. "We are," Cole says, "casualties of the cold war."

The Hollywood Ten, an effective piece of what the Russian Communists called agitprop, was made quickly and secretly by a small crew Jarrico recruited. Though he allowed his name to be openly associated with the film, he promised anonymity to the crew, and he asked John Berry to direct. Berry, a close friend, had received his first director's credit in 1946, and he would add five more before he was blacklisted. When Jarrico came to him, Berry recalled, "and asked [me] if I would direct it, . . . I said no. I didn't want to stick my neck out. . . . [B]ut the [Ten's] defense committee came back to me and gave me that bull shit about my being a man of principle, so would I do it?" Berry said that he "just picked the shots and told them what to do." They shot the film at the end of April and sent it to Carl Lerner in New York to edit. It premiered in four cities in June, the same month that nine of the Hollywood Ten began their prison sentences. (Adrian Scott, who was ill, began his sentence in September.)[16]

Jarrico was also doing what he could to help blacks to break into the industry, a major discussion point for Hollywood Communists. Many had read a report that pointed out that the industry employed 43,322 people, of whom only 185 were black. All but 20 were employed as janitors. The film division members concluded that they had been seriously remiss in their efforts to launch a real fight for black employment and decided to undertake a "sustained, relentless" campaign and relate it to the question of content. For his part, in January 1950, Jarrico contacted his first producer, Nat Perrin, about hiring Mason Roberson, a black cultural affairs writer for *People's World* whom Jarrico had met during his navy days in San Francisco. He wrote Roberson, "I guess you understand without my saying so that if you do get this job we will be cracking another Jim Crow bastion," that "you will be blazing a trail for the employment of Negro writers in Hollywood." Perrin did not hire Roberson, but Jarrico and Adrian Scott later would.[17]

In his ongoing effort to expose the role the United States was playing in escalating the cold war, Jarrico authored an ASP pamphlet on the recently opened war in Korea, accusing the Truman administration of turning the truth inside out and of suppressing the will of the people in South Korea. He demanded that the administration withdraw U.S. troops from Korea and allow the United Nations to take center stage as the keeper of the world's peace.[18] When Congress passed the Internal Security Act in September 1950, Jarrico and other Hollywood Communists joined the Los Angeles Committee for the Protection of the Foreign Born, and ASP sent a telegram to bill author Pat McCarran (D-NV), calling it "a dangerous threat to basic American freedoms."[19]

Despite its efforts to revamp its activities and leadership, the Hollywood party's cultural section membership had declined 12 percent since 1947, and an informant had told the SACLA that those who remained were "extremely 'jumpy' about being uncovered as Party members" and about having a spy in their midst. The SACLA calculated that there were now 332 people in the Hollywood party and 1,100 in ASP.[20]

Jarrico displayed no anxiety about being exposed as a Communist, and his screenwriting career did not seem to be affected by his political activity. When he finished his contract stint at RKO on December 22, 1948, the studio did not exercise its option to renew his contract. Cinematographer James Wong Howe approached him to write and codirect a story about China, but when that project fell through, he traveled to New York to write a script for Michael Todd, which also did not get made. Following his return to Los Angeles, Jarrico was hired by Enterprise Productions to work with Paul Trivers on the script for *Wild Calendar*, a melodramatic triangle movie that he described derisively as "a piece of crap . . . , a project which has been supporting writers of good will for years now." Jarrico wrote

Beatrice Buchman, "They said I should be able to finish it in eight or ten weeks, but it soon became obvious that if I did it their way instead of mine it would take me forever." After two weeks of wrestling with various themes and titles, he gave up on the project.[21]

In early April, Jarrico attempted something no other Hollywood Communist had: an independently made film that clearly favored communism. He rented an office on Sunset Boulevard and began to adapt *Temptation*, a novel set in interwar Hungary, written by John Pen (Janos Szekely). Jarrico had paid Pen $1,000 for a six-month option to buy the book outright for $25,000. He wanted to produce French- and English-language versions, and he wanted to film it in Europe. He asked Beatrice Buchman to be his associate producer and to help raise funds for the English version; he asked Lilo Aisner to translate the script into French and Henri Aisner to codirect. But he told all of them, "I must control the content of the picture." In a letter to Lazar Wechsler, enclosing the script, Jarrico wrote that he wanted the movie to be "honest and realistic, that is to say, progressive," and that he wanted it "to make money."[22]

The novel and screenplay tell the story of Bela, a poor boy from the Hungarian countryside who becomes a bellhop at a hotel. The manager tells him that he must inform on reds working in the hotel or be blacklisted. At first he agrees, but then he decides to join "the organization" and work for the revolution. In his adaptation notes, Jarrico wrote, "In a world like this, there's just two things a man can do—he can become a revolutionist or a scoundrel."[23]

At the end of April, however, Jarrico interrupted work on *Temptation* to take a job that he described as "an attractive if shady proposition from [producer] Jerry Wald," which would, he believed, earn him a fast fee. Wald's brother, Malvin, a screenwriter, had conceived the idea, and Jerry Wald asked Jarrico to collaborate with Malvin on developing it. The story concerned a woman who tries to live a fast life, becomes pregnant, gives the baby up for adoption, despairs, kidnaps another baby, and is saved by the love of a dull, reliable man. In the treatment, which they titled *Bad Company*, Wald and Jarrico made it into a universal story about unwed mothers who are forced to offer their illegitimate children for adoption. Jarrico wanted it to be shot in a documentary style and to demonstrate that "beneath the hard crust of social convention" a drama stirs, "erupting now and then into black headlines, subsiding again to seethe beneath the polite surface." It was, he later said, the fastest script he had ever written. He spent two weeks on the story and screenplay and "was neither happy nor unhappy with the result." But the deal fell through.[24]

On July 3, Jarrico went to New York to discuss his draft of the *Temptation* script with John Pen. Jarrico wrote Sylvia that the sessions "were wonderfully fruitful." He told her that he and Pen had amicably resolved the issues that troubled Pen, that Pen had been "really so pleased" with the draft, and that he had said Jarrico's ending was much better than his. "He's right," Jarrico said.[25] Jarrico then flew to Europe to try to arrange a coproduction of the movie. He spent a total of five weeks in Paris, London, and Rome. While in Europe, Jarrico learned about the indictments that had been issued for the twelve top leaders of the CPUSA.[26] He wrote Sylvia, "This fitted in so completely with the war scare that it took me an hour to regain my conviction that the war could and would be stopped." In London, he touched base with Dmytryk, who was there directing *Give Us This Day/Salt to the Devil*. Dmytryk offered Jarrico a job. Jarrico's first thought, he wrote Sylvia, was "Get him." His second thought was "Well, maybe I'll need it."[27]

Following a series of rejections from western European producers, Jarrico tried to interest the Czechoslovak Republic's movie department in the project. When he experienced difficulty getting a visa to travel there, he sent a telegram to Ota Katz (foreign editor of *Rude Pravo*, the Hungarian Communist newspaper), who arranged the visa for him. While in Prague, Jarrico met with Katz, who demanded to know everything about the Hollywood Ten. "It's really a remarkable thing," Katz told Jarrico. "The Nazis started in the same way, they started with an attack on the movie industry." Jarrico replied that there was one big difference in the two situations—the Hollywood people were not going to lose. Jarrico remembered that Katz "looked at me for a moment. He turned in his swivel chair and looked out the window at the beautiful city of Prague. He turned back to me, and he said, 'We didn't lose.'" At Katz's request, Jarrico wrote an article on the Hollywood Ten for *Rude Pravo*.[28]

Officials in the Czechoslovak Republic's movie department told

Jarrico that the movie could not be made there because of what they called the seething animosity between Czechs and Hungarians. So Jarrico decided to try to arrange a production in Hungary. He traveled to Budapest carrying a letter of introduction written by Katz to the Hungarian secretary of state. Katz referred to Jarrico as among those "in the first rank of struggle of progressive writers in Hollywood." Jarrico thought he had made a deal in Budapest for the Hungarians to produce and him to direct. He wrote Sylvia, "I provide some unspecified technical equipment, they get full European profits and also 20% of the profits of the English version. They put up all the dough for production. I put up the novel, the script, my services, the aforementioned equipment and pay for whatever English dubbing is necessary." Jarrico was confident. "Hell, with a guaranteed production and 80% of the English version for me to play around with, if I can't raise 50 or 60 thousand dollars to pay for the book, our expenses and the equipment, I don't deserve the proud name of entrepreneur." On his way back to the United States, Jarrico received a letter from an official in the Hungarian national film bureau (Filmgartyo Nemzeti Vallalat) informing him that the head of the bureau had read Jarrico's script "and had the best opinion about it." But the reader had found some errors about local conditions that would have to be corrected and had concluded that "the final form of the film must be framed by us, completely, according with our organs." In penciled notes, Jarrico observed that the reader also had said the script was too pessimistic, that Bela was too passive, and that his conversion into "a conscious fighter" for the Communist Party was not convincing. Finally, the Hungarians thought that Jarrico had oversimplified the nature of the ruling class by depicting only its "rotten side."[29]

Jarrico replied with a set of detailed amendments in which he stipulated that he and the Hungarian film bureau would be coproducers, that he would provide a camera dolly and a microphone boom in exchange for Hungarian money to pay his living expenses while he was shooting the film, that they would share artistic control, and that the contract should state explicitly that Jarrico owned the English-language version and all distribution and exhibition rights in the Western Hemisphere as well as in all English-speaking countries in the Eastern Hemisphere.[30]

Back home, Jarrico told a potential backer that *Temptation* was "more than a business deal. It is, I feel, a real struggle for content, for culture, in defiance of the Johnston office and the Thomas committee." When Jarrico could not find any financial backing, he wrote John Pen, "The Iron Curtain propaganda has had its effect, these people are frightened, no question about it. And it is not enough to assure them that they will get their money back. They feel if they're going to gamble they ought to gamble on getting a hell of a lot more than just their money back."[31]

Jarrico received further discouraging news from his contact in Hungary, who wrote, "Our authorities did not accede to this plan; the picture is . . . not in accordance with the actual mentality in Hungary." They (the "authorities") wanted to make movies only about postwar subjects. However, if Jarrico wanted to make *Temptation* in Hungary, he could rent facilities in that country to do so. Jarrico liked that idea, but it would require him to raise even more money. Still hopeful, Jarrico wrote to Pen, asking for a gratis extension of the option. "The fact is," Jarrico wrote, "that having spent some six months and some $7500 direct expenses on this project, I am practically broke. This is not a bid for sympathy—I can probably get a job in Hollywood and get back on my feet quite quickly." Pen agreed to the extension. At the end of 1949, Jarrico wrote his Hungarian film contact, "The political climate in this country is hardly such as to encourage investment in a film to be made 'behind the iron curtain.' After awhile the people who have money begin to believe their own lies. And even those who know better become frightened." When his plan to go to Hungary was thwarted by the U.S. government in March 1950, Jarrico wrote, "I could call the film a casualty of the cold war and let it go at that, but I still have the vague but stubborn hope that it will be made. By me. In Budapest. By gum."[32]

Low on funds, Jarrico turned his attention back to Hollywood studio projects. He made notes for several story ideas, and he and Michael Wilson wrote an original comedy about a French newspaperwoman who comes to the United States, which they titled *Mademoiselle from Armentières*. He then sold *Bad Company* to Emerald Productions, an independent company run by the actress Ida Lupino, and agreed to write the script for a flat fee of $10,000.

Two months after he turned in the completed script, he was told that Lupino and her associate had rewritten it completely and that they wanted sole screen credit. Jarrico objected and submitted the issue to an SWG arbitration panel. He acknowledged that Lupino and her associate had made substantial changes in his original script, but he maintained that those changes constituted not more than 50 percent of the final script. The arbitration committee awarded him sole credit, but Lupino and her associate appealed that decision. Jarrico suggested that the screen credits should be as follows: original story by Paul Jarrico and Malvin Wald, screenplay by Paul Jarrico and Ida Lupino. All the other parties concurred, and the film was released as *Not Wanted*. It is a dull, trite tale of redemption.

In June 1949, RKO decided to revive *The White Tower*. The studio was now controlled by the eccentric entrepreneur Howard Hughes, and Dore Schary had left. Hughes had shut down several productions, fired more than seven hundred workers, and placed an executive committee in charge of production. But all production decisions had to be approved by Hughes, who maintained an office off the lot. He visited RKO only once.[33] A rabid anti-Communist, Hughes must not have been paying attention to hiring decisions when Jarrico was brought back (though as a freelance, not a contract, writer), at $2,000 a week, to polish the script. His revision pleased the studio executives, but when Jarrico asked to be allowed to go to Switzerland for the filming of the script, the director, Ted Tetzlaff, said no. Friends who were involved in the filming wrote to Jarrico that when the lead actor, Glenn Ford, complained about some of the antiwar elements in the screenplay, Tetzlaff simply eliminated them. The finished product puzzled executive producer Sid Rogell, who invited Jarrico to come to the studio and view it. After watching the movie, Jarrico told Rogell that Tetzlaff had cut out all the dialogue that explained the characters' motivations, and he had not substituted others. The result was that the picture "says nothing. It's just confusing." Since it would be too costly to refilm and reedit the movie, it was released as Tetzlaff shot it. But Jarrico was right: stripped of all his antifascist and peace dialogue, there is "a hole" in the meaning of the picture. The few scattered comments relating to the Germans' insistence on superiority and will are made to seem aspects of the fascist character's ego rather than his ideology. The American antifascist (Glenn Ford) is an aimless yokel. The Communist reviewers panned it, but the rest of the press praised it highly.[34]

Scriptwriting jobs, Jarrico wrote Maurice Rapf, were not coming "nearly as often as they used to," but "enough of our friends have worked off and on so that it isn't quite accurate to say that things are tougher than ever. They're tough, but not desperate, not even for the 10, some of whom have picked up a few odd jobs here and there." Hollywood was "still an arena of struggle. On one side, are the forces of monopoly capital and their representatives, the studio executives, who are trying to make films which are subtly or openly weapons of fascist and war propaganda." On the other side were two forces: "the audience, confusedly refusing to support the most reactionary films (*Iron Curtain*, *Red Menace*, *I Married a Communist*, etc.), confusedly crowding in to see a picture like *Home of the Brave*," and some movie producers, "confusedly wanting to make pictures they are not ashamed of." Jarrico thought that Dore Schary, now head of production at MGM, was one of the latter. Though Schary wanted to make progressive pictures (such as *Intruder in the Dust*), making reactionary films (like *Red Danube*) was part of the price he had to pay to run a major studio.[35]

Two months after finishing his work on *The White Tower*, Jarrico received an offer from that picture's supervising producer, Irving Allen, to adapt Georges Simenon's dark and moody novel *The Man Who Watched Trains Go By*. (Allen had recently produced an adaptation of another Simenon novel, *The Man on the Eiffel Tower*.) He offered no cash up front but did offer a $50,000 deferred fee, 10 percent of the total profits, and transportation and expenses. Jarrico's agent, Robert Goldfarb, demanded $3,500 up front and $20,000 for the first draft, and Allen accepted. Jarrico had high hopes for this job, not only because he thought that he might be given the opportunity to be the associate producer or even the director, but also because the script itself would allow him to try something different, to move beyond the romantic comedies that had consumed most of his studio career. He wanted to explore the nature of the revolt of an individual human being, in this case a lower-middle-class man, motivated by abstract concepts of freedom. As Jarrico saw it, the novel's protagonist did not understand freedom in class terms: he was not rebelling as a means to change society for the better; he was rebelling against society in general, against social restrictions per se. The result of his acts was not revolution, therefore, but violent crime. "In our society," Jarrico wrote, "potentially every one is a criminal. In our society, in terms of security and ego-satisfaction, crime *does* pay, or there would be no crime."[36]

He produced an atmospheric script that was much heavier with dialogue than action. The protagonist, a Dutch white-collar worker, learns that his boss has embezzled money from the firm and committed suicide. He tries to seduce the boss's mistress, but she rejects him. He kills her, flees to Paris, meets and physically harms a prostitute, and holes up in a hotel room, where he assiduously follows the accounts of his crimes in the newspapers. He writes to one of the newspapers, "I am not crazy, nor the homicidal maniac some people think. I am merely a man who at the age of forty has determined to live as he thinks fit, without bothering about convention or the laws; for I have discovered, if somewhat late in life, that I was the dupe of appearances and the truth is that nobody obeys the law if he can help it." He is finally captured by the police and incarcerated in a mental asylum. Allen sent the script to Simenon, who responded that Jarrico's treatment had surmounted all the difficulties of adaptation and that he had nothing "very grand to say because everything is kept perfect and brilliant." But Allen could not raise the money for the production.[37]

At the end of December 1949, Jarrico signed a contract with Proser-Nasser Productions to adapt *Shadow of a Hero*, a novel about municipal corruption. He would be paid $2,000 a week and would have to work with the novel's author, Allan Chase. They finished the first draft in mid-February, but the producers did not like it. Jarrico's new agent, George Willner, agreed that the plot was unfocused. When the company refused to pay Jarrico the full amount it owed him, he sued for the additional $14,000 and was eventually awarded $13,372 in damages.[38]

In March 1950, Jarrico was offered a contract with Columbia to adapt another novel, *The Big Eye*, at $1,500 per week for up to ten weeks. Though he was unhappy with the cut in salary, he agreed.

The science fiction novel, written by Max Simon Ehrlich, centers on the efforts of the world's scientists to manufacture a hoax that will prevent a third world war. The producers "hated" Jarrico's first step outline. One told him it was "terrible, stinks, misses the whole point." They approved the second outline, but when Jarrico handed in the completed script, they complained about his decision to have the problems resolved by the United Nations instead of the U.S. government. Following his conference with the producers, Jarrico decided he could not make the changes they wanted during the time remaining on his contract. They decided not to make the picture.[39]

6

The Blacklist Expands, 1951–52

> What if there were a list? A list that said: Our finest actors weren't allowed to act. Our best writers weren't allowed to write. Our funniest comedians weren't allowed to make us laugh. What would it be like if there were such a list? It would be like America in 1953.
>
> —*Paul Jarrico, 1976*

The political situation in Hollywood did not seem too dire to Jarrico in September 1950. He wrote to Abe Polonsky, who was in France, "The only sound is the shuffling of feet, the foolish, embarrassed, legalistic waltz of the nouveaux conquerors. No whooping swooping raids by night, just whittle whittle here, whittle whittle there. No defiant counterattack, just a slow falling back, pretending you don't care." But the slow falling back was on the verge of becoming a massive retreat. In April 1950, *Counterattack* had exposed actor Edward G. Robinson as a member of ASP, and three months later, *Red Channels* linked him to ten subversive organizations and periodicals. Robinson tried various methods to clear himself, including two voluntary appearances before the House Committee on Un-American Activities, on October 27 and December 21.[1] Dore Schary, no longer willing to be accused of employing Communists, went to the FBI's Los Angeles office on December 12. He was, reported the SACLA, "very concerned that MGM not hire any Communists or Communist Sympathizers, especially Betsy Blair. He inquired if there was any assistance the Bureau could give him in matters of this nature."[2] Communists and former Communists, such as Richard Collins, writer Leo Townsend, and actor Sterling Hayden, began contemplating visits to the FBI. Edward Dmytryk, from the federal prison at Mill Point, West Virginia, issued an affidavit avowing: "I am not now, nor was I at the time of the hearing, a member of the Communist Party"; "I am not a Communist sympathizer"; and "I recognize the United States of America as the only country to which I owe allegiance and loyalty." An angry Jarrico wrote, "Out of the anus of Dmytryk has finally been forced the tight shit we all knew was in him."[3]

But Dmytryk was not finished. On February 2, 1951, three months after his release from prison, he met with a committee of the Motion Picture Industry Council (MPIC) and asked the members for advice on how to rehabilitate himself.[4] They told him he had to undergo an interview with the FBI, meet with House Committee on Un-American Activities investigators, volunteer to reappear before the committee, and publish his recantation in a magazine. On February 8, Dmytryk went to the FBI office in Los Angeles, where he told the agents he had joined the CPA but had informally withdrawn at the time of the Maltz controversy. He named more than twenty party members, including Jarrico.[5]

Jarrico did not know that Dmytryk had named him but nevertheless believed that he was "more or less blacklisted as far as major studio assignments go." But he was convinced that he had enough interesting and promising independent projects to sustain him temporarily. He was negotiating with Columbia to purchase screen rights for *The Big Eye*, had been given an option on the *Rip Van Winkle* script by Monogram, and continued to send the *Temptation* script to prospective backers. He wrote to a friend, "My spirits are high, empathetically taut with the birth pangs of that better world."[6]

And then, amazingly, Jarrico was hired (at $2,000 a week) by RKO to rewrite a script titled *The Miami Story*, which had been bouncing around the studio for three years. The story involved a cynical detective, a sexy woman, and a crook. Jarrico noted, "Some of the sex and violence good, but needs much tighter story line, with more clever twists. Main fault is the girl, whose motivations are weak." On January 17, he began a new treatment of what was now called *The Las Vegas Story*. His new approach was approved, and he completed his version of the script in three weeks. During this time, he had no contact with Howard Hughes.[7]

As he was completing his work at RKO, the House Committee on Un-American Activities voted to subpoena Jarrico and three other writers (Waldo Salt, Richard Collins, and Robert Lees) and four actors (Howard Da Silva, Sterling Hayden, Larry Parks, and Gale Sondergaard). Though the committee did not make a public statement about the subpoenas, Da Silva, Sondergaard, and Salt took out an advertisement in *Variety*, announcing their opposition to the committee and their intent to refuse to cooperate with its investigation. But, the SACLA reported, many Communists in Hollywood were "very much worried" that Parks might be inclined to cooperate.[8]

On March 7, the House Committee on Un-American Activities announced the resumption of its investigation of Communist infiltration of the motion picture industry. V. J. Jerome, the first witness, would be followed two weeks later by forty or fifty other Hollywood witnesses. Determined to avoid the bad press of October 1947, the committee had revised its procedures. A committee investigator, usually William Wheeler, met with prospective witnesses before they appeared to determine the nature of their testimony. Those who wished to cooperate and their lawyers then met with committee counsels to rehearse their statements and the lists of the names they would provide. Those who chose not to cooperate understood that they had to invoke the Fifth Amendment if they wished to avoid contempt citations.[9] As a result, during this second round of hearings, there were few surprises and no shouting matches.

Though the U.S. Supreme Court had validated a witness's "privilege to remain silent," the MPIC responded to Gale Sondergaard's publicly stated intent to use the Fifth Amendment with a statement deploring "those who stand on constitutional privileges to hide [the whole] truth, or those who refuse to recognize the authority of the Congress [to ask about the whole truth]." A few days later, Joyce O'Hara, acting president of the Motion Picture Association of America, announced that those witnesses who did not firmly deny any association with Communist or Communist-front organizations would find it difficult to get movie jobs in the future.[10]

Parks, Da Silva, and Sondergaard were scheduled for the opening hearing on March 21. But subpoena servers could not find eleven people, including Jarrico. The Hollywood Communist branch members had decided to test the process by designating some to "disappear." A few others who could not be found had left town to finish projects, to prolong their careers and lives for as long as they could.[11]

Jarrico chose to surface on March 22, after Larry Parks, the first witness, agonized about giving names to the committee in open session but then "provided" twelve names to it in executive session.[12] Jarrico issued a press statement: "I see by the papers there's a subpoena out for me. This is the first I've heard of it, and I assure you I'm available to receive it. If I have to choose between crawling through the mud with Larry Parks or going to jail like my courageous friends the Hollywood Ten, I assure you I'll choose the latter."[13] When he arrived at RKO the following day to make revisions on the *Las Vegas Story* script, he was turned away at the gate. He was not even allowed to go to his office to pick up his personal papers and his whiskey bottle.[14]

Later that year, Jarrico collected the statements of informers for a pamphlet criticizing the committee and those who cooperated with it. He likened the informers, many of whom he had known, to Thomas Paine's "sunshine patriots." He described them as "a thin line of nervous collaborators anxiously await[ing] to bask in the Committee's forgiving sun and to swear under oath that they had been infantile, fools, dupes or just plain dopes," who, upon receiving subpoenas commanding their appearance or being named as Communists "by a previous obedient collaborator," underwent an instant conversion and "now stood ready to renounce all ideas they previously had, denounce all those who ever had similar ideas and to embrace without question the ideology of the Committee's members."[15]

Those who had decided they would not cooperate with the committee met with two of the Hollywood Ten's attorneys, Robert Kenny and Ben Margolis, to plan their strategy. They decided that they needed a fund of at least $15,000 to cover legal, transportation, communication, and publicity costs. Jarrico was assigned the task of writing a fund-raising letter. His humor did not desert him. After trying out two humble openings, he wrote, on his third attempt, "This is a stick-up." The final draft read,

> I never did thank you properly for helping before [with the Ten], and here I am again. This time, of course, I'm involved personally,

> which doesn't disturb me too much—in fact, I'm rather proud of it—but it makes me a little more reluctant to impose on you. . . .
>
> I think you can assume we'll all take the Fifth Amendment position, not only because we're fairly confident it'll keep us out of jail but because, at the moment, it seems to be the only way to fight those bastards.
>
> What they're trying to accomplish with this investigation you know: the militarization of films. The MPA is riding high, threatening to widen the blacklist until it includes practically everyone who ever held a liberal thought. . . .
>
> P.P.S. The stoolpigeon trainers may win a round or two, but they're not going to win the overall fight, believe me.[16]

Jarrico then began to draft the statement he hoped to read at the opening of his testimony. After several false starts, he decided to begin with the story of his father's legacy:

> He taught me to love this country, really love it, not with the demonstrative hypocrisy of a professional patriot but with a profound concern for its people and its future. . . . Your willingness to see the people of the world annihilated, your willingness to see the people of America annihilated, that becomes the sole test of your patriotism. Well, it is not my test, and it is not my patriotism. I am proud of my beliefs. I am proud of my affiliations. I'll be damned, though, if I'll disclose them to my enemies, to be used against my friends.[17]

Jarrico arrived in Washington on April 10, two days before Richard Collins testified. Jarrico and Collins had met for lunch three times in February and twice in March. Collins told the committee that, at one of those meetings, Jarrico asked him "if I would give my personal assurance that I would not give any names. . . . I didn't give that assurance. We then had a long political discussion. Paul Jarrico feels the justice of his position, and he went over the situation, that he believes the Soviet Union is devoted to the interests of all people and is peace-loving as well." Jarrico again urged Collins, based on their "fourteen years of friendship," to assure him that he would not give names. Collins said he would "'if you will give me your personal assurance that in the event of a war between the United States and the Soviet Union you will do nothing to help the Soviet Union.' Paul said, 'You know my answer to that.' He didn't explain the answer." Collins asked again, and when Jarrico did not give him the assurance he requested, "I would not give him mine, and since we would not lie to each other, we had no further conversation."[18]

Sylvia Jarrico remembered, however, that Collins had unequivocally told them that he was cooperating because he felt completely alienated from the Communist Party's lack of democracy and respect for the artist. Jarrico had replied that those criticisms did not matter now, that Collins had to unite with his former comrades to defeat the House Committee on Un-American Activities. Then he and Collins would deal with the other issues. He urged Collins not to "break down now." When Collins questioned Jarrico about taking up arms, Jarrico was startled and laughed. He did not consider the question worth answering, and told Collins, "If you are going to write lines like that, you are finished as a screenwriter." Jarrico and Collins never spoke again.[19]

Collins named twenty-three people. Jarrico always believed that Collins's testimony was "a very personal betrayal" because he had gone out of his way to name the people who had befriended him, helped him, and loaned him money. In response to a friend's comment that Collins had used his testimony to declare his independence from Jarrico, Jarrico replied, "Yes, he wanted to stand on his own two knees."[20]

Jarrico testified on April 13. He took the stand at 11:30 a.m., just after Waldo Salt had invoked the Fifth Amendment when asked if he belonged to the Communist Party. In his agenda book, Jarrico had outlined several types of questions he might be asked. He noted that he would refuse to respond, "on the ground that it might incriminate me," to any questions referring to the Communist Party, "all reputedly red organizations," and any individual he might have known. If asked an "opinion" question—for example, "Would you bear arms?"—he would reply that it was a prowar question and that he would not cooperate with the committee by answering it.[21]

During his testimony, Jarrico's two attorneys, Robert Kenny and Ben Margolis, sat on either side of him. He recalled, "I was getting a little heated in my answers, and Kenny was tugging at my left sleeve and whispering into my left ear, 'Take it easy, take it easy.'

Margolis was whispering into my right ear, 'Give it to 'em! Give it to 'em!'" Jarrico responded fully to counsel Frank Tavenner's questions about his screenwriting career. But when he was asked who actually employed him at RKO, Jarrico fired his first political shot: "It seems to me an attempt to create the basis for a blacklist in Hollywood, on the basis of guilt by employment, guilt by the mere fact that you employ a man. Mr. [Robert] Sparks, a conservative gentleman, I am sure, employed me because he thought I was the best man to do that particular job, and not because of my politics." When asked if he had heard Collins's testimony the day before, Jarrico replied, "I heard him attempting to purge himself before this committee and perjuring himself before this committee." But he refused to explain how Collins had perjured himself or to describe his meeting with Collins in late March. Jarrico then asked if he could read his statement and was told that he could file it for the record. When asked whether he was or had been a member of the Communist Party, Jarrico invoked the Fifth Amendment.[22]

When Tavenner concluded his questions, Clyde Doyle (D-CA) initiated an unusual interchange: he provided Jarrico a platform to speak his mind. Doyle asked whether Jarrico was interested in helping the committee uncover subversive persons. Jarrico replied that he would be happy to do so, "but one man's subversion is another man's patriotism. I consider the activities of this committee subversive of the American Constitution." Doyle asked him how the committee was undermining the constitutional government of the United States. "Sir," Jarrico replied, "I believe this country was founded on the doctrine of freedom, the right of a man to advocate anything he wishes—advocate it, agitate for it, organize for it, attempt to win a majority for it." But, he continued, when the committee voted to cite the Hollywood Ten for contempt, it "subverted the meaning of the American Constitution" and denied the Ten and subsequent witnesses of their right to express themselves freely. When he was asked if the courts that sentenced the Ten to prison and upheld the sentences had also been subversive, Jarrico dodged a direct answer but finally said that they "contributed toward the general destruction of liberty in this country."[23]

Doyle then asked whether Jarrico thought an American citizen had the right to advocate the forceful overthrow of constitutional government in the United States. Jarrico responded, "I believe he may advocate it. I believe that it is unlikely he will get a great response to such a thing. I want to make it clear that I am personally opposed to the overthrow of this Government by force and violence and to the use of force and violence." When asked if he knew of any organization in the United States that advocated the overthrow of the government, Jarrico replied, again after some fencing with Doyle, "If I knew of such an organization, sir, I should help you to expose it."[24]

Finally, Doyle asked Jarrico why he believed the committee was interested in blacklisting people. Jarrico responded,

> You are not interested in that end, but you had better revise your methods, because your methods have had that end. I know of many people who are blacklisted in Hollywood as a result of the hearing in 1947, and I know that today the basis is being laid for an increase of that blacklist, so that anyone who has advocated anything progressive is going to be a suspect. . . .
>
> I feel that if you were sincere in your declarations against blacklisting that you should make it plain that people who claim their constitutional privileges should not be discriminated against in Hollywood, because Hollywood has the impression that you intend everyone who is called before this committee to be driven from the industry.

Congress, Jarrico concluded, has no right to legislate about or "inquire into a man's opinions, his attitudes, his beliefs of any kind."[25]

The day after his testimony, Jarrico and Salt took the train to New York. They talked about all the wonderful projects they intended to undertake once they were blacklisted. At one point, Salt turned to Jarrico and joked, "My God, what if we aren't blacklisted?" In New York, Jarrico and actors Will Geer, Fred Graff, and Victor Killian, all of whom had testified and invoked the Fifth Amendment, spoke about censorship and blacklisting at a midnight meeting sponsored by the New York ASP. Jarrico talked about his meeting with two old friends just out of prison (Lawson and Trumbo) and compared his joy at seeing their growth to his despair at seeing another old friend (Collins) shrink "to the size of a louse."[26]

Shortly after his return to Los Angeles, Jarrico went to Sacramento to speak about political events in Hollywood to the California Legislative Conference. He related to the audience of five thousand the pledge Dalton Trumbo had made shortly after his release from prison: "The end of our careers, hell! This is the beginning of our careers. We're going to write the goddamnedest books and plays this country has ever seen. We're going to have a real people's culture at last!" When Jarrico told the delegates about his plans for independent production, they cheered. And when he told them that his production company would look to them for financial backing, Jarrico wrote George Willner, "they tore the joint apart."[27]

Jarrico also spoke at a Peace Festival in Oakland and, on his return to Los Angeles, appeared on an ASP program with Dalton Trumbo at the Embassy Auditorium. Trumbo spoke about his prison experiences and the emerging people's culture in America. The title of Jarrico's speech was "The Inevitability of Peace," which the SACLA termed "more significant than the usual speech made by local Communists." In it, Jarrico delivered a sharp attack on U.S. foreign policy and a strong defense of the Soviet Union. He told his listeners that they must work to prevent a third world war. He accused the U.S government of pursuing an unreal foreign policy, one based on the premise that communism was analogous to fascism. "Communism," he proclaimed, "is the diametrical opposite of fascism. . . . To speak of Soviet imperialism is a contradiction in terms. Socialism, as an economic system, has no internal need to expand. . . . If the countries of Eastern Europe have gone socialist it was not because socialism was forced on them at the point of a Red Army bayonet, but because socialism makes sense to them, and was long overdue." In fact, he emphasized, the United States was now the aggressor nation in the world; it was the one fighting against every colonial country's liberation effort. Russia, he concluded, was "afraid of the atom bomb! She's also afraid of having to use the atom bomb! She's afraid of war! She hates war! And she has pursued a policy of peace in the years since World War II with the same monomania as she exhibited before World War II."[28]

Shortly after Jarrico's return to Los Angeles, his placement on the blacklist became apparent. The Jaffe Agency informed him there were no further possibilities of his employment in the motion picture industry, and, at its request, Jarrico released it from the obligation of representing him.[29] Despite that, Sylvia remembered that they "felt pretty jaunty about Jarrico's blacklisting. We began to think in terms of living a life independent of Hollywood." Jarrico wrote George Willner, who had also been blacklisted and had left Hollywood for Miami, to invite him to join an independent production company, with *Rip Van Winkle* as the first project. It would use Da Silva, Sondergaard, and other blacklisted actors, working for $100 a week plus stock in the company. But Willner replied that he had no desire to return to Hollywood.[30] Jarrico had more fruitful discussions with Herbert Biberman and Simon Lazarus, a theater owner who had been thinking of forming a corporation that would use the talents of blacklisted people.

In the meantime, Jarrico began to collect unemployment benefits. He retained Edward Mosk as his personal representative, agent, advisor, and attorney. He resumed work on his atomic scientist play, but, as he later wrote a friend, "I kept rewriting it because I was trying to keep ahead of history, which was always passing me by."[31] And he negotiated the sale of the script for *The Man Who Watched Trains Go By* to an English producer, Josef Shaftel.

He then found himself involved in his first significant battle against the blacklist. Unbeknownst to Jarrico, RKO had brought in another writer, Harry Essex, to rewrite *The Las Vegas Story*. Essex turned in his final draft on April 4, 1951. The studio then hired Earl Felton to do another rewrite, which he finished on May 9.[32] When Jarrico learned, in July, that RKO had given sole screenplay credit to Earl Felton, he immediately requested that the SWG arbitrate. According to the analysis he submitted in support of his claim, the dialogue had been almost completely rewritten by Essex and Felton, but the "characters and their relationships, the story line and its basic construction, and indeed the content of a large majority of the scenes, all originated in my screenplay, or in the notes I prepared for the revision of my screenplay." He asked for sole screenplay credit and a cocredit on the original story, despite that he was "far from happy with the screenplay as it stands. Under ordinary circumstances I should be inclined to withdraw from credit entirely, on the ground that the final version perverts and bastardizes my work. The circumstances, however, are far from ordinary. The reason RKO has made this clumsy effort to 'write me off' is, I suppose, common knowledge." The guild arbitration committee decided that the credit should read, "Screenplay by Paul Jarrico, Harry Essex, and Earl Felton. Based on an original story by Jay Dratler." Howard Hughes refused to accept that decision. He claimed he had the right to invoke the morals clause in Jarrico's contract to deny him credit. Hughes also vowed to establish a system at RKO to "screen everyone in a creative position or executive capacity. . . . It is my determination to make RKO one studio where the work of Communist sympathizers will be impossible."[33]

On March 17, 1952, RKO filed a suit asking for a declaratory judgment against the right of the SWG to determine screen credits for writers. Eleven days later, Jarrico countersued, asking $350,000 in damages, basing his claim on the argument that the morals clause had no application to statements made to a committee of Congress. When Hughes, in a press statement, challenged Jarrico to answer the question "Are you now, or have you ever been, a member of the Communist Party?" Jarrico responded,

> Having been caught in a flagrant violation of his contract with the Screen Writers Guild, having been caught in a brazen plagiarism of my work on "The Las Vegas Story," having been caught, in effect, with his hand in my pocket, his only defense is that my understanding of the Constitution differs from his.
>
> Mr. Hughes had better get it straight. The issue before the court is not whether I have a right to my political opinions, but whether he has a right to set himself above the law. He will find, despite his millions, that the law applies to him as well as to every other American.[34]

The guild, faced with a challenge to one of its most important functions, charged Hughes with a violation of the minimum basic agreement, the collective bargaining agreement between the SWG and the studios. But Hughes replied that this was not a labor issue and dared the SWG to strike over it. Gossip columnist Hedda Hopper, *Hollywood Reporter* publisher Billy Wilkerson, Congressmen John Wood and Donald Jackson (R-CA) (both members of the House Committee on Un-American Activities), various

American Legion posts, the Los Angeles City Council, and the Los Angeles County Board of Supervisors praised Hughes's position. When RKO refused to appoint an arbitrator, as the minimum basic agreement required in such a dispute, the guild's attorneys petitioned the court to appoint one. But a superior court judge ruled that RKO had not violated the minimum basic agreement; that the controversy involved only the writer and the producer, not the guild. An appeals court upheld that decision.[35]

The RKO-Jarrico trial began on November 17. Superior court judge Orlando H. Rhodes ruled that Jarrico's case was merely one of breach of contract and that he had not suffered a legal wrong. Thus, even if Jarrico won, he would be entitled only to actual damages, not exemplary (punitive) damages. The judge also ruled that the minimum basic agreement did not supersede the personal contract of a writer with a studio, especially where the morals clause was concerned. On November 25, the judge ruled for RKO. In his formal opinion, the judge wrote that since the American public believed that a Fifth Amendment witness was (or had been) a Communist sympathizer, Paul Jarrico became, when he used that amendment, an "object of public disgrace, obloquy, ill will and ridicule," and thereby violated his contract with RKO. The district court of appeals upheld those findings. Subsequent appeals to the California Supreme Court and the U.S. Supreme Court were refused.[36]

This court action represented one of the several ways that Jarrico, "as a matter of political principle," never stopped fighting the blacklist,[37] even as the number of those standing beside him steadily dwindled, whether because of pessimism, exhaustion, lack of finances, the pressures of life, or death. But in 1951, the force of opposition among Hollywood Communists was strong. They directed their first counterattack against the House Committee on Un-American Activities when its hearings regarding the motion picture industry were transferred to Los Angeles in September 1951. The ASP organized a picket line in front of the federal building. A list of thirty-six slogans was prepared for those who wished to carry signs, including "Welcome Witch Hunters," "Is Peace Un-American?" and "First They Jailed the Hollywood Ten, Then They Jailed the Constitution." A "Help Us Fight Back—for Peace" meeting was held at the Embassy Auditorium on September 21. The circular announcing the meeting proclaimed that the House Committee on Un-American Activities subpoenas were part of a congressional program of "repressive legislation" and that the committee was merely the mouthpiece for those who believed "that the surest way to guarantee the biggest profits is to have a war." It urged all civic groups to fight against the committee, the Smith Act, the McCarran Act, and the Taft-Hartley Act. In his notes for a speech to the gathering, Jarrico wrote, "The funniest thing that happened to me in a long time is that the gigantic excavating machine of a desperate administration unearthed me. They unearthed a gigantic conspiracy of which I was a part, a conspiracy to make better films. And starting tomorrow this marvelous excavating machine is going to be digging up dirt here in our own city. . . . We're going to welcome them."[38]

A second means of fighting back involved individual and collective legal action against the blacklist. The six individual cases filed concerned breach of contract. Lester Cole won at the trial level, but the decision was reversed on appeal. For different reasons, Edward Dmytryk dropped his suit against RKO and Dalton Trumbo dropped his against Loew's. Adrian Scott won a $70,000 verdict from the jury, but the judge overturned it. Ring Lardner Jr. won at the trial level, was reversed on appeal, and settled for $10,000. Jarrico lost against RKO. The collective suits were more successful. *Cole et al. v. Loew's, Inc., et al.* settled for $107,500, and *Nedrick Young et al. v. Motion Picture Association of America, et al.* settled for $100,000. *But Maltz et al. v. Loew's, Inc., et al.* was dropped; *Michael Wilson, et al. v. Loew's, Inc., et al.* was dismissed; and *Independent Productions Corp. and I.P.C. Distributors, Inc. v. Loew's, Inc., et al.* lost at the trial level. Many of the blacklisted writers also contributed money to support the antitrust suit filed by Thurman Arnold on behalf of the SWG, but *Screen Writers Guild v. Motion Picture Association of America, et al.* was eventually dropped.[39]

Jarrico was (and would remain) one of the most aggressive litigants. He responded angrily to Waldo Salt's decision not to press the SWG and Warner Brothers for a credit on *The Crimson Pirate* or for the money owed him by its producer, Harold Hecht. Jarrico wrote Salt,

> I take personal exception to your position that credits must represent a real contribution and that you are unwilling to accept a financial settlement in lieu of credit. Credit is an economic question, and for a blacklisted writer the cash is far more important than the credit. . . . Your purist position seems puerile to me, not only because of my own situation, but because a hundred writers are now trying to win the right to *waive* credit for an additional payment. . . . You must, of course, press for your credit; but I hope you sell it for a goodly sum when you win it.[40]

Left-wing culture offered a third means of struggle. Even though one of the aims of the domestic cold war was to destroy the left-wing (antifascist or Popular Front) culture that had arisen during the 1930s, a leftist culture still functioned in the aftermath of the 1951 hearings.[41] But it was no longer as mass oriented, worker centered, or concerned with major social change. It was now mainly defense oriented: defending the civil liberties of the blacklisted, the civil rights of racial minorities, and the procedural rights of aliens. It also focused greater attention on the creative work of racial minorities and on literary and cinematic style and technique. The fear of fascism remained strong, but uncritical support of the Soviet Union lessened.

Blacklisted Hollywood people contributed in several ways to the left-wing culture of the 1950s. Screenwriter Philip Stevenson cofounded *California Quarterly*, thirteen issues of which appeared between autumn 1951 and 1956. ASP sponsored a film review journal, *Hollywood Review*, edited by Sylvia Jarrico and Helen Slote Levitt. It regularly carried stories on black employment in the industry, racial themes in movies, and the blacklist. Each issue featured a major review of trends in movies. The editors perceived a direct relation between the growth of the blacklist and the increasing emphasis of Hollywood movies on prowar and antihuman themes and violence for the sake of violence. Michael Wilson discussed the increasingly vicious tone of war movies and the changing nature of the film hero. Al Levitt addressed some films' slurring of blacks. John Howard Lawson criticized the antiworker theme of *On the Waterfront*. And Sylvia Jarrico wrote a brilliant, path-breaking article on the changing depiction of women in movies. "Something dreadful has happened to women on the screen," she began. Though the majority of female characters continued to devote themselves to romantic and domestic goals, the minority, "the women of will . . . have undergone a spine-tingling change in the course of the cold war years." She traced the evolution of the independent woman from silent films to World War II movies, and she concluded that in the postwar years, women with a strong will began to be depicted as mortally dangerous persons: "Their lives and their sanity were often in the balance; alternatively, they threatened the lives and sanity of their associates. . . . Some of them, very soon, were monstrously evil." She argued that the complacent theme of submission as the natural state of women had been replaced by an aggressive theme, that submission is the necessary state of women. And this transformation had a political aim: "At a time when American women of varying classes represent a vast force, actual and potential, in preserving world peace, Hollywood's sinister heroines constitute a sharpened attack on the opportunities and capacities of real women to take effective action on behalf of themselves, their families, their communities, and their nation." The final issue of *Hollywood Review* (June–July 1956) noted some positive trends: the demise of the anti-Communist film, the decline in bloody war films, and the increase in naturalistic adaptations of television plays.[42]

This focus on culture was reflected in a series of debates among Hollywood Communists. As previously noted, the role a Marxist writer should play in the motion picture industry had been a regular topic of discussion among the members of the Hollywood section of the Communist Party. That discussion became more intense in the period following the expulsion of Earl Browder and the controversy over Albert Maltz's article in *New Masses*. It now centered on the "base-superstructure debate," an issue with a long history in Marxist cultural analysis. Karl Marx and Friedrich Engels discussed it in several of their works, notably in Marx's preface to *A Contribution to the Critique of Political Economy*. They argued that the sum total of an era's means and forces of production constituted the economic foundation (the base) of that era. This base conditioned the era's social, political, and intellectual processes (the superstructure). But they insisted that the base and the superstructure were composed of a series of dynamic relations and processes. Georgi Plekhanov, the father of Russian Marxism, reduced the concept to a five-part formula in his *Fundamental Problems of Marxism* (1908), and Stalin further rigidified it in his *Marxism and Problems of Linguistics* (1950). John Howard Lawson quoted some of the relevant Marxist texts in his *Theory and Technique of Playwriting* (1936) and *Theory and Technique of Playwriting and Screenwriting* (1949). It is clear from both books that Lawson believed that elements of the superstructure (writers) could affect the base (culture). But when he wrote, in the latter book, that Hollywood had produced worthy movies during and after the war (including one of his own, *Sahara*) and insisted that "there can be no permanent interference with the development of the American motion picture as a people's art," he was chastised by V. J. Jerome, the party's chief ideologue. In his 1953 book *Film in the Battle of Ideas*, Lawson recanted. There, he juxtaposed a quotation from Marx (about a dynamically determined base-superstructure relationship) with one from Stalin (about a rigidly determined one). His absence of comment on the difference between them seemed to indicate that he considered them equivalent and equally authoritative.[43]

Michael Wilson was as serious a student of Marxism as Lawson, but Wilson, who had been a philosophy major in college, was a superior dialectician and a subtler thinker. He, along with Jarrico, Abe Polonsky, and most other screenwriters of their generation, scorned Jerome's (and other party hierarchs') cultural analyses. During the 1940s, Wilson had written several papers on Communist writers and motion pictures. He discussed these papers with Jarrico, and Jarrico concurred with the arguments in them. Wilson was moved to write again on this subject in late 1951, following a number of conferences convened by Jerome to critique the cultural line being followed by members of the western party sections. The participants at these conferences had reached the verdict that "right opportunism" (the notion that the movie screen could be freed from the grip of monopoly capital) had not been uprooted in Hollywood. Wilson responded with a fourteen-page analysis in which he argued that, though the "class-conscious" writer working in Hollywood was constrained by the dictates of "finance capital," which completely shaped the products of the motion picture industry, he or she must struggle within the industry to affect movies to the maximum degree possible and to more closely unite all the workers in the industry for a more organized struggle against what Wilson termed "the increased fascization" of movies. This "on-the-job struggle," Wilson warned, "must be conducted without illusions. By and large it will be a fighting attempt to minimize the damage that movies can do, in an effort to make it more difficult for the producers to create effective propaganda for war and fascism." But he did agree with Jerome that the best means to help develop the class demands of this movement was what Wilson termed "independent cultural production," that is, movies made outside the controls of finance capital.[44]

Now, two years later, with the blacklist nearing its peak, the role of a writer blacklisted from an industry producing reactionary films to satisfy the demands of monopoly capital had become the central topic. The publication that year of Lawson's *Film in the Battle of Ideas* widened the theoretical divide separating Lawson from, among others, Wilson, Jarrico, and Dalton Trumbo. Lawson now fully adhered to Jerome's class-struggle analysis: monopoly capital was in full control of the motion picture industry, and Hollywood movies were a closely controlled propaganda tool of the ruling class. He argued that the only examples of film as "a people's art" were to be found in what he called "the people's democracies" of central and eastern Europe. Only those films "speak the language of human feeling," because, Lawson argued, only they were made by production companies fully controlled by the people. Class-conscious writers in the United States could inject human language into U.S. films not via their scripts but by joining a mass campaign against the corrupting influence of Hollywood films, a campaign to free motion pictures from the dictates of Wall Street.[45]

Lawson's book received a favorable notice in the *Hollywood Review*. Trumbo, in a letter to a friend, wrote that he agreed completely "with the theoretical basis of the book, and with its conclusions." Trumbo also thought that Lawson's analysis of cold war movies was "absolutely brilliant." But he believed that Lawson, by undervaluing the work that progressive filmmakers in Hollywood had accomplished before the onset of the cold war, had undercut his call for a mobilization of artists to change movies. If, as Lawson seemed to be saying, there was no evidence that such a progressive mobilization had ever occurred, nor that it was actually possible, nor that gains resulted, Trumbo asked, why would a future mobilization be warranted?[46]

Jarrico and Wilson clashed with Lawson over their plan to print and circulate a two-page flyer listing about one hundred well-known and (in their view) good movies written by blacklisted people. Jarrico and Wilson envisioned this flyer as part of the ASP's effort to inform the movie audience about the quality of work that the blacklist now proscribed. But Lawson argued not only that many of the movies listed by Jarrico and Wilson were not progressive but that idealizing and exaggerating democratic advances in commercial filmmaking by listing undifferentiated, supposedly great pictures represented "a grave misunderstanding of motion picture history." Jarrico and others, however, believed that the fight against the blacklist demanded that movie audiences be informed that blacklisted people had written many popular films, even though some critics might, in retrospect, label them unprogressive.[47]

In 1954, the Hollywood "cultural leadership" decided to resume the discussion. Three discussion documents were prepared. The first criticized *Hollywood Review* as "self-limiting and sectarian in its approach." Though it lauded the editors for their exposure of war, fascism, white chauvinism, and violence in movies, it criticized them for their failure to point out that there were some traces of virtue and progress in current Hollywood movies and to provide a guide for movie audiences to judge what was worthwhile in mass entertainment. Indeed, all of Hollywood's Communist cultural workers had allowed themselves to be blinded by the strength of the political reaction and had thus become infected by a mood of defeatism.[48]

Wilson accused the "cultural leadership" of employing a "mechanical and abstract approach to the theoretical problems." In order to avoid what he called their "formalistic" approach, Wilson attempted to provide a "concrete statement" of the cultural tasks facing Communist writers. Though socialism remained their ultimate goal, Wilson wrote, contemporary conditions mandated that the Communist writer must "struggle for bourgeois-democratic rights and the defense of the bourgeois-democratic heritage." Since these rights are part of the superstructure of capitalist society, a portion of the struggle for them must occur within the superstructure. "We must," Wilson continued, "utilize and fight within the forms provided by the existent superstructure, the only ones available for the defense of the economic and political rights of the masses and the only forms which the majority of Americans understand." In Hollywood, that meant struggling for humanist, democratic, and patriotic content in movies. "The idea that it is impossible to influence commercial films is a left-sectarian error."[49]

In his contribution, Lawson accused those who opposed him of harboring "a dangerously reformist illusion." His opponents, he charged, lacked a correct understanding of base and superstructure. As a result, they struggled for "democratic and humanist content within the web of monopoly capital's 'culture' . . . like a fish in a net." They did not understand, Lawson continued, that film, since it is a major weapon of monopoly capital, must be fought using the weapons of the class struggle.[50] Lawson seemed to be arguing that no struggle was possible within the capitalist superstructure (the realm of ideas and culture). The class-conscious writer should devote his or her efforts to altering the capitalist base (the means of production).

A climactic meeting on the base-superstructure debate was soon convened. It included Dorothy Healey, then chairperson of the Los Angeles County section of the party. Virtually all the participants sharply criticized Lawson's ideas. Lawson replied, "You all feel I am very stubborn. I consider the whole disc.[ussion] a sweeping abandonment of the concept of the class nature of culture." He thought that Wilson's notions were "non-class, non-Marxist, idealist," and that they diverged from the national cultural line, which he, Lawson, had always advocated. Healey asked Lawson how that cultural line could be correct when all the other elements of the national party line had been proven incorrect. Lawson responded, "No basis is laid for your crit.[icism]. I think it isn't fair. . . . [Your] assumption is I have assumed [the] position [of the leader of the Hollywood party] from above and have not tried to earn it. I never dreamed I could occupy [that] position without [the] respect or love of comrades here."[51]

Meanwhile, Jarrico, Wilson, and Herbert Biberman had become deeply engaged in perhaps the most significant effort to maintain and advance left-wing culture in the United States during the domestic cold war—the fight to produce and exhibit their movie *Salt of the Earth*.

7

Salt of the Earth, 1952–54

At last . . . a real story, about real people.

—*Paul Jarrico, 1954*

In late August 1950, just before Adrian Scott went to prison, he, Jarrico, and Charles Katz formed a partnership to produce independent films. They had two projects in mind. One was an adaptation of Haywood Patterson's memoir *Scottsboro Boy* (cowritten by Earl Conrad);[1] the other was an adaptation of a novel about the Iranian crisis of 1946 (*The Diplomat* by James Aldridge). Jarrico had contracted with Mason Roberson to begin adapting *Scottsboro Boy*, but Scott, on his trip to Washington for sentencing, became interested in another project concerning blacks in the South: *Deep Are the Roots*, a play by Arnaud d'Usseau and James Gow.[2] Scott thought that it would be an easier project to make into a film than *Scottsboro Boy* because it had a smaller cast, fewer crowd scenes, and "a hotcha and daring [interracial] romance." But Jarrico replied that they had already invested too much time and money in the Scottsboro project and that they lacked the resources to do both. In a letter to Katz, Scott expressed a further concern, about Roberson's writing skills. Scott wrote, "I suppose the principle involved here—Mason's understanding would far outreach anything that Paul or I could bring but understanding is not enough. We need something good, the first time, for a minimum—without being accused of being sweatshop operators." Jarrico defended Roberson as a fine writer who had not been able to get a screenwriting job because of his color. Further,

Jarrico promised to "do whatever rewriting may prove necessary to bring it up to my own best standard. I'm not trying to stuff anything here—I just don't see how I can devote full time to this screenplay now, without neglecting many other projects."[3]

But in January 1951, Katz and the financial backer he had found began to have second thoughts about the commercial viability of the Scottsboro project. George Willner, who had once tried to sell an adaptation of Howard Fast's novel about southern blacks, *Freedom Road*, told them that he was not optimistic about the commercial prospects of *Scottsboro Boy*. Katz and his backer, who had not yet paid for the film option rights, withdrew from the project. Jarrico then asked Edward Mosk, his personal attorney, to deal with the option contracts, but after paying the option price, Jarrico did not have enough money to continue paying Roberson. Jarrico was furious with Katz but made up with him a few months later because, wrote Jarrico, it "seemed the wrong time for a vendetta with a progressive lawyer."[4]

At the end of June, Jarrico began meeting with Herbert Biberman, who had also been developing an independent project, *A Woman to Remember*, written by Dalton Trumbo. Biberman later said about Jarrico, "In the many years of our association I do not recall Paul ever having said anything was difficult. . . . Paul never saw anything but potentialities."[5] Jarrico had mixed feelings about Biberman. On the one hand, Jarrico, like most of the other blacklistees, thought there was no more conscientious, devoted, and hard-working organizer than Biberman. On the other hand, Biberman could be rigid, abrasive, arrogant, and insensitive.

In July, Jarrico met with Biberman, Katz, and Simon Lazarus to lay the groundwork for the Independent Productions Corporation (IPC).[6] Jarrico later said that IPC's founders "had no doubt but that under the Waldorf Declaration, under the acquiescence of the imprisoned producers, and under the ecstatic leadership of Roy Brewer, every conspiratorial and illegal action possible would be directed against their effort to produce an independent film." But the producers possessed "faith in their ability to find enough independence around the periphery of the industry to serve their modest needs," and they believed that if they could make just one successful film, they would open the way for many future productions and the employment of many blacklisted people in this and other production companies. The founders also hoped that the competition from these independent productions "would expose the stupidity, the near-suicide and the criminality of the blacklisting climate-of-fear atmosphere in which the whole motion picture industry [is now] clothed." Jarrico further noted that much of IPC's funding "came from individuals who had no belief a film could be completed under such circumstances—but thought the effort worth the risk." Others believed in the skills and the know-how of the organizers of the corporation and were willing to invest in a low-budget film in which administrators, writers, directors, and producers were to receive no cash payment but to be rewarded, if at all, only out of profits.[7]

The partners, Jarrico later said, considered their company a political and commercial enterprise. It was political in that it represented their "responsibility" to create a film that would challenge the pall created by the blacklist and Senator Joseph McCarthy (R-WI). "On the other hand," Jarrico continued, "the pictures that we proposed to make were pictures that we felt would appeal to a very broad audience indeed and not be limited to people who shared our political point of view, whatever it may have been, or who shared each other's political point of view. In that sense, the pictures we proposed to make were not political."[8]

When Scott returned to Los Angeles on July 28, the partners had two possible projects but no acceptable scripts. Though they still intended to make *Scottsboro Boy* their first project, Roberson's outlined story seemed thin and lacking in drama.[9] The second project, the script Trumbo had begun to write for Biberman earlier that year, about a black woman (Jean Field) who had lost a custody hearing when her former husband accused her of being a Communist, had been completed and sent to Biberman at the end of March. Jarrico and Biberman thought that it needed major revisions, and Field commented that it lacked a theme and contained "RANK CHAUVINISM."[10] Fortunately, an idea for a third project would soon come to Jarrico's attention.

That summer, the Jarrico family took a two-week vacation at San Cristobal Valley Ranch in northwest New Mexico.[11] The Jarricos had spent three weeks there the previous year and had become friends with Clinton and Virginia Jencks. He had been an international representative of the International Union of Mine, Mill and Smelter Workers (IUMMSW) in Grant County, southwest New Mexico, since 1947. With his wife's assistance, he and the mainly Mexican American miners in Grant had amalgamated five small local labor unions into Local 890. Shortly after the Jarricos returned to Los Angeles from the ranch, IUMMSW was expelled from the CIO, and the members of Local 890 voted to strike against their employer, the Empire Zinc Corporation. In June 1952, when a federal court judge enjoined the miners from picketing, their wives took over the picket lines.[12] The Jenckses' stories of the strike captured the Jarricos' attention, and they drove to Bayard, the home base of Local 890. There, Sylvia and eleven-year-old Bill were granted permission to join the women's picket line, and Jarrico became convinced that the miners' story should be the first project for IPC. Jencks loved the idea. He remembered thinking, "We in the Silver City area needed help in getting our story out of our little corner of the mountains."[13]

Meanwhile, Biberman, Scott, Lazarus, and Katz had decided to do several more films about black people and were discussing a film on Paul Robeson, to be written by John Howard Lawson and Carlton Moss, and a short film on the life of Frederick Douglass, to be written by Moss and Al Levitt. Jarrico, however, insisted on the mine strike: "It is a story that's got everything. It's got labor's rights, women's rights, minority rights, all in a dynamic package." Biberman and Scott agreed, and Jarrico asked Michael Wilson to write the script. Wilson, who was working on a novel, declined at first. Jarrico persisted, and Wilson agreed to go to New Mexico, look around, and speak with the miners. If he was as excited about the material as Jarrico was, he would write the script. Wilson spent a week with the miners, observing the strike and taking notes. Henrietta Williams, who would appear in the movie, said, "When we saw Mr. Wilson up there on the little hill sitting down, we thought he was a scab. And we always kept an eye on him. We always were watching what he was doing, what time he came, what time he went. . . . We thought he was a company man. That he was writing down names to take us women to jail, like they used to do. He asked a lot of questions."[14]

Aaron Shapiro, 1924. (Courtesy of Lia Benedetti Jarrico)

Jennie Shapiro and baby Israel, 1917. (Courtesy of Lia Benedetti Jarrico)

Israel Shapiro, ca. 1923. (Courtesy of Lia Benedetti Jarrico)

Newlyweds Paul and Sylvia, February 1936. (Courtesy of Lia Benedetti Jarrico)

San Francisco Chronicle, November 1, 1935. Richard Criley (left) and Israel Shapiro address University of California students on the expulsion of UCLA's National Student League leaders. (Courtesy of *San Francisco Chronicle*)

Right to left: Paul Jarrico, Sandy Kibbee, Ring Lardner Jr., Pearl Slutzsky, Richard Collins, Louise Rapf, Vicki Schulberg, Jigee Schulberg, ca. 1938. (Courtesy of Lia Benedetti Jarrico)

Paul Jarrico and Michael Wilson, ca. 1943. (Courtesy of Becca Wilson)

On the set of *Song of Russia* (MGM), early 1943. Back row: Richard Collins, director Gregory Ratoff, Paul Jarrico. Front row: Soviet ambassador, his wife, producer Joe Pasternak. (Courtesy of Lia Benedetti Jarrico)

Dore Schary, vice president in charge of production, RKO Radio Pictures, ca. 1947. (Courtesy of Film and Photo Archives, Wisconsin Center for Film and Theater Research, State Historical Society of Wisconsin, Madison)

The first Christmas political statement: Sylvia, Bill, and Paul Jarrico, 1953. (Courtesy of Lia Benedetti Jarrico)

Lia Benedetti and Paul Jarrico on their wedding day, 1993. (Courtesy of Lia Benedetti Jarrico)

Wilson returned, eager to write the script for what would become *Salt of the Earth*. Jarrico later told an interviewer that the essential themes were already in place (the strike, the Mexican American strikers, and "the most impressive element of this whole episode, that the relations between the men and women had changed in the course of this social battle"), but Wilson created the frame: the personal story of Esperanza and Ramon. Jarrico and Wilson consulted regularly, and Jarrico, Biberman, Scott, and the Bayard people suggested changes. Trumbo also read it and made some suggestions.[15]

In an issue of *California Quarterly* devoted to *Salt of the Earth*, Biberman and Jarrico wrote, "We were agreed that our films must be based in actuality. Therefore, we [were] entering an arena of art to which we as craftsmen brought little experience and in which we found little precedence to guide us. It was clear that the best guarantee of artful realism lay not in fictions invented by us but in stories drawn from the living experience of people long ignored by Hollywood—the working men and women of America." They also acknowledged their lack of experience with Mexican Americans. Jarrico was concerned that they would fail to approach "the people there with sufficient humility, with sufficient awareness of their sensitivity to the most subtle forms of chauvinism. . . . We have all absorbed some of the poisons of this poisonous society. And though we cannot wait until we are all purified before we begin to create a clean culture, we can demand of ourselves a sharp consciousness of our own corruption. And a burning struggle against it."[16]

Jarrico, Biberman, and Wilson shared creative control of the project. Jarrico emphasized in all his later comments on the making of *Salt of the Earth* that the three of them were a solid collective, bound together by friendship and by a common cause. They also formed a collective with the miners, treating the movie as a joint project. Jencks recalled, "We all went through a process of change: At first we held them [Paul, Herbert, and Mike] in awe and they had romantic notions about workers. Both groups had to drop those notions and discover what each had in common with the other." Indeed, they had all been kicked out—the producers out of Hollywood and the IUMMSW out of the CIO—for being left wing. So, as Jarrico regularly told interviewers, IPC and IUMMSW, which had been punished for a crime they did not commit, decided "to commit a crime to fit the punishment." The two groups also shared a hope that they could "demonstrate that a film that expressed the point of view of labor and minority groups could be commercially successful, and to stimulate other unions and minority groups into using the medium of the film to express their aspirations."[17]

Wilson was a dedicated researcher and writer. Jencks recalled that he "sat on the picket line, in our union meetings and in our homes—a wonderful human sponge, soaking up everything and saying very little." When Wilson had finished his first draft, he read it to the assembled miners and their families at the union hall. There were criticisms, Jencks remembered, but Wilson "did not argue or get defensive. He listened, thought, reflected and then went back home to rewrite it."[18]

Though Scott's experience better qualified him to be the producer, he was occupied with personal problems and did not think he could devote the necessary time to the project. So Jarrico was chosen to produce the movie. He hired the technicians and the craftsmen, arranged for the supply of film and the equipment for filming and processing, and supervised the preparation of and adherence to the budget and the schedule. Jarrico later said, "I honestly don't believe that there was any man in the world better qualified to produce this picture than myself." Jencks remembered, "When things looked impossible, he would always find a way to solve them, without a lot of noise."[19]

Jarrico spent much of his time seeking funding for the new company. He traveled to New York, Paris, and London, meeting with dozens of people in each city. Between September 1951 and March 1953, the company accumulated more than $100,000 in loans and contributions. The fund-raising letter stated,

> We are in a most unique and favorable position to produce motion pictures profitably. We have at our disposal a large group of mostly successful motion picture artists, proven in the motion picture industry, who are prepared to work for our company under hitherto unheard of arrangements. For their services, for which motion picture companies have paid hundreds of thousands of dollars we will pay next to nothing or nothing. This will mean that monies expended in production by our company will be confined to the

> barest material essentials—the most expensive elements, namely the creative talent in the most creative department will cost us next to nothing or nothing.

The producers pledged to produce movies for $100,000, to begin production only when all the money was available, and to limit preparatory costs to 5 percent of the proposed budget. In a personal appeal to a friend, Jarrico wrote, "We're not kidding ourselves about the amount of opposition we're liable to run into. We'll be picketed—and worse. Some of the controversy will be good for us, in exploitation value, but it's going to be a fight all the way."[20]

Shortly after Jarrico returned from Europe, he again flew to New York, where he and Scott and Biberman spent five weeks raising money. Jarrico's agenda books are filled with the names of the people with whom he spoke, dined, and drank. On the flight home, he reflectively wrote of himself as "an American Jewish boy, who had grown up concerned with popularity (desire for approval) and sex (desire for experience), but clear on the need for basic social change (socialism). Matured, gained approval of a sort and experience of a sort, and is gradually, painfully, becoming an effective instrument of social changes." Sylvia Jarrico remembered that Jarrico was optimistic that, one way or another, the movie would be made. Biberman wrote later, "In one sense, this picture was more Paul's than anyone's. Not alone that he had found this reality and suggested it as a picture, but that in every moment of everyone else's despair his stubborn optimism, humor and scorn for difficulties became a parachute that went up instead of down. . . . There was no job too ungrateful for him."[21]

Back in Los Angeles, with Wilson's writing going more slowly than they had hoped, the partners contemplated trying to use Trumbo's script for their first project, and they began to think more about what they could do to advance their ideals regarding black people. They reorganized IPC "to include Negro integration on every level." Jarrico wrote to Waldo Salt and Lester Cole to encourage them and others in New York to think about a film combining themes of black liberation and labor. He advised them to invite a group of other blacklisted Hollywood people to meet with a group of black artists and writers because, he noted, "we have found this the most fructifying possible way of working." But the New Yorkers declined to become involved in what they termed speculative work.[22]

In May, IPC ran up against what would be its most formidable obstacle: Roy Brewer, who was in control of the IATSE locals in Hollywood. The producers were determined to use a union crew to shoot *Salt of the Earth*, and Lazarus approached Brewer for permission to use IATSE members. Brewer responded, "I will see you in hell first." An informant told the SACLA that it would be impossible for IPC to hire any union members in Hollywood. So Jarrico went to New York, Chicago, and Denver. He also, very quietly, retried Los Angeles. In line with IPC policy, he made an effort to recruit black workers.[23]

But the company still did not have a completed script or a director. Jarrico wanted John Berry (in Paris), Michael Gordon (in New York), or Jules Dassin (in New York). Jarrico wrote them that they would have to accept the same financial terms as the other partners (no salary draw from the invested funds), and that they must "feel comfortable working in the kind of strict and collective responsibility we have subjected ourselves to create and which we believe we have created." As it turned out, Berry had found a film deal in Paris, and Gordon had made a commitment to direct a play in New York. Dassin was available but had strong reservations. He wrote that the financial situation Jarrico described was "frightening," and he wondered how long blacklisted movie people would continue to victimize themselves monetarily. He appreciated the benefits of collaboration, but he was concerned about making such a difficult film by committee, with so little money, in so short a time. But mostly he was concerned about the script. "This is a wonderful story," Dassin wrote. "But your script is not good enough. There should be no compulsion strong enough to make you shoot before the script is perfect." The characters were not deep enough; the theme was too ideological; the story lacked humanity. "You are in awe of your material and your characters, and it has kept you from getting really close to them. I just don't believe they talk that way—very often they are assigned different sides of an argument so that you can make a social point."[24]

John Howard Lawson also responded negatively to the script. There is no written record of the comments he made when he met with the Jarricos, Wilson, and Dorothy Healey, but Lawson later wrote that the script lacked "a real development of the relationship between the [Anglo] organizer, Barnes, and [the Mexican American] Ramon." It displayed "a certain tendency toward verbalizing the basic issues . . . rather than fully and richly developing these issues in action and human conflict." But the weakest elements, Lawson argued, were a fight near the end, between Esperanza and Ramon, and Ramon's decision to leave the strike and go hunting: "Both these scenes have elements of white chauvinism, suggesting that the Mexican people are more 'likely' to treat women with physical brutality, and that their stamina is not adequate when the going gets tough."[25] Sylvia Jarrico remembered that Jarrico and Wilson were taken aback by Lawson's criticisms but tried to remain respectful in their responses. Sylvia alone responded angrily. After Lawson departed, they decided to disregard what he had said.[26]

After several days of meetings with Dassin in Los Angeles, the partners decided they could not wait any longer to choose a director, and they appointed Biberman. But they still had not recruited a full union crew, and so they again postponed the start of production, until early 1953. Jarrico wanted to use that time to go to Europe to explore foreign markets for IPC, but the Department of State rejected his passport renewal application based on Title 22 of the Code of Federal Regulations, which prohibited the issuing of passports to Communist Party members and other supporters of the Communist movement. An employee of the State Department wrote, "In your case it is alleged that you were a member of the Young Communist League, the Communist Political Association and the Communist Party and that you have been active in Communist Party affairs in Los Angeles." Although he had the right to appeal, Jarrico noted that it was illusory in his case, because he would most likely have been required to make a statement regarding his Communist Party membership.[27]

As it happened, the Communist Party provided no assistance to IPC. Jarrico, Biberman, and Wilson had become convinced that although "we were loyal party people, we were making this film without the party or despite the party, or the party was irrelevant to the making of the film."[28] Though the IUMMSW had agreed to sponsor the movie, it provided little assistance and no funds. Local 890, however, would provide actors, a production committee (to recruit and gather the extras), set constructors, and night watchmen.

On December 16, Jarrico, Biberman, and Sonja Dahl Biberman (the associate producer and Herbert's sister-in-law) left for New Mexico to prepare for the start of production, now scheduled for late January. Jarrico returned to Los Angeles at the end of the month to rent equipment, buy film, and arrange for laboratory processing. On December 29, he learned that the film crew he had hired was reneging on the agreement because its union was negotiating an amalgamation with IATSE. Jarrico was forced to hire inexperienced personnel in many categories. "Some fifteen cameramen refuse employment, in many cases after agreements are reached. In every case but one, the obstacle is fear of reprisal by the IATSE and the movie industry. The one exception is Rosalio Solana, who agrees to bring a complete crew from Mexico City, but is denied a U.S. visa."[29]

Jarrico returned to Bayard on January 15 to oversee budget, payroll, and bookkeeping (with Sonja Dahl Biberman), future set operations, schedules, and laboratory work. The Hollywood people and the miners established a production board, composed of four members of IPC, four members of Local 890, and four members of the women's auxiliary, to handle all matters, from childcare arrangements to questions of content. Jencks recalled, "They treated us with respect, as though we were doing something worthwhile. We were listened to with respect—this was our story." Sonja Dahl Biberman remembered that "Paul so obviously loved them [the local people] that he was immediately accepted."[30]

Shooting commenced on January 20. On February 9, the movie sustained the first of many attacks from the press. *Hollywood Reporter* gossip columnist Mike Connolly told his Rambling Reporter readers, "Herbert and Edward Biberman, Gale Sondergaard, Sonja Dahl, Paul Jarrico, David Wolf (also known as Herbert Waldman), Paul Perlin and other discredited H'wood Reds are shooting a feature-length anti-American racial issue propaganda movie at Silver City, N.M. [ten miles north of Bayard]. SAG Prexy Walter Pidgeon got the tip in a letter from a school teacher fan in N.M. Pidge immediately alerted the FBI, State Department, House Un-American Activities Committee and CIA. Pidge is determined that H'wood shall not be smeared by Reds long since kicked out of the picture biz." The following day, Connolly wrote, with little regard for the facts, that "the anti-American movie the commies are making in New Mexico was ordered by John Howard Lawson, who gets his orders from the Kremlin." That same day, syndicated anti-Communist columnist Victor Riesel, with a similar lack of scrupulousness, noted that the production site was not far from the Los Alamos atomic testing grounds and that "Tovarisch Paul" (Jarrico) had brought two carloads of black people into the mining town. The Hollywood AFL Film Council urged the U.S. government to launch an immediate investigation of the movie, because its purpose "is the recruitment of Party members of Latin American descent here and in South America by use of a discrimination theme." Roy Brewer announced, "No motion picture made by Communists can be good for America. Hollywood has gotten rid of these people and we want the government agencies to investigate carefully."[31]

As a result of these and other attacks (including one by the MPIC), the film and sound laboratories that had begun developing and processing the negatives and tapes refused to continue. On February 24, Congressman Donald Jackson, a member of the House Committee on Un-American Activities, spoke to the House of Representatives about a movie, the title of which he did not know, "now being made under Communist auspices in Silver City, New Mex." He then named all those involved who were, he claimed, Communists, and he incorrectly stated that the "communist-dominated" IUMMSW was financing the production. Jackson continued, "This picture is deliberately designed to inflame racial hatreds and to depict the United States of America as the enemy of all colored peoples. . . . In effect this picture is a new weapon for Russia." He promised that he would do everything in his power "to prevent the showing of this Communist-made film in the theaters of America."[32]

Two days later, Immigration and Naturalization Service officers arrested the lead actress, Rosaura Revueltas, and took her to El Paso for a deportation hearing. Jarrico followed, to post bond, and was joined there by Ben Margolis. While they were trying to get her released and prevent her deportation, in Bayard a mob attacked the crew, and vigilantes attempted to intimidate them.[33] On March 7, production was completed, Revueltas accepted voluntary deportation, and Jarrico flew to New York with the undeveloped negative and untransferred sound tapes. The company was now $20,500 over budget, and Jarrico had to spend a good part of each day raising more money. His personal bank balance was $625.

On March 19, Congressman Jackson introduced letters from Roy Brewer and Howard Hughes. Brewer, on behalf of the Hollywood AFL Film Council, wrote to assure Jackson that everything the council "can do to prevent the showing of the Mexican picture, Salt of the Earth, will be done. . . . The film council will solicit its fellow members in the theaters to assist in the prevention of showing of this picture in any American theaters." Hughes urged every movie person in the industry with film processing skills to refuse to work on the movie, and he urged the U.S. government to prevent its export.[34]

The House Committee on Un-American Activities augmented the offensive by subpoenaing Simon Lazarus and Sol Kaplan, the movie's composer. Lazarus appeared before the committee on March 26–28. He refused to provide any names of IPC personnel because "this Committee is only interested in naming names to blacklist these people." He would talk only about himself, and he claimed ignorance or loss of memory about many matters. Lazarus was clearly frustrated with the committee's questions regarding whether IPC had received funding from the Communist Party and from Russia: "This is absolutely ridiculous. I am not an agent of any government. . . . I have not received any moneys from anybody, from any parties of any sort. I have received money from people." When he tried to tell the committee what *Salt of the Earth* was about, the committee chairman refused to allow him to do so.[35]

One week later, Kaplan, who had not been named by any previous witness in an open session, proved to be one of the committee's most confrontational witnesses. He clashed angrily with Congressman Jackson about the Soviet composer Dmitri Shostakovich and called the congressman a barbarian. He made long statements about the committee's abuse of his rights and compared the committee's members to Nazis. "I am here," he said, "because my father is a workingman, a presser in the garment industry, a Jew. . . . All his life my father . . . was faced with intimidation, blacklist and discrimination, as I am today in this committee room." He demanded to know what was subversive about his music, and he insisted that the committee produce the witness who had accused him.[36] Nine days later, Clinton

Jencks was charged by the Department of Justice with having lied when he signed his Taft-Hartley non-Communist affidavit.

Jarrico, meanwhile, was busy obtaining equipment for editing and screening, hiring and losing one editor after another (four altogether), and trying to find a way to get footage that had been shot in Mexico into the United States. Under U.S. pressure, Mexican authorities had refused Biberman permission to go to Mexico to film Revueltas after her deportation. So a Mexican friend of the producers asked a Mexican film producer to make a "screen test" of Rosaura Revueltas, consisting of the shots IPC needed. As the final shot was completed, somebody on the set yelled, "This isn't a test. It's *Salt of the Earth*!" The Mexican authorities seized the roll of undeveloped negative and locked it in a government warehouse. The partners made several attempts to get the negative released. They even found someone to persuade Lázaro Cárdenas, a former president of Mexico, to intervene. When all had failed, Jarrico recounted later, "I finally arranged for a daring young Mexican I'd met to steal the film. We worked out a plan that involved his flying the film to Tijuana, an open port, where I was to meet him." But when Jarrico reported his plan to Biberman and Wilson, they objected, arguing that the FBI was waiting for him to try something like that. Jarrico replied, "Nonsense. You're being paranoid. With these shots we can finish the film. Without these shots, we could *never* finish the film." They consulted their attorney, who agreed with Biberman and Wilson. If Jarrico were apprehended smuggling the film, he could be sentenced to five years in prison. Since the three had agreed to run the production as a triumvirate and to make no substantive decision unless two of them agreed, Jarrico's plan was vetoed. The next day he and Sylvia drove to Tijuana to abort the smuggling project. Jarrico later recalled,

> We watched as my accomplice's plane came in from Mexico City, watched through a plate-glass window as he came through Mexican customs, unquestioned. He waved at us jauntily, a small suitcase in his hand.
>
> Coming into the waiting room, he handed me the suitcase. I explained, very embarrassed, that I couldn't accept it. My partners had overruled me. I explained their fears. I'd have to ask him, I said, to take the film back to Mexico City. If its disappearance had

> not as yet been noticed, he was to return it to the warehouse from which he'd taken it. We'd have to continue the *legal* fight to recover it.
>
> He looked at me with total contempt, shrugged, accepted the suitcase and started back with it through Mexican customs.

But this time, the inspector demanded that the suitcase and the film can be opened. Realizing that would mean destroying the undeveloped negative, the courier returned to Jarrico and Sylvia, who took the suitcase from him. They drove around Tijuana, looking for a place to stow it. When no place seemed appropriate, Jarrico said, "To hell with it," and with the suitcase in the backseat of their car, they headed back to Los Angeles. At the border checkpoint, they were waved through.[37]

As part of the campaign to get the finished product shown, the partners subsidized the summer 1953 issue of *California Quarterly*, which printed the script and an appeal by Jarrico and Biberman for allies "to defeat the censors and saboteurs." They made a plea to everyone "who is morally concerned with free communication to help provide the atmosphere and the place in which *Salt of the Earth* can be shown and judged on its own merits."[38]

Jarrico also made a vain attempt to appeal to Roy Brewer's labor union conscience. In a letter to him, Jarrico pointed out one of the conundrums of the domestic cold war—that it pitted union against union. IPC had, he wrote, consistently sought to maintain union standards in its labor relations; the film was sponsored by a union; and it dealt with the lives of union people. In sum, IPC had committed no unfair labor practices to justify "your illegal call to boycott our enterprise." He called on Brewer to issue a public statement addressed to all the affiliated guilds and unions of the Hollywood AFL Film Council, assuring them that they might supply IPC with personnel, facilities, and services without fear of discrimination and intimidation by the council.[39] When Brewer did not respond, Jarrico urged his partners to institute an immediate legal action against IATSE. But Biberman was opposed, because, he later wrote, "Our pro-union film was banned by a union and the unions of the country were silent. This was not a background for legal action."[40]

Officers of the IUMMSW, however, expressed concern regarding what they considered to be a lack of worker unity on the *Salt of the*

Earth production. At the end of July, Clinton Jencks wrote Michael Wilson, asking for a "sober re-evaluation of the relationships which must exist between the Production Company and the Union from here on out." According to Jencks, "a completely wrong and artificial separation in the roles" of the cultural workers and the manual trade union workers had occurred. Wilson wrote an apologetic letter to Maurice Travis, the IUMMSW's secretary-treasurer. In September, Wilson spoke at the IUMMSW's national convention in St. Louis. There, he related the history of the film, emphasizing its revolutionary aspects and the full support given it by Local 890. He continued, "The vast majority of the people in and around Silver City were either neutral or friendly to the Union, and ashamed of the un-American antics of a small minority. . . . And there would have been no violence were it not for the incitement and hysteria generated from outside the area—from the self-appointed censors in Hollywood and Washington." The latter, he predicted, would also try to ban it from regular distribution. If they succeeded, and the picture was shown only to miners in the privacy of their union halls, in 16mm, Wilson continued,

> then we will have failed. This picture must be an instrument to build Mine-Mill [IUMMSW], to spread the truth about Mine-Mill. In this sense you need it less than a lot of other people—your potential friends and allies—the unorganized, other trade unionists, middle class and farm groups—all of whom are hit with a daily barrage of anti-union propaganda. . . .
>
> This is the basic issue here—the right of the American people to see and judge this picture on its own merits; the right of a trade union as well as a big corporation to use mass communications to tell its side of the story. But we can be sure that labor's enemies will organize to prevent distribution of this picture.

Wilson concluded by urging the union's members to organize to get the movie shown in their communities.[41]

On December 13, the partners showed a work print to an audience of blacklisted people at Lazarus's Lyric Theater in Los Angeles. Following his viewing of the print, Lawson wrote the ten-page memo discussed above. The memo was, Lawson began, "a purely personal comment." He found the picture to be "a very positive, beautiful and exciting achievement." But, he continued, "there are weaknesses which are so fundamental in the concept and treatment of the material that they cannot be wholly overcome within the limits of the time and money available. . . . The main general difficulty is the somewhat limited appeal and somewhat sectarian character of the material despite its beauty and human warmth." He did not think that the filmmakers had clearly related the struggles of the New Mexico miners "to the whole pattern of struggle in the United States." But, as we have seen, the bulk of his commentary concerned the treatment of Ramon and Esperanza and what to do about correcting it.[42]

Wilson, following a discussion of Lawson's comments with Jarrico and Biberman, composed a seven-page reply. Acknowledging that there might be "sectarian tendencies" in their depiction of the miners, Wilson rejected Lawson's claim that the movie was "a specialized study." To accept it, wrote Wilson, would be to cast doubt not just on the execution of the movie's theme but on the content itself. The content was not sectarian, Wilson wrote, but "vanguard." The partners agreed with Lawson that the final sequence was the weakest portion of the movie, but they attributed that to its having been shot during the height of the violence and the deportation of Revueltas. The scenes could not be reshot.[43]

In early January 1954, Jarrico went to New York to open a distribution office. He called it "Operation New York" in his agenda book, where he listed the tasks he had to undertake: find an office and a theater; plan a public relations campaign; and arrange for foreign sales, domestic sales, and nationwide previews. While Biberman handled technical matters, Jarrico worked on raising more money (they needed another $15,000), talked with lawyers (he still wanted to sue IATSE), and looked for theaters. He wrote Sylvia, "I have never called so many people with so little result or money. Until today, when the ice-jam broke. I now have 1500 in new-found checks in my pocket." He wrote Lazarus that he and Biberman were "working day and night . . . day after day. We are pushing with might and main to move as quickly as good procedure permits. But there is so much to be done . . . that it is taking all our energies to keep abreast of our needs." He told Sylvia that "the problems are overwhelming" and that the estimate of three months before the movie would be in theaters "is probably as screwy as the other time estimates on this flicker." When the IATSE ordered all its laboratory workers and projectionists to refuse to work on or project the film, Jarrico and Biberman possessed only one print. Their solution was to schedule private screenings, something that Jarrico called "sneaky previews," to mobilize support for showing *Salt of the Earth* in public. He reported that the reactions to the private screenings were enthusiastic beyond their wildest expectations, especially from trade unionists.[44]

In the search for a theater, Jarrico and Biberman negotiated simultaneously with several theater owners. Then, Jarrico wrote Sylvia,

> the illiterate boor who owns the 86th St. grande has been calling us for days, drooling to get us to transform his second-rate theatre into a first-run house, on the basis of a super-salesmanship snow job Herbert has perpetrated on him, and he's complaining "I thought we had a deal, whatsamatter?" So we hurry up to 86th St. to conclude the deal before the poor bastard finds out we're not popular. We iron out the details, draft the contract between 5 in the afternoon and 9 that evening, go back to see him and he signs it—without having seen the picture, with a clause that says he can't break the contract even if there are picket lines, labor disputes, stink bombs, municipal interference—you name it, he can't break it. Tomorrow morning we're showing the picture to him. That poor fella. He'll die. I think we got a clause, if he dies, we inherit the theatre.[45]

The afternoon before the scheduled premiere, Jarrico, in a letter to Sylvia, tried to put the event into historical perspective. He noted that "this particular milestone is so much like all the other critical moments we've had—and the prospect of milestones ahead is so endless—that I feel no different than I did before, or expect to later. The sense of history is there, all right, but I like to think it's related to all the other historical things that are happening now—and did—and will." For example, he concluded, "how lucky for us, and how unlucky for all of us, that the economic situation in this country gives our film new meaning and new usefulness every goddam dialectical day."[46]

Salt of the Earth had its world premiere at the Grande on March 14. Jarrico later wrote that the audience was "wildly enthusiastic" and there was "no picketing or hostility." It ran there for nine weeks and two days and grossed over $40,000. The reviews were generally favorable, but no mainstream distributor was willing to handle the film on a national basis. On March 26, it moved to another neighborhood theater, the New Dyckman. Jarrico then composed a three-page, single-spaced letter to Wilson at IPC's Los Angeles office, telling the staff what to expect when the movie opened there. He concluded,

> The trouble is not yet all over. The only guarantee that we can have is the audience which will be ready to go to extraordinary lengths to support us. Each city will have to tackle this main problem all over again. No city will be a free-rider. I am giving you all these hard facts because I believe them to be true. And unless you have the people and the money to undertake this job you had better not try to slip into it because you can ruin yourselves and hurt the picture. I don't say don't do it. I say do it well.[47]

IPC still had not found a national distributor for *Salt of the Earth*, and many independent exhibitors backed out after showing some interest. Biberman, now in charge of distribution, failed to get it shown in Detroit and Chicago. IPC had to lease a theater to show it in Los Angeles, but the major newspapers refused to accept advertisements, distributors refused to supply shorts or other feature films to fill out the program, and the eleven-week run lost money. It would show for one week in Silver City, but Jarrico and Biberman decided not to attend the opening there because it conflicted with another opening in California—a decision that Virginia Jencks said evoked among the mining families "bitter feelings against" them.[48] *Salt of the Earth* ran for four weeks in San Francisco, two weeks in Berkeley, and had five other, brief bookings in the bay area. By the end of October, it had shown in only thirteen theaters and netted $23,000 for the company, which had spent $50,000 in promotion costs and theater rental fees.

The reviews *Salt of the Earth* received during its original run ranged from the enthusiastically positive to the passionately negative. Elizabeth Gurley Flynn, a Communist leader, wrote that the movie "should serve as a herald and a promise of what a truly democratically-minded movie industry could accomplish in our country." The most notorious of the negative reviews was written by Pauline Kael, who was then beginning her illustrious career as a movie critic. She called it "as clear a piece of Communist propaganda as we have had in many years." It was, in her view, a "formulaic melodrama," "dreary and programmatic." Her main specific criticism, which ironically paralleled John Howard Lawson's, was that the strike "has not been placed against the background of American life which would provide perspective and contrast." The makers' focus on local grievances, she continued, was a typical Communist maneuver. She claimed that the filmmakers did what Communist propagandists do, that is, they converted people's desire to alleviate their conditions into a general expression of "anxiety and despair."[49]

The positive reviews could not outweigh the negative press the project had received, and Jarrico's many attempts to break the theater boycott were unsuccessful. He had telegraphed Dore Schary, who had just been appointed to the American Civil Liberties Union advisory council, to ask if Schary could use that position "to persuade local Metro exchange to stop illegal discrimination against us and to allow us to book Metro shorts to run with 'Salt of the Earth' opening at Marcal Theater tomorrow evening? We are particularly interested in booking 'The Flag Speaks' sponsored by American Legion." Schary did not respond. Jarrico went to Denver on August 13 to urge the executive board of IUMMSW to become more involved in the effort. But, Jarrico said, the IUMMSW failed to use its strength in those communities where it had locals to get theater owners to book the film, and the authors of a Communist Party discussion document prepared in the summer of 1954 complained that the distribution effort "has revealed serious weaknesses among trade union leaders who have failed so signally to rally support" for the movie.[50]

The partners now owed $230,000. Their only hope for solvency was international distribution, which seemed promising at first. In July, *Salt of the Earth* was awarded a grand prize at the Karlovy Vary (Czechoslovakia) International Film Festival, and Rosaura Revueltas won the best actress award. The German Democratic Republic purchased the rights to show it for $10,000. But *Salt of the Earth* failed to find mainstream distributors in the United Kingdom, France, Mexico, and Latin America.[51] Jarrico commented dryly: "All our enemies have succeeded in doing is bleeding us white financially, ha ha, they think they're so strong." The investors, of course, could not be repaid. But every year or so, Jarrico would list the loans outstanding and attempt to prioritize repayments.[52]

During a 1960 trip to the Soviet Union, Jarrico learned from a *Variety* correspondent there that the producers' share of the box office receipts amounted to about $5 million. Jarrico had what he termed "an especially charming conversation" with a vice minister of culture in the Russian Republic. The minister, Jarrico wrote,

> gushed that when people ask him the meaning of realism he replies, see "Salt of the Earth." It played, he told me, in every theatre in the S[oviet] U[nion], it had the most enthusiastic reviews, the most tremendous popular reception. "Tell me," he concluded, "how did the picture do financially?" "We lost our shirts," I answered. When this had been translated he seemed utterly bewildered. It was not the phrase that bewildered him, but the fact. "How is it possible?" he marveled. "Well," I said, "for one thing we had the illusion that the socialist countries would pay enough for it to make it possible to make other such films." He grew very embarrassed. "I cannot speak for the socialist countries," he said. "Specifically," I said, "we had that illusion about the Soviet Union." He blushed, Herbert, I swear. He was extremely upset. "It was not my department," he apologized. "I don't know anything about that, it's possible that we made a mistake."[53]

In mid-1955, the partners and their attorneys concluded that their only hope of recouping their investment was legal action. Jarrico began to draft a chronology of events, with appendices listing the names of those who had refused to be employed on the film, including sixteen cameramen, five soundmen, and twenty-nine editors. The suit would be filed in June 1956.

Over the years, Jarrico wrote and spoke many times about his perspective on *Salt of the Earth*. For a Feminist Press showing at Carnegie Hall, he wrote, "*Salt of the Earth* is the only film I ever worked on that got better instead of worse over the years. I suspect that's because the struggles we tried to reflect have grown more urgent, more determined—especially that of women for unequivocal equality." Indeed, *Salt of the Earth* is clearest and most compelling in its depiction of the rise of the women's consciousness, activism, and courage. In his oral history, Jarrico said of the film,

> For many years I could only see the defects. But lately when I do see the kind of audience reaction it still gets thirty-five years later,

> I really am very proud of it. I think the difficulties we had are reflected in certain technical crudities. I don't think the direction is as good as it should be. I think the performances of some of the amateur actors are so clearly amateur that they're somewhat embarrassing, though the leading performances are very good. I think probably the content is a little too much on the nose, that the social conflicts are presented in terms that are too black and white and not gray enough, not ambiguous enough, not ambivalent enough. On the other hand, when I see some of the freewheeling films that have been hailed over the past twenty-five or thirty years as great artistic breakthroughs but whose meaning is very hard to discern, I'm very pleased about the fact that Salt of the Earth is so very crystal clear about what it's trying to say.[54]

The film's particular claim on posterity is the Marxist vision that Jarrico, Wilson, and Biberman brought to the project. The values that informed their political lives gave an aesthetic coherence to the story of Mexican American miners and their families that had been lacking in all previous movies, and has been missing from all subsequent movies, about working people.[55]

8

The Black Market and Khrushchev's Speech, 1954–58

> The atmosphere here has improved enormously since the [U.S.-USSR] meeting at the summit [Geneva, July 1955]. . . . Personally I'm finding it increasingly easy to make a living again, and I also find time to fight the good fight for a lasting peace and a people's democracy. Not, however, by making decent films. That is my one great frustration.
>
> —*Paul Jarrico, 1956*

The year 1954 was the height of the domestic cold war. Public opinion polls registered overwhelmingly anti-Communist sentiments,[1] and Congress enacted the Communist Control Act, which effectively stripped the party of most of its due process rights.[2] Though the Senate condemned Senator Joseph McCarthy in early December, one month later, it unanimously approved a resolution stating, "The Communist Party of the United States is recognized to be a part of the international Communist conspiracy against the United States and all the democratic forms of government. It is the sense of the Senate that its appropriate committees should continue diligently and vigorously to investigate, expose, and combat this conspiracy and all subversive elements and persons connected therewith."[3]

As we have seen, the full weight of this anti-Communist apparatus had been employed against the makers of *Salt of the Earth*. Jarrico, back in Los Angeles, now felt its weight on him as an individual. He immediately began to seek work on the black market using the pseudonym "Peter Achilles." He wrote to a prospective agent, "As you know, I'm blacklisted. But if you know anyone who wants a $2000 a week writer at a considerable discount, on either a movie or a TV script, let me know."[4] Few did. Jarrico had earned thirteen Academy credits between 1937 and 1949. He would not receive another credit until 1969. He had earned $28,500 on average per year in the decade prior to the blacklist (1941–51); he would earn $14,000 total between 1952 and 1957.

Jarrico noted that the black market for scripts went through several phases:

> At first, it was really so far under the table that it was under the floor. I mean by that that if a producer discovered he'd bought something by a blacklisted writer, sold to him under another name or through a front, the chances were very real that the deal would be broken. . . . That was the earliest stage. That was the early fifties, or for the . . . Hollywood Ten, the late forties. But by the mid-fifties, by the time I really began to depend on the black market, producers were beginning to look the other way. I'd say by the late fifties, they were even courting blacklisted writers, still insisting, though, that they work under phony names or through fronts. It was very complicated. There were as many stories as there were black market deals.[5]

In the summer of 1954, Jarrico and Adrian Scott spent two days writing a speculative treatment for an episode of the television show *Lassie*, but it was rejected. Jarrico was then approached by the newly blacklisted Frank Tarloff, who had written a screen story that would be fronted and produced by Edward Lewis.[6] Tarloff offered Jarrico one-third of his 50 percent interest in the project. They decided to title it *Malvourneen (The Stud with a Delicate Ear)*, after an Irish song, "Kathleen Malvourneen." It involved a bachelor in a small Irish village who loved three women. They had big hopes for it and worked on it steadily for the rest of the year. But Lewis was unable to get it made.

Jarrico also worked on developing a speculative original by Michael Wilson (*The Flying Carpet*). Ostensibly about a music teacher who teaches the children of U.S. oil workers based in a Middle Eastern country, the story was actually a critical commentary on international oil dealings. Jarrico also tried to work with Sylvia on two projects. The first, "The Loser," was a half-hour television script about rehabilitating criminals in prison and restoring them to a useful place in society, for which the Jarricos received $750. The second, about delinquent girls in a reform school, was offered to them by Dalton Trumbo and Adrian Scott. Scott would be the associate producer, the Jarricos would write the treatment, and Trumbo would write the script. The Jarricos based their treatment on the precept that "there are no bad girls—there are only bad circumstances. So-called bad girls are all potentially good. Like all other girls, they are full of gaiety, beauty and promise. They are, in fact, the flowers of an evil world." But no one involved in the project liked the Jarricos' treatment. Trumbo decided to go ahead with the script on his own.[7]

In his journal, the forty-year-old Jarrico evaluated the personal and professional progress he had made in the previous decade. He congratulated himself

> on certain evidences of increased maturity. I'm much less worried about whether people like me (though still not free of that worry) and more confident generally. But I still concentrate for days on jobs that would be almost as good (good enough?) if done in hours, a torturous perfectionism that I criticize Sylvia for. . . . On the other hand, I watch Herbert [Biberman] pound out documents lacking in grammar, organization and modesty, and prefer being a perfectionist. Or rather, I wish I could work with his methods and my results.[8]

In his journal, Jarrico also considered his son's personal development. He was honest about the demands he made of Bill: "I want him to make a maximum personal contribution to society because I think it will make him happy. I want him to learn to love people, to work with them, to love life—and to bring to a Socialist America as many of the great treasures of the bourgeois democratic past as he can. Learning, that's the ticket." Sylvia Jarrico, however, was concerned that he was setting the standard too high for Bill. She did not want Bill "to be bright and unhappy, think he's better than others."[9]

The question of what to do next with *Salt of the Earth* still lurked. Jarrico suggested that IPC give up the search for theatrical exhibition and distribute it in a 16mm format so that it could more easily be shown in homes and union halls, but Biberman and Wilson opposed him. They met with representatives of unions from the Southwest, but they failed to produce a plan to improve distribution in that region. Meanwhile, IPC's attorneys had filed an action in Chicago, charging the projectionists' union there with violation of the Sherman Anti-Trust Act. In June, a federal district court judge decided in favor of IPC. He ordered that the ban against projecting the film be lifted and ruled that a huge fine would be imposed if it were not. He also refused to order the IPC officers to answer interrogatories about their political beliefs. But IATSE lawyers managed to get a different judge assigned to the case, and the new judge ordered the IPC officers to answer the interrogatories. When they refused, they were forced to withdraw their complaint.[10]

Jarrico struggled to determine in what direction he should be heading. At the end of March 1955, he confessed in his journal that he was feeling "pretty restless. . . . As I told Sylvia yesterday, my conflict is now whether to work on commercial assignments or on my [atomic scientist] play, but the fact [is] that I don't really feel like doing either. Or much of anything else. I feel considerable guilt about not doing more politically these days, but I don't think my desire to get away from it all or my feeling that the world is too much with me has any basic political motivation. If it does, it's pretty well distorted by subjective filters and prisms." Several weeks later, he wrote that he was feeling "very foolish and self-indulgent on the whole question of what I should be doing these days." It had at first seemed clear to him that he should concentrate on commercial jobs until he had made a substantial amount of money. But, he continued, "my decisive feeling didn't last too long, and now I wonder again."[11] He had even applied for a job as a copywriter in an advertising firm.[12] His plans to undertake independent productions of *Mademoiselle from Armentières* and *Rip Van Winkle* ran aground when he could not raise the funds to make the former nor the $15,000 Allied Artists wanted for the rights to the latter. And he was concerned that he was drinking too much.[13]

Nor did Jarrico have much success in his effort to become a television writer, although he had several opportunities. He and Sylvia helped Al Levitt with a speculative television script, *The Legend of Johnny Moccasin*, about an Indian boy who lives with white settlers. Levitt could not pay them immediately, but he was a close friend, they liked the topic, and it gave them practice in writing for a different medium. Shortly thereafter, Frank Tarloff told Jarrico that

Arthur Stander, producer of the television series *It's Always Jan* (CBS), would buy original scripts from him for $1,500 each. The show was a situation comedy about a widow (Janis Paige) who has a young daughter and sings in a nightclub. Jarrico and Tarloff wrote three scripts, two of which ("The Playboy" and "The Doctor") were purchased. But the show lasted only one season. At the end of August, Jarrico received a letter from Ring Lardner Jr., advising him that Albert Ruben, a scenario editor for Hannah Weinstein, was coming to Hollywood to recruit writers for a series of English television programs, including *The Adventures of Robin Hood* and *The Highwayman*. The company would pay $700 for a first draft, $300 for a rewrite, and 10 percent of the producer's net profit on the episode. Lardner and Ian Hunter were already hard at work on these projects. Jarrico recommended himself and six others, but Ruben offered none of them immediate assignments.[14] Jarrico was able to earn some money at the end of the year when he and Michael Wilson were hired to write some scenes for a television program featuring Kay Starr.

With no script projects on the horizon, Jarrico thought about renting a cabin in the Sierras, taking along a large collection of Marxist material, and cowriting with Sylvia a popular approach to Marxism for what he called the intelligent but nonintellectual American. That suggestion precipitated a crisis with his wife, who responded angrily, "I don't want to be dominated by you and I don't want to work with you on a project in which you tell me what to read and when, and what to think about it! And you're not thinking about whether this would be good for Bill!" Jarrico confided to his journal that he had been selfish and insensitive. Unsure what he himself should be doing, he was relegating Sylvia to the position of his assistant in whatever he decided to do. He finally understood, he claimed: "She wants to make her own major contributions. And can. If I'd stop nagging her and forcing her to help me."[15]

He and Sylvia did work together to aid Elizabeth Poe Kerby with her research for what would be a groundbreaking exposé of the blacklist. They introduced her to blacklisted people, who were understandably reluctant to speak to reporters or researchers. Jarrico wrote in his journal, "Betty's study of the blacklist for the Fund for the Republic is a most deserving project, and we've tried to help as much as we can, but there's always the possibility that the information we give her will fall into the wrong hands and serve to increase the blacklist instead of fighting it."[16] Kerby, however, proved worthy of her interviewees' trust: she guarded her interviews and files steadfastly, and when she donated them to the Academy of Motion Picture Arts and Sciences' library, she removed the names of all those to whom she had promised anonymity.

Jarrico also continued his efforts to break the motion picture blacklist. Despite the setbacks he had experienced, he believed that legal actions were the best means to do so. He encouraged Michael Wilson to sue Allied Artists for refusing to give him a screen credit for *Friendly Persuasion*, and he advised Albert Maltz to sue Paramount Pictures, which was refusing him a credit on the remake of his first film, *This Gun for Hire*.[17] For his part, Jarrico contemplated suing RKO for two screen credits. On April 17, 1956, KHJ-TV in Los Angeles began a week's showings of *Tom, Dick and Harry*. Billy Wilkerson, publisher of the *Hollywood Reporter*, publicly criticized the station for showing a movie written by and credited to a blacklisted writer. "What's going to happen now," Wilkerson asked, "when pictures with the names like Paul Jarrico are released to TV and will probably be seen by ten times the number of people that viewed them in particular theaters? Will the public get the idea that all our fight and high standards were just a piece of momentary exploitation to gain the public's favor and we have no interest in the product now being passed over to TV? This is a dangerous situation, posing one of serious consequences, unless stopped right at its incubation." That very day, when the movie was shown again, Jarrico's credit had been removed. Jarrico issued a press statement in protest: "The illogic of the blacklist has been reduced to an absurdity. Fifteen years ago I was nominated for an Academy Award for writing this picture. Today, re-released on TV, its authorship is treated like a military secret. The public, it appears, is not to be protected from my work—however beguiling and subversive it may be—the public is only to be protected from my name." Future prints of the movie would be released with no writer's credit.[18]

The following year, RKO remade *Tom, Dick and Harry* as *The Girl Most Likely*. The studio notified the Writers Guild of America, west (WGAw)[19] that sole screenplay credit would be given to one Devery Freeman and that there would be no credit assigned for the original story. Jarrico wrote the WGAw, protesting that neither it nor RKO had notified him of the tentative credit submission, and he sent a similar protest to RKO. When RKO did not respond, Jarrico asked the guild to arbitrate the credit dispute. Jarrico argued that he should be awarded both a story credit and a co–screenplay credit, since "the screenplay of the original version represents a major portion of the current screenplay." The guild's arbitration committee agreed with Jarrico, and Ben Margolis threatened RKO with legal action if the ruling was not enforced. But RKO, clearly relying on the anti-Communist clause in the bargaining agreement, ignored the letter. "I want to sue the bastards," Jarrico wrote Margolis. "I wrote that picture under a contract that had *no morals clause*, and that guaranteed me credit. . . . A credit on the remake, and I'm not inflating this for the sake of an argument, could easily be worth $50,000 a year to me, for the next few years, since it would mean I was no longer blacklisted. That's aside from other damages." He also wanted to sue the WGAw for signing an agreement with the studios allowing them to take a writer's name off a script. "They had no right to give RKO something that belongs to me, and I think we can prove it. The fact that they're a union doesn't mean a goddam thing to me. They're enforcing the blacklist, and it will do the membership good to have their union licked on this." Margolis replied that he did not think a winnable case could be made against the guild and that the case against RKO would require a considerable amount of money, which Margolis's firm could not advance. Jarrico finally decided not to pursue the matter.[20]

Jarrico also served on a committee to raise money for a public relations campaign in support of *Wilson et al. v. Loew's Inc. et al.* A Los Angeles superior court had dismissed the case; the California court of appeals had upheld the dismissal; and the California Supreme Court had refused to review it. But the U.S. Supreme Court, in January 1957, had issued a writ of certiorari. Jarrico's appeal for funds, however, met resistance. Those who bothered to reply had no more money to contribute, and one of them, Sam Moore, wrote that the case "has the appearance of being a stubborn, isolated, last-ditch, won't-quit kind of an effort, with no support from anywhere." Those favoring the litigation strategy were dealt a severe blow in January 1958 when the Supreme Court issued a per curiam opinion dismissing the writ because it had been "improvidently granted."[21]

As regarded the Communist Party, Jarrico remained a stalwart. He did not express any particular emotion over the death of Stalin in May 1953, but he watched approvingly as Stalin's successors came and went in what Jarrico considered an orderly fashion. His main focus was altering the strategy and tactics of the CPUSA. In a report to his party section meeting, following the August 1955 meeting between Soviet premier Nikolai Bulganin and President Eisenhower, Jarrico argued that the party needed to build a mass base by conducting a "struggle within the organizations of the people." They should recruit workers, blacks, and Mexican Americans to run for political office on a platform that included opposition to U.S. war provocations.[22]

At the end of 1955, Jarrico arranged a tribute to John Howard Lawson, sponsored by the ASP. He wrote letters to intellectuals and artists all over the world, asking for messages of appreciation. He edited the souvenir program, produced the show, emceed it, and oversaw the cleanup. The dinner, on December 11, was the last significant event for the ASP. On December 14, the ASP executive board voted to dissolve the council because, the directors wrote, "There is a new spirit abroad in the land. There are opportunities for expanded and intensified activity among scientists, artists and professionals," and ASP no longer "offers the best organizational form for the realization of these potentialities."[23]

Personally, Jarrico felt optimistic about world affairs. In March 1956, he wrote Jules Dassin, "The fact that American imperialism has been forced to recognize its inability to conquer the world has been healthy for all of us. . . . The promise of peace is like the sun, it thaws the long winter, flowers begin to grow." Jarrico's positive attitude was also evident in his report that spring on the February 16 public speech of First Secretary Nikita Khrushchev to the twentieth congress of the CPUSSR. Jarrico described the speech as "one of the most significant documents of our time," one that "raises and proposes answers to some fundamental questions of Marxist theory and practice, questions that concern us all." The bulk of Jarrico's report focused on Khrushchev's discussion of the international position of the Soviet Union. But he also offered some commentary on Khrushchev's analysis of the internal situation of the Soviet Union and his criticism of some aspects of Stalin's leadership. "It is my personal opinion," Jarrico wrote, "that the criticism of Stalin has to be seen in perspective"; Khrushchev's criticism did "not loom so large if seen against the monumental victories of socialism and peace recorded in this document." Besides, Jarrico continued, both Khrushchev and Anastas Mikoyan, in another speech, had publicly condemned the cult of the individual leader "as being alien to the spirit of Marxism-Leninism."[24]

In his summation of the February 16 speech, Jarrico reached five conclusions:

> 1. The Soviet Union is in wonderful shape. It is led by men who are first-rate Marxists, it is re-establishing socialist democracy, and it is well on the historic road to the most democratic system of society ever conceived—communism. What it needs least of all is our blind adherence.
> 2. The Communist Party of America is in terrible shape. It has been isolated from the American people not only because of the attacks of reaction but because it has defended everything that has happened in the Soviet Union, however scandalous and tyrannical.
> 3. It is time for the most thorough-going re-examination of our theory and practice, of our political program and of our organizational structure—from the bottom to the top. And that is how people should be listened to—the rank and file first, the leadership last.
> 4. If we draw the right conclusions from this re-examination—if we admit our mistakes with sincerity—the opportunities for unity which will open to us will be breathtaking. If we do not, if we try to treat this as just another change in line in which the membership is to be calmed down by the leadership, we shall be more isolated than ever.
> 5. Don't underestimate the shock and confusion in our ranks.[25]

It was only in late April or May that Jarrico (and the rest of the world's Communists) learned that the rumors of another, "secret," speech were true. Khrushchev had delivered this speech on the night of February 24. In it, he addressed what he called the "gradual" growth of the "Stalin cult," which became "at a certain specific stage the source of a whole series of exceedingly serious and grave perversions of Party principle, of Party democracy, of revolutionary legality." On May 1, Jarrico wrote in his journal, "The XXth Congress has made a lot of people think very hard. What it made me think was that we had contributed to our isolation from the American people by our slavish defense of everything that happened in Russia, and that we must tell people that we were *wrong* and make sure it never happens again if we are to have any hope of unity and effectiveness in the United States."[26]

On June 17, Jarrico prepared a report for the cultural section of the Hollywood party that reemphasized the conclusions he had reached in his April report. He wrote, "There is no denying it. The explosion of the Stalin myth has shaken us to the hard core. In the glaring light cast by the explosion we can see how deep the chasm separating us from the American people has really been. We can see how poorly we have been equipped to cross that chasm. We can now see how profoundly we have to change our theory and practice if we are serious about helping our people achieve a better life." Jarrico counseled his readers not to attempt to comfort themselves with the rationale that their failures resulted from the cold war offensive against them, because those attacks did not and could not "account for the cynicism and scorn with which a large part of the American people" viewed Communists. It was, rather, their slavish adherence to Soviet policy that had laid them wide open to the charge that they were agents of a foreign power. That they were not, he continued, "that we felt we were serving the best interests of our own country in defending the Soviet Union, does not excuse our stupidity. Objectively our apologetics were of advantage to neither the United States nor the Soviet Union. It merely compromised whatever reputation for brains and honesty we had won in other fights, and seriously weakened our effectiveness." Some might protest "that we did not know about Stalin's crimes and should not be accused of defending them. The answer to that is that we did not want to know. We either refused to read works critical of the Soviet leadership or refused to believe what we read."[27]

U.S. Communists, he continued, must face up to the issue of freedom and accept the meaning given to it by most Americans: democratic elections; the right to think as one pleases; the right to say what one thinks, pray as one wants, go to the meetings of one's choice;

the right to refuse to talk to the police; the right to get a lawyer, a fair trial, and due process. The American people would not listen to Communists "if we equivocate on the question of personal liberty." They would not buy socialism unless they were absolutely guaranteed that they would have more civil liberties under it than they did under capitalism. And, Jarrico concluded, American Communists must admit that they had regularly equivocated—on free speech for anti-Semites, on the relocation of Japanese Americans, on the trial of the Trotskyites. These were more than just tactical errors. "They sprang," Jarrico argued, "from basic theoretical principles, principles which were developed in other countries under other conditions and which we adopted wholesale." His thesis, he continued, was a simple one: "We must become an American party. It is my conception that we must re-examine every concept—Stalinist, Leninist, even Marxist, and see what applies to the situation in this country and what does not. . . . [W]e must stop talking a language the American people don't understand. We should not only learn how to speak differently but how to think differently."[28]

When party secretary Eugene Dennis sent a draft resolution to party branches in early October, Jarrico criticized it for not going far enough. He thought Dennis did not fully appreciate the party's deep crisis and that his economic analysis was neither penetrating nor clear. Jarrico proposed that the Hollywood cultural section discard it and write a new resolution that contained a clear statement of why the party had failed, as well as "unequivocal declaration[s]" of "independence from the Communist Party of the Soviet Union," their belief in democratic freedom, their belief in socialism, their intention to reexamine every Marxist concept on the basis of American experience, and their "desire to join with others who believe in an independent American movement for freedom and socialism."[29] The Soviet invasion of Hungary on November 4, 1956, increased Jarrico's determination to seek far-reaching change in the party.

The Hollywood branch scheduled a meeting at Jarrico's house at the end of January 1957 to discuss the position it would take on the question of party reform, which was to be the main item at the national convention the following month. The national office had prepared and distributed an alternative draft resolution on party reform, but Jarrico thought that it too fell well short of what was needed. He proposed, as topics of discussion at the branch meeting, methods of achieving a nationally independent party that was democratic in form and substance and socialist in purpose.[30] The meeting began with a report on the national party by Lawson. The members then discussed what their section should do in terms of the blacklist, black employment, the content of movies and television programs, and independent cultural production. Jarrico did not record what was said or what decisions, if any, were taken.

At the national convention, when a resolution critical of the past and a new party constitution were approved, the reform advocates thought they had won. But the old leadership remained in place. In early 1958, William Z. Foster declared invalid the decisions taken at the 1957 convention and regained control of the party. Jarrico had finally had enough. "I was," he recalled, "at a meeting [in New York] with Dorothy [Healey] and five or six others early in 1958. One by one each of us said, 'That's it, I'm getting out.' Dorothy said to me, 'You can't do that, you're a stalwart.' 'No,' I said, 'I'm leaving and you should too.' And she said, 'I'm not going to let those bastards have the Party.'"[31] For all intents and purposes, the Hollywood branch dissolved. And, because of lack of funds, *Hollywood Review* folded.

Jarrico believed that a phase of his life had ended. He wanted a break from political activity; he wanted to try something new; and he wanted to be adventurous. He wanted to write, but not at a studio and not under the table. He believed that in a different environment he could complete his atomic scientist play and write the popular book he had originally suggested cowriting with Sylvia, to be titled *Marxism for Americans: What Communism Is All About (in Plain English).* He envisioned it as a means to promote socialism as the only real solution to the current world crisis. He wrote in his journal, "I don't think the level of Marxist understanding is very high in this country, and I think if I applied myself to it I could make some original contributions." In May 1957, he proposed to Carl Marzani, cofounder of the publishing firm Cameron and Associates, a six-chapter book or six pamphlets that would explain Marxism as social science, philosophy, history, economics, and political movement, and socialism as a realistic alternative for the United States.[32]

Sylvia Jarrico argued that they should stay in Los Angeles because they were an important source of strength and assistance to many people. But Jarrico felt they had already given enough, and there was nothing in Los Angeles requiring their presence. There was certainly nothing left to do on *Salt of the Earth*. IPC's lawyers had completed the papers for an antitrust suit against sixty-eight individuals and organizations, charging them with violation of the Sherman Anti-Trust Act. Ben Margolis advised Jarrico, Herbert Biberman, and Sonja Dahl Biberman that if they remained as officers and directors of the company, they would have to testify, and that if they refused to answer questions about their political beliefs by invoking the Fifth Amendment, the complaint might be dismissed. They resigned on May 31, 1956, and the complaint was filed on June 21. *Independent Productions Corp. and I.P.C. Distributors, Inc. v. Loew's, Inc., et al.* would remain in the courts for eight years.[33]

The Wilsons had moved to Paris, and, Jarrico wrote, "Mike writes tantalizing letters about the opportunities in France; he's hot as hell; says if I was there I could make a fortune." But when the Jarricos applied for passports, they received identical letters from the Department of State informing them that they must execute and have notarized the enclosed affidavit: "I [name in full] residing at [street address, city, state] am not and never have been a Communist; . . . I am not and never have been a member of the Communist Party or any other organization which advocates the overthrow of the United States Government by force of arms." Jarrico wrote to the Department of State that he had already sworn to support and defend the Constitution.

> It seems to me that you are now inviting me to join you in a conspiracy to violate some of the fundamental principles of that Constitution, namely its guarantees of free speech and assembly. I shall not do so. I consider your request that I take an additional oath—a political test oath which is clearly unconstitutional—both unnecessary and insulting.
>
> In brief, Sir, my political beliefs and associations are none of your business. Nor are they the business of any other government employee or Department.

The passport office replied that there would be no further consideration of the Jarricos' pending applications. Jarrico wrote Tarloff that the "only thing about this whole fucking blacklist that's really made me feel *personally* gypped is the travel restriction." Ben Margolis referred Jarrico to Leonard Boudin, a New York lawyer who had become expert at winning passport cases for left wingers.[34]

At Jarrico's insistence, he and Sylvia decided to await the outcome of their passport case in New York. They sold their house and, on July 3, drove east. They spent a few weeks with the Polonskys on Martha's Vineyard and arrived in New York City in late August. They rented an apartment on East Ninety-third Street.

In New York, Jarrico compiled ten script ideas for Hannah Weinstein's consideration, three television series ideas for the producer Alfred Crown, and four television spectaculars for the producer David Susskind. None were accepted. He also sent letters to directors and producers offering his services and his old scripts. (Michael Wilson once commented that Jarrico was "a ghoul about old scripts, always digging them up again.") Jarrico and Sylvia wrote three outlines for *The Phil Silvers Show*, but only one was purchased (for $1,100). In November, he noted, "In 1956, I made $6,416.25. In the first eleven months of 1957, $400. But oh the promises, oh the speculations, oh the possibilities." To Bill, who was now at Reed College in Portland, Oregon, he wrote, "I'm not getting much better jobs here than I was not getting in L.A. . . . Do you know that I've made less as a writer this year than in any year for twenty years?"[35]

The Jarricos' financial situation was eased somewhat when Wilson sent Jarrico a treatment, *The Grand Tour*, to polish (for $500), and Sylvia was hired by McGraw-Hill as an assistant editor. (She also did some editorial work for C. Wright Mills.) Edward Lewis, who had fronted for *Malvourneen* and was now an executive at Kirk Douglas's Bryna Productions, asked Jarrico to rewrite a western script, *The Silent Gun*, for which he would be paid $7,500. It concerned a gunslinger, Johnny Ringo, who learns that real men know how to live without killing. When Lewis rejected Jarrico's first outline because it lacked conflict, action, and tension, Jarrico farmed it out to another blacklisted writer, Arnaud d'Usseau. But Jarrico ended up rewriting d'Usseau's version. Even though Lewis reported that Douglas "was crazy about" the new approach, Bryna dropped the project. Wilson, however, made a deal for *The Grand Tour*, which Jarrico would cowrite with him.[36]

Alfred Crown then came through with a more substantive project, a jazz musician version of *Othello* originally titled *The Night They Waited*. He paired Jarrico with Nel King, a jazz enthusiast who had been a film editor at Paramount, and they closed the deal. Crown agreed to pay them $2,500 in advance for the outline, $5,000 for the script, and another $5,000 if it was produced. Jarrico and King envisioned it as "a classic tragedy" played out in "a high-voltage," all-night jazz session in a Manhattan loft. Delia, a retired white singer married to a black bandleader, decides to resume her career with a new band. But there are complications: the new band is being started by the drummer in her husband's old band, who, Iago-like, tries to get what he wants via lies and innuendos. Arguments, fights, and deaths result.[37]

Sylvia Jarrico, meanwhile, was succeeding as a freelance editor, getting all the work she could handle. She edited books on antibiotics, psychiatric nursing, and business forecasting. But they still had not decided where they wanted to live after their apartment lease expired in June. Jarrico wrote Ed Kraus, "The peculiar fact is that economically it doesn't seem to matter very much where we live, as far as my work goes. New York is better for Sylvia's work, as there are many more publishers here and her services are in considerable demand." If they got their passports back, he continued, Europe would be their first choice, especially if the Wilsons stayed there.[38]

That spring, Leonard Boudin argued before the U.S. Supreme Court the case of the artist Rockwell Kent, who had been denied a passport when he refused to answer questions regarding his political views and refused to sign a non-Communist affidavit. On June 16, 1958, by a 5–4 vote, the Supreme Court ruled that Congress had not given the Department of State the authority to withhold passports from citizens because of their beliefs or associations.[39] One month later, Jarrico and Sylvia applied for passports. On August 12, they received their passports and decided to move to France. Jarrico admitted years later that, in terms of work, he did not need to leave the country then. But, he continued, "I'd worked up such a head of steam on wanting to get out of here that I took off."[40] They drove west, spent three weeks in Los Angeles, where Jarrico finished writing the jazz musician script (now titled *All Night Long*), then flew to New York on September 27 and to Paris on October 1.

The FBI, however, had not lost sight of Jarrico. Four months before the Jarricos moved east, the SACLA compiled an eleven-page report of his political activities. It included his continued membership in the Communist Party and his work on behalf of the California Legislative Conference, the Southern California Peace Crusade, and *Salt of the Earth*. The SACLA recommended that Jarrico's name be kept on the Los Angeles office's security index.[41]

PART 3

EMIGRATION

9

Europe, 1958–75

> Confidential [FBI] source advised on 1-14-59 that [name blacked out] received correspondence from Paul Jarrico from 226 Rue de Rivoli, Paris, France, and an individual in Los Angeles advised that he has learned from [name blacked out] that subjects are residing in Paris and that Paul Jarrico is attempting to find employment in the movie industry and, if successful, will take up residence in Paris for an indefinite period. Information concerning subjects' travel previously furnished to State, CIA, and abovementioned Legal Attachés [Paris, Rome, London].
>
> —*J. Edgar Hoover, 1959*

Within five days of Jarrico's arrival in Paris, he and Michael Wilson met with Dino De Laurentiis to make a deal to adapt Ugo Pirro's novel *Jovanka e le altre* (Jovanka and the Others), a story about World War II Yugoslavian partisans. De Laurentiis agreed to pay them $45,000. Two weeks later, Jarrico and Sylvia moved into a five-room apartment in the first arrondissement, at 226 Rue de Rivoli. It was situated on the Right Bank, halfway between the Place de la Concorde and the Louvre, overlooking the Jardin des Tuileries. It was rented to them at a very low price by a doctor who maintained a love nest in a room closed off from the rest of the apartment. The Jarricos began their Paris lives with liquid assets of $9,623.

Jarrico later claimed that it was not difficult being a writer in exile, given that most of his work was on English-language movies, mainly financed by American companies and intended for an international market. But his earliest letters from Paris indicate that he was experiencing great difficulties and that his life had changed dramatically. On Christmas Day, 1958, Jarrico wrote to Clinton and Virginia Jencks,

> It's really very strange, being here. In the sense that the Wilsons are here, it's home. In the sense that Mike was able to line up a good assignment for me, it's business as well as pleasure. In the sense that we'd spent six years trying to get another passport, it's a satisfying but rather anti-climactic victory. . . .
>
> But the fact is, after all, that we're aliens. It's not only the language, with which we struggle. It's the sense of not being able to affect our society. And without kidding ourselves about how much we've been able to do so at home, and without minimizing how much we still have to learn about being effective, we do miss the day to day feeling of belonging where we are, and the longer term feeling that we're changing something for the better.

They did not, he concluded, plan to stay in Europe for any great length of time, because they were "not meant to be expatriates."[1]

Jarrico never mastered French well enough to function comfortably in France or to feel integrated into French society. The Jarricos would spend most of their leisure time with English-speaking couples, the Wilsons, Dassins, Berrys, and Golds. Wilson brought him virtually all of his projects, and he and Wilson spent a huge amount of time together.

Their *Jovanka* script progressed slowly. They faced two difficulties: the novel was too unstructured and episodic to serve as the basis for an intelligible script, and they did not know enough about Yugoslavian history. The novel is set in German-occupied Yugoslavia in spring 1942. Five Slovenian women who have slept with a German army sergeant have their heads shaved by Yugoslav partisans and are then driven from the town by the Germans. They quickly learn that survival requires cooperation with one another and a kill-or-be-killed mentality. When they join forces with the partisans who shamed them, they have to learn "guerrilla discipline," which includes a ban on love affairs. But romances do blossom. That theme, Jarrico and Wilson wrote De Laurentiis, was the key to the drama: "In the most brutal circumstances, in the midst of the most violent carnage, the human animal is still capable of love, human life is still precious. Love transcends national, political and even military boundaries. But love is a function of life, not of death, of liberty, not of fascism. For women especially, the bearers of life, the fight for freedom is a fight for the right to love freely, to love whomever they choose to love, for the right to emotional as well as social equality."[2]

But when Jarrico and Wilson traveled to Rome in January 1959 to discuss their treatment with De Laurentiis, he told them that they had deviated too far from the novel and that they were too stubbornly adhering to the "American school" of filmmaking. (De Laurentiis seemed to mean that they had oversimplified the plot and smoothed over too many rough edges.) Jarrico and Wilson replied that "an exceptional motion picture" must be an entity, not a series of episodes. Back in Paris, they prepared a step outline, which pleased De Laurentiis because "it is much closer than the preceding one to the type of film 'I saw' when reading Ugo Pirro's story."[3]

Jarrico then traveled to Ljubljana, where he spent four days, and he and Wilson began to write the screenplay in February. The next month they went to Rome, where they stayed for two months, writing and conferring with De Laurentiis and the director, Martin Ritt.[4] De Laurentiis admired the script's logical construction, but he believed that the powerful antiwar elements of the novel had been lost. He wanted the script to be about "the protest of a group of girls who want to live, against an absurd war, or in any event against a war which they do not understand and to which they are extraneous. Instead of being primarily a love story, it should be a denouncement: in brief, a condemnation of that absurd Fascist and Nazi slogan used during the war: 'Hate the enemy.' A slogan which reprisals, intolerance and often desperation drove many partisan leaders to adopt."[5]

Jarrico and Wilson wrote two more drafts, but they refused to stay in Rome to make revisions while the movie was being shot. In late September, Jarrico wrote Ritt asking what changes had been made and who had made them. When Ritt replied that the character of one of the women had been changed, as had the main love relationship, Jarrico asked Ritt to send him a copy of the revised script. Ritt said that there was none and that De Laurentiis was letting his Italian writers make the script more propartisan and "a bit more left."[6]

Retitled *Five Branded Women*, the movie was released by

Paramount, with screenplay credit assigned to Ivo Perilli. The *New York Times* reviewer noted that the story "moves like molten lead under Martin Ritt's direction." The reviewer for *Variety*, however, thought that the "film's strength lies in Ritt's direction" and had only tepid praise for the script. Ritt, for his part, disowned the movie. He claimed that it was the only movie he made of which he was ashamed and that, if he had had enough money, he would have bought all the copies of it. He never listed it among his credits, and when he donated his papers to the Academy of Motion Picture Arts and Sciences' library, he included no material about it.[7]

Before Jarrico had seen it, he asked Ritt, "How is the picture politically?" Ritt, as Jarrico remembered it, "sputtered and exclaimed that he couldn't care less." That statement, Jarrico said, "convinced me he must have fucked it up good, which we already suspected." Jarrico thought the finished product was terrible. In a letter to his son, Jarrico wrote, "They ripped out our love story, our theme (the necessity for humanism as well as discipline in a revolutionary fight), our realism, and left a dull, stupid masquerade. The direction was really miserable, lacking pace, feeling, reality, wholly aside from the mutilation of our script." In a note to himself, weighing his prospects in May 1961, Jarrico wrote, "The new career which began to develop when Mike got me on 'Jovanka' pretty well fizzled out when Martie fucked the picture up."[8]

Five Branded Women is not as bad as Ritt and Jarrico thought. Jovanka clearly expresses Jarrico and Wilson's themes: She does not hate the Germans, she hates war. She regularly takes a stand against the ways in which war depersonalizes and dehumanizes combatants and citizens alike. She speaks always of the need for kindness and love. And Velko, the partisan leader, delivers the message about revolutionary discipline. The Germans are not demonized, the partisans are not glorified, and the three romances that develop are reasonably well integrated and do not slow down the action.

Meanwhile, *All Night Long*, the *Othello*-themed jazz script Jarrico had cowritten with Nel King, had run into problems. The producer, Alfred Crown, wanted a more extensive rewrite than Jarrico thought the contract called for, and Crown reported that United Artists would distribute the movie only if Lena Horne (a light-skinned black actress) played the Desdemona-like role. Jarrico and King angrily responded that such casting defeated the whole point of the screenplay, which was the issue of miscegenation. When Crown replied that United Artists did not want to handle a film about miscegenation, Jarrico thought that he and King should buy the script from Crown and look for another producer. In mid-December, he flew to London to try to interest Bob Roberts in the script.[9] Roberts liked the project, and at the end of January 1959, Jarrico began, in his words, "the fastest rewrite ever seen." He hoped that Roberts would buy it and allow Jarrico to direct it, because, as he wrote King, "I'm forty-four years old, Nel, and I'm nowhere. I'm so sick and tired of being a writer, an assistant to the director, that I could scream."[10] Roberts did agree to buy the script (for $25,000 against percentages of budget and profits), but he did not hire Jarrico to direct.

The project's chances for success deteriorated when it turned out that the director Roberts had chosen, Basil Dearden, liked neither jazz nor black people. Jarrico disapproved of the alterations Dearden and Roberts made to the script, especially their decision to cut the embrace of the black man and white woman at the end. Jarrico also thought that not enough blacks were involved in the project. After seeing a rough cut in October, he wrote King, "It isn't that good. It isn't *bad*, you understand. It just isn't good. . . . We are finding ourselves with our names on a picture (are you sure that you want your name on it?) that may turn out to say the very opposite of what we intended." To Bill Jarrico, he wrote, "I'm just going to have to become a director." When the film was released, the London critics were, on the whole, even more critical. The *Sunday Times* called it "an extremely silly story"; the *Sunday Pictorial* critic bemoaned, "Oh, that script!"; the *Daily Telegraph and Morning Post* called it "a writing failure."[11] But *All Night Long* is actually a well-constructed version of *Othello*, with well-realized characters. Unfortunately, it is lethargically directed; there is little of the heat one would expect from an all-night jazz session involving rivalries and romantic tangles. And no one dies.

Following the completion of the *Jovanka* script and the production of *All Night Long*, Jarrico felt a recurrence of his malaise. Jarrico chided himself, "Man, you've never had it so good, you're living in the most beautiful city in the world in the book-lined elegance you deserve overlooking fantastic sunsets behind the Eiffel Tower and making money. You're working on or promoting scripts with something to say." He admitted that his political effectiveness depended on what he wrote, not what he did. "You're not going to lead the revitalized left in America, or advise its leaders, or run for Congress, and you're as much in touch with what's going on there as you were when you were there and preferred taxis to subways." He did not miss "the barometric reactions of the Hollywood liberals, how warmly or how coldly are they addressing or avoiding me today," and he did not "miss the bagels or the dogshit or the Times Square crowds of New York." But he sorely missed the English language.[12]

Jarrico's attitude worsened in late 1959 when what had seemed like a grand opportunity unraveled. An Italian producer had approached him to work with the established neorealist screenwriter Sergio Amidei (*Open City* and *Paisan*) and a second-generation neorealist director, Francesco Rosi. They would adapt and film *The Gallery*, John Horne Burns's novel about the U.S. occupation of Naples. "The material is interesting, the money good, and all in all it looks like a good assignment," Jarrico wrote to John Berry. But when he and Sylvia flew to Rome at the end of November to confer with Rosi and Amidei, they discovered that Amidei was antagonistic toward the project. In his mind, the novel painted too negative a picture of Naples. Sylvia wrote in her notes, "He [Amadei] is frankly scared of making a picture about the Gallery, but he knows that the producers are going to go ahead with him or without him. Let's have no criticism of the Neopolitans, he says, and no criticism of the Americans; let's, in fact, make the most superficial picture that will still hold the audience's attention. Make it gutsy, human, stark, and don't say much. To say that he has mixed feelings toward Paul is to make a very dry understatement." Jarrico, for his part, thought that Amidei was "temperamental, arrogant, chauvinistic," a bully who always vented his fury on the weakest person in the room. During one meeting, when they disagreed over how to depict a black soldier, Amidei blew up, screamed that American writers "write shit," and stormed out of his own house. Amidei did not attend the last two conferences, and the producer and director told Jarrico not to proceed with the treatment. Rosi finally told Paul, in August 1960, that they had decided to postpone the production for at least another year, because it was "too complex" to do it that year.[13]

Sylvia Jarrico seemed more satisfied with her own work. She had met with the actress and dancer Josephine Baker to gather material for a documentary that Joris Ivens planned to film and was studying French, helping Jarrico on his writing projects, and, Jarrico noted in one of his letters, enduring "with remarkable poise the snarling I tend to hurl at her when I'm working and drinking hard." But Jarrico's patience with her waned, and he began to associate his dissatisfaction with his life and work with what he called "the binds of matrimony." In May 1961, shortly after Sylvia flew to the United States to attend their son's graduation from Reed College, the woman with whom Arnaud d'Usseau was living told Jarrico that d'Usseau was having an affair with another woman. In a letter to himself, Jarrico asked what one could learn from this sad tale. "The concept of emotional exclusivity, . . . the idea of monogamy, of anybody's monopoly on anyone else's love, is as dead as the propeller plane. Oh, it's still around, and even useful, but it's outmoded, it's been superseded, it's the product of an earlier time. . . . Fidelity, infidelity, jealousy, possessiveness—these were old-hat concepts, no longer valid, cliches, déja vu." And he told himself, "One can love more than one person, even, at one time. [Love] is a resource that grows as it is spent, expands as it is expended. Demand of it that it be exclusive and you will slowly constrict it, you will harden its arteries, and you will finally destroy it. And the one you love. And yourself."[14]

Jarrico apparently took these reflections quite seriously. When, on June 7, he met Yvette Le Floc'h, he was immediately smitten. A few months later, he described her:

> My lady is French [born in Quimper, January 25, 1925], a writer, very left, the mother of an eleven year old girl, and recently divorced. She has been living in Prague for some years, adapting Czechoslovakian plays into French, and writing screenplays for the Czech film industry. She studied to be a doctor but decided she'd rather be a writer. Meanwhile, she'd been studying Slavic languages, in which she became an expert (Russian, Bulgarian, Polish, Czech, and one or two others). She understands English almost perfectly, and reads it, but she's somewhat shy about speaking it.

> So she talks to me in French, and I talk to her in English. We don't *always* understand each other—verbally—but we're very close.[15]

Others who knew Yvette described her as "a remarkable woman," intelligent, attractive, warm, and caring, but tough—"harder-edged than Sylvia." She seemed to make Jarrico feel more sophisticated and glamorous. But she could also be "a very tense person."[16] Though Yvette was only thirty-two years old, she had a complex medical history. She had been sick with a fever for two months (1949); had been sick for three months after the birth of her daughter (1950); had spent two months in a sanatorium to recover from depression (1953); had spent another few months in a clinic to recover from pleurisy, pneumonia, and kidney stones (1956); and had suffered another three-week bout of depression (1959). She would continue to have health problems all the time Jarrico knew her.

After their first meeting, Jarrico saw Yvette a few more times in June, both in the company of others and alone. Sylvia and Bill returned to Paris on June 21. In early July, Jarrico went to London to work on *All Night Long*, and Yvette joined him there. Six weeks later, when Sylvia and Zelma Wilson left for a trip to Greece, Jarrico and Yvette spent ten days in Brittany. Jarrico later wrote Nel King, "Flipped. Gone. Hooked. Hung up." In addition to her obvious physical and emotional appeal, Yvette provided a bridge to a part of French society previously unavailable to Jarrico, though he still did not feel integrated. She also introduced him to Czechoslovakian society, in which she had spent twelve years. Jarrico recalled, "Her circle of acquaintances there was wide and interesting, and I got to know more Czech people in the relatively short time I spent there—three months in '67 and about five months in '68—probably than I ever got to know in Paris, French people in Paris."[17]

When Sylvia returned from a trip to Greece, Jarrico followed her everywhere she went. Finally, she recalled, she asked him, "'Is there something you want to tell me?' He replied, 'I'm in love with another woman.' I laughed. I thought it was just Jarrico being witty. I kissed him and said, 'what is it you really want to tell me?' He replied: 'I am in love.'" Sylvia was shocked and hurt by his revelation. Jarrico reported to Yvette a somewhat different account:

> I got home Thursday evening [August 31], about an hour and a half after Sylvia got home from Greece. I said I'd only been in England briefly, I'd spent some time in Brittany. It was not until the next morning that she asked, mildly, what I'd been doing in Brittany. We went out for coffee and croissants, and I finally answered her question. I finally told her my unspeakable secret. I loved my wife, I said, but I was in love with a woman who was not my wife.
>
> She was surprised, she was sad, but she was wonderful—warm, generous, whimsical, all of the things I had dared to hope she would be. . . . [N]o one could have accepted it as gracefully and with as much genuine friendship as she did. She was truly gallant.

Her empathy, though, had its limits: When Jarrico told her he did not have to leave her, that it was possible for him to have two women in his life, Sylvia replied that it would not work. Nor did she share Jarrico's desire that the two women become friends. She thought Jarrico was making a big mistake.[18]

Jarrico told his son that he was "deeply in love" with Yvette and that he was "very serious" about her. Bill was not surprised. He was already aware of Jarrico's feelings for Yvette. In fact, Bill had long been aware of his father's feelings for other women and thought they had become more pronounced in recent years.[19]

Jarrico continued to live with Sylvia for a few more weeks while continuing to see Yvette. On September 16, Sylvia told Jarrico that they would have to separate. She remembered saying, "You have a real need to be with Yvette. Your central drive at this moment is to develop a rich and enduring relation with her. You also have a rich and enduring relation with me, which you want to keep. But the two drives are colliding." Jarrico admitted that Yvette was central but claimed that she was not fundamental. He did not wish to replace Sylvia with her.[20]

Jarrico moved first into a friend's apartment and then into a hotel. Finally, in early October, Jarrico and Yvette moved in together. But Jarrico continued to see Sylvia regularly, and both tried to explain their relationship to their son. Jarrico told Bill that Sylvia "continues to demonstrate enormous resiliency and resources, though she cries a little, in a smiling way, from time to time." Sylvia reported that Jarrico "gets a little irritable or depressed if I'm less than saintly in my attitude toward [Yvette], but mostly we have fun together, which is ridiculous."[21]

Jarrico went to great lengths to explain his feelings for Yvette to those who had known only Paul and Sylvia. To Nel King, he wrote, "It's a real problem, leaving a wife you love for a woman you love, and not without pain, terrible pain, at times. But I'm genuinely in love with this lady, insofar as I understand the concept at all, and there is a great happiness in being with her." To Ed Kraus, Jarrico wrote, "I wanted to live with someone else—I fell in love with someone else. . . . I feel guilty about having left Sylvia, of course. She had done me no injury, and I had no justification for leaving her, in that sense. The guilt I feel is, however, a price that I'm prepared to pay."[22]

Jarrico was also taken with the idea of acting as a father to a young girl. Yvette's daughter Armelle remembered him as

> an exceedingly tender and generous father to me. We didn't have a common language for several years, but I learned English quicker than he learned French. Fluency in foreign languages was never his forte. Our relationship was an arduous one for a long time, because I wasn't ready to accept him as a substitute for my father. Paul laughed more and moved more than others I had known, and he was quite the opposite of my biological father. Despite my resistance, [Jarrico's] commitment to me was total, and true to his style in other areas of his life, he was demonstrative. Once we devised a common tongue, we got along quite well. He taught me humor, the pleasures of story telling, and tried to instill me with his optimism.[23]

Looking back, Sylvia Jarrico thought her husband "felt a great need to leave me. He wanted to be free from the commitments he had made with and to me." She recognized that he was in the grip of a strong desire to make significant changes in his life, which included a declaration of his independence not only from her but also from the Wilsons. "Mike's success was enormous," Sylvia continued; "we spent a great deal of time with the Wilsons, and Mike regularly consulted with Paul about those projects." Zelma Wilson remembered that she and Mike took the news of the Jarricos' split very hard.[24]

Jarrico now had to earn money to support both his families. Sylvia, who was seeing the actor William Marshall, wrote to Ed and

Dot Kraus, asking, in confidence, for a loan: "I've never seen Paul so deeply disturbed in all the time I've loved him as he is right now, by the temporary standstill in his professional life." It probably did not help his mood that, as Sylvia noted, "the Wilsons are going through an idyllic period right now. Mike can still afford to refuse jobs on stories he doesn't like and indulge his preference for writing stories he does like on a speculative basis." A few months later, she finally told the Krauses about the separation. "His scripts are here, his correspondence is here, and I'm here, so it's still his home in a sense. . . . [But he] lives not far away, with a handsome and accomplished French woman whom he loves, and who loves him. This is a somewhat puzzling situation, but Paul and I would be the last to say that life is anything less than fascinating."[25]

Jarrico had to fly to New York on December 13, 1961, for the long-delayed deposition in the IPC case. Yvette had planned on accompanying him there, but they did not have the money for her airfare. She ended up going to Prague for medical treatment. On the eve of his departure, he wrote her,

> I have a cold, I drink too much wine, I have a sense of estrangement from my friends, from society in general, connected with my feelings of guilt about Sylvia, and with the fact that tomorrow and for at least two weeks afterward I'll be seeing many close friends who will be critical of me, and whose good opinion I want. I also have my usual worries about money, about my career, intensified somewhat by my imminent trip to New York. I write imaginary letters and conduct imaginary interviews with potential employers and financiers, and I don't like my role, my imaginary role. Or even my real role.[26]

A week later, he wrote to Sylvia that their New York friends' attitudes regarding the separation had not been as bad for him as he feared, but that the disapproval was widespread. "I've disarmed them a little bit," he wrote, "by not trying to defend myself. 'Everybody is on Sylvia's side,' I sigh, 'including me.'" In addition, Sylvia, who wanted to lighten Jarrico's burden, had written what he called a "charming note" to their friends: "The bearer, Paul Jarrico, having been an encouraging, tender, and amusing husband to me, courtesies to him will, as heretofore, be courtesies to me."[27]

The deposition took twenty-two days, and the trip did little for Jarrico's professional prospects. In a letter he wrote to Arnaud d'Usseau, he remarked, "I'm beginning to realize . . . that my optimism is constitutional rather than rational." He returned to Paris on January 27, 1962, and four days later drove to Prague, where he remained until March 2. The political atmosphere in Prague did not appeal to him, however, and he had begun to be irritated with Yvette's lack of organization and efficiency. His agenda books for 1962 record at least one quarrel or fight per month, plus several crises. When he returned to Paris, he saw Sylvia regularly. After he had found a new Paris apartment for himself and Yvette (and before she returned), he wrote in a note to himself, "Ah, Paul, you have become a drunkard again. Presumably because of your moral conflict about Sylvia."[28]

Yvette joined Jarrico at their new apartment on March 18. They spent June and July on the French Riviera while Jarrico assisted Sidney Buchman on an adaptation of Romain Gary's memoir, *Promise at Dawn*. In early August, they moved to London, where Jarrico thought he would have a better chance of getting writing jobs and, perhaps, establishing himself as an independent producer.

His professional prospects did not immediately improve, but in October producer Albert (Cubby) Broccoli offered Jarrico a "fast rewrite" of a Bob Hope picture, *Call Me Bwana*. It had been in production for two weeks, six writers had come and gone, hundreds of jokes had been written about a bumbling explorer and a CIA agent searching for a U.S. space capsule in Africa, but no filmable story had emerged. Jarrico read the script; conferred with the producers, the director, and Hope; and, he commented wryly, "said profound things like 'what this script needs is some logic.' They looked at me like I was a genius." Broccoli offered to pay Jarrico $2,500 for four weeks' work, but there was no talk of a screen credit. He wrote his agent, George Marton, "It's like the old days in Hollywood—total confusion. I'm happy, I'm prosperous."[29]

But no other jobs developed from this one, and Jarrico's personal life remained troubled. He told Yvette that he felt something was wrong between them:

> It sometimes seems to me that it is just when you need me most that I'm in love with you least—and vice versa. I'm in bad shape, darling, worse than you in many ways, though my nature is optimistic and energetic, though my health is quite good, though I seem to have many more resources than you. I cannot go on always being the one who helps, the one who gives, the one who takes responsibility, the one who supports. I know objectively that when you become demanding, unreasonable, it's because of your insecurity. But subjectively I find myself closer and closer to the end of my rope, as the saying goes.

In her reply, Yvette admitted that Jarrico was very generous. But, she added, he was also impatient and critical. She thought he was punishing her for the guilt he still felt toward Sylvia and Bill. And she put her finger on what she thought was probably the main problem for Jarrico: he wanted to be close with all three of them, but no one of the three could fulfill him.[30]

Not surprisingly, Jarrico was again drinking too much. In a summary of his "wagon history," he noted that he was completely dry in 1960, drank only beer and wine in 1961, resumed drinking whiskey in the summer of 1962, and drank two-thirds of the days of 1963. On May 13, he wrote, "Well, Paul, here you are, 48 years old, still making an up & down living as a screen writer, married to one woman, living with another, father of a 23 yr. old boy & responsible for a 12 yr. old girl. Revisionist but still concerned. Liked by many & liking many. Only problem is that you still lv [love] your wife, and you're not sure if you still lv your mistress. Headed south & once again you have to decide whether it's the beginning of the end, or not."[31]

At the end of the year, to avoid a tax penalty, Jarrico and Yvette decided to move to Cannes. Personally and professionally, 1964 marked the beginning of Jarrico's leanest years. He remained torn between Sylvia and Yvette. He was concerned about Bill, who was unemployed and seemed to lack plans for the future. Jarrico was drinking constantly and gaining weight. And, in a fit of righteous anger, he permanently alienated one of his oldest and closest friends, Adrian Scott.

Scott, who had been employed as a producer for MGM British Studios, had hired Jarrico in May 1963 to adapt Agatha Christie's

ABC Murders. Jarrico would be paid $17,500, and the credit would go to "Peter Achilles." Jarrico began writing on May 1, and he submitted a first draft screenplay on July 21. MGM then offered him a bigger assignment, to adapt Jack London's *Call of the Wild*, for which he would be paid $50,000. But just after Jarrico and Yvette arrived in Cannes, Jarrico was informed that MGM's lawyers had discovered a copyright problem with *Call of the Wild*. He was asked to undertake instead another Agatha Christie mystery, *They Do It with Mirrors*, for $15,000. Jarrico threatened to sue, and he wrote Marton, "I expect you to be very tough on this issue, even with my friend Adrian Scott, who is in the middle, but who has to be treated, for purposes of this fight, as part of management." He copied that letter to Scott and added, "I swear to you that I love you and that I don't blame you for *any* of this—on the contrary, I know how hard you've tried to help me. But I simply have no alternative to fighting this. If I have to settle for $5,000 instead of $15,000 for a treatment, I'm up shit creek, having already rented an apartment and made other commitments based on the expectation of the 15." But MGM raised the price a little, to $20,000, and Adrian said he would be fired if Jarrico did not accept it. So, Jarrico wrote to John Berry, "I settled for the lesser deal on the Christie."[32]

While Jarrico was working on the treatment for the second Christie book, he received from Scott a sixteen-page, single-spaced critique of his adaptation of *ABC Murders*. An angry Jarrico wrote in his agenda book, "Adrian's criticism of ABC impossible." He asked Michael Wilson to read the script and Scott's comments. Reluctantly, Wilson read the material. His criticisms were substantive enough—he said the script lacked logic and legitimacy as a detective story—to convince Jarrico that it needed more work than he thought it did. Following his discussions with Wilson, Jarrico had a long, strained telephone conversation with Scott. In his notes of that conversation, Jarrico summarized what he had told Scott: "We are, nevertheless, still in trouble, as between you and me, because the more I study your notes the more convinced I am that our values are so different on this project that the chances of our coming to an agreement on it are very slim. . . . [T]he man who could make the proposals you made to fix this script is not a man who is likely to be pleased with the changes I would be likely to make."[33]

Jarrico had convinced himself that Scott was acting too much like a boss, like the studio producers Jarrico so disliked. Scott believed that Jarrico had overreacted; although he (Scott) had asked for a substantial revision, he had not demanded that the revision be done in a specific manner. They finally agreed that Jarrico would continue to work on *They Do It with Mirrors* and that Scott would discuss the *ABC Murders* script with Zero Mostel, who was to play the lead. (Jarrico had sent Mostel a copy of the script.) Jarrico admitted to Wilson that he felt terrible on two accounts: because "this is what always happens, this is how I've spent my entire professional life," watching producers screw up scripts, and because this particular producer was a good friend. "I'm sure," Jarrico continued, that Scott "thinks I'm just being subjective and stubborn, my feelings have been hurt because my script has not been sufficiently appreciated, I'm revenging myself by insulting him in turn, deriding his proposals, writers have large, sensitive egos, and blacklisted writers have been so frustrated that they are especially quick to resent criticism. Well, there are some minor elements of truth in that."[34]

Scott cabled Jarrico at the end of December, "Zero very unhappy with script, no possibility of seeing eye to eye with Achilles." On January 14, Lawrence Bachmann, Scott's boss, told Jarrico that the *They Do It with Mirrors* treatment was "not right" and that Jarrico would not be assigned the screenplay. Jarrico wrote Daniel Mainwaring, "I've been trying to rise above it, the friendship is more important than the job, blood is thicker than ketchup, and so on, but the scar tissue hasn't quite formed yet. Sad, really is, but nobody ever said the class struggle was a picnic."[35]

When several months passed without a word from Scott, Jarrico wrote a "Dear Paul" letter from Scott's perspective and sent it to him:

> As far as I'm concerned, I got you the jobs in the first place, I did everything I could to help you. . . . You're simply an ungrateful bastard. . . . You claim to be a professional about criticism. Your reactions to my criticisms were childish, stubborn, and extremely insulting. That's what I'm paid for: to express my best judgment. If you disagree, that's your privilege, but why revile my proposals as "horseshit"? . . . You keep repeating that our friendship is more important than the script, but you keep attacking the friendship, to

> the extent of complaining to mutual friends that I act like a boss, as though I'm to blame for the "position of the writer." . . . The script may not be more important than our friendship, but my health, my peace of mind, must be. I'm not going to allow you to tear me apart inside, it will kill me. You're a good writer, despite your egotism. But you lack the most important gift of a writer—the ability to put himself in another's place.

But in Scott's mind, the friendship had ended. He believed that he had acted professionally as a producer but that Jarrico had not responded professionally as a writer. Scott also did not like Jarrico's involving Wilson. He thought Jarrico had failed him, both as a writer and as a friend. Joan Scott, Adrian's widow, said that though Scott was slow to anger, once he became angry, he was an icicle.[36]

While this break was occurring, Jarrico and Yvette realized that the move to Cannes had been a mistake. They felt isolated, but they could not decide if they should go back to London or Paris or try New York instead. Their interpersonal conflicts intensified. He complained about her proneness to depression and hysteria; she complained of his impatience and hostility. He wrote Bill, "I plod along on [the] Genghis [Khan script], I'm on the wagon, then off, then on, I get along well with Yvette and Minou [their name for Armelle], then badly, then well, I worry about money, and Syl, and you—I would not say it was one of my better periods."[37]

Finally, Jarrico and Yvette decided that she and Minou would spend the summer in Prague, where Yvette could get some medical treatment and perhaps secure some writing assignments, and Jarrico would stay at a friend's apartment in Paris and look for work from there. If they could afford it, that fall they would move to New York, where George Willner and Lou Solomon thought Jarrico could probably scrounge enough television work to live.[38] Meanwhile, Jarrico was borrowing from friends and family to stay afloat.

Just before Yvette departed for Prague, she applied for her visa to the United States. Though American officials grilled her about her political past, she was granted a temporary visa. Jarrico and Yvette arrived in New York on September 3 for the IPC trial and sublet an apartment.[39] When the trial was over, they moved to another apartment in Manhattan. Yvette discovered that she liked New York more than she expected; Jarrico, however, was drinking heavily and gaining weight steadily. When Sylvia asked him for a divorce, he feared that she was, in effect, ending their friendship. Jarrico admitted to her that he could not let go of her; he wanted Yvette and Sylvia both. Their marriage, he wrote, was only one aspect of their relationship—their friendship had preceded their marriage and could survive it. He said that he missed her and felt both a sense of responsibility for her and "piercing guilt" for having left her.[40]

One bright spot for Jarrico during this period came via Abe Polonsky, who had developed *Seaway*, a dramatic series for Canadian television. He secured writing assignments for Jarrico and Ian Hunter and a directing assignment for John Berry. Jarrico wrote four originals and did one rewrite for the program, which paid $5,000 per completed script. He liked writing those scripts, he told a reporter, because it gave him the opportunity to turn out something original.[41]

But the cold war once again complicated Jarrico's existence. Yvette's visa expired in June 1965. When she applied for a one-month extension, she was told she would have to submit to an interrogation by FBI agents. When asked if she had been a Communist, she said no but that she had worked for *Cultura*, a magazine published by the Communist government of Czechoslovakia. Several days later, she was told that her visa would not be extended and that she must leave the country by June 21. She did so. When she applied for a new visa in August, her application was denied because, she was told, the McCarran Act forbade entrance to the United States to foreigners who had advocated Communist ideas and had Communist relations.[42]

Neither Jarrico nor his lawyers could find a means to reverse or overcome the decision. When his legal efforts came up empty, Jarrico decided to move back to Europe. He wrote to friends, "Not a fate worse than death, but I was beginning to feel that the United States was ready for me." Jarrico was thus forced back to the meager pickings of the European market for English-speaking writers. For the next eleven years, he would be constantly changing his address, traveling to work on or promote various jobs. At one point, he wrote, "I have been in so many cities, so many countries, these past months that I'm dizzy."[43] He spent hours duplicating and mailing scripts, treatments, and prospectuses; making telephone calls and sending telegrams; and, more than anything else, receiving rejection after rejection. His drinking increased, his weight soared, his debts deepened, and his temper frayed.

Jarrico reunited with Yvette in Geneva in early September 1965. In February 1966, he returned to the United States to accompany Sylvia to El Paso–Juarez to obtain their divorce. He returned to New York, sublet the apartment, sold some of the furniture, and went to Toronto to finish a *Seaway* script. Afterward, he flew to Puerto Rico to visit Bill, and then to Prague, where he installed Yvette in a sanatorium. She would spend three months there.

Jarrico returned to Paris and then spent seven weeks in Madrid rewriting *Beyond the Mountains* for Landau-Unger Productions. The original script was written by Alexander Ramati, who had written the novel and was directing the film, which had a glittering international cast (Maximilian Schell, Irene Pappas, and Raf Vallone). Jarrico was paid $12,500 in four installments and $100 a week in expenses, but he did not receive a screen credit. Released as *The Desperate Ones*, it did not receive good reviews. The *Variety* reviewer noted its "uninspired direction, soporific editing, and faulty scripting."[44]

From Madrid, Jarrico went to Zurich to rewrite some scenes for an English-language version of a Lazar Wechsler film about a gynecological clinic (*Der Arzt Stellt Fest/The Doctor Says*). He dramatized various dilemmas faced by women with unwanted pregnancies (and their doctors) in a country with strict abortion laws. Wechsler accepted Jarrico's argument that birth control was the best answer to women's demands for abortion, and Jarrico had the doctor in the story give specific advice to women about birth control pills and intrauterine devices. Jarrico also inserted a new moral theme: no child should come into the world unwanted, unloved, and without parents to care for him or her. Wechsler permitted Jarrico to direct the scenes he had added. "I was," Jarrico wrote Sylvia, "hardly nervous at all."[45] Jarrico was paid $5,000 for the script (and nothing for his directing), and he again did not receive a screen credit.

Jarrico spent July in London, where he and Yvette had decided to live. She joined him there in mid-August, and they married on October 3. It was, he wrote years later, a marriage that "lasted 15 largely unhappy years."[46] After the wedding, Jarrico's professional and personal fortunes steadily spiraled downward, and he seemed powerless to extricate himself from the vortex. He and Yvette moved constantly: to Prague, to London, to Nice, to Prague, to London, to Geneva, to London, to Paris. They occasionally spent months apart because of her health or his work. The one bright spot was his first screen credit since 1950. He undertook an extensive rewrite of a script titled *The Day the Hot Line Got Hot*, for which he was paid $1,250 a week for six weeks and another $5,000 when filming began. The resulting spoof of spies and spying is sillier than it is clever.[47]

Jarrico and Yvette attempted on several occasions to collaborate on movie scripts, but none of these efforts were produced. Their best work, *Big Brother*, was an innovative representation of Czech Communist leader Alexander Dubček, the Prague Spring of 1968, and the Warsaw Bloc invasion of Czechoslovakia. To a prospective producer, Jarrico wrote, "As you know this is a subject very close to our hearts. We believe, in fact, that the attempt to humanize the inhuman system of Eastern Europe which calls itself 'socialist' may be the most significant development of our troubled time. And though it has been set back for the present, it *must* reassert itself, for it is the only alternative to both the American way of death and the Soviet way of death. It is the road to life, in short." Jarrico wrote another producer that the movie would be "a suspense drama, like Z. . . . The inside story of the conspiracy to stop the Prague Spring."[48] Shortly thereafter, Jarrico and Yvette made a deal with Thomas R. Bransten (Telemont S.A., Geneva) to write the Dubček script. Bransten agreed to pay them $5,000 immediately and $5,000 on completion of the first draft and to allot them two-thirds of the profits.

Jarrico and Yvette had high hopes for the script. They believed that they were in the process of creating a new genre, what they called "a political gangster comedy drama with music." They tried to write the script in a nonrealistic, Brechtian style, interweaving the activities and discussions of a group of student demonstrators, Czech Communist Party meetings, and meetings between Soviet and Czech leaders. The script opens with a student demonstration brutally suppressed by the police in October 1967. A student narrator, who is also a folk singer, briefly recounts the history of his country. The action is intercut with parodies of Soviet and Czech songs that satirize communism, party lines, and faction names. One of the students states, "We are *for* socialism! But why should freedom and democracy be thought of as bourgeois values? *Genuine* socialism *includes* democracy! And that's what we want!" Jarrico and Yvette proposed using animated cartoons for satirical purposes. One parodied "Casey Jones":

> *Stalin's bones, grinding at the throttle,*
> *Stalin's bones, back and doing fine,*
> *Stalin's bones, Brezhnev as his fireman,*
> *The resurrected driver of the Party line.*

When the invasion occurs and the demonstrations erupt, a series of choruses satirizes the conceits of socialist brotherhood. The script ends with a dialogue between a Soviet soldier and two of the students. When the soldier understands the motives for the invasion, he kills himself.

Jarrico asked a number of big-name directors (John Boorman, Janos Kadar, Lindsay Anderson, Jules Dassin, Joseph Losey, and Milos Forman) to commit to the project, but none would. Several of the producers who read it thought that the Brechtian effects did not work, that they reduced rather than heightened the dramatic possibilities, complicated the narrative, and falsified the story. Dore Schary wrote, "I simply don't believe that it's a commercial movie." When Jarrico queried a literary agent in London about its potential as a stage play, he was told, "It needs a colossal amount of work to condense it and . . . , above all, the characters need to be written into life. At the moment, it does seem to me that they are more puppets than people."[49]

While the *Big Brother* script was making the rounds of directors and financiers, Jarrico and Yvette's relationship deteriorated further. In June 1971, he told her that he no longer wished to be married to her, and in September they agreed to separate. He wrote Lou Solomon that he was thinking of returning to the United States, and he asked Solomon for a job writing a program for *The Great American Dream Machine*, a television series Solomon was producing. Jarrico wrote another friend, "I feel, more and more, that my place is [in the United States]. I'm a very political animal, as you know; I think the old left has something to offer the new left, difficult though some of my old comrades may find it to make themselves heard; I think I'm more in tune with what's happening (and where and how) than most of my generation; and I want to come home." He planned to go with Yvette if possible, without her if necessary.[50]

Jarrico stayed in Europe for the next four years but made regular trips to the United States. He contracted to write a variety of scripts, none of which were made into movies. In February 1972, he wrote to Sylvia, "I'm in debt to almost everybody I love, and even a few people I don't, so it's hard to know where to turn." A few months later, he wrote, "I used to say anything was easier than writing; producing for sure. But after you've been stalled by John Boorman, Lindsay Anderson and a couple of others, while you're jockeying to keep Jean-Louis Trintignant and Peter Ustinov lined up at the starting-gate [for *Big Brother*], writing's a cinch." Other than that, he was "in good shape. Fat, drunk, crippled by nicotine, overcommitted emotionally but just fine."[51]

In July 1974, Oliver Unger approached Jarrico to revise a script about the August 1914 assassination of Archduke Franz-Ferdinand at Sarajevo. Unger was overseeing a Czechoslovakian-Yugoslavian coproduction, but the project was saddled with a Chinese-English script that Unger thought needed substantial rewriting. He agreed to pay Jarrico $1,000 a week for ten weeks and another $15,000 when the movie began shooting. (Jarrico was also entitled to a share of the profits, which he would sell for $10,000 in January 1976.) Jarrico agreed to go to Zagreb to meet with the director, Veljko Bulajiĉ, who was married to the niece of the wife of Yugoslavian leader Josip Tito and was Tito's favorite director. Bulajiĉ was, Jarrico said, "otherwise unqualified to handle this film."[52]

Unger wanted Jarrico simply to craft an entertaining film based on a historical event. Jarrico, however, decided to prepare a truthful and dramatic account of the event and use it to examine what he called "the psychology of idealistic terrorism," as well as the positive and negative sides of nationalism and "the relation between social revolution and national liberation." Jarrico met with Unger, Bulajiĉ, and the other producers at the end of August, and they approved Jarrico's thematic points. Jarrico completed his first draft on October 5 and sent it to Yugoslavia. After reading it, the Yugoslavian producer asked Jarrico to come to Zagreb for "further serious discussion" with the director. When Jarrico arrived on December 18, he was handed a very different script, Bulajič's revision. When Bulajič insisted that any further revisions be incorporated into this revised script, Jarrico refused and returned to Paris.[53]

The producers backed Jarrico, and he completed the shooting script in February. But just before shooting began, Bulajič once again insisted that the script be altered, to incorporate a "Leninist point of view." Jarrico recounted the ensuing argument:

> "But where is the *Leninist* point of view in the script you had?" (Which [the Yugoslav comrades] were defending.) "Where do you say that political assassination, individual terror, is *not* the way to advance the socialist revolution?" They fell back in (individual) terror before the peculiar onslaught of this Hollywood Red. My capitalist boss [Unger], who obviously couldn't have cared less about Lenin, backed me up, and I finally won. "You shoot the script as Paul wrote it or I will pull out my million bucks," he said. They signed a treaty to that effect, and presumably are living up to it. I was supposed to hold the hand of the prick who's directing it (or, as I like to say, the prick of the hand who's directing it), during the production; but the Czechs have refused to let me into Czechoslovakia. The script, yes; me, no. Which makes me feel very proud. To be blacklisted not only in the West but the East.[54]

Bulajič finally shot the script as written. When Jarrico saw the rough cut in August, he thought it could be a good film if it were cut by about thirty minutes, and he sent a detailed list of those cuts to Unger. But he was disappointed with the edited version he saw in December. He wrote Unger, "We're in trouble on this picture." He had hoped that his editing suggestions would overcome Bulajič's "wooden direction," but the editing had not been "judicious," the music had not been used properly, and the dubbing was uneven. In Jarrico's opinion, the film, as it now stood, could not be a success, "either critically or commercially," unless it were recut.[55] The Yugoslavs demurred, but they did agree to give Jarrico sole screenplay credit. *Atentat u Sarajevu/The Day That Shook the World*, featuring Christopher Plummer and Maximilian Schell, received tepid reviews but was nominated by the Academy for best foreign picture of 1976. It did not win, however, and perhaps deservedly so, for it lacks a first-rate script and direction. The story needed much more background about the nationalist assassins and much less footage on the royal couple. Jarrico's message about nationalist revolutionaries was reduced to one exchange: "Is individual violence the way to advance the revolutionary movement?" "The assassination will be a signal for revolution."

In June 1975, Jarrico left Paris to spend three months in Los Angeles, where he would lay the groundwork for his permanent return to the United States.

10

Political Battles, 1958–75

> I consider myself as an active element in a large social movement.
>
> —*Paul Jarrico, circa 1977*

As an exile, Jarrico could not become involved in French politics without risking the loss of his residency permit.[1] But he did not cease to be political. He remained involved in the organized fight against the blacklist and the IPC litigation. In addition, he kept himself well informed about, and occasionally participated in, a variety of international and American issues, including those pertaining to the Soviet Union and world communism. And he continued to reassess his ideological outlook.

The Blacklist

Though Jarrico's move to Europe separated him from the daily struggles against the blacklist, he remained in close touch with those who were leading the fight. Toward the end of 1958, a major breakthrough seemed possible when rumors began circulating that Nathan E. Douglas, cowriter (with Hal Smith) of the hugely popular and critically successful *The Defiant Ones*, was a pseudonym for the blacklisted writer Nedrick Young. Realizing that the screenplay might be nominated for an Academy Award and wanting to avoid the rumors that swirled around *The Brave One* and *The Bridge on the River Kwai*, the Academy board of governors rescinded its bylaw prohibiting blacklisted people from winning Academy Awards. In March 1959, "Douglas" and Smith won the Academy Award for best original screenplay. They came forward to accept their Oscars but did not make any comments about the blacklist. Dalton Trumbo, however, used the occasion to reveal that he was the Robert Rich who had won the 1956 award for best original story (for *The Brave One*), and two local newscasters, Bill Stout (CBS) and Lou Irwin (ABC), ran long stories on the blacklist.[2]

A pessimistic Arnaud d'Usseau kept Jarrico apprised of the situation in Hollywood. He doubted that "there will be such a thing as a general amnesty. . . . Whoever gets jobs will have to make a fight individually. For those who appeared before committees it is still tough." Tiba Willner told Jarrico that her husband, George, had failed in his effort to get back into the agency business. "Everyone was sweet and full of smiles but no business. It was made amply clear to him [George] that if he cleared himself, everything would be open to him." George Willner had told Ring Lardner Jr. that "the only real sign of activity [in Hollywood] was the seasonal flow of old Jarrico scripts out of Bekin's warehouse." D'Usseau reported to Jarrico in May that the major studios "are still demanding a clearance from the Un-American Committee, the independents are not so particular but jobs are scarce and the money is wretched." But d'Usseau reported that he had found an agent who was currently submitting his name to the studios, just like in the old days. One month later, however, d'Usseau reported that the American Legion, George Murphy, and Adolphe Menjou were all leveling blasts at the Academy and that some ground had been lost in the fight against the blacklist. He inquired about the work situation in Europe, and Jarrico wrote back that, although he had had some good luck recently,

> what it boils down to is that Mike and Mike alone among our writing friends here is in demand, and he's in enormous demand. . . . I was able to get work because Mike was willing to collaborate with me, and was in a position to demand that they hire me too if they wanted him. . . . But without this kind of direct lift from Mike, I don't know what I should have done, and I don't think he'd be willing to do it for anyone else. Nor am I flying high enough as yet to give you a similar boost.

Jarrico mentioned a number of producers that d'Usseau might want to contact, but, he added, d'Usseau would have to bring a property to them, because they would not be likely to hire him to write one they already owned.[3]

As d'Usseau had noted, the American Legion had not ceased its effort to maintain the blacklist.[4] The indefatigable Myron C. Fagan issued another incendiary publication: "Urgent Warning to All Americans: The Reds Are Back in Hollywood!!!"[5] Nevertheless, Otto Preminger announced on January 19, 1960, that he had hired Dalton Trumbo to script *Exodus*, and that Trumbo "naturally will get the credit on the screen that he amply deserves." The article about the *Exodus* credit also noted that Trumbo had written *Roman Holiday* and was working on *Spartacus*.[6] One month later, Stanley Kramer termed the American Legion's attempt to dictate employment conditions in the industry "un-American," and he stated that he would hire any writer he pleased.[7]

But neither act broke the blacklist. Indeed, the blacklist was not a stone tablet that could be hurled to the ground and shattered, as Moses did with the decalogue. It was a conspiracy not to hire that had become a familiar protective device for most studio executives. The day after Preminger made his statement about hiring Trumbo, it was reported that "important executives at major studios" said they intended to continue their policy of not hiring writers who refused to cooperate with congressional investigating committees.[8]

From that point forward, the blacklist became increasingly arbitrary. Paramount Pictures purchased for distribution in the United States a movie (*Blind Date*) written by Ben Barzman and Millard Lampell and directed by Joseph Losey, none of whom had used pseudonyms. Retitled *Chance Meeting*, it came under attack by the American Legion, and Paramount executives decided to cancel the publicity campaign it had planned for it and open it instead as the second feature of a double bill. Though pressure from the American Legion led Frank Sinatra to renege on the agreement he had made with Albert Maltz to write the script for *The Execution of Private Slovik*, similar pressure did not discourage Otto Preminger from adhering to his contract with Ring Lardner Jr. to adapt Patrick Dennis's *Genius*. When 20th Century-Fox made a deal with Sidney Buchman to produce *Genius* in England, he wrote

Jarrico, "All is forgiven. The blacklist is thoroughly smashed." But Adrian Scott observed a few months later, "Many thought that after Trumbo's break through that there would be many more. Not so. . . . Trumbo is secure now, mining a narrow vein but of pure gold." And the *New York Times* reported in September that producers were asking those blacklisted writers who were under consideration for assignments to write letters saying that they were not now members of the Communist Party.[9]

The opportunity to write such a letter came Jarrico's way in February 1961, when Buchman invited Jarrico to come to London to collaborate with him on a rewrite of the script for *Cleopatra*. (Shooting was scheduled to begin in March, and the new director, Joseph Mankiewicz, had deemed the script unacceptable.) Buchman offered Jarrico $25,000 for eight weeks' work. When Jarrico arrived in London, he met with Spyros Skouras, the head of 20th Century-Fox. Skouras offered to use Jarrico on another project and to clear him if Jarrico wrote a letter stating he was no longer a Communist. Two days later, Skouras changed his mind about Jarrico's salary. He now said that the studio would use him only on a week-to-week basis. Inexplicably, in direct opposition to his best interests, Jarrico refused to accept those terms and returned to Paris. One year later, he wrote Ben Margolis, "I now think that I made a mistake, that I should have signed the letter. . . . [And] I do mean to surrender on this issue, the next chance I get."[10]

That opportunity arose, in a different manner and in a different venue, nearly three years later, when the IPC suit came to trial. As noted earlier, in spring 1956, prior to filing the complaint, Ben Margolis had advised Jarrico and Herbert Biberman to resign as officers of the IPC corporations. Margolis hoped that this would shield them from questions about their political pasts. But following a series of motion hearings in 1961, Judge Sidney Sugarman declared that Biberman and Jarrico were managing agents within the meaning of the Federal Rules of Civil Procedure and thus subject to being deposed. Biberman, the first to be deposed, refused to answer questions about his political beliefs and activities, and Judge Sugarman ruled that those questions were irrelevant.[11]

When it was Jarrico's turn, Margolis advised him not to answer any questions concerning his political beliefs or affiliations because "we have been engaged for many years in a battle to protect the rights to refuse to answer political questions. This case is part of that fight. You and others are being asked to surrender the very right you are fighting for as a condition of protecting it. This I think should not be done." But Edward Labaton, one of the New York attorneys, wrote to Margolis, "Up to now the failure to answer these questions has cast a cloud upon this lawsuit that has obscured all the real issues and has delayed the trial for at least four years. Refusal to answer these questions has not only not helped us but it has immeasurably helped the defendants for it has enabled them to transform this action into a Smith Act prosecution." Labaton, however, failed to acknowledge what was a major sticking point for both Jarrico and Margolis: once Jarrico testified about his political beliefs and associations, he waived his Fifth Amendment privilege with respect to the political beliefs and affiliations of other people. In a draft of his affidavit, Jarrico indicated he would not answer any questions about his political beliefs or associations. But when he arrived in New York City in December 1961, Jarrico wrote Sylvia that he had decided to answer no to the "are you now [a Communist] question" and to say that he had not been a Communist for more than three years. He would refuse to answer any further questions in that area.[12]

The defendants' attorneys, however, had decided to change their strategy. Instead of focusing on political questions to get the case dismissed, they focused on *Salt of the Earth* (its production, distribution, and so forth) to demonstrate that the movie would have failed no matter what the defendants did or did not do. Only after three weeks on that topic did the defendants' attorneys switch to direct political questions. When asked if he was a member of the Communist Party, Jarrico replied no. When asked if he had ever been a member, he refused to answer. When asked when he severed his relation with the party, he refused to answer specifically. But, he said, "I will tell you that I have not been a member of the Communist Party since leaving the United States for France, which was on October 1, 1958, and was not for some time before that." He then refused to answer a long series of questions about the party and people who may have been members. He answered questions about people who had provided loans to IPC, but he declined to answer questions about their political beliefs and associations.[13]

Three years later, in August 1964, shortly before he left Europe for the IPC trial, Jarrico wrote to Ben Margolis and Herbert Biberman, expressing his fear that the trial would set him back "five more years economically," because "producers have told me to my face that I was more blacklisted than other guys because I was more litigious, more militant, had more publicity (mostly because I sued Hughes), etc. And I don't see how we can sue the movie industry about SALT without getting some people in the industry sore at us. I don't have to add, but I will, that I'd consider it my duty to tell the truth about what the producers did to us—and that I'd testify—even if I knew it was the end of all further work possibilities for me, even under the table." Their best approach, he continued, would be to pretend the blacklist was over, that the conspirators were no longer in control, and that the black market was a necessary evil.[14]

Jarrico also thought that he and Biberman "should answer the political questions. I think we should say we were Communists. I think we should answer every question except questions about others." They should do this, he continued, not simply for tactical legal reasons but for "profound political reasons," to reverse what Jarrico now believed to have been the party's fundamental political error—its insistence on secrecy. He exclaimed,

> How illusory that secrecy was! And how unnecessary! What nonsensical charges of conspiracy it opened to us! I know all the arguments about the right of a group to be secret, and I know the necessity as well, under certain circumstances. . . . But what did we ever accomplish *in Hollywood* with our childish pretense that we were underground? Nothing that was done, positively, would not have been done better if the Party had been open. It would have been smaller, I grant you. And especially would it have been smaller in the number of shits within it.

Jarrico also now believed that the Hollywood Ten should have told the press (but not the House Committee on Un-American Activities) in October 1947 that they were Communists. If he were now asked the party membership question, Jarrico wrote, he would respond,

> No, I'm not a member of the Communist Party. But I'm still profoundly sympathetic to the communist movement—I think it has to be changed in many ways—I'm a "revisionist" and would be glad to discuss what that means if it's germane. I'm for the left-socialist movement in the U.S., one that is independent of both Russia and China as far as policy goes. I'm for Cuba. I'm against the American policy in Vietnam. I'm for the Negro revolution, etc. I'm for peaceful co-existence, etc. etc. I never committed any crime against my own country, whatever stupidities I may have been guilty of—and not one of your filthy informers would dare to testify otherwise.[15]

Jarrico and Yvette arrived in New York on September 3, 1964. The trial began the following day and lasted until November 12. The jury found for the defendants because, the jury members later said, the plaintiffs had provided no credible evidence to support the conspiracy charges. Jarrico told reporters, "We have just finished fighting."[16] The following February, Simon Lazarus wrote to all those who had loaned money to IPC and IPC Distributors, advising them to take a tax write-off. In June, the two corporations dissolved, assigning all rights in the negative to Jarrico, Wilson, and Biberman.

Although all efforts to get the 35mm version into theaters failed, *Salt of the Earth* would enjoy a second life, on college campuses, in its 16mm version. In 1992, the Librarian of Congress listed it on the National Film Registry, marking it as a film to be preserved for its "cultural, historical, or aesthetic significance."

Becoming a Left Socialist

Jarrico's attitudes concerning the Soviet Union and communism underwent significant changes while he was in Europe. On August 2, 1959, the Jarricos flew to the Soviet Union to attend an international film festival in Moscow. Their impressions of the Soviet Union, Jarrico wrote, were similar to those of Harrison Salisbury, who had written a series of articles for the *New York Times* in early September. Salisbury reported that the Soviet Union had changed, that Russians living under Khrushchev's rule were no longer afraid of each other, that a new era of toleration existed in creative matters, and that there was a halting effort to come to grips with government-directed anti-Semitism. Jarrico wrote to his uncle Chaim, "We were generally pleased with what we saw there. We found no personal evidence of anti-Semitism, and indeed met Jews who had once been in jail but were now restored to rather eminent positions. But that it had existed now seems clear to us; you were certainly right about that." To his uncle Abram and aunt Esther, he wrote, "We went to Russia with the illusion that we had shed all our illusions, but we may have acquired some new ones, for it was very heartening. The people we met there were so friendly and optimistic, so full of curiosity about everything American, so pleased with the improvement in their lives (not only materially but in terms of liberty, to judge by the many anti-Stalinist jokes we heard) that we felt very much at home."[17]

In August 1960, Dorothy Healey wrote Jarrico regarding a rumor she had heard that he and Wilson were involved in financing and writing for an anti-Communist journal. Jarrico responded that the rumor was not true but that he did not want to give the impression "that there's nobody here but us orthodox chickens." He told her that he subscribed and contributed to *New Left Review*, *People's World*, *National Guardian*, *Monthly Review*, and *I.F. Stone's Weekly*. But none of these publications, he commented, "begin to satisfy me as an expression of my own ideas on the need for an American road to socialism. In brief, I am still what your complaining friends would call a revisionist, and they're still what I used to call left-sectarian, and the name-calling gets us nowhere."[18] He now referred to himself as a left socialist. In his Christmas poem for 1963, composed to the tune of "Which Side Are You On?" he wrote,

They say in Lenin's doctrine
There are no neutrals here
You're either a revisionist
Or a gung ho left sectaire

Which side are you on, which side are you on?

A right wing opportunist
He serves the bosses well
But left wing dogmatism
Will blow us all to hell[19]

During a stay in Prague in March 1962, Jarrico realized that he had become disenchanted with the way socialism worked there. He wrote to Bill, "What they do is distribute poverty. Oh, it's true that everybody has a kind of minimum security, and that's all to the good, but it isn't enough. . . . [T]here's a sad sense of separation between the government and the people. There's a continuing fear of being marked lousy for protesting, for not conforming. There's a defeatism about improving things." If the United States could learn from such failures, Jarrico thought, socialism might have a better future there. He began to envision a new American radical party based on seven principles: the repudiation of all of the crimes of the past; the repudiation of dogmatic Marxism; the repudiation of existing socialist countries as models for American socialism; the reexamination of every Marxist and Leninist principle; the reaffirmation that socialism's goals are justice, plenty, freedom, and cooperation; the insistence that truth is revolutionary (and lies are counterrevolutionary); and the avowal that the freedom to disagree is essential to progress.[20]

Jarrico was also reexamining his thoughts about the relation of art to politics. He had concluded in early 1963 that there is neither socialist art nor bourgeois art but only "good art and bad art." In his journal, he wrote, "I happen to believe that most good art—not all, most—is humanistic. And if you happen to believe that socialism is the highest contemporary expression of humanism, you may say that good art tends to support the socialist reconstruction of society." Most good art, he continued, is also rebellious and critical. Truth is revolutionary, and art, which is a way of searching for and asserting truth, may also be termed revolutionary. He concluded, "Long live freedom of the arts! Long live the revolutionary function of art, not only under capitalism but under socialism as well! Long live the revolutionary transformation of Stalinist socialism, so that socialism may become worthy of its future, worthy of the future of Man!"[21]

Along those same lines, in 1964, Jarrico encouraged an English friend, William Blake, to write a primer on Marxism for Americans, a project Jarrico had once considered undertaking himself. He advised Blake to "translate what is still valid in Marxist thought into good American English—to get rid of the German and Russian vocabularies entirely," and to organize it "within categories of thought which are familiar to American kids, and even bright high school kids, yes, 'bourgeois' categories." In the last chapter, Blake should "demonstrate the relevance of Marxism to the problems people actually face, and will be facing, in the U.S., and . . . hit the question of democratic freedom vs. dictatorial force head on."[22]

Jarrico himself remained active. When he was in the United States in the spring of 1965, he marched in an anti–Vietnam War demonstration in Washington DC and, after the United States sent troops to the Dominican Republic in April, wrote to *Time* magazine, "We shatter Vietnamese bodies to save American face, and lose what little support we have in the Orient. We plunge a dagger into Dominican democracy, claiming to be aiming at communism. . . . My country right or wrong, but this is ridiculous."[23] He also attended a memorial for Malcolm X, who had been assassinated in February. Intrigued with Malcolm X's life, Jarrico began amassing a research file on him and sent out feelers about a biographical movie, which he would write.

Prague Spring

Five years after he had deplored the state of socialism in Czechoslovakia, at the end of February 1967, Jarrico joined Yvette in Prague, just as a clash between reformers and hardliners was brewing. While he was there, the Union of Czechoslovak Writers launched a demand for more democratic practices, and the government responded by depriving them of control of their weekly journal. When Dorothy Healey arrived on May 2, Jarrico and Yvette greeted her at the airport with a banner reading "Healey Is Our Leader." Yvette introduced her to an interdisciplinary research team of Czech intellectuals set up by the Czech Academy of Sciences to discuss the problems of power in a socialist society.[24]

They returned to western Europe in the summer, but Jarrico's 1967 Christmas poem, "The Revisionist Internationale," clearly reflected his continuing preoccupation with events in Czechoslovakia.

Arise, ye prisoners of stagnation
Revise that old dogmatic pap
The science of emancipation
Shall not finally drown in crap

Karl Marx was not the son of Mary
And Lenin was not the one guru
Their view was revolutionary:
We change the world and we change too

'Tis the final conflict
For the method they taught
Revision is the essence
Of scientific thought

'Tis the final conflict
Let us dogma erase
The courage to guard the evidence
Shall free the human race

Yvette returned to Prague at the end of January 1968, and Jarrico followed one week later. Alexander Dubček had just been elected first secretary of the Czech Communist Party. He had relaxed the censorship; come out in support of what the reformers called the Action Program, designed to end the dictatorial, sectarian, and bureaucratic practices of the Czech Communist Party and government; and begun rehabilitating the party members who had been purged after 1948. But Dubček knew he had to move carefully. He lacked a reform-minded majority in the party, he was a Slovak in a Czech-dominated governing apparatus, and he hesitated to remove the pro-Soviet elements he inherited. Events outside the apparatus moved much more swiftly. The students had become politicized, the writers' union had established a new journal, *Literarni Listy*, and a democratic counterculture flourished. It was a period that would come to be known as the Prague Spring.

Jarrico wrote Dorothy Healey at the end of May that he was determinedly optimistic about the changes occurring in Czechoslovakia under Alexander Dubček. The events there seemed to him to be "the most important experiment since socialism got off on the wrong foot in 1927 or so, and if it can be proved that it's possible to have the best fruits of the bourgeois democratic revolution in terms of personal freedom and the best fruits of the proletarian revolution in terms of social justice, it could be the best of all possible worlds. . . . I mean if you see a turning point in history right before your eyes, you have to believe in it." Nevertheless, he was forced to admit that the current news was on the pessimistic side, "pressure and more pressure from big brother [the Soviet Union], and a retreat by the radicals, who are now the centrists. Not just a brake on the heady headlong democratization but a real attempt to reverse it." He would, he concluded, try to cling to his "long-term optimism"; even if the Czechs did not succeed, "maybe we still can make it in the U.S. someday."[25]

In July, two weeks after Jarrico and Yvette returned to London, the so-called Warsaw letter was issued by the leaders of the USSR, the German Democratic Republic, Poland, Hungary, and Bulgaria. It sharply criticized the Czech reforms as counterrevolutionary. On August 20, just before midnight, without warning, the authors of the Warsaw letter dispatched 165,000 soldiers and 4,600 tanks to Czechoslovakia, seized Dubček and sent him to Moscow, and began a process of "normalization." The Czech government chose not to resist with arms, but the citizens, virtually unanimously, opposed the military occupation politically and culturally. As a result, it required six months for the Soviet Union to install a new, more reliable government. Only ten of the world's eighty-eight Communist parties approved the invasion.[26] Jarrico wrote to Abram and Esther Shapiro, "We were hopeful that they [Czechs] were really beginning to solve the problem of making individual liberty and economic justice compatible. But that was exactly what the Russian leaders couldn't bear. If the Czech ideas spread, it would mean the end of *their* power. It was as simple as that, in my opinion." To a friend, he wrote, "We're all upset, obviously, about Czechoslovakia, and trying, rather fruitlessly, to be of some help. . . . I must say, ancient though my disillusion was, I was rather surprised to find myself picketing the Russian Embassy the other evening." He had carried a "Hands Off Czechoslovakia" sign.[27]

Jarrico and Yvette pitched in to help Czechs stranded in England by the invasion. They attended several other demonstrations and a cocktail party hosted by Communists for Czechoslovakia. Yvette believed that all Czechs should return to fight the occupation, but when she stated she wanted to return as well, Jarrico demurred. He thought she could be more effective where she was. For his part, Jarrico worked hard on behalf of eastern European anti-Stalinists, writing letters, pulling strings, and using whatever prestige he had as a former Communist and blacklisted Hollywood writer.[28] His Christmas poem that year was titled "A Battle Hymn for 1968."

> *Oh mine eyes have seen the glory of the coming of the tanks,*
> *They are countering the counter-revolutionary cranks.*
> *On our glorious red banners see emblazoned o'er our ranks*
> *The proud cry 'Censorship!'*

Jarrico and Yvette had become friends with Eduard Goldstücker, who had been president of the Czech writers' union and was now in exile in London. They worked with him to gather names and messages of support for a special edition of the writers' union now-banned *Literarni Listy*, which would be smuggled into Czechoslovakia on the second anniversary of the invasion. Jarrico asked Jules Dassin (and through him Melina Mercouri and Mikis Theodorakis, composer of the music for *Z*), Edgar Snow, and James Jones for written statements. To Jones, Jarrico wrote, "It's getting worse in Czechoslovakia, and quickly. Eleven intellectuals expect to go on trial in mid-July, and three other large trials are planned for the Fall. And the accused, of course, are the most courageous personalities of the Prague Spring. The way to help them—the way to inhibit the savagery of the bastards persecuting them—is for guys like you to protest publicly; and in a journal like Listy, which will reach *into* their country."[29]

In December 1969, Jarrico wrote to Dorothy Healey, who was arguing that the old guard should fight to save the word "Communist" from the invaders, "Me I'm for letting the bastards have the word and raising the banner of REVOLUTIONARY HUMANISM instead." Three years later, after she had read a draft of the *Big Brother* script, Healey wrote Jarrico that it neglected "the larger truths." In particular, she thought it failed to address the claim that the Soviet Union still represented a force against U.S. imperialism, a claim that Healey very strongly believed to be true. Jarrico disagreed. He argued that the Soviet Union and the People's Republic of China acted only according to their respective national interests. Former CPUSA members should have learned, he wrote, "from 40 years of bitter and exhilarating experience . . . that left-wing colonialism *is* an infantile disorder." In a postscript, he added, "It now becomes clear: we should have turned the Party into a debating society. Thrown the baby out with the bath water, and not have cracked eggs to make omelettes."[30]

A few years later, Jarrico read an article by Ernst Fischer, a noted scholar of Marxism, that, he told Michael Wilson, "expresses my own political views these days, and I therefore found it brilliant." Fischer praised the new Left as a "force impelling progress" but criticized it for misunderstanding the events in Czechoslovakia and for dismissing its socialism with a human face as mere revisionism. Fischer also urged the new Left not to disdain the parties of the old Left. "The tactics of the left must be highly flexible in their attempt to achieve a firm alliance of all different types of organizations and groups, salvaging all they possibly can from the older ones." Fischer warned against what he saw as tropism toward one-party systems. The concentration of power in one party, he cautioned, inevitably leads to the deformation of democracy and the domination of a power apparatus.[31]

Nevertheless, Jarrico supported several efforts to aid Communist dictators' wars against the United States. He assisted Anne-Marie Roy, a friend of Yvette's, with her documentary film about the Vietnam War, *Sur les chemins de la victoire/Le fleuve rouge*, for which she had secured the cooperation of the Democratic Republic of Vietnam (DRV). To help her raise the $40,000 she needed to finish the movie, Jarrico wrote fund-raising letters and tried to negotiate a television deal. With John Berry, he tried to organize an international brigade to go to the DRV to help repair the flood-control dikes, which had been damaged by U.S. bombing raids over the Red River delta. They spoke with representatives of the DRV and sent out a confidential memorandum to influential people, trying to win their support. Jarrico envisioned that the brigade members would share the life and labor of the Vietnamese villagers and, by their presence, perhaps, deter the bombing or, at the very least, call attention to the issue. He told DRV representatives that he would raise the money to transport the brigade there, but he was told that the DRV government was not interested.[32]

In late 1973, Jarrico realized that he had retained more of his revolutionary consciousness than he had thought. At the Cannes film festival that summer, he had met Henrik Stangerup, a Danish writer and film director. Stangerup proposed that they cowrite a film script based on a story idea that he had titled *The Glass of Water Theory*, about a love affair between an idealistic young woman and a cynical ex-Communist. Jarrico thought that this project offered him a promising vehicle for contrasting the old and new Left and commenting on political theory versus political practice.

After several congenial meetings, however, they quarreled over the movie's message. In Stangerup's mind, the personal was political, and the moral of the movie had to be "You can't change the world if you don't love it." Jarrico, however, wanted the movie to emphasize that ex-Communists who renounced personal political responsibility were "dead wrong," that they were "cop-outs." On that question, he told Stangerup,

> I think I am more radical than you, and you are more liberal than I, and we cannot "paper over" this difference. We have to resolve it, if we're to collaborate. And we cannot resolve it by repeating over and over a lovely catch phrase like "you can't change the world if you don't love it." I find that it sounds beautiful but does not withstand analysis. Lots of people have changed the world without loving it. . . . You can't change the world without fighting like hell to do so. Our film must say something far more profound about the *necessity* to change the world. If we deal with socialism at all (and nobody forces us to), what we have to say must throw some light on real problems—the problems of building "socialism with a human face"—actual conflicts (Dubček, Allende)—not some Christian (or "existential") platitudes.

The two argued heatedly, and Jarrico abruptly ended the collaboration. One year later, he wrote Stangerup to apologize and request the rights to the script in exchange for 10 percent of anything realized on it. Stangerup agreed, but nothing came of the plan.[33]

Jarrico's last major investment of political time and energy in Europe was to assist Yvette with her efforts to raise money to find UNITA (National Union for the Total Independence of Angola), the smallest of the three groups fighting for Angola's independence from Portugal.[34] Jonas Savimi had formed it in 1966. Though UNITA was the smallest of the three groups, it was the most tribally and locally based. It received support, at first, from the People's Republic of China and Tanzania. Two summits, in 1972 and 1974, failed to unify the independence groups, but, following Portugal's announcement of a grant of independence, a unified transitional government was formed in January 1975.

UNITA's leaders invited Yvette to come to Abidjan, Ivory Coast, to meet with Savimbi and help him prepare for negotiations with the other Angolan independence movements. At Yvette's behest, Jarrico drafted a nine-page letter to the leaders of UNITA regarding the future of Angola. He clearly saw this letter as an opportunity to put into practice the principles of the revisionist manifesto that he had written ten years earlier. He began with a rhetorical question: What kind of socialism were they pursuing? He urged them, in their answer, to eschew the "problem-ridden" Soviet and Chinese models and pursue instead democratic socialism. "If you can prove," he continued, "that a socialist society can be built on a democratic base—that social justice and individual liberty *can* co-exist—you will be turning a new page. Not only in African history but in world history. Generations to come will thank you." He admitted that the socialist precedents had not been encouraging but argued that the opportunity to participate in the construction of a provisional government for an independent Angola provided UNITA with a great opportunity. Jarrico advised UNITA's leaders to represent the will of the villagers, the Angolan majority, and to fight for a better life for them. He admonished them not to adopt a paternal attitude toward the people: UNITA must start where the Angolan people were; it must respect the traditions of the people (even as UNITA was struggling to change those traditions); it must speak to the people on the basis of their own experiences; and it must help the people of Angola to see that UNITA's program offered them a better life than the one they were now living. Yvette and Jarrico met with Jorge Sangumba, UNITA's foreign minister and London representative, to discuss the letter. Upon meeting Savimbi, however, Yvette decided that he would not be receptive to Jarrico's advice and did not give him the letter. She returned from the meeting sorely disillusioned. "I think," she told Jarrico, "I like revolutions better before they win."[35]

Two years later, just before leaving Europe for good, Jarrico told a French interviewer, "Since I spent twenty-five years of my life as a Communist, . . . I still feel deeply involved in the efforts to transform the international movement which calls itself Communist, and specifically in the effort to democratize it. Basically I believe that socialism does not have to be tyrannical, that social justice and individual liberty can co-exist."[36]

PART 4

HOME AGAIN

11

Back in the USA, 1975–97

> One of the reasons I came back here is that it's become an honor instead of a handicap to have been on the blacklist. It's become part of nostalgia now, and the revolts of the 1960s—the student and black movements—have made some of our radicalism of the 1930s and 1940s look pretty tepid.
>
> *—Paul Jarrico, 1977*

By early 1975, Jarrico and Yvette had reached an impasse. When they were together, they quarreled constantly. When they were apart, they wrote letters to each other that revealed near-murderous loathing for the other's personality tics. She began leaving their apartment for long periods without telling him where she was going, and he flew to the United States in June and stayed three months.

The atmosphere in the United States regarding the blacklist had completely changed. The new generation of writers and film-oriented people admired the blacklistees and wanted to tell their story sympathetically. On this trip, Jarrico met Deborah Rosenfelt, who was researching her book on the making of *Salt of the Earth*, and David Talbot and Barbara Zheutlin, who were interviewing old and new Hollywood radicals for their book *Creative Differences*. Jarrico attended "blacklist evenings" in Pasadena and North Hollywood at which the sympathetic documentary *Hollywood on Trial* (Cinema Associates, 1976) was shown.[1] The following year, he assisted Gregg Heacock with a retrospective of movies by blacklisted people and appeared on the panel following the showing of *Salt of the Earth* at the Los Feliz theater. He granted interviews to people whose books would significantly alter the debate on the blacklist (Nancy Schwartz, Larry Ceplair, and Victor Navasky).[2] Jarrico also joined a new socialist-feminist organization, the New American Movement, and began attending meetings of the chapter to which Dorothy Healey, Ben Margolis, John McTernan, and other former Communist friends belonged. (Bill Jarrico was also a member.)

For the next two years, he divided his time between Europe and the United States, spending more and more time in the latter. When he was away, he and Yvette had little communication. Their financial situation was "dire," he wrote in one letter, and he was "still fighting, unsuccessfully, that ol' debbil (black talk for old devil) drink-smoke-and-weight." Despite all this, he told Ed Kraus, he still believed that he was "going to be able to break through again into good credits and good money."[3]

In the spring of 1977, he and Yvette decided to live apart. He flew to Los Angeles in May; one week later, he ran into Lia Tjordmann (née Benedetti), whom he had briefly met the year before. She had been in the process of divorcing her husband when she met Jarrico, and, she remembered, they experienced a mutual fascination. Though she had been active in the anti–Vietnam war movement, she knew little about the blacklist or *Salt of the Earth*. Jarrico moved in with her in early August. He promised her he would stop drinking, go on a strict diet, and start saving money.[4] He still faced serious financial problems, and he felt obligated to continue sending money to Yvette. Jarrico did not tell Yvette about Lia, even after Lia's divorce became final in February 1978. Nor, obviously, did he initiate divorce proceedings. Yvette would remain ignorant of Jarrico's new love for eight years.

After two years of living together, Lia began to put pressure on Jarrico to divorce Yvette, but he continued to resist. In January 1979, he brought Yvette to Los Angeles, where she stayed four months, undergoing a variety of medical treatments under Jarrico's WGAw health plan. By day, he ferried Yvette from one doctor to another; by night, he was with Lia. When Yvette returned to Paris, she informed Jarrico that she would need $26,550 per year for her separate maintenance. Minou was asking him for money to help pay her rent in New

York, and Jarrico was berating himself that he had left Sylvia without medical insurance, social security, or savings. And, of course, he had to pay his share of the living expenses with Lia.[5]

Toward the end of 1984, Jarrico wrote Yvette a letter telling her "almost" all. He then flew to Paris to talk with her, but he again shied away from the divorce issue. The status quo continued until October 1991, when he met with her again in Paris. She agreed to accept service of divorce papers in exchange for Jarrico's promise to pay her an immediate $5,000, underwrite her health plan, and thereafter pay her alimony of $1,000 a month. The divorce decree was granted on September 1, 1992, and Jarrico and Lia married on September 30. Jarrico and Yvette spoke by telephone fairly regularly, and occasionally heatedly, until April 1993. After that, they communicated only through Minou. Jarrico and Lia purchased a house in Ojai in 1992, and they moved there in December 1996.

Writing in Hollywood, Act 2

Between 1977 and 1997, though he developed dozens of ideas and wrote many treatments and scripts, Jarrico grossed slightly less than $600,000 from movie and television writing assignments. In five of those years, he earned no income from his writing. Jarrico blamed his agents for his failure to get more assignments, and he changed agents constantly.

Others in Hollywood suggested that the problem lay not with Jarrico's agents but with his age. Heidi Wall, who along with Harry Chandler ran Dream City, a production company, recalled,

> Paul sent us a number of projects, but our subjective opinion was that they were too tough to sell to the broadcasters. . . . Paul's ideas had great merit, but didn't seem particularly timely or "commercial," which is the sad reality we had to contend with. Personally, I was never so painfully aware of ageism as I was with Paul. He was such an outstanding writer and, in my opinion, a national treasure, but he seemed to walk into a room (at that point in his life) knowing that little or nothing would come of it. The ideas he presented, for the most part, did seem out of date in terms of what was "hot" at that particular moment.

Don Newman, who worked with him on a remake of *Salt of the Earth*, recalled that Jarrico was "an anomaly, a man of deep convictions, who never diluted his principles." Though he had a "youthful soul," Newman said, Jarrico was bucking a youth-oriented Hollywood system whose decision makers had difficulty seeing the talent and energy behind Jarrico's age. Another agent wrote Jarrico, "I believed and still do believe that you are a marvelous writer. But I did not find any of your screenplays to be immediately saleable."[6]

Television

Jarrico had not written for television since the mid-1960s, and though he landed several remunerative television assignments, he regularly faced difficulties with the producers, including protracted battles over salary and credits.

On August 1, 1977, Arnaud d'Usseau's brother Loring, a producer at KCET, the public broadcasting television station in Los Angeles, asked Jarrico to write two half-hour shows on midlife crises. Jarrico counterproposed a series, with him as writer-producer, to be titled *Mid-Life Transitions*. His outlines for three one-hour shows were approved and the production schedule was set, but then the project was canceled.

The following year, via Michael Wilson, Jarrico was assigned to write a script for a television series, *The First Americans*, that Marlon Brando was developing for ABC. Wilson had been hired as script supervisor for this series about the destruction of the Indian tribes of North America. Wilson planned to write the first script, concerning the massacres of the Cheyenne at Sand Creek and Washita, and he asked Jarrico to write the second, about Sitting Bull. (Jarrico was to be paid $12,500 in advance, $12,500 on completion of the first draft, and $10,000 for the second draft.) But six days after the producer had agreed to Jarrico's participation, Wilson died from a heart attack, having written only a single-page outline of his script.

Wilson's death represented a major loss for Jarrico. They had collaborated often, both politically and professionally, and they viewed events in a similar fashion. Wilson had been Jarrico's closest friend.

After the funeral, however, Jarrico resumed work on the project. He began to develop his ideas for the script he had titled *The*

Ghosts of Paha Sapa. He decided to make it a paradigm "of the war between the whites and the Indians for the continent as a whole," and to depict Sitting Bull as the representative of "all that was indomitable—even in defeat—of the Indian people as a whole." He told the producer, John Beck, he would not use a "white frame of reference," treat the Indians as "noble savages," or sentimentalize or patronize them. But Jarrico had difficulty translating those ideals into a script, and he fell behind schedule. Though Beck was willing to give him more time, Jarrico said that he wanted out, that he could not work at what he called "a television tempo."[7] The series was not made.

In the summer of 1984, Jarrico found a short-lived career as executive story editor for several television series. The first was *Call to Glory*, a series about the family of an air force officer during the Kennedy administration. Jarrico was to be paid $10,000 per episode, whether or not his script was used. But he became caught in a conflict between the producers and the network over the steady decline in ratings. As a result, what had begun as a show with a critical perspective about the politics of the 1960s became a family-based series. When Jarrico submitted a critical memorandum summarizing his thoughts about the program's new direction, he was excluded from all future story discussions and decisions. The show was canceled after eleven episodes.[8]

The following year, Jarrico was hired as one of three story editors for *Fortune Dane*, a television series starring Carl Weathers as a troubleshooter for a female mayor. (Abe Polonsky was one of the story editors.) Jarrico was paid $10,000 per episode. He rewrote two scripts for the show, but once again he had major conceptual differences with the show's producer and also with Polonsky, who had become, as he grew older, even feistier than Jarrico.

In 1991, Jarrico received an assignment that allowed him to deal straightforwardly with the history of the Soviet Union. He was asked to revise a script for a four-hour television movie about Stalin, which had originally been written by Paul Monash, for HBO. Jarrico was guaranteed $30,000 for the revisions, and, if the producers asked him to make a final polish, he would be paid an additional $10,000. Jarrico cut twenty-six pages from Monash's script, changed the opening, radically altered the scenes concerning the death of Sergei Kirov (the prelude to the purge trials), enhanced Nikolai Bukharin's role by giving him a longer speech against forced collectivization and adding a speech calling for a return to Leninism, and added two scenes, one in which Stalin and Maxim Litvinov discuss the need to make a deal with Germany, and another in which Stalin, in the face of reliable intelligence, denies that Germany will invade the Soviet Union.

Monash did not like Jarrico's changes, and, following a series of rancorous meetings in September, Jarrico was notified that HBO would not exercise the polish option and did not owe him any more money. To the producer, Mark Carliner, Jarrico wrote, "You had me rewriting and polishing at the same time and your requests forced me to work an extra three days past the deadline." He concluded with the question, "Have you associated yourself with an attempt to defraud me of a hard-earned $13,000?" Jarrico petitioned the WGAw legal services department to submit the salary disagreement to a producers arbitration tribunal. HBO offered $5,000 to settle. Jarrico rejected it. HBO then offered $7,500, which Jarrico also rejected. Both parties finally agreed upon a settlement of $8,000 plus an HBO contribution to Jarrico's WGAw pension and health plans.[9]

The producers of *Stalin* decided to cut Jarrico's scenes concerning the lead-up to the German invasion of the Soviet Union. That decision left a significant historical and dramatic gap, and the movie as a whole lacks narrative drive. It contains too many personal scenes, which slow the pace and do not help the viewer to understand Stalin's psychology.

Movies

Jarrico received only one screen credit during these years, despite writing several screenplays (on President Warren Harding, a miners' strike in late-nineteenth-century Colorado, a panda-hunting adventure in China, and heroin trafficking) and making revisions on a script about pool players, *The Baltimore Bullet*.

Jarrico's last sole screenplay credit came to him in 1988 via Pancho Kohner, the son of his former agent. Kohner had produced several successful movies featuring Charles Bronson. Their latest project, *Messenger of Death*, had been adapted by Richard Sale from a Rex Burns novel, *The Avenging Angel*. When Sale's failing eyesight prevented him from making the necessary revisions, Kohner hired Jarrico to do a polish job on a week-to-week basis. But, Kohner recalled, "Paul, being Paul," decided Sale's script did not work, so he began a complete rewrite. On the first day of shooting, Jarrico appeared with two new pages, and he rewrote all through the production. It was "annoying," Kohner said, but the results were very good. Jarrico simplified and streamlined the plot into a well structured investigative journalist procedural. There were no political inserts and no romantic triangle. Though there were grisly death scenes, it was the first movie in which Bronson did not kill anybody in the course of solving the mystery. Kohner paid Jarrico $45,000 for his work, but when he proposed that Jarrico share the credit with Sale, Jarrico objected—he had written a completely new screenplay, even changing the story line. When the movie came out, Jarrico received sole credit. The critic for *Variety* wrote, "In these days of mindless mayhem and random plotting, Paul Jarrico's script at least offers some substance."[10]

Stage

In the early 1980s, Jarrico refashioned into a two-act stage play a screenplay about Leonardo da Vinci that he had been working on for more than ten years, using themes that he had tried to develop in his atomic scientist play. Jarrico saw a strong parallel between Leonardo's involvement with the tyrant Cesare Borgia and J. Robert Oppenheimer's involvement with the Manhattan Project, and he was fascinated by Leonardo's genius, curiosity, and omnicompetence. The play opens with Leonardo questioning the logic of loyalty to a particular city or country. He decides he will live according to the dictates of reason rather than the promptings of emotion and that he will try to find in his scientific work the enduring truths of existence. He convinces himself that it is the invention itself that matters, not the use to which it is put. The play closes with Leonardo's realization that one cannot separate what one does from the effects it has, that one cannot serve an ideology or cause (or scientific project), no matter how good or interesting it may seem, by means that are cruel or harmful or have harmful effects.

In November 1982, the Department of Dramatic Art at the University of California, Santa Barbara produced the play. To subsidize Jarrico while the play was being prepared, university officials appointed him a regents lecturer. Jarrico devoted his lecture to the problems attendant to dramatizing history. He told his audience that he had based Leonardo on three basic themes: the idea of progress, the belief that individuals do affect history, and respect for truth as a liberating element for humanity. He had tried, he continued, both to be true to Leonardo and his times and to make Leonardo's dilemmas relevant to the present. In a program note, he wrote,

> Defined absolutely, there is no such thing as historical truth. However objective the historian may try to be, his subjective values cannot but affect his emphasis—the facts he selects as significant from the multiplicity of facts available. As for the dramatist, who emphasizes whatever suits his theme and structure, inventing and imagining freely, there is not even a pretense of objectivity.
>
> The question of accuracy remains—the respect for such facts as are known—whatever the emphasis, whatever the invention. There are scenes in my play that cannot possibly be documented. There are no scenes, however, that are inconsistent with the documents that do exist.[11]

Following the production, Jarrico received an offer to teach a variety of film courses at the university. He taught three: The Hollywood Studio, The Social Roots of the American Film: From *The Birth of a Nation* to *Judgment at Nuremberg*, and a course on screenwriting. He found teaching interesting and educational but noted that it was "very hard work for someone not used to it (and at all conscientious)." When he was asked to continue teaching, he proposed a different relationship: "I produce a film, using the resources of the university. I bring in a handful of professionals into the project, some of the funding. The students learn by participating in the making of a professional feature film; and I get a lot of free labor."[12] But the university decided against it.

In 1994, Jarrico began to focus his writing energy on Genghis Khan, another subject on which he had been working for many years. In a note to himself, he wrote, "I was trying to decide what to work on last month and my mind went back to Leonardo and to Genghis Khan. . . . Of all the scripts I've written, they're the two on which I worked the hardest. I spent more time creating them and more effort trying to promote them than I did on any other project, and they remain my pride and my frustration."[13]

That year he had discovered a book titled *The Secret History of the Mongols*, which had been compiled in 1240. It was, he wrote, "an account of [Genghis Khan's] life so intimate that he may well have dictated part of it himself! . . . [I]t is a writer's dream come true." But he made little progress on the project. He wrote Pierre Rissient one year later, "I've been brooding about Genghis Khan. I feel as I get older that I'm spreading myself too thin. I don't feel old. My doctor says I'm 20 years younger physiologically than I am chronologically. But the actuarial odds tell me it's time to concentrate. And the project that interests me most is Genghis." In June 1996, he reconceived it as a "mega-musical play in two acts," using songs, dances, and pantomime. In act 1, Genghis seeks immortality through religion; he invites representatives of all the religions to relate to him their respective visions of death. In act 2, however, Genghis decides that the only form of immortality available to him is a record of his deeds. As he recollects his life for a scribe to record, the script calls for entertainers downstage to act it out. Jarrico noted, "Some of the stories will be accompanied by silent pantomime, some by acrobatic ballet, some will mimic warfare, with flowing streamers and the clash of cymbals. Think Chinese Opera crossed with Cirque de Soleil."[14] Jarrico did not write a complete script, however, and he was unable to interest a producer in the project.

Politics in Hollywood, Act 2

After his return to Los Angeles, Jarrico continued to think of himself as an active participant in a large social movement. But aside from picketing during several WGAw strikes, his political activities consisted mainly of writing letters to the editor. In a letter to the *Los Angeles Times* regarding the former Ugandan leader Idi Amin, who had been labeled a racist murderer by former United Nations ambassador Daniel Patrick Moynihan, Jarrico noted that "everyone who supported America's intervention in Vietnam was to some extent a racist murderer; though it may take some time for decent Americans to recognize our genocidal role in that war. . . . Amin is in fact a racist murderer. But no more so than Johnson, Nixon, Kissinger and, to a lesser extent, all who went along with them."[15]

Jarrico also continued to follow events in Czechoslovakia. He wrote an open letter to Gustav Husak, the first secretary of the Czech Communist Party, and collected signatures for it. It stated,

> We who fight for socialism in our own land are shamed and crippled by the violations of socialist legality in your land. We appeal to you to honor the commitment you made in signing the Helsinki Accord of 1975—a solemn commitment to respect the human rights of your citizens. We condemn the jailing, blacklisting and harassment of those who signed Charter 77. . . . Do not tell us your internal affairs are none of our business. During the McCarthy period, when we ourselves were jailed, blacklisted and harassed, it was international outrage that helped us to regain our rights.

The letter was signed by six of the blacklisted, as well as Dorothy Healey, Clinton Jencks, Linus Pauling, Jessica Mitford, and Ben Margolis.[16]

The appearance of Warren Beatty's film *Reds* (1981), about the life of John Reed and his role in the Russian Revolution, prompted Jarrico to reflect once again on his Communist past. In notes he made in preparation for an interview about the movie, he wrote, "Having spent some twenty-five years of my life as a fan of the Soviet Union, a fervent admirer, and another twenty-five years increasingly hostile, this film reminds me of what I saw in the Russian Revolution in the first place. Like the American Revolution, and the French Revolution, and more recently, the Chinese Revolution, the Russian Revolution *did* shake the world." Just as Nixon and Reagan did not invalidate the American Revolution, Stalin and Brezhnev did not invalidate the Russian Revolution.[17]

Jarrico repeated many of those themes at a WGAw forum on the blacklist in January 1989. It was not, he said, "total imbecility to believe that a better world was indeed in birth in Soviet Russia and that it had to be supported against the attempts of the great powers, including our own, to strangle it. The continuation of that support into the thirties also made historical sense, especially after the rise of Hitler." But he acknowledged that he was not trying to minimize the "utter stupidity" of American Communists "in accepting Stalin as the fount of all wisdom, in refusing even to listen to those who told the truth about him. But stupidity is not treason. We believed in all sincerity that what was good for the Soviet Union was good for the U.S.A."[18]

Jarrico later described the promises and threats of combining democracy and socialism.

> I'm exhilarated by the notion that Stalinism and neo-Stalinism have been defeated, that there's a recognition that you cannot call a tyrannical command system socialism, that that's not what socialism really means. Socialism has to be democratic if it's to be socialism, and therefore the rapidity with which the various countries that call themselves socialist have been throwing out their dictatorial leaderships and opting for democratic forms of government, that has been very exhilarating. On the other hand, like a lot of other people, I'm very nervous about what's going to happen in these countries, because it seems to me that in their eagerness for the advantages of a free-enterprise system, of a recognition that self-interest is a useful motor to get things produced and get things done, that they might forget that social justice is still the basic aim of a socialist government, or should be. And if they embrace the evils of capitalism as well as the advantages of genuinely free enterprise, then they're going to be in terrible trouble. . . . We have to find a way of harnessing the motor of self-interest to social ends, and we haven't found it.[19]

Jarrico continued to use his Christmas poems, which he was now sending to nearly three hundred people, to comment on the year's political events. For 1991, he wrote a satire on the Reagan and Bush administrations.

Mine eyes have seen the glory of the Reaganomic boom
'Twas morning in America, an end to gloom and doom
Malaise had given way to pride, the market was in bloom
Our hype was marching on

We built the greatest war machine the world has ever seen
We humbled Caribbean isles, taught Libya not to preen
We could have won in Lebanon if only they'd fought clean
Our hype went marching on

We contrad Sandinistas. Noriega? Cleaned his clock
We kicked the Russian backside, put their Empire into hock
We exorcised Vietnam at last by taking on Iraq
Our hype kept marching on

We won in eighty, eighty four and eighty eight as well
The secret word is money and it hasn't lost its spell
We help the rich and they provide the wherewithal to sell
The hype that's marching on

We may not know the way to solve our nation's many woes
But how to muddle issues, man, on that we're really pros
With kinder, gentler racism we addled all our foes
Our hype keeps oozing on

But if perchance our thousand points of hate get people sore
Our recourse will be simple, we'll just start another war
Few eyes are clear when they're suffused with patriotic gore
Our hype will win once more.

Jarrico regularly received invitations to appear on blacklist panels and at *Salt of the Earth* showings from Silver City, New Mexico, in May 1982 to Helsinki's Oulu University in April 1995. In July 1996, the European Film College in Denmark invited him to deliver a lecture and discuss *Salt of the Earth*. His speech, "What's Playing at Plato's Cave?" addressed what he called the "historic failure of the movies to achieve their promise. A medium unprecedented in its capacity to capture reality has given the world, by and large, a pale imitation of reality—shadows instead of substance." He stressed, as he always had, the significance of content, especially latent content and covert messages. Though he offered his listeners a nine-point sliding scale for analyzing content, he did not provide a very convincing strategy for making movies with more humane and uplifting content.[20]

When he learned that AMC was producing a documentary on the blacklist, the first to be shown on television, Jarrico provided an enormous amount of time and resources to researcher Stephanie Jenz.[21] The result, *Blacklist: Hollywood on Trial* (1995), which included an interview with Richard Collins, won a Presidential Emmy.

Salt of the Earth, Act 2

Jarrico spent significant time, thought, and energy on a variety of projects involving films about *Salt of the Earth* or remakes of it.[22] He had first been approached, in August 1978, by Tony Grutman and Richard Smith, who had written *The Patriots*, a script based on Herbert Biberman's book about the making of *Salt of the Earth*. But he did not think their script captured the suspense, tension, and drama of the actual event.[23]

In 1984, Marine Dominguez of Silver City began to raise money for a film about the making of *Salt of the Earth*. In June, Jarrico met with Lisa Kernan, the director of script development, who had prepared an eight-page treatment. The following April, Dominguez and Jarrico agreed that Jarrico would write the script. But he balked at the two proposed contracts they sent him. He had asked for a coproduction contract, and they were offering him employment contracts. He wrote Dominguez on July 13, "After three months of waiting for an agreement, I've finally done what I should have done in the first place: I've written my own story about the subject, with a wholly original focus, and I've registered it with the Writers Guild. I shall be offering it—under my own conditions and terms—to a number of people; and I shall also give you and your associates a crack at it. In short, Marine, our negotiations—such as they were are off. This is a new ball game."[24]

Jarrico's project, *Hugger-Mugger*, told the story of *Salt of the Earth* from the viewpoint not of the filmmakers but of those who tried to stop the film from being made. He had decided to write it in the form of "a detective story—the suspenseful closing of a police dragnet, McCarthyism through the eyes of the McCarthyites." He invented an FBI agent who had been given the task of investigating and stopping the production, and he placed the agent in a romantic triangle involving the agent, the agent's wife, and the Chicana who is first blackmailed by the agent into cooperating and then becomes his lover. But Jarrico could not find a producer willing to commit to it. When his friend Frank Gruber asked him, "Why make a movie about a good FBI agent?" Jarrico replied, "Why not? It is just a movie, and it is a good story idea."[25]

In 1991, Jarrico was approached by Tony Ludwig, of Group W Productions, and Don Newman about a remake of *Salt of the Earth*. They agreed that they would stay as close to the original script as possible but would add some hooks to make it appealing to producers of independent features and cable companies. They sent copies of Wilson's script to a variety of producers and production companies, and, in November, Robert Katz and Moctezuma Esparza expressed strong interest. They discussed casting, selecting a director, and the scope of Jarrico's participation. A deal memorandum was prepared and several actors and directors expressed an interest, but in February 1994, Jarrico noted, "Salt remake almost dead."[26]

In September 1993, Jarrico and Sonja Dahl Biberman were approached by Karl Francis of Bloom Street Productions, who wanted to make a feature film based on Herbert Biberman's book. At first, Jarrico was to cowrite and coproduce, but he came to see that such a collaboration would not work, and he focused his efforts on helping Sonja Dahl Biberman receive the best deal possible for the rights to her brother-in-law's book. Francis also wanted the right to incorporate or reproduce Wilson's screenplay and to use clips from the movie, but Jarrico and the Wilson daughters did not think Francis was paying them an adequate fee for those rights. And, though Sonja Dahl Biberman was paid $25,000, Jarrico believed she should have received much more.

Francis wrote the script, which he titled *One of the Hollywood Ten*, and sent it to Jarrico in March 1995. In his agenda book, Jarrico wrote, "Oy vay." In his letter to Francis, he said that though the script "is good, and potentially very good," he was dismayed at how much it departed from what actually happened. In January 1997, Francis sent him a revised draft, and Jarrico responded with a two-page general critique and a six-page detailed critique. In sum, Jarrico thought that there was an overwhelming lack of historical research and an incredibly confused story line. Though he acknowledged that the script came to life in the final third, which contained the scenes recreating the filming of *Salt of the Earth* in New Mexico, Jarrico stated that Francis still got most of the facts wrong. Francis responded cordially to all of Jarrico's concerns, and he made the movie. It has not, however, been distributed or shown commercially.[27]

Finally, in 1996, a *Salt of the Earth* project reached fruition and an audience. Kathleen McElroy wanted to produce an opera based on the strike and the movie. Jarrico, the Wilson daughters, and Sonja Dahl Biberman agreed to provide her with whatever rights she needed. The opera, *Esperanza*, which was sponsored by the Wisconsin AFL-CIO and the Wisconsin Labor History Society, debuted in Madison on August 25, 2000.[28]

His Final Bow

Most of Jarrico's activities in 1997 focused on the restoration of screen credits to blacklisted writers, working with the committee to construct a monument to the blacklist on the campus of the University of Southern California,[29] and working with an all-guild committee to prepare a program to commemorate the fiftieth anniversary of the Hollywood blacklist. The program director, Judy Chaikin, wanted to feature Jarrico's work to restore credits, but he refused. He did, however, like her idea of a scene dramatizing his appearance before the House Committee on Un-American Activities. Chaikin chose Kevin Spacey to portray Jarrico because she thought Spacey embodied one of Jarrico's finest qualities—his understated approach. She told Spacey, "Jarrico is a measured man. He always takes a moment to think about his responses."[30]

On October 27, 1997, "Hollywood Remembers the Blacklist" featured various actors and actresses reading documents and reenacting House Committee on Un-American Activities encounters. Following speeches by the current presidents of the Screen Actors Guild, the Screen Directors Guild, the Writers Guild of America, west, and the American Federation of Television and Radio Artists, Ring Lardner Jr. and Jarrico accepted their apologies. Jarrico could not resist the urge to lighten the solemnity, and he began his reply by saying, "There's been a mistake. I am Kevin Spacey." He continued, "The Guilds have come a long way since they failed to protect the Hollywood Ten and the Hollywood hundreds. What you and your fellow presidents have reaffirmed tonight is the guiding principles of unionism: that an injury to one is an injury to all."[31]

The following day, at a luncheon honoring all those involved in the project, Chaikin remembered, Jarrico exhibited a "glow of appreciation." Others remembered how exhausted he seemed. Driving back to Ojai after the luncheon, he fell asleep at the wheel of his automobile. It went off the road and crashed into a tree, and Jarrico died instantly. A memorial was held at the Writers Guild Theater on December 7. He was given the guild's Robert Meltzer award for "a singular act of courage in defense of freedom of expression and the rights of writers" the following year.[32]

EPILOGUE

> People are dying and sources are drying up.
>
> —*Paul Jarrico, 1991*

Some of the blacklisted writers, notably Albert Maltz and Paul Jarrico, were preternaturally watchful of the historical record regarding the blacklist. Their files are filled with drafts of letters to newspaper editors and letters to friends (and former friends) setting the record straight. They were the keepers of the blacklist historical flame. Their example has deeply influenced my own research and writing on this subject. I wrote in 1991,

> The blacklist period was born and it thrived in the darkest, meanest shadows of American politics. The historian, confronted with the specters of government agents sneaking around Hollywood, hate groups secretly compiling lists of "subversives," and individuals informing anonymously and secretly to save their careers at the expense of others, should shine a glaring spotlight into every corner. Unless it means violating a confidence or gratuitously hurting a living person, the historian should endeavor to fill in every blank and clarify every obscurity.[1]

The largest and most obscure page in the blacklist story at the time I wrote those words was the huge number of movie and television scripts written behind fronts or under pseudonyms. But disclosing the identities of the actual authors turned out to be an enterprise fraught with crosscurrents. My immersion in that enterprise began in 1979 when Albert Maltz told me, in the strictest secrecy, that he had written *Broken Arrow* and that it had been fronted by his then friend Michael Blankfort. (Blankfort had been nominated for an Academy Award and had won an SWG award for the script.) When Maltz died in May 1985, I told this story in the form of a eulogy I wrote for the *Los Angeles Herald-Examiner*. I concluded the story by arguing that the WGAw should follow the lead of the Academy of Motion Picture Arts and Sciences, which had given posthumous Academy Awards the previous month to Carl Foreman and Michael Wilson for their screenplays for *The Bridge on the River Kwai*.[2] When nothing happened, I wrote a longer version of the story for *Cineaste*.

I spoke with Jarrico about revealing the original writers of these old screenplays, and I learned that he was engaged in an ongoing (albeit theretofore unsuccessful) effort to convince the WGAw to give Michael Wilson screen credit for *Lawrence of Arabia*. I also learned that Jarrico had been helping a Finnish writer, Matti Salo, who was writing a book about fronts and pseudonyms during the blacklist period.[3] Jarrico had begun his campaign to get Wilson the *Lawrence of Arabia* credit in June 1988, when he learned that a director's cut of the movie was going to be released. He made a pitch to the WGAw board on May 1, 1989, to award Wilson a cocredit. Executive Secretary Brian Walton told the board that a further investigation would be made.[4] One month later, Jarrico sent Walton the full correspondence on the subject, including letters from the British Screenwriters Guild. The two exchanged several letters, but no action was taken. According to former WGAw president Del Reisman, board members believed that Hollywood had moved past the blacklist.[5]

In May 1991, I sent a letter to WGAw president George Kirgo, enclosing the article I had written for *Cineaste* and a copy of the *Broken Arrow* contract Maltz and Blankfort had signed. I was asked to present my case to the WGAw board. I did so, and the board voted to add Maltz's name to the WGAw award for the script. The guild's journal reprinted my article.[6] When news of this decision was made public, Steven Barr contacted the board to make a strong case for adding Dalton Trumbo's name to the award for *Roman Holiday*.[7] On the night of March 22, 1992, at the forty-fourth annual WGAw

Awards ceremony, Warren Beatty presented awards to Esther Maltz for her late husband's screenplay and to Cleo Trumbo for her late husband's original story.

In October 1994, an article on *Lawrence of Arabia* was published in *Cineaste*. The author, Joel Hodson, undertook a side-by-side comparison of the scripts written by Wilson and Robert Bolt and concluded that the structure of Wilson's screenplay had been appropriated by Bolt and the director, David Lean. Jarrico sent copies of Hodson's article to every WGAw executive. After Hodson's article was reprinted in the *WGAw Journal* the following March, guild spokesperson Cheryl Rhoden said that the question of Wilson's cocredit remained an "'open matter,' which, along with other unacknowledged or pseudonymous credits for blacklist-era films was reviewed 'from time to time' by an ad hoc committee."[8] Finally, in September 1994, the board announced that it had formally recognized Wilson as co-writer of the *Lawrence of Arabia* screenplay and would urge Columbia Pictures to change the writing credit on all future releases. Columbia and the Academy agreed to make the change.

On January 3, 1996, the WGAw board appointed an ad hoc blacklist credits committee composed of George Kirgo, Del Reisman, the guild's credit administrator Cathy Reed, and Paul Jarrico. The committee was authorized to review credits from the blacklist period and make recommendations for changes. At its second meeting, in March, the committee established its purpose: "to investigate and make recommendations concerning credits for blacklisted writers who worked under the Guild's jurisdiction or an affiliate Guild's jurisdiction." It would investigate three types of cases: writers who had been denied credit because of the blacklist, writers who had used fronts because of the blacklist, and writers who had used pseudonyms because of the blacklist. It would not, however, investigate cases in which the guild had already determined that no credit was due; that is, it would not reopen arbitration cases. It would use guild records, all pertinent documents and correspondence, written acknowledgments by fronts, first-person statements, and any other relevant historical records.[9]

The committee began working with lists supplied by Jarrico and Bernard Gordon, which grew to more than ten pages. Reisman said that Jarrico "was the driving force; he was the committee." Reed said that "he had a quiet insistence and if thwarted, would come back with more information. He had this underlying passion driving him." Stephanie Jenz, a researcher for the committee, agreed; she recalled that when some of the members did not believe that enough evidence existed to award a credit Jarrico believed in, he would not let it go—"not in an annoying way, but in a strong, ethical, and firm way." But, said Reed, Jarrico tried not to be partisan; he always tried to separate his personal feelings from the process. Reisman said that Jarrico "never pounded the table."[10]

The unanimity rule prevailed: all committee members had to agree on the decision about a particular credit. At the beginning, Jarrico was very protective of the blacklistees' rights (though he insisted that his own credits be the last ones investigated), and he urged the other committee members to consider subjective or hearsay evidence. Gradually, though, he acceded to the evidence requirement demanded by Reisman, Kirgo, and Reed. "The decisions," said Reed, "had to be beyond reproach." They tried to contact the families of everyone involved to obtain their permission to make the credit change. Reisman said that some families wanted to leave the past buried. But the committee members had become determined to find and restore true authorship in all cases.[11]

In June, the committee recommended to the board that credit changes be made to three movies: *Friendly Persuasion*, *Odds against Tomorrow*, and *The Day of the Triffids*. But in July, Jarrico became concerned that the guidelines were being interpreted too mechanically and that some credits might be in jeopardy, particularly those for *The Robe* (Albert Maltz), *Cry, the Beloved Country* (John Howard Lawson), and *Ivanhoe* (Marguerite Roberts). He articulated his concerns in an extensive memorandum to the other members. He first pointed out that "there was a long period during which our predecessor Guild [the SWG] had surrendered control of credits (a period that extended into our own Guild's history). It was unlikely during that period, that the rightful claimants to a credit would even be known, much less heard, by an arbitration committee. Why then should the Guild's determination of credits be so respected as to even exclude an *investigation* into a case?" He emphasized that he was not arguing in favor of new arbitrations, but he did insist that if the committee could and did find significant evidence "that ran counter to some lopsided 'Guild determination,'" that evidence should be the determining factor. His second point concerned the clash between a script whose front had been chosen by a producer and the guideline requiring written acknowledgment by that producer. He mentioned two producers notorious for putting their names on scripts written for them by blacklistees. To resolve this predicament, Jarrico proposed that if the committee members were convinced by the weight of the evidence that the blacklistee had written the script and that the front or producer was unreasonably refusing to approve a credit for that writer, then they should recommend that the credit be awarded.[12]

In March 1997, the committee sent twenty-four recommended credit changes to the board, which approved them all. But the list did not include the three credits that concerned Jarrico the most. The fronts for *Cry, the Beloved Country* and *Ivanhoe* were dead, and the committee did not have scripts written by Lawson and Roberts. But Jarrico believed that the circumstantial evidence had crossed the threshold of credibility. In the case of *The Robe*, the producer had taken Maltz's name off the script and given it to Philip Dunne to rewrite. But other writers who had worked on that script had claimed a credit, and an arbitration committee had awarded the credit to Dunne. Dunne did not know at the time that Maltz had written the original script but had since learned about and acknowledged it. A committee member contacted Amanda Dunne, Philip Dunne's widow, who agreed that Maltz deserved a cocredit. Jarrico located Maltz's original script in the 20th Century-Fox collection at the University of Southern California, and he asked me to compare it with Dunne's final script. I did so, and in a memorandum I wrote to Jarrico, I concluded that Dunne had extensively rewritten the dialogue but that he had retained Maltz's structure, scenes, and characters. After extended discussion, the other committee members accepted Jarrico's arguments on *The Robe*, *Cry, the Beloved Country*, and *Ivanhoe*.

One credit, that for *Roman Holiday*, put Jarrico in an awkward position. He had been very close friends with Ian Hunter, the credited scriptwriter, and good friends with Dalton Trumbo, who had written the original story. When he informed the Trumbo family that the committee members had decided to assign only story credits to Trumbo for *The Brave One* and *Roman Holiday*, Christopher Trumbo objected. He claimed that his father had written the original screenplay for both movies and thus deserved co–screenplay credit for both. When Jarrico told Christopher Trumbo that the credits would stand as the committee members had determined them, Trumbo replied that he would publicly criticize the committee's methods if it did not reconsider. Reisman said that Jarrico felt "a personal embarrassment" about this impasse. Eventually, the committee members concurred with the Trumbo family regarding *The Brave One*, but they held firm to their decision regarding *Roman Holiday*.[13]

As of July 2000, ninety-one films, including five to which Jarrico had contributed, had been designated for credit changes. The surviving members of the committee decided not to tackle the much thornier task of correcting blacklist television credits. No one has since emerged to champion that cause. As John Berry, in his eulogy of Jarrico, wrote, "There are few of us who have the courage and the will for generous humanity and the fierce determination to never give up the fight, to right the wrong and to obtain what is just. Paul was one of those few."[14]

FILMOGRAPHY

No Time to Marry
(Columbia Pictures, January 10, 1938, b&w, 63–64 minutes)
Romantic comedy
Executive producer: William Perlberg
Assistant producer: Nat Perrin
Director: Harry Lachman
Screenplay: Paul Jarrico
Based on a story by Paul Gallico
Featuring Richard Arlen, Mary Astor, Lionel Stander

The Little Adventuress
(Columbia Pictures, October 24, 1938, b&w, 60–62 minutes)
Romantic comedy
Executive producer: Irving Briskin
Producer: Ralph Cohn
Director: D. Ross Lederman
Screenplay: Michael L. Simmons
Story: Michael L. Simmons and Paul Jarrico
Original screen story: Mary McCarthy
Featuring Edith Fellows, Richard Fiske, Jacqueline Wells, Cliff Edwards

Beauty for the Asking
(RKO Radio Pictures, February 10, 1939, b&w, 68 minutes)
Romantic comedy
Producer: B. P. Fineman
Director: Glenn Tryon

Screenplay: Doris Anderson and Paul Jarrico
Story: Edmund L. Hartmann
Original idea: Grace Norton and Adele Buffington
Featuring Lucille Ball, Patric Knowles, Donald Woods

The Face behind the Mask
(Columbia Pictures, January 16, 1941, b&w, 66 or 69 minutes)
Drama
Executive producer: Irving Briskin
Director: Robert Florey
Screenplay: Allen Vincent and Paul Jarrico
Story: Arthur Levinson
Based on a radio play by Thomas Edward O'Connell
Featuring Peter Lorre, Evelyn Keyes, Don Beddoe

Men of the Timberland
(Universal Pictures, June 6, 1941, b&w, 61 minutes)
Modern western
Associate producer: Ben Pivar
Director: John Rawlins
Screenplay: Maurice Tombragel and Griffin Jay
Original story: Paul Jarrico
Featuring Richard Arlen, Andy Devine

Tom, Dick and Harry
(RKO Radio Pictures, June 13, 1941, b&w, 85–86 minutes)
Romantic comedy
Producer: Robert Sisk
Director: Garson Kanin
Story and screenplay: Paul Jarrico
Featuring Ginger Rogers, George Murphy, Alan Marshal, Burgess Meredith

Thousands Cheer
(MGM, September 13, 1943, Technicolor, 125–26 minutes)
Musical comedy
Producer: Joseph Pasternak
Director: George Sidney
Screenplay: Paul Jarrico and Richard Collins
Based on their story "Private Miss Jones"
Featuring Kathryn Grayson, Gene Kelly

Song of Russia
(MGM, February 10, 1944, b&w, 106–7 minutes)
War
Producer: Joseph Pasternak
Director: Gregory Ratoff
Screenplay: Paul Jarrico and Richard Collins
Original story: Leo Mittler, Victor Trivas, and Guy Endore
Featuring Robert Taylor, Susan Peters, John Hodiak

Little Giant
(Universal Pictures, February 22, 1946, b&w, 91–92 minutes)
Comedy
Producer: Joe Gershenson
Director: William A. Seiter
Screenplay: Walter De Leon
Original story: Paul Jarrico and Richard Collins
Featuring Bud Abbott, Lou Costello

The Search
(MGM, March 23, 1948, b&w, 105 minutes)
War refugees
Producers: Lazar Wechsler and Oscar Duby
Director: Fred Zinnemann
Screenplay: Richard Schweizer
Collaborator on screenplay: David Wechsler
Additional dialogue: Paul Jarrico
Featuring Montgomery Clift, Aline MacMahon, Wendell Corey

Not Wanted
(Emerald Productions, July 23, 1949, b&w, 91 minutes)
Social drama
Producers: Ida Lupino and Anson Bond
Director: Elmer Clifton
Screenplay: Paul Jarrico and Ida Lupino
Original story: Paul Jarrico and Malvin Wald
Featuring Sally Forrest, Keefe Brasselle, Leo Penn

The White Tower
(RKO Radio Pictures, June 14, 1950, Technicolor, 98 minutes)
Mountain climbing

Producer: Sid Rogell
Director: Ted Tetzlaff
Screenplay: Paul Jarrico
Based on the novel by James Ramsey Ullman
Featuring Glenn Ford, Valli, Claude Rains

The Hollywood Ten
(Hollywood Arts, Sciences and Professions Council, 1950, b&w, 32 minutes)
Agitprop
Producer: Paul Jarrico
Director: John Berry
Screenplay: Paul Jarrico and the Hollywood Ten
Featuring the Hollywood Ten

The Las Vegas Story
(RKO Radio Pictures, January 9, 1952, b&w, 87 minutes)
Gangster
Producer: Robert Sparks
Director: Robert Stevenson
Screenplay: Paul Jarrico, Harry Essex, and Earl Felton
Original story: Jay Dratler
Featuring Jane Russell, Victor Mature

The Paris Express/The Man Who Watched Trains Go By
(Eros Film, June 1953, Technicolor, 80 minutes)
Policier
Producers: Raymond Stross and Josef Shaftel
Director: Harold French
Screenplay: Paul Jarrico and Harold French
Based on the novel by Georges Simenon
Featuring Claude Rains, Marius Goring, Marta Toren

Salt of the Earth
(Independent Productions Corporation, 1953, b&w, 94 minutes)
Women and workers
Producer: Paul Jarrico
Director: Herbert Biberman
Screenplay: Michael Wilson
Featuring Rosaura Revueltas, Juan Chacon

The Girl Most Likely
(RKO Radio Pictures, December 14, 1957, color, 98 minutes)
Producer: Stanley Rubin
Director: Mitchell Leisen
Screenplay: Paul Jarrico (originally uncredited) and Devery Freeman
Story: Paul Jarrico (originally uncredited)
Featuring Jane Powell, Cliff Roberston, Keith Andes

Five Branded Women
(Paramount Pictures, March 28, 1960, color, 100 minutes)
War
Producer: Dino De Laurentiis
Director: Martin Ritt
Screenplay: Michael Wilson, Paul Jarrico, and Ivo Perilli
Based on the novel by Ugo Pirro
Featuring Silvano Mangano, Vera Miles, Barbara Bel Geddes, Jeanne Moreau, Van Heflin

All Night Long
(J. Arthur Rank, February 6, 1962, b&w, 98 minutes)
Musical drama
Producer: Bob Roberts
Directors: Michael Relph and Basil Dearden
Screenplay: Nel King and Paul Jarrico
Featuring Patrick McGoohan, Keith Mitchell, Paul Harris, Betsy Blair

Le rouble à deux faces/The Day the Hot Line Got Hot
(Balcazar P.C.-Inter-Continental, December 24, 1969, color, 100 minutes)
Spy
Producer: Francisco Balcazar
Director: Etienne Périer
Screenplay: Paul Jarrico
Story: Guerdon Trueblood and Dominique Fabre
Featuring Charles Boyer, Robert Taylor, George Chakiris

Atentat u Sarajevu/The Day That Shook the World
(Yugoslavian Film, August 10, 1976, color, 136 minutes)
Historical
Producers: Jadran Film-Kinema Sarajevo and Barandov Studios
Director: Veljko Bulajiċ

Screenplay: Paul Jarrico
Based on a scenario by Stevan Bulajiĉ and Vladimír Bor
Featuring Christopher Plummer, Florinda Bokan, Maximilian Schell

Messenger of Death
(Cannon Group/Golan-Globus, June 1988, color, 90 minutes)
Mystery
Producer: Pancho Kohner
Director: J. Lee Thompson
Screenplay: Paul Jarrico
Based on the novel *The Avenging Angel* by Rex Burns
Featuring Charles Bronson

Uncredited Contributions

I Am the Law
(Columbia Pictures, 1938, b&w, 83 minutes)
Crusading attorney
Producer: Everett Riskin
Director: Alexander Hall
Screenplay: Jo Swerling
Featuring Edward G. Robinson
Contributor to treatment

Saboteur
(Universal Pictures, April 22, 1942, b&w, 108 minutes)
Espionage
Producer: Frank Lloyd
Director: Alfred Hitchcock
Screenplay: Peter Viertel, Joan Harrison, and Dorothy Parker
Featuring Priscilla Lane, Robert Cummings
Additional scene with Richard Collins

The Pride of the Yankees
(Samuel Goldwyn, 1942, b&w, 128 minutes)
Biography
Producer: Samuel Goldwyn
Director: Sam Wood
Screenplay: Jo Swerling and Herman J. Mankiewicz
Original story: Paul Gallico

Featuring Gary Cooper, Teresa Wright
Additional scene with Richard Collins

Hers to Hold
(Universal Pictures, July 16, 1943, b&w, 93–94 minutes)
Producer: Felix Jackson
Director: Frank Ryan
Screenplay: Lewis R. Foster
Based on a story by John D. Klorer
Featuring Deanna Durbin, Joseph Cotten
Draft of screenplay with Richard Collins

The Heavenly Body
(MGM, March 23, 1944, b&w, 95 minutes)
Comedy
Producer: Arthur Hornblow
Director: Alexander Hall
Screenplay: Michael Arlen and Walter Reisch
Adaptation: Harry Kurnitz
Based on a story by Jacques Thery
Featuring Hedy Lamarr, William Powell
Minor revisions with Richard Collins

Bayou
(American National, June 1957, color, 88 minutes)
Melodrama
Producer: M. A. Ripps
Director: Harold Daniels
Story and screenplay: Edward J. Fessler
Featuring: Peter Graves
Script revisions

The Green-Eyed Blonde
(Warner Brothers, November 29, 1957, b&w, 76 minutes)
Social drama
Producer: Sally Stubblefied
Director: Bernard Girard
Screenplay: Dalton Trumbo
Featuring Susan Oliver, Tommie Moore
Treatment

Call Me Bwana
(J. Arthur Rank/United Artists, June 6, 1963, color, 93 minutes)
Comedy
Producers: Harry Saltzman and Albert R. Broccoli
Director: Gordon Douglas
Screenplay: Nate Monaster and Johanna Harwood
Featuring Bob Hope, Anita Ekberg, Edie Adams
Script revisions

The Long Ships
(Warwick Film Productions, Avala Film, distributed by Columbia Pictures, June 24, 1964, color, 125 minutes)
Adventure
Producer: Irving Allen
Director: Jack Cardiff
Screenplay: Beverley Cross and Berkely Mather
Featuring Richard Widmark, Russ Tamblyn, Sidney Poitier
Script revisions

Der Schatz der Azteken
(CCC-UltraScope-Farbfilm, 1965, color, 102 minutes)
Western
Producer: Artur Brauner
Director: Robert Siodmak
Screenplay: Ladislas Fodor, R. A. Stemmle, and Georg Marischka
Based on the novel by Karl May
Featuring Lex Barker
Screenplay

Die Pyramide des Sonnengottes/Pyramid of the Sun God
(CCC-UltraScope-Farbilm, 1965, color, 100 minutes)
Western
Producer: Artur Brauner
Director: Robert Siodmak
Screenplay: Ladislas Fodor, R. A. Stemmle, and Georg Marischka
Based on the novel by Karl May
Featuring Lex Barker
Screenplay

Der Arzt Stellt Fest/The Doctor Says
(Praesens/CCC/Fono, January 1966, color, 86 minutes)
Documentary
Producer: Lazar Wechsler
Director: Alexander Ford
Writer: David Wechsler
Script revisions

Wer kennt Jonny Ringo?/Who Killed Johnny R.?
(1966, color, 91 minutes)
Western
Producer: Artur Brauner
Director: Jose Luis Madrid
Screenplay: Ladislas Fodor
Featuring Lex Barker
Screenplay

The Desperate Ones
(Pro Artis Iberica/David Productions/Landau-Unger Company, distributed by American-International Pictures, November 27, 1967, color, 104 minutes)
War
Producer, director, and writer: Alexander Ramati
Featuring Maximilian Schell, Irene Papas, Theodore Bikel
Screenplay

The Baltimore Bullet
(Avco Embassy, February 1980, color, 103 minutes)
Pool hall drama
Producer: John F. Brascia
Director: Robert Ellis Miller
Screenplay: Robert Vincent O'Neil and John F. Brascia
Featuring James Coburn, Omar Sharif
Script revisions

Television

It's Always Jan
(CBS, September 1955–June 1956, 30 minutes)
Situation comedy
"The Playboy" and "The Doctor"

The Lord Don't Play Favorites
(NBC, September 17, 1956, 90 minutes)
Producers' showcase
Featuring Kay Starr
Scenes with Michael Wilson

The Phil Silvers Show
(CBS, September 1955–September 1959, 30 minutes)
Situation comedy
"Homesteaders" (September 1957)

The Defenders
(CBS, September 1961–September 1965, 60 minutes)
Drama
"No-Knock" (October–November 1964)

The Seaway
(filmed in Toronto, Ontario, syndicated, 1965–66, 60 minutes)
Drama
"What the Rats Knew," "The Provocative Mademoiselle," "Over the Falls," and "Ghost Ship"

Nurse
(CBS, 1981, 60 minutes)
Drama
"Strike"

Call to Glory
(ABC, August 1984–February 1985, 60 minutes)
Drama

Fortune Dane
(ABC, February–March 1986, 60 minutes)
Crime drama
Executive story editor

Stalin
(HBO, November 21, 1992, 180 minutes)
Biography
Producer: Mark Carliner
Director: Ivan Passer
Writer: Paul Monash
Uncredited revisions

NOTES

Preface

Epigraph: Paul Jarrico, "Notes for an Autobiography," January 1, 1984, Paul Jarrico Papers, in the possession of Lia Benedetti Jarrico. After I had perused them, Lia Benedetti Jarrico donated the bulk of Jarrico's voluminous papers to the Margaret Herrick Library of the Academy of Motion Picture Arts and Sciences (AMPAS). At the time of this writing, they had not been catalogued, so I can provide only descriptions and dates of the documents I am citing. Items from the collection will hereafter be cited as PJP-MHL if they are at the Margaret Herrick Library, Academy of Motion Picture Arts and Sciences, Beverly Hills, CA, and as PJP-LBJ if they remain in the possession of Lia Benedetti Jarrico.

1. *Los Angeles Times*, November 3, 1997, F3; *LA Weekly*, November 7–13, 1997, 28.

1. The Early Years, 1915–36

Epigraph: Paul Jarrico to Sylvia Jarrico, October 1, 1943, PJP-LBJ.

1. The universal military service statute (1874) required all Russian males between sixteen and twenty to register for conscription. The conscriptees were chosen by lot for fifteen-year terms. Males who were only sons could request an exemption, and many Jewish families with more than one son sent the others to families without sons. Aaron, however, told his son that they were both the oldest sons of the oldest sons and so on, going back to a revered sixteenth-century rabbi known as Tosvos Yomtov.

2. Nora Levin, *While Messiah Tarried: Jewish Socialist Movements, 1871–1917* (New York: Schocken Books, 1977), 2–5, 258–59; A. L. Patkin,

The Origins of the Russian-Jewish Labour Movement (Melbourne: F. W. Cheshire, 1947), 217–21.

3. Israel Shapiro, "A Young Man Must Not Sleep," [ca. 1936], PJP-MHL.

4. In 1923, Aaron traveled to Riga (Latvia) to bring his mother, sister, and sister's family to the United States. He had to bribe border guards to let them out of the Soviet Union.

5. Sylvia Jarrico, interview by the author, September 20, 2002; Paul Jarrico, note, November 1, 1993, PJP-MHL. Rose died from tuberculosis, as did many other Jewish immigrants. Aaron and Chaim helped found the Jewish Consumptive Relief Association and a sanatorium for tuberculars in Duarte. This city of tents became the City of Hope. Ed was sixteen years old when Jarrico was born. Jarrico described him as having a "nice face, well made, good features, not smart, but pleasant, experienced, wears nice clothes well, nice looking." Zelma Gussin, Sylvia Jarrico's younger sister, described Ed as "a rag-a-muffin," a boarder whom Rose Gussin took in and then married. Zelma Wilson, *Rebel and Architect*, Oral History Program, University of California, Los Angeles (1994), interview in 1994 by Marlene L. Laskey, collection 300/399, Department of Special Collections, Charles E. Young Research Library, University of California, Los Angeles, 40. There is no genealogy in Jarrico's records for Jennie's birth family. Jennie had two sisters and one brother, but Jarrico's sketchy genealogy does not indicate whether any of them married or had children.

6. Sylvia Jarrico, interview; Lillian Blake, interview by the author, June 22, 2002. Insulin as a treatment for diabetes was discovered in 1921 and became widely available in 1923. But home testing and dosing remained a clumsy process until the late 1940s. Jennie was one of the first patients in Southern California to inject herself, but she always struggled to keep her blood sugar stabilized.

7. Paul Jarrico, *Hollywood Blacklist: Paul Jarrico*, Oral History Program, University of California, Los Angeles (1991), interview in 1988 and 1990 by Larry Ceplair, collection 300/360, Department of Special Collections, Charles E. Young Research Library, University of California, Los Angeles, 9. Jarrico and I began and finished this oral history in the summer of 1988. Five of the tapes were stolen from the oral history office in January 1989, and we redid those tapes in March 1990.

8. Ibid.; Jarrico, note, n.d., PJP-MHL; Sylvia Jarrico, interview; Blake, interview.

9. Max Vorspan and Lloyd P. Gartner, *History of the Jews of Los Angeles* (San Marino, CA: Huntington Library, 1970), 109–24.

10. Israel Shapiro, "Success Story," [ca. 1931], PJP-MHL. In the law school yearbook, Chaim summarized the socialist doctrine and urged

other law students to investigate and study thoroughly the principles of socialism. *Stare Decisis, Being the Year Book of the Students of the College of Law, University of Southern California*, 1913, 41, 81. This material was provided to me by John G. Tomlinson Jr., associate dean of the law school.

11. Jarrico, *Hollywood Blacklist*, 5–6, 4; note on fiftieth birthday celebration for Aaron Shapiro, n.d., PJP-MHL. The Workingmen's Circle (Der Arbayter Ring) was formed by two Jewish cloak makers in New York City, in 1892, for mutual assistance, education, and the organization of cooperative business enterprises. It was renamed the Workmen's Circle, in 1900, when it became a national order. It opened its first Yiddish volkshule (school for children) in 1917 and began establishing Young Circle Clubs in 1925. Maximilian Hurwitz, *The Workmen's Circle: Its History, Ideals, Organization and Institutions* (Workmen's Circle, 1936).

12. Job Harriman (1861–1925) led the Socialist Party in California from 1890 to 1920. He ran for governor of California in 1898, for vice president as Eugene V. Debs's running mate in 1900, and for mayor of Los Angeles in 1911. Following the last election, he renounced politics and, in 1914, founded the Llano del Rio Cooperative Colony in Antelope Valley.

13. Aaron Shapiro, speech, n.d., PJP-MHL; Israel Shapiro, journal entry, May 4, 1933, PJP-MHL.

14. Jarrico, *Hollywood Blacklist*, 11.

15. Ibid., 12–13; Paul Jarrico, interview, in *Tender Comrades: A Backstory of the Hollywood Blacklist*, by Patrick McGilligan and Paul Buhle (New York: St. Martin's Press, 1997), 330. Mooney, a socialist, served twenty-three years in prison, having been falsely convicted of killing ten people with a bomb in 1916. The anarchists Nicola Sacco and Bartolomeo Vanzetti were convicted of a 1920 robbery and murder and executed in 1927. All were considered martyrs by the Left, who organized movements to free Mooney and save Sacco and Vanzetti.

16. Jarrico, *Hollywood Blacklist*, 19.

17. Paul Jarrico, notes, April 6, 1991, October 9, 1995, PJP-MHL. Aaron fathered a daughter with another woman, but no one in the family ever met her.

18. Jennie Shapiro to Ed Kraus, [1930s?], PJP-LBJ.

19. Israel Shapiro, "Boys and Girls," n.d., PJP-MHL; Paul Jarrico, "Autobiographical Musings," October 8, 1995, PJP-MHL.

20. Israel Shapiro, "Education, the Solution of the World's Problems," speech, n.d., PJP-MHL.

21. Sylvia Jarrico, interview.

22. Israel Shapiro to Sylvia Gussin, October 19, 1931, PJP-MHL. Busick was a socialist and an organizer for the International Ladies' Garment Workers' Union.

23. Israel Shapiro, "Thomas Paine," April 15, 1932, high school oratory folder, PJP-MHL; Israel Shapiro, *Rough Rider*, January 8, 1932.

24. Israel Shapiro to Jennie Shapiro, October 27, 1931, PJP-MHL; Jarrico, *Hollywood Blacklist*, 21; Israel Shapiro to Sylvia Gussin, April 19, 1932, PJP-MHL.

25. Israel Shapiro to Esther Schaffer, [ca. November 1932], December 20, 1932, PJP-MHL.

26. Shapiro, journal entries, March 23, 27, May 4, 1933, PJP-MHL.

27. Jarrico, *Hollywood Blacklist*, 103, 105; Israel Shapiro to Sylvia Gussin, February 21, 1933, PJP-LBJ.

28. Israel Shapiro, speech for English 9, spring 1933, PJP-MHL.

29. Israel Shapiro to Sylvia Gussin, July 25, August 18, 1933, PJP-LBJ. Jarrico wrote that Sylvia had once said to him, "I knew you liked women, but I never thought you did something about it." Jarrico added, to himself, "I bedded more than a few, but [my] wives aside, I'll be damned if I'm going to kiss and tell." Paul Jarrico, note, [mid-1990s?], PJP-LBJ.

30. Shapiro to Gussin, July 25, 1933, PJP-MHL; Israel Shapiro to Aaron Shapiro, July 25, 1933, PJP-MHL; Aaron Shapiro to Israel Shapiro, July 27, 1933, PJP-MHL.

31. Israel Shapiro to Cyril Endfield, November 10, 1933, PJP-MHL; Jarrico, *Hollywood Blacklist*, 14; Haskell Shapiro (Jarrico's cousin), interview by the author, May 8, 2002.

32. Israel Shapiro, journal for an English course, December 1933, PJP-MHL.

33. Israel Shapiro to Cyril Endfield, January 18, 1934, PJP-MHL; Israel Shapiro to Gershon Legmann, February 11, 1934, PJP-MHL; Sylvia Jarrico, interview; Israel Shapiro, "My Father Is Dead," *Occident*, April 1935, 8.

34. Israel Shapiro to Diana Bricks, February 21, 1934, PJP-MHL.

35. The New York Student League was organized in 1931 by Communist college students deeply concerned about the effects of the Depression. A few months later, it was renamed the National Student League, and in December it helped organize the Student Congress Against War. See James Wechsler, *Revolt on the Campus* (New York: Covici, Friede, 1935); Hal Draper, "The Student Movement of the Thirties: A Political History," in *As We Saw the Thirties: Essays on Social and Political Movements of a Decade*, ed. Rita James Simon (Urbana: University of Illinois Press, 1967), 151–89; Philip G. Altbach, *Student Politics in America: A Historical Analysis* (New York: McGraw-Hill, 1974). ROTC was complusory for first- and second-year male students at land-grant (Morrill Act, 1862) colleges.

36. Israel Shapiro, "The Dilettante," *California Daily Bruin*, April 9, 1934, 4.

37. On May 9, the International Longshoremen's Association struck to

demand a coastwide contract and union control of the hiring halls. Harry Bridges, soon to become the bête noire of American anti-Communists, headed the vanguard group, the San Francisco Strike Committee. See David F. Selvin, *A Terrible Anger: The 1934 Waterfront and General Strikes in San Francisco* (Detroit: Wayne State University Press, 1996).

38. Sylvia Jarrico, interview; Israel Shapiro to Diana Bricks, May 15, 1934, PJP-MHL.

39. Israel Shapiro to Jennie Shapiro, June 5, 1934, PJP-MHL; Israel Shapiro, speech, n.d., PJP-MHL.

40. Israel Shapiro to Jennie Shapiro, June 5, 1934, PJP-MHL; Blake, interview; Violet Gershenson, interview by the author, June 25, 2002.

41. Israel Shapiro to Sylvia Gussin, July 12, 1934, PJP-LBJ.

42. Jarrico, *Hollywood Blacklist*, 26; Israel Shapiro, "Superior Boy Goes Traveling," n.d., PJP-MHL.

43. Sylvia Jarrico, interview; Israel Shapiro to Cyril Endfield, September 25, 1934, PJP-MHL. According to Harvey Klehr, the CPUSA intended the YCL to be its main feeder, to politicize young workers and farmers. But it remained much smaller than anticipated, probably peaking at around eight thousand members in 1935. Students may have composed 15–20 percent of its membership. Harvey Klehr, *The Heyday of American Communism: The Depression Decade* (New York: Basic Books, 1984), 307–9. But Ben Dobbs, who joined the YCL in 1932 and became head of its California section in 1934, stated that it was not intended as a mass recruiting device. "It was very selective" and represented a "life choice" for those who joined. Ben Dobbs, *Democracy and the American Communist Movement*, Oral History Program, University of California, Los Angeles (1990), interview in 1990 by Michael Furmanowsky, collection 300/328, Department of Special Collections, Charles E. Young Research Library, University of California, Los Angeles, 1:38.

44. Wechsler, *Revolt on the Campus*, 273–82.

45. Israel Shapiro to Cyril Endfield, January 29, 1935, PJP-MHL; Israel Shapiro to Cyril Endfield, April 8, 1935, PJP-MHL. Jarrico's arrest record was later expunged.

46. Israel Shapiro to André Marrin, April 23, 1935, PJP-MHL; Jarrico, *Hollywood Blacklist*, 24.

47. Israel Shapiro to Hal Smith, June 25, 1935, PJP-MHL. Jack Woodford's *Trial and Error: A Dithyramb on the Subject of Writing and Selling* (New York: Carlyle House, 1935) was a straightforward approach to writing for the market. He advised his readers that the most salable type of novel was the honest sex novel. Donald Henderson Clarke's *Impatient Virgin* (New York: Triangle Books, 1931) was just such a novel, featuring a very strong woman.

48. Israel Shapiro to Cyril Endfield, August 2, 1935, PJP-MHL.

49. Israel Shapiro to Cyril Endfield, October 16, 1935, PJP-MHL. Jarrico was referring to the seventh congress of the Communist International; see chap. 2.

50. Israel Shapiro to Hal Smith, October 26, 1935, PJP-MHL; Israel Shapiro, manuscript, n.d., PJP-MHL. The USC film program, sponsored initially by the Academy of Motion Picture Arts and Sciences to train filmmakers, was based on earlier, studio-initiated courses at Columbia University and Harvard University. It began in 1929 with Introduction to the Photoplay and began awarding bachelor's degrees in cinematography in 1932. Peter Decherney, *Hollywood and the Culture Elite: How the Movies Became American* (New York: Columbia University Press, 2005), 70.

51. Israel Shapiro to Cyril Endfield, January 26, 1936, PJP-MHL; Israel Shapiro to Cyril Endfield, December 4, 1935, PJP-MHL. Phelan, a former U.S. senator, had endowed fellowships in literature and arts. For the academic year 1936–37, the trustees had announced two fellowships of $1,000 each, including one "open to competition by writers of fiction, biography, historical narrative, and verse narrative."

52. Shapiro, "Young Man Must Not Sleep," PJP-MHL.

53. Chas B. Lipman to Israel Shapiro, April 8, 1936, PJP-MHL.

54. Bill Jarrico, interview by the author, July 17, 2002.

55. Israel Shapiro, "Tomorrow I Graduate" (typescript), June 5, 1936, PJP-MHL.

2. Screenwriting and Communism, 1936–39

Epigraph: Paul Jarrico, journal entry, January 14, 1944, PJP-MHL.

1. Jarrico believed that Knopf had treated him more courteously because Knopf had, in effect, invited him to come to the studio. Israel Shapiro to Cyril Endfield, mid-June 1936, PJP-MHL.

2. Edwin H. Knopf to Israel Shapiro, August 12, November 21, December 18, 1936, PJP-MHL; Paul Jarrico to Whitney Bolton, "Me," February 14, 1941, PJP-MHL; Israel Shapiro to Hal Smith, October 10, 1936, PJP-MHL; Israel Shapiro to Cyril Endfield, August 6, 1936, PJP-MHL.

3. Israel Shapiro to Hal Smith, October 10, 1936, PJP-MHL.

4. Jarrico, *Hollywood Blacklist*, 8.

5. Israel Shapiro to Cyril Endfield, November 20, 1936, PJP-MHL.

6. Jarrico recorded his state of mind in the first of what he would refer to as his "agenda books." Beginning in December 1936 and continuing through the rest of his life, he recorded in those books his daily activities, the people he saw, the telephone calls he made and received, the letters he

wrote, the books he read, the movies he saw, and some of his thoughts and dreams. For twelve years, he used desk calendar pages, but during a 1948 trip to Europe he discovered Hermès pocket calendars. He used those for the rest of his life. (They remain in the possession of Lia Benedetti Jarrico.)

7. Jarrico, *Hollywood Blacklist*, 33.

8. Paul Jarrico to Cyril Endfield, May 12, 1937, PJP-MHL; Paul Jarrico to Hal Smith, July 20, 1937, PJP-MHL.

9. Neal Gabler, *An Empire of Their Own: How the Jews Invented Hollywood* (New York: Anchor/Doubleday, 1989), 198, 200.

10. Paul Jarrico to Hal Smith, August 10, 1937, PJP-MHL.

11. Jarrico to Bolton, "Me," February 14, 1941, PJP-MHL. *No Time to Marry* had a long afterlife as an anecdote about "red infiltration of the screen." The actor playing the photographer, Lionel Stander, one of the first and staunchest Hollywood Communists, was asked by the director to whistle a tune while he and the reporters were waiting for an elevator. Stander whistled a few bars from "The Internationale," the Soviet national anthem. No one at the studio recognized it. But a few years later, the Columbia vice president in charge of foreign sales asked Jarrico what was wrong with the movie. Perplexed, Jarrico asked, "Wrong?" The vice president told him it had been banned in Brazil, Argentina, and Venezuela. "I've run the picture a dozen times, trying to figure out why." Paul Jarrico and Lionel Stander, interviews, in McGilligan and Buhle, *Tender Comrades*, 327, 612.

12. Paul Jarrico to Dore Schary, October 19, 1937, PJP-MHL.

13. Paul Jarrico to Hal Smith, November 30, 1937, PJP-MHL. Sidney Buchman was one of the most successful Communist screenwriters, and he would become vice president in charge of production at Columbia. In a sketch intended for his memoir, Jarrico wrote, "Of all the film makers who fell from grace during the witch hunt, Sidney fell the farthest, for he'd been the most highly placed." Buchman had not, however, been a very active party member. "It was his wife, Beatrice Buchman, who was the activist of that menage." Paul Jarrico, notes, January 13, 1984, PJP-MHL. For more on Buchman, see Max Wilk, *Schmucks with Underwoods: Conversations with Hollywood's Classic Screenwriters* (New York: Applause Theatre and Cinema Books, 2004), 29–41.

14. Paul Jarrico to Hal Smith, January 5, 1938, PJP-MHL. Though studios regularly lent writers without assignments to other studios, which then compensated the lending studio for the writer's salary, Samuel Goldwyn was famous for hiring only "eminent" authors.

15. Paul Jarrico to Erwin Ellmann, January 28, 1938, PJP-MHL.

16. Paul Jarrico to Hal Smith, May 4, 1938, PJP-MHL; Paul Jarrico to Cyril Endfield, June 27, 1938, PJP-MHL.

17. There is an interesting link between Jarrico's research into consumer protection and the future Hollywood blacklist. When a group of workers struck Consumer Research, the leading consumer research organization, J. B. Matthews, one of its board members, charged Communist instigation and became director of research for the House Committee on Un-American Activities. See Lawrence B. Glickman, "The Strike in the Temple of Consumption: Consumer Activism and Twentieth-Century American Political Culture," *Journal of American History* 88 (June 2001): 99–128. Matthews, a great believer in the power of lists, laid the foundation for the committee's vast dossier system. See Frank J. Donner, *The Un-Americans* (New York: Ballantine, 1961), 14.

18. *Hollywood Reporter*, January 20, 1939, 3; *Variety*, January 20, 1939, 3; Paul Jarrico to Hal Smith, October 3, 1938, PJP-MHL.

19. Paul Jarrico to Hal Smith, August 27, 1938, PJP-MHL.

20. Paul Jarrico to Bill Jarrico, January 1, 1942, PJP-MHL.

21. Paul Jarrico to Hal Smith., November 28, 1938, PJP-MHL. Frank Morgan was a successful comic actor who would later portray the wizard in *The Wizard of Oz*.

22. In May 1939, Jarrico signed a contract with Zeppo Marx Inc., which later became Marx, Miller and Marx Inc. It would represent Jarrico until October 1947. Between then and his blacklisting in April 1951, he would be represented by MCA Artists Ltd., the Goldstone-Willner Agency, and the Sam Jaffe Agency.

23. Collins was a member of the YCL in New York City. When he came to Hollywood in 1936, Budd Schulberg invited him to join a Marxist study group, and Schulberg and Ring Lardner Jr. later took him to a party branch. Maurice Rapf, a member of that circle of young screenwriters, "always felt that Collins was riding a little bit on Jarrico's coattails, but at the same time Collins was a nice guy to be around." Maurice Rapf, interview, in McGilligan and Buhle, *Tender Comrades*, 529. Sylvia Jarrico thought he was a very lonely and unhappy person. "He was uncomfortable with the leadership of those he considered less cultured than he. He mocked the Party leadership and was especially contemptuous of the Los Angeles Section's functionaries. He was ambitious [to be an artist], superior, and possessed of a cutting humor." Sylvia Jarrico, interview. Isobel Lennart though he was "a very rigid man and a fanatic." Quoted in Victor S. Navasky, *Naming Names* (New York: Viking Press, 1980), 257. For Collins's background, see Richard Collins testimony, April 12, 1951, House Committee on Un-American Activities, *Communist Infiltration of Hollywood Motion Picture Industry* (Washington, DC: GPO, 1951–52), pt. 1. I interviewed him on September 5, 2001; his papers are at the University of Oregon Library, Eugene.

24. Jarrico, *Hollywood Blacklist*, 47–49; Michael Wilson, *I Am the Sum of My Actions*, Oral History Program, University of California, Los Angeles (1982), interview in 1975 by Joel Gardner, collection 300/196, Department of Special Collections, Charles E. Young Research Library, UCLA, University of California, Los Angeles, 105–6.

25. Larry Ceplair and Steven Englund, *The Inquisition in Hollywood: Politics in the Film Community, 1930–1960* (Garden City, NY: Anchor Press/ Doubleday, 1980), 56. The party created the American Artists Congress and the American Music League in 1936.

26. Dimitrov quoted in Larry Ceplair, *Under the Shadow of War: Fascism, Antifascism, and Marxists* (New York: Columbia University Press, 1987), 91.

27. Earl Browder, report to tenth national convention of the CPUSA, reprinted in *A Documentary History of the Communist Party of the United States*, ed. Bernard K. Johnpoll (Westport, CT: Greenwood Press, 1994), 5:325.

28. SACLA (Special Agent in Charge, Los Angeles) to J. Edgar Hoover, February 18, 1943, 23, Freedom of Information Act documents, Margaret Herrick Library, Academy of Motion Picture Arts and Sciences, Beverly Hills, CA (hereafter cited as FOIA-MHL); *Hollywood Red: The Autobiography of Lester Cole* (Palo Alto, CA: Ramparts Press, 1981), 139.

29. Martin Berkeley testimony, September 19, 1951, House Committee, *Communist Infiltration of Hollywood Motion Picture Industry*, pt. 4, 1581–86; see also Lawson's autobiography, John Howard Lawson Papers, Morris Library, Special Collections, Southern Illinois University, Carbondale. When Jerome was subpoenaed by the House Committee on Un-American Activities in March 1951, he invoked the Fifth Amendment in response to all questions about his work in Hollywood. House Committee, *Communist Infiltration of Hollywood Motion Picture Industry*, pt. 1, March 8, 1951, 69–76.

30. Paul Jarrico, interview, in McGilligan and Buhle, *Tender Comrades*, 331. Rapf and Schulberg, both sons of studio executives, had traveled to the Soviet Union in the summer of 1934. There they met Ring Lardner Jr., who was a member of the Socialist Club at Princeton University. On their return to Hollywood, Rapf and Schulberg joined a Marxist study group, and when Lardner came to Hollywood in 1936, they recruited him into the party. Ring Lardner Jr., *I'd Hate Myself in the Morning: A Memoir* (Emeryville, CA: Thunder's Mouth/Nation Books, 2000), 37, 45–46, 98–99; Maurice Rapf, *Back Lot: Growing Up with the Movies* (Lanham, MD: Scarecrow Press, 1999), 69–72, 76–78, 85–86.

31. Sylvia Jarrico, interview.

32. Paul Jarrico to Cyril Endfield, December 21, 1937, April 25, 1938, PJP-MHL.

33. Jarrico, *Hollywood Blacklist*, 118. Leon Trotsky, one of the main figures in the Russian revolution and the civil war that ensued, had been outmaneuvered by Stalin and exiled from the Soviet Union. As an exile, living in a variety of countries, Trotsky wrote many articles and books criticizing the Soviet leader and attempted to organize an international Communist opposition. Followers of Trotsky's ideas called themselves Trotskyists; foes called them Trotskyites.

34. Jarrico, *Hollywood Blacklist*, 117.

35. See Ceplair and Englund, *Inquisition in Hollywood*, 16–46, and Nancy Lynn Schwartz, *The Hollywood Writers' Wars* (New York: Knopf, 1982).

36. Roland Kibbee testimony, June 2, 1953, House Committee on Un-American Activities, *Investigation of Communist Activities in the Los Angeles Area* (Washington, DC: GPO, 1953), pt. 6, 2323.

37. Sylvia Jarrico, interview.

38. Ring Lardner Jr., interview, in *Backstory 3: Interviews with Screenwriters of the 1960s*, ed. Patrick McGilligan (Berkeley: University of California Press, 1997), 207–8; Rapf, *Back Lot*, 111.

39. In 1933, the Motion Picture Producers and Distributors of America, under pressure from officials of the Catholic Church, created the Production Code Administration, with a Catholic, Joseph I. Breen, at its head. All scripts had to be submitted to his office before shooting could begin, and all negatives had to be approved by it prior to their being printed. No movie could be released unless all the changes demanded by the Production Code Administration had been made.

40. Paul Jarrico to Cyril Endfield, June 27, 1938, PJP-MHL. For the story behind the making of *Blockade*, see Larry Ceplair, "The Politics of Compromise in Hollywood," *Cineaste* 8, no. 4 (1978): 2–7.

41. Jarrico, *Hollywood Blacklist*, 119–23; Paul Jarrico, interview, in *A Crime to Fit the Punishment*, directed by Barbara A. Moss (New York: First Run Features, 1983).

42. John Howard Lawson, interview by Dave Davis and Neal Goldberg, "Organizing the Screen Writers Guild," in *The Cineaste Interviews: On the Art and Politics of the Cinema*, ed. Dan Georgakas and Lenny Rubinstein (Chicago: Lake View Press, 1983), 193.

43. Paul Jarrico, interview, in McGilligan and Buhle, *Tender Comrades*, 334–35.

44. Norma Barzman, *The Red and the Blacklist: The Intimate Memoir of a Hollywood Expatriate* (New York: Thunder's Mouth Press/Nation Books, 2003), 361; Dorothy Healey, interview by the author, May 25, 2002; Mary Yohalem, interview by the author, June 12, 2002; Jarrico, *Hollywood Blacklist*, 113; Sylvia Jarrico, interview.

45. Jarrico, *Hollywood Blacklist*, 113–14.

46. Ibid., 111–12.

47. Walter Chambers had just written a book that was markedly antagonistic to New Deal labor legislation, the AFL, and the CIO: *Labor Unions and the Public* (New York: Coward-McCann, 1936).

48. Paul Jarrico to Hal Smith, August 6, 1936, PJP-MHL.

49. Paul Jarrico, "The Jew-Baiters Crash Hollywood," May 2, 1939. It was rejected, the editor wrote, because "it is only an opinion article. Buttress it with a few facts and illustrations and it'll be just what we want." Byron Pumphrey to Paul Jarrico, May 18, 1939, PJP-MHL.

3. World War II, 1939–45

Epigraph: Paul Jarrico, "Or have we eaten on the insane root / That takes the reason prisoner?" *Written By*, October 1997, 39.

1. The letter was reprinted in the *Nation*, August 26, 1939, 228.

2. Jane Degras, ed., *Soviet Documents on Foreign Policy* (London: Oxford University Press, 1953), 3:359–61; *Communist International* 16 (September 1939): 957.

3. Reprinted in Johnpoll, *Documentary History*, 6:158, 160.

4. Dore Schary, *Heyday: An Autobiography* (Boston: Little, Brown, 1979), 105.

5. *Fortune*, June 1940, 162; Warren B. Walsh, "What the American People Think of Russia," *Public Opinion Quarterly* 8 (Winter 1944–45): 515.

6. Frist Morstein Marx, "Totalitarian Politics," in "Symposium on the Totalitarian State: From the Standpoints of History, Political Science, Economics and Sociology," *Proceedings of the American Philosophical Society* 82, no. 1 (February 1940), 1–38.

7. Lyons took much of his information from an article by William Bledsoe, even though Bledsoe had argued that the nonaggression pact had pretty much destroyed the "Hollywood revolution." William Bledsoe, "Revolution Comes to Hollywood," *American Mercury*, February 1940, 152. For other examples, see M. J. Heale, *American Anticommunism: Combating the Enemy Within, 1830–1970* (Baltimore: Johns Hopkins University Press, 1990), 99–121.

8. The U.S. House committee was formed in May 1938. For its first two incursions into communism in Hollywood, in August 1938 and July 1940, see Ceplair and Englund, *Inquisition in Hollywood*, 109, 156–57. On the California committee, see Edward L. Barrett Jr., *The Tenney Committee: Legislative Investigation of Subversive Activities in California* (Ithaca, NY: Cornell University Press, 1951).

9. Alien Registration Act, reprinted in Henry Steele Commager, ed., *Documents of American History*, 8th ed. (New York: Appleton-Century-Crofts, 1968), 2:433; Athan G. Theoharis, *Chasing Spies: How the FBI Failed in Counterintelligence But Promoted the Politics of McCarthyism in the Cold War Years* (Chicago: Ivan R. Dee, 2002), 12.

10. Jarrico, *Hollywood Blacklist*, 115–16; Healey, interview; Sylvia Jarrico, interview.

11. Paul Jarrico to Hal Smith, October 14, 1939, PJP-MHL; Jarrico, *Hollywood Blacklist*, 116; Haskell Shapiro, interview; Paul Jarrico, agenda book entry, October 18, 1939, PJP-LBJ.

12. Paul Jarrico to Hal Smith, January 8, July 21, 1940, PJP-MHL.

13. Paul Jarrico to Hal Smith, February 10, 1940, PJP-MHL.

14. Paul Jarrico, *Star Light Star Bright* (original story), July 18, 1939, PJP-MHL; Paul Jarrico, memo to Pandro Berman, July 18, 1939, PJP-MHL.

15. Paul Jarrico, notes for revision of original outline, August 1, 1939, PJP-MHL.

16. Paul Jarrico to Hal Smith, April 28, 1941, PJP-MHL; Paul Jarrico to Diana Bricks, May 19, 1941, PJP-MHL.

17. *Hollywood Reporter*, July 14, 1941, 3; *Variety*, July 14, 1941, 3; *Newsweek*, July 28, 1941, 52; *New Yorker*, July 19, 1941, 39–40; Otis Ferguson, "Garson's Guard," *New Republic*, July 28, 1941, 117; *Life*, July 28, 1941, 59–62; other reviews in PJP-MHL; Paul Jarrico to Otis Ferguson, August 4, 1941, PJP-MHL; Otis Ferguson to Paul Jarrico, August 11, 1941, PJP-MHL; Otis Ferguson, October 6, 1941, *New Republic*, 437. The review and Ferguson's response are reprinted in *The Film Criticism of Otis Ferguson*, ed. Robert Wilson (Philadelphia: Temple University Press, 1971), 378–80, 389.

18. Alvah Bessie, *New Masses*, July 29, 1941, 29–30; *Daily Worker*, clipping in PJP-MHL; Joy Davidman, "Women: Hollywood Version," *New Masses*, July 14, 1942, 28–31. Davidman (1915–60), a Communist and a published poet (*Letter to a Comrade*), had come to Hollywood in April 1939 as a junior screenwriter for MGM. She stayed for about five months, wrote perhaps four scripts, none of which were produced, and returned to New York, where she wrote a series of very critical comments on movies for *New Masses*. She was also a member of the League of American Writers and compiled for it an anthology of anti-imperialist poems (*War Poems of the United Nations*). She would leave the party in 1946, convert to Christianity in 1948, and marry C. S. Lewis in 1956. See Lyle W. Dorsett, *And God Came In* (New York: Macmillan, 1983).

19. Paul Jarrico, outline and draft, n.d., PJP-MHL. *New Masses* printed only one letter in response to Davidman's review, an approving one from a Cape Cod woman (August 4, 1941). A subsequent article endorsed

Davidman's attack on Hollywood's caricatures of human relationships but accused her of romanticizing the "reality" in Hollywood movies. Charles Humboldt, "Caricature by Hollywood," *New Masses*, July 28, 1941, 29–30.

20. Paul Jarrico to Garson Kanin, May 23, July 30, 1941, PJP-MHL; Jarrico, *Hollywood Blacklist*, 58.

21. *New York Times*, February 7, 1941, 23; *Weekly Variety*, February 12, 1941, 14.

22. Paul Jarrico, "Completed Script: Satire on Success Story" (typescript), April 19, 1942, PJP-MHL.

23. Garson Kanin to Paul Jarrico, March 8, 1942, PJP-MHL; Paul Jarrico to Garson Kanin, May 25, 1942, PJP-MHL; Dore Schary to Paul Jarrico, June 10, 1943, PJP-MHL. Several years later, their script was rewritten as an Abbott and Costello vehicle, *Little Giant* (Universal, 1946), and Jarrico and Collins received original story credit.

24. Reprinted in Johnpoll, *Documentary History*, 6:1080.

25. Jarrico quoted in Ceplair and Englund, *Inquisition in Hollywood*, 182. The "Trotskyites" were twenty-six members of the Socialist Workers Party (SWP) and leaders of Minneapolis Local 544 of the International Brotherhood of Teamsters (the AFL) who were indicted for violating the Alien Registration Act. The Communist Party supported the indictments, claiming that the SWP was a "Trotskyite Fifth Column" and that its members were "agents of fascism." Eighteen of those indicted were convicted and given prison sentences ranging from one year to sixteen months. Art Preis, *Labor's Giant Step: Twenty Years of the CIO* (New York: Pioneer, 1964), 138–43. In a Communist Party "study outline" titled "Trotskyism," circa 1939, Trotskyism is described as "the expression of the attitude of a certain class, namely the petty bourgeoisie," which is counterrevolutionary. Their dream "is to see the Soviet Union destroyed, to see the leaders of Bolshevism assassinated, to see the world Communist movement crushed, and to see the Communist International wiped off the face of the earth." Michael Wilson Papers, in the possession of his daughter, Becca Wilson (hereafter cited as MWP-BW).

26. John Houseman, *Front and Center* (New York: Simon and Schuster, 1979), 149–50.

27. *Communiqué*, February 7, March 20, 1942; Paul Jarrico to Charlie Page, May 21, 1942, PJP-MHL; Collins testimony, April 12, 1951, House Committee, *Communist Infiltration of Hollywood Motion Picture Industry*, pt. 1, 243.

28. Paul Jarrico, "Coordination Committee," n.d., PJP-MHL; Paul Jarrico, "Our Approach to Content of Pictures" (outline), n.d., PJP-MHL; Paul Jarrico, "Points to Be Included," n.d., PJP-MHL.

29. Paul Jarrico, "The Writers' Clinic," August 9, 1942, PJP-MHL.

30. Writers' clinic notes, February 1–August 2, 1942, PJP-MHL.

31. A fifth columnist is a member of a secret subversive group working within a country to undermine it militarily and politically. The term was coined in 1936 in Spain to describe the rebel sympathizers in Madrid, who were trying to weaken the city's resistance to the four columns of rebel troops besieging the city.

32. Writers' clinic notes, March 29, 1942, PJP-MHL.

33. Although the international organization known as the United Nations was not founded until 1945, the Allies regularly referred to themselves as the United Nations.

34. Writers' clinic notes, April 19, 26, 1942, PJP-MHL.

35. Ibid., August 2, 1942; Michael Wilson, "Notes on Change in Character," August 1, 1942, PJP-MHL.

36. James K. McGuinness testimony, October 22, 1947, House Committee on Un-American Activities, *Hearings Regarding the Communist Infiltration of the Motion Picture Industry* (Washington, DC: GPO, 1947), 139; Writers' clinic notes, June 28, 1942, PJP-MHL.

37. Thomas Cripps, "Movies, Race, and World War II: *Tennessee Johnson* as an Anticipation of the Strategies of the Civil Rights Movement," *Prologue*, Summer 1982, 62–65; "Tennessee Johnson" in *The American Film Institute Catalog of Motion Pictures Produced in the United States*, vol. F4, *Feature Films, 1941–1950* (Berkeley: University of California Press, 1999), 2453; *Tennessee Johnson* file, MPAA/PCA files, AMPAS. This was the first time that a Hollywood studio significantly revised a finished movie in response to a Popular Front–U.S. government alliance.

38. Clayton R. Koppes and Gregory D. Black, *Hollywood Goes to War: How Politics, Profits, and Propaganda Shaped World War II* (Berkeley: University of California Press, 1990), 84–90; James M. Myers, *The Bureau of Motion Pictures and Its Influence on Film Content during World War II: The Reasons for Its Failure* (Lewiston, NY: Mellen, 1998), 128–30; reviews in *Tennessee Johnson* clipping file, AMPAS. The Production Code Administration noted that the "colored servants" received "sympathetic" characterization.

39. Daniel Fuchs, *The Golden West: Hollywood Stories* (Boston: Black Sparrow Press, 2005), 244; Richard Collins, interview by the author, September 5, 2001; Frank Tarloff, interview, in *Red Scare: Memories of the American Inquisition; an Oral History*, ed. Griffin Fariello (New York: Norton, 1995), 326.

40. Jarrico to Kanin, May 25, 1942, PJP-MHL; *Private Miss Jones*, idea outline, dialogue sketches, 1942, PJP-MHL; writers' clinic notes, July 7, 1942, PJP-MHL.

41. *Private Miss Jones*, scripts and revisions, 1942–43, MGM Collection, Cinema-Television Library, University of Southern California, Los Angeles; *New York Times*, September 14, 1943, 27; *Variety Film Reviews*, 1943–1948 (New York: Garland), September 15, 1943. The Jarricos saw *Thousands Cheer* in a theater in early January 1944. Jarrico wrote in his journal, "I rather liked it. I was only embarrassed at two points, really embarrassed." Jarrico, journal entry, January 11, 1944, PJP-LBJ.

42. *New York Times*, November 6, 1942, 26, November 20, 1942, 9; *Time*, January 4, 1943; *Life*, March 29, 1943. The Production Code Administration registered strong reservations about *Mission to Moscow* because it featured a very sympathetic image of Joseph Stalin, but it did not find any problems with *The North Star*. The House Committee on Un-American Activities would subpoena Howard Koch, the writer of *Mission to Moscow*, in 1947; Richard Collins, the cowriter of *Song of Russia*, in 1947 and 1951; Paul Jarrico, the cowriter of *Song of Russia*, in 1951; Dan James, the cowriter of *Three Russian Girls*, in 1951; and Lillian Hellman, the writer of *The North Star*, in 1952. Ironically, the most laudatory movie about the Soviet Union, *The Battle of Russia* (1943), made by Frank Capra's U.S. Army Signal Corps for the *Why We Fight* series, was not cited.

43. Nat Goldstone to Kenneth MacKenna, 1942, MGM Collection, Cinema-Television Library, University of Southern California; *Scorched Earth* reader's report, MGM Collection, Cinema-Television Library, University of Southern California; Louis B. Mayer testimony, October 20, 1947, House Committee, *Hearings Regarding the Communist Infiltration of the Motion Picture Industry*, 80. See also *American Film Institute Catalog*, F4:2263.

44. Other writers were still on the project: Trosper, Laslo Benedek, and Michael Blankfort made some notes on revision in July and August, and Trosper and Blankfort completed a forty-three-page treatment on September 14. On that same day, Strong completed still another treatment. Jarrico and Collins had begun work on their version on August 31. Jarrico did not note, in his records, whether he and Collins knew about the other writers.

45. Jarrico, *Hollywood Blacklist*, 65; Richard Collins, "Sources of Writers' Ideas," *Authors' League Bulletin*, September 1944, 21.

46. Paul Jarrico to Michael Wilson, December 3, 1942, PJP-MHL.

47. Jarrico, *Hollywood Blacklist*, 67–68; Collins testimony, April 12, 1951, House Committee, *Communist Infiltration of Hollywood Motion Picture Industry*, pt. 1, 235.

48. Joseph Breen to Louis B. Mayer, December 9, 1942, PJP-MHL; Gregory Ratoff to Joe Pasternak, December 11, 1942, PJP-MHL; Lowell Mellett to Joe Pasternak, December 29, 1942, PJP-MHL; Vladimir I. Bozykin to Joe Pasternak, January 12, 1943, PJP-MHL.

49. *PM*, "Louis B. Mayer Manicures Russia for M-G-M," clipping in PJP-MHL; Paul Jarrico and Richard Collins to *PM* editor, March 20, 1943, PJP-MHL; David Platt to Paul Jarrico and Richard Collins, March 27, 1943, PJP-MHL.

50. *Los Angeles Daily News*, December 2, 1942, 25, 28.

51. John Wexley, interview, in McGilligan and Buhle, *Tender Comrades*, 715; *Song of Russia*, treatments, memoranda, letters, and scripts, MGM Collection and Joe Pasternak Collection, Cinema-Television Library, University of Southern California.

52. *Los Angeles Times*, February 18, 1944; *Los Angeles Herald-Examiner*, February 18, 1944; foreign commissar of the Soviet Writers Union to the editor of *Communiqué*, December 1, 1944, PJP-MHL.

53. Ayn Rand testimony, October 20, 1947, House Committee, *Hearings Regarding the Communist Infiltration of the Motion Picture Industry*, 83–90. For a laudatory account of Rand's testimony, see Robert Mayhew, *Ayn Rand and "Song of Russia": Communism and Anticommunism in 1940s Hollywood* (Lanham, MD: Scarecrow Press, 2005).

54. Collins testimony, April 12, 1951, House Committee, *Communist Infiltration of Hollywood Motion Picture Industry*, pt. 1, 237.

55. Robert Taylor testimony, October 22, 1947, House Committee, *Hearings Regarding the Communist Infiltration of the Motion Picture Industry*, 166–67; Robert Taylor and Louis B. Mayer statements, *Hollywood Reporter*, May 19, 1947, 17.

56. Scott Eyman, *Lion of Hollywood: The Life and Legend of Louis B. Mayer* (New York: Simon and Schuster, 2005), 350; Jarrico, *Hollywood Blacklist*, 65–66; Collins quoted in Mayhew, *Ayn Rand*, 27.

57. Louis Russell testimony, October 30, 1947, House Committee, *Hearings Regarding the Communist Infiltration of the Motion Picture Industry*, 517. There is no reference to this meeting in Jarrico's papers. Peters, also known as Alexander Goldfarb and Isador Bernstein, headed the "secret apparatus" (Soviet spy network) in the United States from 1932 to 1938. Following the defection of one of his top agents, Whittaker Chambers, Peters was reassigned to work on "special assignments" for the CPUSA Central Committee. John Earl Haines and Harvey Klehr, *Venona: Decoding Soviet Espionage in America* (New Haven, CT: Yale University Press, 1995), 60–61, 120.

58. Jarrico to Kanin, May 25, 1942, PJP-MHL; Michael Wilson to Paul Jarrico, November 11, 1942, PJP-MHL; Paul Jarrico to Michael Wilson, November 26, 1942, PJP-MHL; Paul Jarrico to Jimmy Henderson, March 2, 1943, PJP-MHL.

59. Jarrico, journal entry, July 1943, PJP-LBJ. Jarrico may have learned about the merchant marine from Otis Ferguson, who joined it right after Pearl Harbor and was killed in 1943.

60. Paul Jarrico to Blackie Myers, July 21, 1943, PJP-MHL; Paul Jarrico to Leo Huberman, July 21, 1943, PJP-MHL; Paul Jarrico to Patrick McGilligan, May 6, 1996, PJP-MHL. Jarrico was one of thousands of merchant marines who had never seen a ship before they arrived at a training center for a very hasty induction course. See John Gorley Bunker, *Liberty Ships: The Ugly Ducklings of World War II* (Annapolis, MD: Naval Institute Press, 1972).

61. SACLA to J. Edgar Hoover, September 15, October 6, 1943, and J. Edgar Hoover to SACLA, January 12, 1944, Freedom of Information Act documents in the author's possession (hereafter cited as FOIA-author). House Committee on Un-American Activities investigator Louis Russell testified that while Jarrico was gone, Sylvia Jarrico hosted a gathering at her house addressed by Joseph North, a Communist writer, and attended by Hanns Eisler. Russell testimony, October 30, 1947, House Committee, *Hearings Regarding the Communist Infiltration of the Motion Picture Industry*, 513. Hoover started the custodial detention index in September 1939 to identify those "national security threats" who might need to be detained during war. When the attorney general ordered him to terminate that list in August 1943, Hoover simply renamed it the security index.

62. Paul Jarrico to Jennie Shapiro, September 25, 1943, PJP-MHL; Paul Jarrico to Michael Wilson, December 20, 1943, PJP-MHL.

63. Paul Jarrico, notes on *A Woman's Place*, December 29, 1943, PJP-MHL.

64. Paul Jarrico to Michael Wilson, April 9, 1944, PJP-MHL.

65. Paul Jarrico to Jules Carson, May 14, 1944, PJP-MHL.

66. Jarrico, journal entries, January 1, January 8, May 31, 1944, PJP-LBJ.

67. Bill Jarrico, interview; Jarrico, agenda book entry, October 26, 1954, PJP-LBJ.

68. *New York Times*, January 11, 1944, 3.

69. Jarrico, journal entry, January 17, 1944, PJP-LBJ; Sylvia Jarrico, interview.

70. Jarrico, agenda book entry, February 14, 1945, PJP-LBJ; Paul Jarrico to Sylvia Jarrico, April 13, 1945, PJP-LBJ; Scott quoted in Barzman, *Red and the Blacklist*, 58.

71. Jarrico, journal entry, January 3, 1944, PJP-LBJ; Paul Jarrico to Nat Goldstone, [ca. early 1944], PJP-MHL.

72. Jarrico, journal entries, January 3, 14, 1944, PJP-LBJ.

73. Paul Jarrico to Sylvia Jarrico, April 13, 1945, PJP-LBJ.

74. Sanora Babb to Paul Jarrico, August 4, 1945, PJP-MHL; Paul Jarrico to Sanora Babb, August 8, 1945, PJP-MHL. Jarrico's papers contain no other

correspondence with or references to Babb. She later married the cinematographer James Wong Howe, with whom Jarrico was very friendly.

75. Jarrico, *Hollywood Blacklist*, 76–78; Paul Jarrico to Phillip Borsos, November 8, 1994, PJP-MHL.

76. Jarrico, *Hollywood Blacklist*, 124–25.

77. Paul Jarrico to Alan Miller (handwritten draft), [ca. September 1945], PJP-MHL.

4. The Cold War in Hollywood, 1945–47

Epigraph: Paul Jarrico, "If This Be Treason" (notes for a play), September 30, 1946, PJP-MHL.

1. The second front of attack demanded by the Soviet Union and Communist parties in the Allied countries was western Europe (the first front being eastern Europe).

2. J. Edgar Hoover to SACLA, September 8, 1942, FOIA-MHL; SACLA, "Communist Infiltration of the Motion Picture Industry," report to J. Edgar Hoover, February 18, 1943, FOIA-MHL.

3. SACLA, report to J. Edgar Hoover, August 9, 1943, FOIA-MHL; SACLA, report to J. Edgar Hoover, February 16, 1944, FOIA-MHL.

4. J. Edgar Hoover to SACLA, May 8, 1944, FOIA-MHL; J. Edgar Hoover to Francis Biddle, October 31, 1944, FOIA-MHL; J. Edgar Hoover to Colonel Henry Hawkins Vaughan, May 4, 1945, FOIA-MHL.

5. *Los Angeles Times*, February 5, 1944, 1.

6. Lela Rogers wrote Hoover in November to inform him that Communists had infiltrated the industry, especially at her daughter's studio (RKO). J. Edgar Hoover to Clyde Tolson (assistant director), November 10, 1944, FOIA-MHL; J. K. Mumford to D. M. Ladd (domestic intelligence division), November 16, 1944, FOIA-MHL. The SACLA prepared a lengthy report detailing the extent of "Communist infiltration" of RKO. SACLA, report to J. Edgar Hoover, November 23, 1944, FOIA-MHL.

7. *Los Angeles Times*, April 29, 1944, 1; *Hollywood Citizen-News*, April 29, 1944, 1. The SACLA reported that the MPA had not yet undertaken any activities worth mentioning. SACLA to J. Edgar Hoover, December 12, 1944, FOIA-MHL. Most of the documents available on the MPA are in the Hedda Hopper Collection, AMPAS.

8. It passed by a margin of 208–186, with 40 not voting. *Congressional Record*, 79th Cong., 1st sess., January 3, 1945, 13. Sixteen months later, an appropriation of $75,000 was approved by a vote of 240–81. *Congressional Record*, 79th Cong. 2nd sess., May 17, 1946, 108.

9. *Congressional Record*, 79th Cong., 1st sess., July 9, 1945, 7386; *Los Angeles Examiner*, June 12, 1945, 1.

10. SACLA to J. Edgar Hoover, September 12, 1945, FOIA-MHL; D. M. Ladd to J. Edgar Hoover, October 9, 1945, FOIA-MHL.

11. In 1941, Herbert K. Sorrell, the head of Painters Local 644, organized the CSU to assist unrecognized unions and guilds and to promote a democratic alternative to the IATSE. The CSU had grown during the war, and Sorrell was clearly ready for a new battle. For the CSU strikes, see Gerald Horne, *Class Struggle in Hollywood, 1930–1950: Moguls, Mobsters, Stars, Reds, and Trade Unionists* (Austin: University of Texas Press, 2001); Cole, *Hollywood Red*, 212–13; Bernard Gordon, *Hollywood Exile, or How I Learned to Love the Blacklist* (Austin: University of Texas Press, 1999), 8; and SACLA to J. Edgar Hoover, March 17, 23, 1945, FOIA-MHL.

12. *People's World*, "End the Movie Strike at Once!" March 15, 1945, 1; Roy H. Brewer, oral history (unfinished transcript), 1980, record series 507, box 16, pp. 91, 96, 116, 146, 157, University Archives, University of California, Los Angeles. Brewer visited the Los Angeles office of the FBI in November to tell the SACLA that the Communists had taken control of the CSU strike and that they had complete control over the congressmen from Southern California and the National Labor Relations Board. SACLA to J. Edgar Hoover, November 6, 1945, FOIA-MHL. See also Roy H. Brewer, interview, in Fariello, *Red Scare*, 115.

13. Jacques Duclos, "A Propos de la dissolution du parti communiste américain," *Cahiers du communisme* 6 (April 1945): 21, 36. Documents from the recently opened Soviet archives demonstrate that the article was written in Moscow, published in a Soviet journal, translated into French, and sent to Duclos, who appended his name and had it published in *Cahiers*. Harvey Klehr, John Earl Haynes, and Kyrill M. Anderson, *The Soviet World of American Communism* (New Haven, CT: Yale University Press, 1998), 96, 100–106.

14. James G. Ryan, *Earl Browder: The Failure of American Communism* (Tuscaloosa: University of Alabama Press, 1997), 252–62; Joseph R. Starobin, *American Communism in Crisis, 1943–1957* (Berkeley: University of California Press, 1975), 86, 103; Earl Browder, "How Stalin Ruined the American Communist Party," *Harper's*, March 1960, 45–47; William Z. Foster, "One Year of Struggle against Browderism," *Political Affairs* 25 (September 1946): 772, 791.

15. Michael Wilson, interview by the author, November 6, 1976; Jarrico, *Hollywood Blacklist*, 125–26; Paul Buhle and Dave Wagner, *A Very Dangerous Citizen: Abraham Lincoln Polonsky and the Hollywood Left* (Berkeley: University of California Press, 2001), 90.

16. Albert Maltz, "What Shall We Ask of Writers?" *New Masses*, February 12, 1946, 19–22; Howard Fast, "Art and Politics," *New Masses*, February 26, 1946, 6–8; Joseph North, *New Masses*, "No Retreat for the Writer," February 26, 1946, 8–10; Bessie Alvah, "What Is Freedom for Writers?" *New Masses*, March 12, 1946, 8–10; Leopold Atlas testimony, March 12, 1953, House Committee, *Investigation of Communist Activities in the Los Angeles Area*, pt. 5, 946; Albert Maltz, "Moving Forward," *New Masses*, April 9, 1946, 8–10, 21–22.

17. Jarrico, *Hollywood Blacklist*, 126–27. Subsequently, others such as Abe Polonsky, Jules Dassin, and Ben and Norma Barzman said they had also supported Maltz.

18. Paul Jarrico, "The Writer in Hollywood," February 18, 1946, PJP-MHL.

19. Paul Jarrico, "The White Tower: Analysis," April 6, 1946, PJP-MHL.

20. Paul Jarrico to Sylvia Jarrico, July 21, 1946, PJP-MHL.

21. Paul Jarrico to Sylvia Jarrico, August 17, 1946, PJP-MHL. The year before, Dmytryk had also objected to the political content of John Wexley's script for *Cornered*, which Wexley had situated in Argentina to show that the Juan Perón government harbored Nazis. An angered Wexley asked Lawson and Maltz to intercede, but they did not think that the changes Dmytryk wanted were significant. John Wexley, interview, in McGilligan and Buhle, *Tender Comrades*, 716; Edward Dmytryk testimony, April 25, 1951, House Committee, *Communist Infiltration of Hollywood Motion Picture Industry*, pt. 2, 416–17. During his testimony, Dmytryk said that in late 1945 he had decided "to drift away from the party" (434). But Albert Maltz, who was incarcerated with him at the federal prison in Mill Point, West Virginia, in 1950–51, said that Dmytryk's "drift" was not apparent to the other members of the Hollywood Ten. Albert Maltz, interview by the author, October 21, 1976.

22. Paul Jarrico to Sylvia Jarrico, August 25, September 1, 1946, PJP-MHL.

23. James Francis Crow to Peter Rathvon, January 3, 1947, PJP-MHL.

24. Paul Jarrico to Sylvia Jarrico, September 8, 1946, PJP-MHL; Jarrico, "If This Be Treason" (notes for a play), PJP-MHL.

25. Paul Jarrico, "If This Be Treason" (an outline for a play in three acts), October 3, 1946, PJP-MHL.

26. Paul Jarrico, *Report on China* (Los Angeles: Southern California Committee to Win the Peace, 1946), PJP-MHL; Paul Jarrico to Allen Metcalf, January 23, 1947, PJP-MHL.

27. SACLA to J. Edgar Hoover, January 10, 1946, FOIA-MHL; Sylvia Jarrico to Paul Jarrico, August 29, 1946, PJP-MHL.

28. Paul Jarrico, *Studio Ghost* (original story), March 21, March 30, 1947, PJP-MHL.

29. Paul Jarrico to Dore Schary, April 8, 1947, PJP-MHL.

30. Paul Jarrico to Dore Schary, April 9, 11, 1947, PJP-MHL; Dore Schary to Paul Jarrico, April 10, 14, 1947, PJP-MHL; Paul Jarrico to Nel King, April 24, 1947, PJP-MHL.

31. Praesens-Film was founded in 1924 by Lazar Wechsler (1896–1981), a Polish Jewish emigré, and Walter Mittelholzer, a pioneer in aviation. Though it was one of the leading Swiss production companies for many decades, it was well known for its low budgets, meager filming equipment, "cramped muggy studio," and use of nonprofessional actors. Dean Jennings, "He Breaks Hollywood Rules," *Saturday Evening Post*, May 26, 1956, 48–49, 63–65.

32. Paul Jarrico to Maurice Rapf, June 24, 1947, PJP-MHL; Paul Jarrico to Anne and David [no last name], June 30, 1947, PJP-MHL.

33. Fred Zinnemann to Kjeld Vierup, August 24, 1996, PJP-MHL; Fred Zinnemann to Matti Salo, April 26, 1985, PJP-MHL.

34. Paul Jarrico to Lazar Wechsler, July 2, 1947, PJP-MHL; Joanna Rapf, "Mythic Figures: Women and Co-Being in Three Films by Fred Zinnemann," *Film Criticism*, Spring–Fall 1994, 151. After his blacklisting, Jarrico would receive several more assignments from Lazar Wechsler. (See chap. 9.) Most of them ended unsatisfactorily for both. Jarrico told Rapf that Wechsler was "a hands-on producer, only he had rough and insensitive hands" and was a "pain in the ass." Paul Jarrico to Joanna Rapf, December 1993, PJP-MHL.

35. Paul Jarrico to Dore Schary, August 29, 1949, PJP-MHL.

36. Fischer quoted in Eric Bentley, ed., *Thirty Years of Treason: Excerpts from the Hearings before the House Committee on Un-American Activities, 1933–1968* (New York: Viking, 1971), 73.

37. In 1944, as part of the effort to ensure Roosevelt's reelection, liberals and Communists formed two significant groups, the National Citizens Political Action Committee and the Independent Voters Committee of Artists, Writers and Scientists (which would become the Independent Citizens Committee of the Arts, Sciences and Professions in 1945). They allied with the CIO Political Action Committee, formed in 1942, to sidestep the War Labor Disputes Act's restrictions on direct labor contributions to political campaigns. Following the election of 1946, the National Citizens Political Action Committee, the Independent Citizens Committee of the Arts, Sciences and Professions, and eight smaller progressive groups, with Communist assistance, formed the PCA.

38. House Committee on Un-American Activities, *Investigation of Un-American Propaganda Activities in the United States: Hearings on H.R. 1884 and H.R. 2122*, 80th Cong., 1st sess., March 24–27, 1947, 39, 46, 244, 246, 264, 290–91, 293–96.

39. Ibid., May 7, 1947, 1; Robert E. Stripling, *The Red Plot against America* (Drexel Hill, PA: Bell, 1949), 72; David F. Prindle, *The Politics of Glamour: Ideology and Democracy in the Screen Actors Guild* (Madison: University of Wisconsin Press, 1988), 50.

40. *Hollywood Reporter*, May 7, 1947, 1, May 9, 1947, 1, 3, May 16, 1947, 1, May 19, 1947, 1; L. B. Nichols to J. Edgar Hoover, August 21, 1947, FOIA-MHL; SACLA to J. Edgar Hoover, August 22, 1947; D. M. Ladd to J. Edgar Hoover, September 3, 1947, FOIA-MHL; J. Edgar Hoover to L. B. Nichols, September 13, 17, 1947, FOIA-MHL. Hanns Eisler had been subpoenaed independently, and he appeared as the sole witness on September 24. He testified that he had not been a member of the German Communist Party "in any real sense" and stated, "I am not now a Communist." House Committee on Un-American Activities, *Hearings Regarding Hanns Eisler*, 80th Cong., 1st sess., September 24–26, 1947, 3–61. He was deported the following March.

41. Sylvia Jarrico, interview.

42. Nineteen witnesses had been immediately labeled as unfriendly: Alvah Bessie, Herbert Biberman, Bertolt Brecht, Lester Cole, Richard Collins, Edward Dmytryk, Gordon Kahn, Howard Koch, Ring Lardner Jr., John Howard Lawson, Albert Maltz, Lewis Milestone, Samuel Ornitz, Larry Parks, Irving Pichel, Robert Rossen, Waldo Salt, Adrian Scott, and Dalton Trumbo. Koch, Milestone, and Pichel were not Communists. Brecht, who planned to testify in a manner that would allow him to leave the United States after the hearings ended, retained separate legal counsel. See Larry Ceplair, "The Unfriendly Hollywood Nineteen," in *The Political Companion to American Film,* ed. Gary Crowdus (Chicago: Lake View Press, 1994), 437–40.

43. Herbert Biberman, *"Salt of the Earth": The Story of a Film*, new ed. (New York: Harbor Electronic, 2003), 22–23; Lardner, *I'd Hate Myself*, 119–20. In retrospect, it is difficult to see why the attorneys thought the Supreme Court would sustain their challenge to the committee. In no prior case had the Supreme Court granted certiorari to discuss the contention that the right to free speech implied the right to remain silent when asked about one's political opinions and affiliations. Carl Beck, *Contempt of Congress: A Study of the Prosecutions Initiated by the Committee on Un-American Activities, 1945–1957* (New Orleans: Hauser Press, 1959), 35, 49–50.

44. Dore Schary testimony, October 29, 1947, House Committee, *Hearings Regarding the Communist Infiltration of the Motion Picture Industry*, 471–76. Schary later told Adrian Scott that the other studio executives who testified, Jack Warner and Louis B. Mayer, were supposed to have taken the same position that Schary had but had been "chicken-hearted." Quoted in Jennifer Langdon-Teclaw, "Caught in the Crossfire: Antifascism, Anticommunism and

the Politics of Americanism in the Hollywood Career of Adrian Scott" (PhD diss., State University of New York, Binghamton, 2000), 451–52.

45. Paul Jarrico, interview, in McGilligan and Buhle, *Tender Comrades*, 347; Patrick McGilligan, "Tender Comrades," *Film Comment*, December 1987, 45.

46. William Fadiman to Paul Jarrico (with handwritten note by Jarrico), December 14, 1947, PJP-MHL; Paul Jarrico to Dore Schary, November 13, 1947, PJP-MHL.

47. The Waldorf statement is reprinted in Ceplair and Englund, *Inquisition in Hollywood*, 445. See also Dore Schary, statement, November 15, 1947, Dore Schary Collection, Wisconsin Center for Film and Theater Research, State Historical Society of Wisconsin, Madison (hereafter cited as WCFTR); Dore Schary deposition, *Independent Productions Corp. and I.P.C. Distributors, Inc. v. Loew's, Inc., et al.*, civ. 110-304 (S.D. N.Y. 1961), 16–17, 39–42; Biberman, *"Salt of the Earth,"* 232; and Schary, *Heyday*, 164–66.

48. Schary deposition, *Independent Productions Corp. and I.P.C. Distributors, Inc. v. Loew's, Inc., et al.*, 76. Many of the blacklisted screenwriters I interviewed for *The Inquisition in Hollywood*, including Jarrico, gave me this account of Schary's speech. Interviews by the author, 1976–78.

49. Paul Jarrico, note, n.d., PJP-MHL; Jarrico, agenda book entry, November 20, 1947, PJP-LBJ. Jarrico later said, "Schary was in a sense the cliché liberal who says, 'I'm going to make this compromise now so that I will be in a stronger position to be effective for what I really believe later.' He kept making these compromises from the beginning of his career, as far as I could see." Jarrico also said that he had a certain amount of sympathy for Schary, who contributed to causes Jarrico supported but always insisted that these contributions be kept quiet. So, when Schary spoke to the writers, Jarrico's reaction was not "'Oh, my god, here's my friend doing the dirty work of the reactionaries.' It was sort of 'Here he is again,' I mean in an impossible position." Jarrico, *Hollywood Blacklist*, 87–88; Paul Jarrico to Patrick McGilligan, April 11, 1996, PJP-MHL.

50. Petition to the board of the SWG, December 16, 1947, photocopy in PJP-MHL.

51. Paul Jarrico to Henri and Lilo Aisner, December 18, 1947, PJP-MHL; SACLA to J. Edgar Hoover, January 29, 1948, March 22, 1951, FOIA-author.

5. The Interregnum, 1948–50

Epigraph: Jarrico quoted in McGilligan, "Tender Comrades," 45.

1. Paul Jarrico, *Are You Intimidated?* n.d., PJP-MHL; Paul Jarrico, *Can Wallace Win?* n.d., PJP-MHL.

2. Alfred Friendly, in a detailed article implying that the third party was a Communist Party creation, stated, "There is nothing to suggest that Wallace was a party to, or had direct knowledge of, the Communists' inception and creation of the third party." *Washington Post*, May 2, 1948, 1. See also Starobin, *American Communism in Crisis*, 178–90.

3. Thomas G. Paterson, *Meeting the Communist Threat: Truman to Reagan* (New York: Oxford University Press, 1988), 84; Kenneth O'Reilly, *Hoover and the Un-Americans: The FBI, HUAC, and the Red Menace* (Philadelphia: Temple University Press, 1983), 176; Mary Sperling McAuliffe, *Crisis on the Left: Cold War Politics and American Liberals, 1947–1954* (Amherst: University of Massachusetts Press, 1978), 38, 44.

4. Lauren Kessler, *Clever Girl: Elizabeth Bentley, The Spy Who Ushered in the McCarthy Era* (New York: HarperCollins, 2003), 155–56, 179. See also Kathryn S. Olmstead, *Red Spy Queen: A Biography of Elizabeth Bentley* (Chapel Hill: University of North Carolina Press, 2002).

5. Right after the election, most of the liberals who had remained with the campaign departed the Independent Progressive Party. One year later, in November 1949, the CIO expelled eleven international unions.

6. The CSU had won a second strike in July 1946 for a large wage increase. The third strike, launched in September 1946, was a rematch of the jurisdiction dispute of the first strike. Brewer and the Producers' Labor Committee had set a trap into which Sorrell fell, allowing the producers to lock out CSU workers. Brewer then set up parallel locals within IATSE, and the producers began employing their members as replacement workers. The strike again became violent, and hundreds of picketers were arrested. The CSU lost the strike and disappeared three years later. Sorrell was later expelled from the painters' union.

7. Paul Jarrico, typescripts, August 20, 1948, PJP-MHL. He was also composing an article for the *New Republic* condemning Hollywood's efforts to inundate Europe with American films and praising European efforts to resist this flood. He argued that Hollywood films were as propagandistic as films made in eastern Europe. The difference was that the latter were openly "national in form, socialist in content." Paul Jarrico, "They Are Not So Innocent Abroad," *New Republic*, January 31, 1949, 17–19.

8. Report to the executive board, n.d., PJP-MHL; *Hollywood Reporter*, April 28, 1949, 2; *People's World*, April 18, 1949, 5; Paul Jarrico, *North Atlantic*, n.d., PJP-MHL.

9. The House Committee on Un-American Activities, in its report on the New York conference, labeled it "a supermobilization of the inveterate wheelhorses and supporters of the Communist Party and its auxiliary organizations." This report must have been a boon to the red-baiting organiza-

tions that would soon appear, because it listed sponsors and supporters by name and organization (nearly 400); front organizations and their affiliates (74); signers of petitions and statements; supporters of Communist candidates, defendants, and publications; and supporters of the Soviet Union. House Committee on Un-American Activities, *Review of the Scientific and Cultural Conference for World Peace, Arranged by the National Council of the Arts, Sciences, and Professions, and Held in New York City, March 25, 26, and 27, 1949*, April 19, 1949.

10. Paul Jarrico to Abe Polonsky, May 14, 1949, PJP-MHL.

11. Theoharis, *Chasing Spies*, 85; Barzman, *Red and the Blacklist*, 150; Carey McWilliams, "Hollywood Gray List," *Nation*, November 19, 1949, 491–92. The graylist, which forced the studios to institute political clearance procedures they would have preferred to avoid, was mainly a product of the red-smear industry. In April 1947, three former FBI agents founded American Business Consultants Inc., which published a monthly periodical, *Counterattack*, and, in 1950, a special report, *Red Channels: The Report of Communist Influence in Radio and Television*. This 213-page booklet, whose cover depicted a red hand reaching for a microphone, contained the names of 151 people employed in the entertainment industry and a list of subversive organizations to which each belonged. Almost all of the individuals listed had or still worked in the movie industry. The booklet was sent free of charge to the nearly four thousand subscribers of *Counterattack* and sold for one dollar on some newsstands. In 1949, two other smear organizations began their work: the Wage Earners Committee of the United States, which picketed subversive films, and Jacoby and Gibbons and Associates, Anti-Subversive Public Relations Specialists, which published *Alert*, a periodical that exposed the subversive pasts of those associated with selected movies. Also that year, Myron C. Fagan began his publishing career with *Red Treason in Hollywood*; he followed it, in 1950, with *Documentation of the Red Stars in Hollywood*. In 1952, the American Legion sent to studio heads a list of more than three hundred subversives.

12. Sylvia Jarrico, interview. The nonsigners were fired that summer. See John Caughey, "A University in Jeopardy," *Harper's*, November 1950, 68–75, and David P. Gardner, *The California Oath Controversy* (Berkeley: University of California Press, 1967).

13. Paul Jarrico, ASP film division chairman's report, February 27, March 7, 1950, PJP-MHL. When John Howard Lawson began his prison term that summer, Jarrico became chairman of ASP, but he did not replace Lawson as head of the Hollywood party branch. The younger generation, led by Jarrico and Michael Wilson, decided that they no longer wanted to operate under the supervision of a single individual. CPUSA national headquarters, preoccupied

with the arrests and trials (or flight) of its administrators, did not intervene. John Weber has claimed that he became the party leader; the SACLA reported in 1950 that Weber "has been right-hand man of John Howard Lawson." SACLA to J. Edgar Hoover, February 19, 1951, FOIA-MHL; Healey, interview; John Weber, interview, in McGilligan and Buhle, *Tender Comrades*, 694; SACLA to J. Edgar Hoover, September 13, 1950, FOIA-MHL.

14. *Lawson v. United States and Trumbo v. United States*, 176 F.2d 52 (1949); *Lawson v. United States and Trumbo v. United States*, 339 U.S. 934 (1950).

15. Paul Jarrico deposition, December 20, 1961, *Independent Productions Corp. and I.P.C. Distributors, Inc. v. Loew's, Inc., et al.*, 209. Herbert Biberman claimed that he wrote the script. Herbert Biberman, interview, in *Positif* 107 (Summer 1969): 20. A copy of the next-to-final draft of the script is in PJP-MHL.

16. John Berry, interview, in McGilligan and Buhle, *Tender Comrades*, 72–73. They also tried to arrange distribution in Europe. The SACLA estimated that the film had cost $14,000. SACLA to J. Edgar Hoover, March 22, 1951, FOIA-author.

17. Anne Millar, "Negro Employment in the Motion Picture Industry" (typescript), [ca. 1950], MWP-BW; ASP film division, outline of discussion on blacks in the motion picture industry (typescript), n.d., MWP-BW; Paul Jarrico to Mason Roberson, January 13, 24, 1950, PJP-MHL.

18. Paul Jarrico, *The Truth about Korea* (Los Angeles: Southern California Chapter of the National Council of the Arts, Sciences and Professions, 1950). It contained thirty-five footnotes, mainly citations of the *New York Times* and the *New York Herald Tribune*.

19. ASP, telegram to Pat McCarran, September 23, 1950, PJP-MHL. The American Committee for the Protection of the Foreign Born, established in 1933, was closely allied with the Communist Party. There is extensive documentation of its work in the Norman Leonard Papers, Labor Archives and Research Center, San Francisco State University, San Francisco, CA. See also Fred Rinaldo, "Defending Foreign Born Workers," in Ann Fagan Ginger and David Christino, *The Cold War against Labor: An Anthology* (Berkeley, CA: Meiklejohn Civil Liberties Institute, 1987), 553–60, and Jeffrey M. Garcilazo, "McCarthyism, Mexican-Americans, and the Los Angeles Committee for Protection of the Foreign Born," *Western Historical Quarterly* 32 (Autumn 2001): 273–95. Among its many provisions, the McCarran Act excluded from the United States any alien who was or had ever been an anarchist, a member of any organization advocating or teaching opposition to all organized government, or affiliated in any way with the Communist Party, or who advocated any communistic doctrines

or advocated, taught, wrote, or published doctrines supporting the overthrow of the U.S. government.

20. SACLA to J. Edgar Hoover, January 11, April 13, 1950, FOIA-MHL.

21. Paul Jarrico to Beatrice Buchman, April 27, 1948, PJP-MHL. Max Ophuls, who had been hired to direct, brought in Arthur Laurents to rewrite the script. When it was released, as *Caught*, Laurents received sole credit. Arthur Laurents, *Original Story By: A Memoir of Broadway and Hollywood* (New York: Knopf, 2000), 140–44; *American Film Institute Catalog*, F4:396.

22. Paul Jarrico to Lilo and Henri Aisner, March 17, 1948, PJP-MHL; Paul Jarrico to Lazlo Wechlser, June 14, 1948, PJP-MHL. Henri Aisner had assisted Max Ophuls with *Werther* (1938) and *Sans Lendemain* (1939). A Polish Jew and Communist, he and his wife, Lilo, and his brother, Robert, spent the war years in Hollywood. Robert Aisner was technical advisor on *Casablanca* (Warner Brothers, 1943) and had cowritten, with his sister-in-law, the story for *Cross of Lorraine* (MGM, 1949). When Henri Aisner returned to France, he directed *Le mystère de la chambre jaune*, but he did not have another credit for almost a decade. Pierre Rissient, e-mail message to the author, October 31, 2002.

23. Paul Jarrico, notes for adaptation of *Temptation*, April 2, 1948, PJP-MHL.

24. Paul Jarrico to Beatrice Buchman, April 27, 1948, PJP-MHL; Paul Jarrico to Matti Salo, February 27, 1987, PJP-MHL.

25. Paul Jarrico to Sylvia Jarrico, July 10, 1948, PJP-MHL. Ten days after Jarrico left Los Angeles, the SACLA recommended installation of a "technical or microphone surveillance" of the Jarricos' house. SACLA to J. Edgar Hoover, July 13, 1948, FOIA-MHL.

26. Their trial commenced on January 1, 1949. All the defendants were convicted; ten were sentenced to ten years in prison; and all their attorneys were convicted of contempt and sentenced to prison. The convictions and the constitutionality of the act were upheld on appeal. In the following years, 132 other party leaders would be indicted and 98 convicted. These cases decimated party governance and drained the party treasury. *Dennis v. United States*, 341 U.S. 494 (1951); Michael R. Belknap, "Cold War in the Courtroom: The Foley Square Communist Trial," in *American Political Trials*, ed. Michael R. Belknap (Westport, CT: Greenwood Press, 1981), 233–62; Edward P. Johanningsmeier, *Forging American Communism: The Life of William Z. Foster* (Princeton, NJ: Princeton University Press, 1994), 328.

27. Paul Jarrico to Sylvia Jarrico, July 22, 28, 1948, PJP-MHL.

28. Jarrico, *Hollywood Blacklist*, 145–46. In June 1943, the Jarricos vacationed in Mexico, where they met and formed a friendship with Katz, who had called himself André Simone when he came to Hollywood in the 1930s to raise money for international Popular Front organizations. In November

1951, he and thirteen other Czechoslovakian Communist leaders, eleven of whom were Jewish, were arrested and charged with treason. They were tried and found guilty one year later, and eleven, including Katz, were hanged. Jarrico knew Katz well enough to know that his trial was contrived: "It was put up. This was not on the level. The accusations were not true, and certainly I was deeply troubled by that. . . . I knew [Katz] to be a very loyal international Communist and couldn't believe the charges against him, that he was a tool of the imperialists trying to overthrow the socialist regime." It was, he continued, "just utter nonsense" to accuse him of treason. For the first time, Jarrico began to feel that there was "something radically wrong, basically wrong, terribly wrong [with communism]." But, he later said, "I didn't quit, I didn't quit the party because of that." Jarrico, *Hollywood Blacklist*, 117, 142, 146–47. Four months after Katz's arrest, Jarrico referred to Czechoslovakia as "Lower Slobovia" and opined, "What an outrage that we have to defend such a travesty of socialism. . . . Nothing but fear. Nothing but Stalinism on top and fear below. Isn't there a way of overthrowing such governments? Not counter-revolutions, but pro-revolutions?" Paul Jarrico to Carl Marzani, March 10, 1952, PJP-MHL.

29. Paul Jarrico to Sylvia Jarrico, August 18, September 2, 1948, PJP-MHL; André Simone to Ivan Boldizsar, August 21, 1948, PJP-MHL; Revai Deszi (for Magyar Film) to Paul Jarrico, September 7, 1948, PJP-MHL; Paul Jarrico, "Hungarian Critique" (handwritten notes), n.d., PJP-MHL.

30. Paul Jarrico to Revai Deszi, September 15, 1948, PJP-MHL.

31. Paul Jarrico to Paul Rosenfeld, October 8, 1948, PJP-MHL; Paul Jarrico to John Pen, October 11, 1948, PJP-MHL.

32. Deszo Révai to Paul Jarrico, October 14, 1948, PJP-MHL; Paul Jarrico to John Pen, October 22, 1948, PJP-MHL; Paul Jarrico to Deszo Révai, December 5, 1949, PJP-MHL; Paul Jarrico to Michael Burn, March 24, 1950, PJP-MHL. Jarrico could not afford to renew the option, but Pen agreed not to sell the screen rights without giving Jarrico a chance to bid. A British producer, Christopher Brunel, showed some interest in it in 1957, but nothing came of the exchange of letters.

33. In May 1948, Hughes had purchased 24 percent of outstanding RKO stock for $8.8 million. According to movie historian Joel W. Finler, Hughes "ran the studio as though he had little interest in whether it earned a profit or not." Joel W. Finler, *The Hollywood Story* (New York: Crown, 1988), 177. John Houseman wrote that Hughes was never seen, "but his influence was pervasive and sinister. . . . It was a distasteful and unproductive atmosphere." Houseman, *Front and Center*, 316–17. For Jarrico's comments on Hughes, see Paul Jarrico, interview by Anne A. Morris, November 19, 1982, Oral History Collections, California State University, Long Beach.

34. Jarrico, *Hollywood Blacklist*, 90–91. Later, Ford said that he always tried "to whittle down" the lines of dialogue his character spoke because he thought "motion pictures talk too much." *Los Angeles Times*, September 1, 2006, E15.

35. Paul Jarrico to Maurice Rapf, October 4, 1949, PJP-MHL. *Home of the Brave* and *Intruder in the Dust* were two of a handful of postwar movies dealing with racial prejudice. For a discussion of the anti-Communist films mentioned, see Michael Barson and Steven Heller, *Red Scared! The Commie Menace in Propaganda and American Culture* (San Francisco: Chronicle Books, 2001).

36. Paul Jarrico, *The Man Who Watched Trains Go By* thematic statement, October 15, 1949, PJP-MHL.

37. Georges Simenon to Irving Allen, January 28, 1950, PJP-MHL. When Allen failed to make a production deal, he returned the screenplay to Jarrico. In June 1951, Jarrico arranged to sell the script to Josef Shaftel and to revise it for $5,000 up front, $10,000 deferred, and 3 percent of the profits. Shaftel intended to coproduce it with Raymond Stross of Eros Film. Jarrico convinced Shaftel to hire John Berry to direct, but Claude Rains, the star, had heard that Berry was blacklisted and prevailed on Shaftel to get rid of him. Jarrico later learned that Berry's replacement, Harold French, "was drunk and incompetent during the entire shooting." Paul Jarrico to Matti Salo, January 24, 1987, PJP-MHL. When *The Paris Express* (1953) was released, Shaftel gave the writing credit to French. Bosley Crowther criticized both the writing and directing and opined that the movie lacked "quality, character, sympathy and suspense." *New York Times*, June 6, 1953, 6. The version I viewed did not have a writing credit. All of Jarrico's narrative and dialogue regarding freedom and the individual have been eliminated, making the movie drag once the setup is finished and the scenario shifts to Paris.

38. George Willner to Paul Jarrico, February 27, 1950, PJP-MHL.

39. Paul Jarrico, "The Big Eye: Record," March–April 1950, PJP-MHL.

6. The Blacklist Expands, 1951–52

Epigraph: Paul Jarrico, advertisement, [ca. September 1976], PJP-MHL. Jarrico wrote this tongue-in-cheek advertisement after he saw *The Front*, written by former blacklistee Walter Bernstein.

1. Paul Jarrico to Abe Polonsky, September 30, 1950, PJP-MHL; Edward G. Robinson Collection, Cinema-Television Library, University of Southern California; SACLA to J. Edgar Hoover, December 14, 1950, FOIA-MHL. Robinson would be called to appear a third time, on April 30, 1952.

2. SACLA to J. Edgar Hoover, January 2, 1951, FOIA-MHL. Hoover noted in the margin of the report, "I would view with some reservations Schary's professions of anticommunism now."

3. *New York Times*, September 11, 1950, 18; Jarrico to Polonsky, September 30, 1950, PJP-MHL.

4. The MPIC was created in December 1947 to improve the image of the industry. Its members included representatives from the producers' associations, talent guilds, and craft unions.

5. On the SACLA's report of his meeting with Dmytryk, Hoover wrote in the margin, "Dmytryk is obviously more interested in expediency than clearing his record." SACLA to J. Edgar Hoover, February 3, 1951, FOIA-MHL. Almost fifty years later, some blacklistees' anger at Dmytryk had not abated. At a panel discussion in Barcelona, he was attacked by Jules Dassin (whom Dmytryk had named) and Walter Bernstein. *Weekly Variety*, July 6, 1988, 13, 16.

6. Paul Jarrico to George Tabori, January 9, 1951, PJP-MHL.

7. Paul Jarrico, *The Miami Story* (outline), January 16, 1951, PJP-MHL.

8. *Variety*, "In Our Opinion," March 5, 1951, 11; SACLA to J. Edgar Hoover, March 14, 1951, FOIA-MHL; SACLA to J. Edgar Hoover, March 22, 1951, FOIA-author.

9. The Supreme Court did not determine the Fifth Amendment's scope until 1955. Beck, *Contempt of Congress*, 63–90.

10. Gale Sondergaard, *Variety*, March 6, 1951, 5; MPIC statement, *Hollywood Reporter*, March 8, 1951, 3; *Variety*, March 14, 1951, 1. Johnston had taken a ten-month leave of absence from the Motion Picture Association of America, from January to November 1951, to serve as economic stabilization administrator in the Truman administration.

11. Karen Morley (one of the missing witnesses), interview by the author, August 19, 1976. Hugo Butler and Joseph Losey were traveling around the state, working on a script for Columbia. When Dalton Trumbo was released from prison, the Butlers went to his ranch, and the two families decided to move to Mexico. Butler never testified, though he was named by seven witnesses. Jean Rouverol Butler, "Stranger in a Strange Land," *Written By*, October 1997, 26–28. Losey, who was named once, went to France to avoid testifying.

12. The transcript indicates that Parks named the twelve himself, but Betty Garrett, his wife, has written that he, with the committee counsel, went down a list he had been given, saying the names of those he knew to be Communists. "He was not volunteering. He was reading." Betty Garrett with Ron Rapoport, *Betty Garrett and Other Songs: A Life on Stage and Screen* (Lanham, MD: Madison Books, 1998), 137. In any event, the day following

his testimony, Parks was fired from Columbia. His testimony was made public by the committee in 1953. House Committee, *Investigation of Communist Activities in the Los Angeles Area*, pt. 6, 2303–6.

13. Paul Jarrico, press statement, *Los Angeles Times*, March 24, 1951, 1. Jarrico received a few letters from people he did not know in response. A screenwriter from Italy wrote, "You have molti friends who sending heart feeling applause for your splendid struggle for the freedom of the artist." A woman wrote, "If I had to make any choice at all it would be to see you crawling through the mud of Korea with some true Americans." [Name withheld] to Paul Jarrico, March 26, 1951, PJP-MHL; Rose Monte to Paul Jarrico, [date obscured], PJP-MHL.

14. Jarrico, *Hollywood Blacklist*, 96–97.

15. Paul Jarrico, "Nothing but the Truth—So Help Me: An Exposé of the Committee on Un-American Activities and Its Collaborators" (materials for an unpublished pamphlet), [ca. September 1951], PJP-MHL.

16. Paul Jarrico to Michael Gordon, March 30, 1951, PJP-MHL. The fund was named the Kenny-Morris Trustee Fund after attorneys Robert Kenny and Robert Morris. People were asked to contribute what they could afford; reimbursements of travel expenses from the committee were paid back into the fund. Howard Da Silva contributed $1,500; Waldo Salt, Robert Lees, Gale Sondergaard, Harold Buchman, Joseph Bromberg, George Willner, Abraham Polonsky, and Jarrico each contributed $1,000. In May 1952, Jarrico became financial secretary. Correspondence and records in PJP-MHL. When this round of hearings ended, about $4,000 remained in the fund, half of which was given to the attorneys handling the main class-action suit against the studios, *Wilson v. Loew's, Inc.*

17. Paul Jarrico, drafts of statement to House Committee on Un-American Activities, n.d., April 11, April 12, 1951, PJP-MHL; final statement reprinted in Jarrico, *Hollywood Blacklist*, 172–73.

18. Collins testimony, April 12, 1951, House Committee, *Communist Infiltration of Hollywood Motion Picture Industry*, pt. 1, 251–56.

19. Sylvia Jarrico, interview.

20. Paul Jarrico, interview, in Fariello, *Red Scare*, 277. Isobel Lennart, who appeared as a cooperative witness the following year, believed that Collins "testified out of conviction," that he had "turned violently against the Communist Party for the most honest reasons." Quoted in Navasky, *Naming Names*, 257. Collins said that he never regretted his testimony and that the experience of being a pariah (among his former friends) served him in good stead; it made him tougher. Collins, interview.

21. Jarrico, agenda book entry, April 1951, PJP-LBJ.

22. Paul Jarrico, interview, in Fariello, *Red Scare*, 279; Paul Jarrico testimony, April 13, 1951, House Committee, *Communist Infiltration of Hollywood Motion Picture Industry*, pt. 1, 275–78.

23. Jarrico testimony, April 13, 1951, House Committee, *Communist Infiltration of Hollywood Motion Picture Industry*, pt. 1, 278–79.

24. Ibid., 279–81.

25. Ibid., 281–83.

26. Paul Jarrico, interview by Philippe Haudiquet, "Du sel de la terre à la liste noire," *La revue du cinéma: Image et son* 329 (June 1978): 115; Paul Jarrico, speech, New York Council of the Arts, Sciences and Professions, April 14, 1951, PJP-MHL.

27. Paul Jarrico, speech to the California Legislative Conference, Sacramento, [ca. early May 1951]; Paul Jarrico to George Willner, May 25, 1951, PJP-MHL. Howard Da Silva and Gale Sondergaard used the same words the following week at a meeting of the San Francisco Council of Arts, Sciences and Professions and received a similar response. The California Legislative Conference was created by Robert Kenny in January 1946 as a grass-roots, ad hoc consultative assembly on the war-to-peace conversion process. Its delegates wrote a political platform for the 1946 elections and Kenny's run for governor.

28. SACLA to J. Edgar Hoover, July 23, 1951, FOIA-author; Paul Jarrico, "The Inevitability of Peace," speech, Embassy Auditorium, Los Angeles, California, June 8, 1951, PJP-MHL.

29. Robert Goldfarb, who had joined the Jaffe Agency in 1950, sympathized with the Left and admired the stand of the Hollywood Ten. He recalled that most of his coworkers were liberal, and he did not remember whether a company policy regarding blacklisted people existed. He did not want to know if a script he was handling had been written by a blacklisted writer, either behind a front or under a pseudonym, but once he did know, he enthusiastically conspired to help. He estimated that perhaps only three or four other agencies knowingly represented left-wing writers. Robert Goldfarb, interview by the author, July 1, 2002.

30. Sylvia Jarrico, interview; Jarrico to Willner, May 25, 1951, PJP-MHL.

31. Paul Jarrico to George Feifer, July 20, 1992, PJP-MHL.

32. The various versions are in the RKO Collection: Scripts, Arts Library Special Collections Library, University of California, Los Angeles.

33. Paul Jarrico to SWG arbitration committee, July 12, 1951, PJP-MHL; Hughes quoted in Howard Rushmore, interview, in *New York Journal-American*, March 5, 1952, quoted in Donald L. Bartlett and James B. Steele, *Empire: The Life, Legend and Madness of Howard Hughes* (New York: Norton, 1979), 180. Jarrico later wrote that he had researched and

drafted a fairly convincing dossier proving that Hughes had broken every one of the Ten Commandments. "Since the issue was his right to take my name off a film under a morality clause . . . , I did think his morality was pertinent; after all, his name was on the film too—and remained on." But his lawyer assured him that Hughes's morality was irrelevant "under the rules of the legal game we were playing." Paul Jarrico to Clifford Irving, August 8, 1971, PJP-MHL.

34. *Variety*, March 31, 1952, 6.

35. The Motion Picture Association of America offered to reword the credit arbitration clause if the Writers Guild of America, west (WGAw; see chap. 8) allowed studios to refuse screen credits to "Communists" and Fifth Amendment witnesses. The WGAw agreed, and the anti-Communist clause remained part of the collective bargaining agreement for two decades.

36. The coverage by the *Los Angeles Times*, *Los Angeles Examiner*, *New York Times*, and the trade papers was extensive.

37. Paul Jarrico, interview by Haudiquet, 114.

38. Picketing instructions and circular, September 1951, PJP-MHL; Paul Jarrico, notes for a speech, n.d., PJP-MHL.

39. A radio personality, John Henry Faulk, won the most famous blacklist legal action. See John Henry Faulk, *Fear on Trial* (Austin: University of Texas Press, 1983).

40. Jarrico to Salt, April 17, 1952, PJP-MHL. Salt wrote that he could not fight for the credit from New York because the cost would exceed the value. Waldo Salt to Paul Jarrico, n.d., PJP-MHL.

41. See W. T. Lhamon Jr., *Deliberate Speed: The Origins of a Cultural Style in the American 1950s* (Washington, DC: Smithsonian Institute Press, 1990), and Stephen J. Whitfield, *The Culture of the Cold War*, 2nd ed. (Baltimore: Johns Hopkins University Press, 1996). For a comparison of the cold war cultures of the United States and the Soviet Union, see David Caute, *The Dancer Defects: The Struggle for Cultural Supremacy during the Cold War* (Oxford: Oxford University Press, 2003).

42. Michael Wilson, "Conditioning the American Mind: War Films Show Vicious Over-all Policy," *Hollywood Review*, January 1953, 1, 3; Michael Wilson, "Hollywood's Hero: Arrogant Adventurers Dominate Screen—Goodbye Mr. Deeds," *Hollywood Review*, April–May 1954, 1, 3; Al Levitt, "Film Slurs Negroes: Member of the Wedding Shows Industry Fails to Clear House," *Hollywood Review*, March–April 1953, 1, 3; John Howard Lawson, "Hollywood on the Waterfront: Union Workers Are Gangsters, Workers Are Helpless," *Hollywood Review*, November–December 1954, 1, 3; Sylvia Jarrico, "Evil Heroines of 1953: Women of Will and Purpose Shown by Films as Lethal Borgias Destined to Kill," *Hollywood Review*, June–July 1953, 1, 3–4.

43. Lawson, *Theory and Technique of Playwriting and Screenwriting* (New York: Putnam's, 1949), 361; V. J. Jerome, *The Negro in Hollywood Films* (New York: Masses and Mainstream, 1950), 54–55.

44. Michael Wilson, "The Writer in the Motion Picture Industry," [ca. late 1951], MWP-BW.

45. John Howard Lawson, *Film in the Battle of Ideas* (New York: Masses and Mainstream, 1953), 88, 91.

46. *Hollywood Review*, April–May 1954, 3; Dalton Trumbo to Sam Sillen, December 5, 1953, in Trumbo, *Additional Dialogue*, 281–83.

47. Jarrico, *Hollywood Blacklist*, 149. Lawson restated his criticism in a forty-three-page typescript he prepared for a party discussion: John Howard Lawson, "Toward a People's Culture," [ca. 1955], MWP-BW.

48. Untitled typescript, [ca. summer 1954], MWP-BW. The first sentence reads, "The following document is submitted by the cultural leadership as a basis for discussion, evaluation and criticism of the work in our field."

49. Michael Wilson, "A Note on the Organization Document" (typescript), [ca. summer 1954], MWP-BW.

50. John Howard Lawson, "Basis and Superstructure" (typescript), [ca. summer 1954], MWP-BW.

51. Los Angeles County section of the CPUSA meeting, transcript, [1954], MWP-BW.

7. *Salt of the Earth*, 1952–54

Epigraph: Jarrico, suggestion for trailer, agenda book entry, February 1954, PJP-LBJ.

1. The Scottsboro case involved nine young black males, ages thirteen to twenty-one, who were accused of raping two white women in Alabama (1931). Eight were convicted and sentenced to death before the Communist-run International Labor Defense took control of the case and launched a legal and political campaign on behalf of the condemned. After a series of appeals, trials, and bargains, four were released and five served lengthy prison terms. Patterson escaped in 1947.

2. Directed by Elia Kazan, *Deep Are the Roots* had played on Broadway for 477 performances between 1946 and 1947. The reviewer for the *New York Times* wrote that it "is the first work of the fall with an idea, the first not to shy away from a problem." *New York Times*, September 27, 1945, 24. For discussions of the play, see Judith E. Smith, *Visions of Belonging: Family Stories, Pop Culture, and Postwar Democracy, 1940–1960* (New York: Columbia University Press, 2004), 128–34, and Richard Schickel, *Elia Kazan: A Biography* (New York: HarperCollins, 2005), 128–32.

3. Adrian Scott to Paul Jarrico, September [21?], 1951, PJP-MHL; Adrian Scott to Charles Katz, September 23, 1950, PJP-MHL; Paul Jarrico to Adrian Scott, November 4, 1950, PJP-MHL.

4. Adrian Scott to Paul Jarrico, September 23, 1950, PJP-MHL; Paul Jarrico to Ken McCormick (editor in chief, Doubleday), September 28, 1950, PJP-MHL; George Willner to Paul Jarrico, December 20, 1950, PJP-MHL; Paul Jarrico to Lee Barker (executive editor, Doubleday), January 11, 1951, PJP-MHL; Paul Jarrico to Adrian Scott, February 16, 1951, PJP-MHL; Paul Jarrico to George Willner, May 25, 1951, PJP-MHL. See also Howard Fast, *Being Red* (Boston: Houghton Mifflin, 1990), 80.

5. Biberman, *"Salt of the Earth,"* 31, 38.

6. Lazarus was president, Katz was secretary-treasurer, and Jarrico, Biberman, and Scott were vice presidents. Jarrico, Biberman, and Scott thought that they needed the support of a community of businesspeople to make their films and that theater owner Lazarus provided an entry into that community. They also needed the backing of people who knew the business end of motion picture production. Jarrico deposition, *Independent Productions Corp. and I.P.C. Distributors, Inc. v. Loew's, Inc., et al.*, 40, 1167, 1169.

7. Paul Jarrico, manuscript (probably written for the attorneys in the IPC suit), n.d., PJP-MHL.

8. Jarrico deposition, *Independent Productions Corp. and I.P.C. Distributors, Inc. v. Loew's, Inc., et al.*, 75–76.

9. Paul Jarrico to Mason Roberson, September 13, 1951, PJP-MHL. Roberson tried a new approach, but on January 11, 1952, Jarrico informed him that it did not work either and that they may have chosen the wrong book for the movie. Jarrico later admitted to John Berry that IPC had "made a real mistake, picking that [book], and our Negro friends have pointed it out in no uncertain terms. They want a story of their liberation struggle, not the story of a victim but of a victor." Paul Jarrico to John Berry, March 1, 1952, PJP-MHL.

10. Dalton Trumbo to Herbert Biberman, March 24, 1952, PJP-MHL; outlines and Fields's comments, PJP-MHL. For Trumbo's comments on the script, see Dalton Trumbo to Herbert Biberman, [August] 1951, and Dalton Trumbo to Hy Kraft, May 4, 1952, Trumbo, *Additional Dialogue*, 228, 230. For an extensive analysis of Trumbo's reaction to the others' criticisms, see Ronald Radosh and Allis Radosh, *Red Star over Hollywood: The Film Colony's Long Romance with the Left* (San Francisco: Encounter Books, 2005), 212–17.

11. Jenny and Craig Vincent had converted their summer camp to a guest ranch in 1949. It attracted mainly liberal, left-wing families. Bill Jarrico recalled

that Jenny's folk singing brought many musical people as well. Bill Jarrico, e-mail message to the author, August 4, 2004. The Vincents closed the camp in 1953 because FBI agents were congregating there, "looking over everyone's shoulder." Jenny Vincent, interview by the author, August 17, 2004.

12. The union had been chartered by the American Federation of Labor in 1916, and it joined the CIO in 1936. By the end of World War II, IUMMSW represented most of the nonferrous metal workers in the United States. Eighty-five percent of its members in Arizona and New Mexico and 90 percent of the Empire Zinc employees were Mexican Americans. After the union's expulsion from the CIO, its membership declined by 55 percent, to about 44,000. A history of the union, focusing mainly on its leaders, can be found in Vernon H. Jenson, *Nonferrous Metals Industry Unionism, 1932–1954: A Study of Leadership Controversy* (Ithaca, NY: Cornell University Press, 1954). The best accounts of the strike and the making of the movie are in James J. Lorence, *The Suppression of "Salt of the Earth": How Hollywood, Big Labor, and Politicians Blacklisted a Movie in Cold War America* (Albuquerque: University of New Mexico Press, 1999), and James J. Lorence, "Mining *Salt of the Earth*," *Wisconsin Magazine of History*, Winter 2001–2, 29–43. See also Biberman, *"Salt of the Earth,"* and Michael Wilson, with commentary by Deborah Silverton Rosenfelt, *Salt of the Earth* (Old Westbury, NY: Feminist Press, 1978). Ellen R. Baker's *On Strike and on Film: Mexican American Families and Blacklisted Filmmakers in Cold War America* (Chapel Hill: University of North Carolina Press, 2007) arrived too late for me to incorporate its findings in this biography. Most of the details in this chapter are from Paul Jarrico, "A *Salt of the Earth* Chronology," compiled in 1955 and regularly updated, in PJP-MHL.

13. Jencks quoted in Robert Nott, "On the Line," *Pasatiempo*, February 21–27, 2003, 41. For further comments by the Jenckses on the strike and the movie, see their interviews in Ginger and Christino, *Cold War against Labor*, 2:595–601. Coincidentally, blacklisted screenwriter Philip Stevenson, using the name Lars Lawrence, had just begun writing *The Seed*, a multivolume novel about a miners' strike in Gallup, New Mexico, in August 1933. The first two parts, *Morning, Noon and Night* and *Out of the Dust*, were published by Putnam's in 1954 and 1956. The second two parts, *Old Father Antic* and *The Hoax*, were published by International Publishers in 1962. The fifth part was never published.

14. Jarrico quoted in Lorence, *Suppression*, 58; Henrietta Williams, interview, in *A Crime to Fit the Punishment,* directed by Barbara A. Moss (New York: First Run Features, 1983).

15. Paul Jarrico, interview by Haudiquet, 106–7; Jarrico deposition, *Independent Productions Corp. and I.P.C. Distributors, Inc. v. Loew's, Inc., et al.*, 45, 50, 54, 1881.

16. Paul Jarrico and Herbert Biberman, "Breaking Ground," *California Quarterly*, Summer 1953, 60–63; Paul Jarrico to Jules Dassin, August 2, 1952, PJP-MHL.

17. Jarrico, *Hollywood Blacklist*, 136; Clinton Jencks, interview by the author, June 27, 2004; Jarrico quoted in Rosenfelt, *Salt of the Earth*, 108 ("crime"); Jarrico deposition, *Independent Productions Corp. and I.P.C. Distributors, Inc. v. Loew's, Inc., et al.*, 1882.

18. Jencks quoted in Nott, "On the Line," 41.

19. Jarrico deposition, *Independent Productions Corp. and I.P.C. Distributors, Inc. v. Loew's, Inc., et al.*, 77–78, 208, 442; Jencks, interview.

20. IPC to Henry Willcox, October 6, 1951, PJP-MHL; Paul Jarrico to Harold Rosen, December 24, 1951, PJP-MHL.

21. Jarrico, agenda book entry, March 1, 1952, PJP-LBJ; Sylvia Jarrico, interview; Biberman, *"Salt of the Earth,"* 57.

22. Jarrico to Berry, March 1, 1952, PJP-MHL; Paul Jarrico to Waldo Salt, March 6, 1952, PJP-MHL; Paul Jarrico to Lester Cole, March 7, 1952, PJP-MHL; Lester Cole to Paul Jarrico, March 10, 1952, PJP-MHL. Writer Carlton Moss and actress Frances Williams had been made full partners, and they were trying to gather the names of black film technicians. Jarrico later stated, "We felt very strongly the need to integrate Negroes into our company. We felt the need to develop projects which would have an appeal to the Negro people. . . . Most Negroes have never had the opportunity to become film producers and we wanted to provide that opportunity, and so it was in that spirit that we invited these two people to join us and discussed with them the possibility of their sharing equally with us in the stock of the company." Jarrico deposition, *Independent Productions Corp. and I.P.C. Distributors, Inc. v. Loew's, Inc., et al.*, 237–38.

23. Jarrico, "*Salt of the Earth* Chronology," August 1, 1993, 5, PJP-MHL; SACLA to J. Edgar Hoover, September 24, 1952, FOIA-author; Biberman, *"Salt of the Earth,"* 58.

24. Paul Jarrico to John Berry, June 2, 1952, PJP-MHL; Jules Dassin to Paul Jarrico, August 5, 1952, PJP-MHL.

25. John Howard Lawson, "Important Memo, *Salt of the Earth*," John Howard Lawson Papers, supplement, file cover 34, Special Collections Research Center, Morris Library, Southern Illinois University, Carbondale (copy provided by Katherine Salzmann). Lawson vaguely remembered writing it in 1954, but it was most likely written after he saw a rough cut on December 13, 1953.

26. Sylvia Jarrico, interview; Jarrico, *Hollywood Blacklist*, 165. Although Lawson was privately critical, in public he lauded Wilson's script: "If the possibilities of the story are realized on the screen, *Salt of the Earth* will be a vital contribution to the development of a people's and working class art film in the United States." Lawson, *Film in the Battle of Ideas*, 120–21.

27. Department of State to Paul Jarrico, November 25, 1952, PJP-MHL; Paul Jarrico to Barney Dreyfus, December 1, 1952, PJP-MHL.

28. Jarrico, *Hollywood Blacklist*, 165.

29. Jarrico, "*Salt of the Earth* Chronology," August 1, 1993, 7, PJP-MHL.

30. Jencks quoted in Nott, "On the Line," 41; Sonja Dahl Biberman, interview by the author, July 7, 2002.

31. Mike Connolly, Rambling Reporter, *Hollywood Reporter*, February 9, 1953, 2, February 10, 1953, 2; Riesel quoted in Lorence, *Suppression*, 78; film council and Brewer quoted in Mike Connolly, Rambling Reporter, *Hollywood Reporter*, February 13, 1953, 1, 8. Brewer had founded the Hollywood AFL Film Council in 1948 to fight communism in the movie industry.

32. *Congressional Record*, 83rd Cong., 1st sess., February 24, 1953, 1371–72.

33. The best contemporary account of the efforts to stop the filming is Elizabeth Kerby, "Violence in Silver City: Who Caused the Trouble?" *Frontier*, May 1953, 5–10.

34. *Congressional Record*, 83rd Cong., 1st sess., March 19, 1953, 2127.

35. Simon Lazarus testimony, March 26–28, 1953, House Committee, *Investigation of Communist Activities in the Los Angeles Area*, pt. 2, 478–98.

36. Sol Kaplan testimony, April 8, 1953, ibid., pt. 4, 826–36.

37. Paul Jarrico, *Hugger-Mugger*, July 1985, PJP-LBJ. This was a nine-page film treatment about the effort to disrupt the filming of *Salt of the Earth*.

38. Jarrico and Biberman, "Breaking Ground," 63. IPC paid the publisher $500. "We wanted a great many copies so that we could send it out to people who had heard what we considered to be falsehoods about the picture, so that the script would help us to clarify some of the atmosphere." Jarrico deposition, *Independent Productions Corp. and I.P.C. Distributors, Inc. v. Loew's, Inc., et al.*, 1665. Ira Wallach, who read the script in this format and reviewed it for a Communist cultural journal, termed it a "deeply humane and powerful document." Ira Wallach, "Major Screenplay," *Masses and Mainstream*, September 1953, 54.

39. Paul Jarrico to Roy Brewer, July 28, 1953, PJP-MHL. Copies were sent to eight laboratories and to the sound technicians' and film editors' locals.

40. Biberman, *"Salt of the Earth,"* 147.

41. Clinton Jencks to Michael Wilson, July 31, 1953, box 45, folder 12, Michael Wilson Papers, Arts Library Special Collections, University of California, Los Angeles (hereafter cited as MWP-ALSC); Michael Wilson,

speech, IUMMSW national meeting, St. Louis, MO, September 16, 1953, box 45, folder 13, MWP-ALSC.

42. Lawson, "Important Memo: *Salt of the Earth*," John Howard Lawson Papers, supplement, file cover 34, Special Collections Research Center, Morris Library, Southern Illinois University, Carbondale.

43. Michael Wilson, "Comments on the Memo," n.d., box 45, folder 14, MWP-ALSC.

44. Paul Jarrico to Sylvia Jarrico, January 10, 1954, PJP-LBJ; Paul Jarrico to Simon Lazarus, January 17, 1954, PJP-MHL; Paul Jarrico to Sylvia Jarrico, January 20, 1954, PJP-LBJ; Paul Jarrico to Sylvia Jarrico, January 31, 1954, PJP-LBJ.

45. Paul Jarrico to Sylvia Jarrico, March 3, 1954, PJP-LBJ.

46. Paul Jarrico to Sylvia Jarrico, March 14, 1954, PJP-LBJ.

47. Jarrico, "*Salt of the Earth* Chronology," August 1, 1993, 22, PJP-MHL; Paul Jarrico to Michael Wilson, March 7, 1954, PJP-MHL.

48. Jencks quoted in Lorence, *Suppression*, 103–7, 140.

49. Elizabeth Gurley Flynn, "What *Salt of the Earth* Meant to Me," *Political Affairs* 33 (June 1954): 65; Pauline Kael, "Morality Plays Right and Left—Advertising: *Night People* and Propaganda: *Salt of the Earth*," *Sight and Sound*, October–December 1954, 67–73. In an analysis written at the end of his life, Jarrico noted that seven of the dialogue quotations Kael criticized did not appear in the finished product—they appeared in the version of the screenplay printed in *California Quarterly*. Jarrico concluded that Kael had not seen the movie. He wrote, "I do not question Kael's right to dislike *Salt*, and to give it a negative review. . . . My reaction is subjective, admittedly, but what she seems to have lost at the movies was not her innocence but her honor." Paul Jarrico to Mark Le Fanu, September 28, 1996, PJP-MHL.

50. Paul Jarrico, telegram to Dore Schary, May 19, 1954 (copy provided by James Lorence); Jarrico deposition, *Independent Productions Corp. and I.P.C. Distributors, Inc. v. Loew's, Inc., et al.*, 396, 705; Untitled typescript, [summer 1954], 13, MWP-BW.

51. Rights would be sold to Poland, Romania, the Soviet Union, and the People's Republic of China. The Department of State blocked the deal with China under the Trading with the Enemies Act, and the Chinese government appropriated the movie. By October 1956, IPC had realized about $55,000 from international sales, half of which went to repay loans and the other half to start a legal fund. Jarrico wrote to a Czechoslovakian friend, "Foreign countries, including your own, have praised the film in the highest terms—and offered to buy it on the lowest terms. That may sound unfair. What seems low to us may seem high to those in charge of film imports in the Eastern Democracies. But it seems to us to be a serious underestima-

tion of the value of cultural work." Paul Jarrico to Jiri Weiss, March 5, 1955, PJP-MHL. In May 1959, the United States Information Agency provided Congress with a list of eighty-two Hollywood movies it had blacklisted, including *Salt of the Earth*. Any profits those films earned in the twelve countries with "blocked" currencies could not be converted into U.S. dollars. *New York Times*, May 24, 1959, 46.

52. Paul Jarrico to Solomons, May 23, 1954, PJP-MHL. Jarrico and Biberman came close to selling the movie to the American Federation of Labor for $400,000, with the proviso that IPC's and IUMMSW's names be removed from the film. But even under those conditions, IATSE president Richard Walsh refused to remove his union's proscription. See Lorence, *Suppression*, 155–67.

53. Paul Jarrico to Herbert Biberman, June 25, 1960, PJP-MHL.

54. Jarrico, agenda book entry, June 1978, PJP-LBJ; Jarrico, *Hollywood Blacklist*, 163–64. Biberman later wrote, "The degree of our skill [as filmmakers] must be drawn from the fact that we NEVER HAD ONE DAY OF NORMALITY in the entire course of making the film." Herbert Biberman, "What Kind of Company Was This? How Normal Was It? What Were the Relationships among Its Members?" [1964?], PJP-MHL.

55. See Larry Ceplair, "A Crime to Fit the Punishment," *Cineaste* 13, no. 3 (1984): 26–27, and Larry Ceplair, "The Many Fiftieth Anniversaries of *Salt of the Earth*," *Cineaste* 29, no. 2 (2004): 8–9.

8. The Black Market and Khrushchev's Speech, 1954–58

Epigraph: Paul Jarrico to Jiri Weiss, February 8, 1956, PJP-MHL. At Geneva, the United States, the Soviet Union, the United Kingdom, and France met but accomplished little of substance. The meeting did, however, mark a relaxation of cold war tensions.

1. One survey, taken that summer by the Fund for the Republic, recorded the following: 66 percent of the respondents favored removing from the public libraries any book written by a Communist; 91 percent favored firing any Communist teacher; 90 percent favored firing any Communist working in a defense plant; 68 percent favored the prohibition of any Communist speaking in public; 77 percent favored taking away the citizenship of any Communist; 73 percent stated that they would report to the FBI any neighbor or acquaintance suspected of being a Communist; 78 percent believed that a Communist could not be a loyal American; and 72 percent of Republicans and 62 percent of Democrats had a favorable opinion of congressional committees investigating communism. Reported in Samuel

A. Stouffer, *Communism, Conformity, and Civil Liberties: A Cross-Section of the Nation Speaks Its Mind* (Garden City, NY: Doubleday, 1955).

2. See Jeff Broadwater, *Eisenhower and the Anti-Communist Crusade* (Chapel Hill: University of North Carolina Press, 1992), 172–75.

3. *Congressional Record*, 84th Cong., 1st sess., January 14, 1955, 361. The resolution was approved 84–0, with twelve senators not voting.

4. Paul Jarrico to Dick Irving Hyland, November 10, 1954, PJP-MHL.

5. Jarrico, *Hollywood Blacklist*, 138.

6. Lewis, whom several blacklisted writers considered a progressive, became, in 1955, an executive vice president at Kirk Douglas's production company, Bryna Productions. He secured assignments for John Howard Lawson and Dalton Trumbo. See Bernard F. Dick, *Radical Innocence: A Critical Study of the Hollywood Ten* (Lexington: University Press of Kentucky, 1989), 64.

7. Paul Jarrico and Sylvia Jarrico, *Greeneyes* (outline), January 4, 1955, PJP-MHL. Under the original deal, the Jarricos were to receive 50 percent, but when Trumbo decided to forego their treatment, the deal was revised, and the Jarricos were paid $1,200. It was released in 1957 as *The Green-Eyed Blonde*, and the writing credit was given to the producer, Sally Stubblefield.

8. Jarrico, journal entry, January 16, 1955, PJP-LBJ.

9. Jarrico, journal entry, February 7, 1955, PJP-LBJ; Sylvia Jarrico quoted in ibid.

10. Jarrico, journal entry, February 15, 1955, PJP-LBJ; Jarrico, agenda book entry, February 1955, PJP-LBJ. For more on *IPC Distributors, Inc. v. Chicago, Moving Pictures Machine Operators Union, Local 110*, see Lorence, *Suppression*, 171–73.

11. Jarrico, journal entries, March 28, April 20, 1955, PJP-LBJ.

12. He responded to an advertisement in *Variety* for an "unusual advertising copywriter." He wrote, "I'm unusual, all right. In the spring of 1951 I was a $2000 a week screenwriter at RKO." Then he was blacklisted, but, he continued, "If you're interested in my ability rather than my politics, I'm your man." For the most helpful book he had ever read, Jarrico filled in "Chicken Little (taught me how to read)." He was rejected, but the rejection letter noted that it was a matter of complete indifference to the agency that he had been "accused" by the House Committee on Un-American Activities. Paul Jarrico to Guild, Bascom and Bonfigli Inc., April 15, 1955, PJP-MHL; Guild, Bascom and Bonfigli Inc. to Paul Jarrico, May 9, 1955, PJP-MHL.

13. Jarrico and his screenwriting friends drank heavily. Ring Lardner Jr. recalled that the young Hollywood writers of his generation "worked hard and drank hard" because of the stress of deadlines, creative problems, working in isolation, and personal demons. Lardner, *I'd Hate Myself*, 43,

55. Although Bill Jarrico remembered that his father always had a bottle of scotch on his desk when he wrote at home, Sylvia Jarrico said he never seemed to be drunk. Bill Jarrico, interview; Sylvia Jarrico, interview.

14. Ring Lardner Jr. to Paul Jarrico, August 28, October 6, 1955, PJP-MHL. Weinstein, who had worked on the Wallace campaign, had moved her family to England to escape the domestic cold war. In 1952, she established Sapphire Films, which produced *The Adventures of Robin Hood* and other costumed adventure series.

15. Jarrico, journal entry, September 30, 1955, PJP-LBJ.

16. Jarrico, journal entry, February 5, 1955, PJP-LBJ. When her article, "The Hollywood Story," appeared in *Frontier* (May 1954), it attracted the attention of Robert Hutchins, president of the Fund for the Republic. He proposed that she expand the article into a book for the fund. But when his advisors told him that she appeared too close to the Communists (the blacklistees who had granted her interviews), Hutchins gave the job to John Cogley, editor of the liberal Catholic periodical *Commonweal*. Cogley then contracted with Kerby to research and write the Hollywood blacklist chapter of *Report on Blacklisting* (1956).

17. Ben Margolis filed a complaint in superior court, charging Allied Artists and director William Wyler with fraudulent conspiracy to deprive Wilson of his legitimate credit. Ben Margolis to Michael Wilson, July 25, 1956, March 22, 1957, PJP-MHL; Albert Maltz to Paul Jarrico, April 13, 1957, PJP-MHL; Paul Jarrico to Albert Maltz, May 20, 1957, PJP-MHL. Wilson also brought an action in France to enjoin the movie from being shown there. He eventually settled both suits for $5,000. Maltz did not file a suit.

18. Billy Wilkerson, *Hollywood Reporter*, April 19, 1956, 1; Paul Jarrico, press statement, April 19, 1956, PJP-MHL. A portion of it was quoted in *New York Times*, April 23, 1956, 51.

19. In 1954, the SWG merged with the Radio Writers Guild and the Television Writers Guild to form the Writers Guild of America, west and the Writers Guild of America, east. Screenwriters were placed in the former.

20. Paul Jarrico to Screen Writers Branch, WGAw, January 16, 1957, PJP-MHL; Paul Jarrico to William Nutt, January 16, 1957, PJP-MHL; Paul Jarrico to Arbitration Committee, WGAw, March 6, 1957, PJP-MHL; Ben Margolis to RKO Radio Pictures, March 28, 1957, PJP-MHL; Paul Jarrico to Ben Margolis, March 19, 1958, PJP-MHL; Ben Margolis to Paul Jarrico, March 25, 1958, PJP-MHL. Only the reviewer for the *Hollywood Reporter* noted that *The Girl Most Likely* was based on *Tom, Dick and Harry*. *Hollywood Reporter*, December 17, 1957, 3.

21. Sam Moore to Michael Wilson, November 12, 1956, PJP-MHL; *Wilson, et al. v. Loew's Incorporated, et al.*, 355 U.S. 597 (1958).

22. Paul Jarrico, "Geneva Report," August 4, 1955, PJP-MHL.

23. ASP executive board, press statement, December 14, 1955, PJP-MHL.

24. Paul Jarrico to Jules Dassin, March 10, 1956, PJP-MHL; Paul Jarrico, "The Twentieth Party Congress of the CPSU," April 5, 1956, PJP-MHL. Anastas Mikoyan was a member of the CPUSSR Central Committee Presidium and the first deputy chairman of the USSR Council of Ministers. The congress met in February, but CPUSA members received transcripts of the speeches in March.

25. Jarrico, "Twentieth Party Congress of the CPSU," PJP-MHL.

26. Jarrico, journal entry, May 1, 1956, PJP-LBJ. CPUSA leaders knew the details of the "secret" speech almost immediately, but the text was not printed in the *Daily Worker* until June, following its printing by commercial newspapers. Gates, *Story of An American Communist*, 167.

27. Paul Jarrico, report to the CPUSA cultural section, June 17, 1956, PJP-MHL.

28. Ibid.

29. Paul Jarrico, "Criticism of Draft Resolution," October 6, 1956, PJP-MHL. See also Paul Jarrico, cultural section resolution, draft, November 1, 1956, and final copy, November 14, 1956, PJP-MHL.

30. Paul Jarrico to Jim Allen, January 4, 1957, PJP-MHL; Jarrico, agenda book entry, October 1956, PJP-LBJ.

31. Jarrico, *Hollywood Blacklist*, 150–51; Jarrico quoted in Dorothy Healey and Maurice Isserman, *Dorothy Healey Remembers: A Life in the Communist Party* (New York: Oxford University Press, 1990), 150. Party secretary Eugene Dennis wrote, "The heaviest loss of membership took place after the publication of the special report of Khrushchev on Stalin; there was another notable exodus after the events in Hungary. Following the [1957] convention, quite a few left the organization in New York. . . . This process continues and one of the big factors was the damaging role of the protracted factional struggles." Eugene Dennis to John Williamson, [ca. 1957], quoted in Peggy Dennis, *The Autobiography of an American Communist: A Personal View of a Political Life, 1925–1975* (Westport, CT: L. Hill, 1977), 232. Healey did not leave the party until 1968, following the Warsaw Bloc invasion of Czechoslovakia.

32. Paul Jarrico, journal entry, September 30, 1955, PJP-LBJ; Paul Jarrico to Carl Marzani, May 21, 1957, PJP-MHL.

33. The law firm of Margolis, McTernan and Branton (Los Angeles) engaged the law firm of Rosston, Hart and Brussel (New York) to try the case. George Brussel Jr. and Edward Labaton handled the pretrial depositions and motions.

34. Paul Jarrico to Ring Lardner Jr., June 1, 1957, PJP-MHL; S. M. Jeppson to Paul Jarrico, June 28, 1956, PJP-MHL; Paul Jarrico to S. M. Jeppson, July 17, 1956, PJP-MHL; John T. White to Paul Jarrico, August 7, 1956, PJP-MHL; Paul Jarrico to Frank Tarloff, November 17, 1956, PJP-MHL. Boudin had been appointed as counsel for the Emergency Civil Liberties Committee, and in their first major test case, they secured a passport for Paul Robeson. See Susan Braudy, *Family Circle: The Boudins and the Aristocracy of the Left* (New York: Knopf, 2003).

35. Paul Jarrico to Alfred Crown, October 23, 1957, PJP-MHL; Paul Jarrico to Bill Jarrico, October 12, 1957, PJP-MHL; Paul Jarrico, "The Week the Dam Finally Began to Break" (list of possible deals), November 25, 1957, PJP-MHL.

36. Paul Jarrico to Michael Wilson, April 9, 1958, PJP-MHL. *The Grand Tour* was a romantic comedy involving a tourist bus in France filled with people of different nationalities. It was a spoof of tourists, a satirical look at various nationality traits, and a study in human loneliness. The title page of a revised draft, dated November 1962, gives screenplay credit to Peter Achilles and original story credit to Michael Wilson. PJP-MHL.

37. Paul Jarrico and Nel King, *The Night They Waited*, April 2, 1958, PJP-MHL; Paul Jarrico and Nel King, *All Night Long*, notes and drafts, 1958–59, PJP-MHL.

38. Paul Jarrico to Ed Kraus, April 28, 1958, PJP-MHL.

39. *Kent v. Dulles*, 357 U.S. 116 (1958). See Stanley J. Kutler, *The American Inquisition: Justice and Injustice in the Cold War* (New York: Hill and Wang, 1982), 101–16. The Department of State asked Congress for the necessary legislation, but the Senate failed to act on the request.

40. Paul Jarrico, interview, in Fariello, *Red Scare*, 279.

41. SACLA to J. Edgar Hoover, February 27, 1957, FOIA-author.

9. Europe, 1958–75

Epigraph: J. Edgar Hoover to Office of Security, Department of State, February 4, 1959, FOIA-author. The legal attaché in Paris reported to the State Department the following month that he had received a report (from an agency whose name is blacked out): "The present activities of PAUL JARRICO are unknown. He claims to be a writer and reportedly receives frequent visits from non-French persons. These visitors, who are occasionally extremely noisy, are reported to leave very late at night. The neighbors have protested because of this noise." American Embassy in Paris to J. Edgar Hoover, March 9, 1959, FOIA-author.

1. Paul Jarrico to Clinton and Virginia Jencks, December 25, 1958, PJP-MHL.

2. Paul Jarrico and Michael Wilson to Dino De Laurentiis, December 5, 1958, PJP-MHL.

3. Dino De Laurentiis to Paul Jarrico and Michael Wilson, January 24, 1959, PJP-MHL.

4. Ritt had been blacklisted as an actor but was hired by MGM to direct *Edge of the City* (1957). See Martin Ritt, interview, in McGilligan and Buhle, *Tender Comrades*, 554–70.

5. Dino De Laurentiis to Michael Wilson, May 29, 1959, PJP-MHL.

6. Paul Jarrico and Michael Wilson to Dino De Laurentiis and Martin Ritt, June 7, 1959, PJP-MHL; Paul Jarrico to Martin Ritt, September 26, 1959, PJP-MHL; Martin Ritt to Paul Jarrico, October 8, 1959, PJP-MHL; Paul Jarrico to Martin Ritt, October 12, 1959, PJP-MHL; Martin Ritt to Paul Jarrico, October 24, 1959, PJP-MHL. Two weeks after their return to Paris, Jarrico and Wilson learned that Mike Connolly, in his *Hollywood Reporter* gossip column, had exposed their employment by De Laurentiis. *Hollywood Reporter*, July 20, 1959, 2.

7. *New York Times*, February 2, 1960, 27; *Variety Film Reviews*, *1959–1963* (New York: Garland, 1983), April 6, 1960; Martin Ritt, interview by Bruce Cook, "Norma Rae's Big Daddy," *American Film*, April 1980, reprinted in *Martin Ritt: Interviews*, ed. Gabriel Miller (Jackson: University Press of Mississippi, 2002), 53; Gabriel Miller, *The Films of Martin Ritt: Fanfare for the Common Man* (Jackson: University Press of Mississippi, 2000), 37.

8. Paul Jarrico to Bill Jarrico, April 27, October 16, 1960, PJP-MHL; Paul Jarrico, "Portrait of an Artist in Search of a Buck and a Road," May 8–14, 1961, PJP-MHL. A recently translated biography of Dino De Laurentiis states that Ritt was completely bewildered by the outdoor, mountainous location and the large Italian company. De Laurentiis had to ask Pietro Germi to assist Ritt. Tullio Kezich and Alessandra Levantesi, *Dino: The Life and Films of Dino De Laurentiis*, trans. James Marcus (New York: Miramax Books / Hyperion, 2004), 144. Many years later, when congratulating Ritt for *The Front* and *Norma Rae*, Jarrico wrote him, "You're aware, of course that I'd not forgiven you for *Five Marked Women*. Not, be it said, for not making a good movie but (1) for having declared, when I phoned you in Austria and asked about the changes I'd heard were being made, 'I take full responsibility,' and (2) when we all had dinner in Paris, and I asked you how it had turned out politically, for having answered, 'I couldn't care less.' So I have held you responsible." Paul Jarrico to Martin Ritt, December 1, 1980, PJP-MHL.

9. Paul Jarrico to Nel King, November 19, 1958, January 22, 1959, PJP-MHL; Paul Jarrico to Matti Salo, December 19, 1986, November 24, 1991,

PJP-MHL. Roberts, who had cofounded Enterprise Productions with John Garfield, was named by Martin Berkeley in September 1951, but the House Committee on Un-American Activities did not subpoena him.

10. Paul Jarrico to Bob Roberts, September 24, 1959, PJP-MHL; Paul Jarrico to Nel King, September 28, 1959, PJP-MHL.

11. Paul Jarrico to Nel King, October 21, 25, 1961, PJP-MHL; Paul Jarrico to Bill Jarrico, October 22, 1961, PJP-MHL; Paul Jarrico to Matti Salo, December 19, 1986, PJP-MHL; review clippings in *All Night Long* file, PJP-MHL.

12. Paul Jarrico to Edith and Carl Marzani, October 30, 1959, PJP-MHL.

13. Paul Jarrico to John Berry, December 4, 1959, PJP-MHL; Sylvia Jarrico, conference notes, December 2–10, 1959, PJP-MHL; Paul Jarrico to Solomons, December 8, 1959; Sylvia Jarrico to Bill Jarrico, December 6, 1959, PJP-MHL; Francesco Rosi to Paul Jarrico, August 11, 1960, PJP-MHL. The movie was not made.

14. Paul Jarrico to John Berry, October 26, 1959; Paul Jarrico to Nel King, November 29, 1959, PJP-MHL; Paul Jarrico to himself, May 27, 1961, PJP-MHL.

15. Paul Jarrico to Neuma Agins, September 13, 1961, PJP-MHL. Yvette Le Floc'h had met her husband, Marcel Aymonin, while they were both taking classes at the Oriental Language School in Paris. They were either members of or very close to the French Communist Party, and when he applied for a position in the foreign service, he was posted as a chargé d'affaires to Sofia, Bulgaria, where their daughter, Armelle, was born in 1950. Aymonin was then posted to Prague as cultural attaché. He would eventually become a professor of literature at the University of Algiers and a translator of Czech books, including one by Milan Kundera.

16. Zelma Wilson, *Rebel and Architect*, 402; Bill Jarrico, interview; Daniel Mainwaring to Paul Jarrico, May 11, 1971, PJP-MHL; Clancy Sigal, interview by the author, June 19, 2002; Betsy Blair, interview by the author, April 18, 2004; Sonja Dahl Biberman, interview. Despite repeated requests, Yvette Jarrico chose not to provide me with any information regarding her life with Paul Jarrico.

17. Paul Jarrico to Nel King, October 8, 1961, PJP-MHL; Jarrico, *Hollywood Blacklist*, 155.

18. Sylvia Jarrico, interview; Paul Jarrico to Yvette Le Floc'h, September 2, 1961, PJP-LBJ.

19. Paul Jarrico to Yvette Le Floc'h, September 8, 1961, PJP-LBJ; Bill Jarrico, interview.

20. Sylvia Jarrico, interview; Jarrico, agenda book entries, September 16, 17, 1961, PJP-LBJ.

21. Paul Jarrico to Bill Jarrico, September 24, 1961, PJP-LBJ; Sylvia Jarrico to Bill Jarrico, October 20, 1961, PJP-LBJ.

22. Paul Jarrico to Nel King, October 31, 1961, PJP-MHL; Paul Jarrico to Ed Kraus, August 25, 1962, PJP-MHL.

23. Armelle Aymonin, e-mail message to the author, November 20, 2004. Jarrico supported her ambition to become an artist, and he and Yvette paid for her college and graduate studies in the United States. She is currently an interpreter, living in Paris.

24. Sylvia Jarrico, interview; Wilson, *Rebel and Architect*, 314, 405.

25. Sylvia Jarrico to Ed and Dot Kraus, October 17, 1961, March 22, 1962, PJP-LBJ.

26. Paul Jarrico to Yvette Le Floc'h, December 12, 1961, PJP-LBJ.

27. Paul Jarrico to Sylvia Jarrico, December 19, 1961, PJP-LBJ; Sylvia Jarrico to whom it may concern, n.d., PJP-LBJ.

28. Paul Jarrico to Arnaud d'Usseau, January 6, 1962, PJP-MHL; Paul Jarrico, note, March 15, 1962, PJP-MHL.

29. Paul Jarrico to George Marton, October 11, 27, 1962, PJP-MHL.

30. Paul Jarrico to Yvette Le Floc'h, February 5, 1963, PJP-LBJ; Yvette Le Floc'h to Paul Jarrico, February 6, PJP-LBJ.

31. Paul Jarrico, "Wagon History," 1963 agenda book, PJP-LBJ; Jarrico, agenda book entry, May 13, 1963, PJP-LBJ.

32. Paul Jarrico to George Marton, October 22, 1963, PJP-MHL; Paul Jarrico to Adrian Scott, October 22, 1963, PJP-MHL; Paul Jarrico to John Berry, October 26, 1963, PJP-MHL.

33. Jarrico, agenda book entry, December 9, 1963, PJP-LBJ; Paul Jarrico, "The Scott-Jarrico Conflict," December 15, 1963, PJP-MHL.

34. Jarrico, "Scott-Jarrico Conflict," PJP-MHL; Paul Jarrico to Michael Wilson, December 17, 1963, PJP-MHL.

35. Adrian Scott, telegram to Paul Jarrico, quoted in Jarrico, agenda book entry, December 26, 1963, PJP-LBJ; Lawrence Bachmann to Paul Jarrico, January 14, 1964, PJP-MHL; Paul Jarrico to Bill Jarrico, January 18, 1964, PJP-MHL; Paul Jarrico to Daniel Mainwaring, March 19, 1964, PJP-MHL. Although Jarrico and Mostel were friends, Mostel did not respond to Jarrico's letters regarding this screenplay or others in which Jarrico tried to interest him. When Jarrico later ran into him in New York, Jarrico refused to shake his hand and told him he was a "nothing." Jarrico, agenda book entry, February 2, 1965, PJP-LBJ. *The ABC Murders* was not made, and a few years later, Jarrico rewrote it as *Eyeball to Eyeball*.

36. Paul Jarrico to Adrian Scott, March 4, 1963, PJP-MHL; Joan Scott, interview by the author, July 4, 2002. In August 1971, Jarrico approached Scott at the memorial for Herbert Biberman. "When I said, 'Look, Adrian,

with Mike [Wilson] having a stroke and Herbert dying and none of us getting younger, don't you think we ought to settle this ridiculous business?' To which he replied no. I pressed him to explain what the hell was so important about a dispute over a script. '*You* knew,' he said, 'how insecure I was in that job.' And for the first time I did know." Paul Jarrico to Sylvia and Bill Jarrico, January 2, 1973, PJP-LBJ.

37. Paul Jarrico to Bill Jarrico, April 12, 1964, PJP-LBJ.

38. Yvette Le Floc'h to Lester and Kay Cole, May 27, 1964, PJP-MHL; Paul Jarrico to John Berry, May 28, 1964, PJP-MHL.

39. For the IPC trial, see chap. 10.

40. Paul Jarrico to Sylvia Jarrico, February 5, 1965, PJP-LBJ.

41. *Toronto Globe and Mail*, October 23, 1965, 18.

42. Leonard Boudin to Congressman Philip Burton, June 20, 1967, PJP-MHL; Yvette Le Floc'h to Paul Jarrico, n.d., PJP-LBJ; Paul Jarrico, notes, August 26, 1965, PJP-LBJ. Yvette applied again, in late 1966, after she and Jarrico had married, and was again refused. Jarrico asked a friend of a California congressman to inquire into the matter. Democratic congressman Jeffery Cohelan replied that the Department of State was not prepared to allow Yvette Jarrico to reenter the country for "a number of reasons," but he did not disclose those reasons. Jeffery Cohelan to Dave Jenkins, January 30, 1967, PJP-MHL. Dorothy Healey, in her memoirs, wrote that Yvette considered herself a Communist. Healey and Isserman, *Dorothy Healey Remembers*, 225.

43. Paul Jarrico to Naomi and David Robison, September 18, 1966, PJP-MHL; Paul Jarrico to Carl Marzani, August 3, 1966, PJP-MHL.

44. *Variety Film Reviews, 1968–1970* (New York: Garland, 1983), April 3, 1968.

45. Paul Jarrico to Sylvia Jarrico, June 26, 1966, PJP-LBJ. In 1929, Wechsler had contracted with Sergei Eisenstein to direct a film on abortion, *Frauennott—Frauenglück* (*Women's Misery—Women's Happiness*).

46. Paul Jarrico to Erwin Ellmann, May 27, 1996, PJP-MHL.

47. The movie was titled *Le rouble à deux faces* and dubbed into English as *The Day the Hot Line Got Hot*. Ironically, one of the stars of the movie was Robert Taylor, appearing in what would be his last film. The movie opened in San Francisco on December 24, 1969. It was not reviewed by the *New York Times*, *Variety*, or the *Hollywood Reporter*, and there are no reviews in the AMPAS library's clipping file or in Jarrico's papers.

48. Paul Jarrico to Lazar Wechsler, July 14, 1970, PJP-MHL; Paul Jarrico to Max Schoen, July 24, 1970, PJP-MHL.

49. Max E. Youngstein to Paul Jarrico, November 10, 1971, PJP-MHL; Richard Lester to Paul Jarrico, January 25, 1972, PJP-MHL; Gordon Davidson to Paul Jarrico, November 16, 1972, PJP-MHL; Dore Schary

to Paul Jarrico, December 29, 1972, PJP-MHL; Anthony Jones to Paul Jarrico, January 26, 1972, PJP-MHL.

50. Paul Jarrico to Lou Solomon, September 13, 1971, PJP-MHL; Paul Jarrico to David Jenkins, September 29, 1971, PJP-MHL.

51. Paul Jarrico to Sylvia Jarrico, February 1, 1972, PJP-LBJ; Paul Jarrico to Ian Hunter, July 4, 1972, PJP-MHL.

52. Jarrico, *Hollywood Blacklist*, 140–41.

53. Paul Jarrico to Sandy Ruben, January 6, 1975, in the possession of Sandy Ruben.

54. Paul Jarrico to Sylvia and Bill Jarrico, May 31, 1975, PJP-LBJ.

55. Paul Jarrico to Oliver Unger, December 19, 1975, PJP-MHL.

10. Political Battles, 1958–75

Epigraph: Paul Jarrico, interview by Haudiquet, revised ending, [ca. 1977], PJP-MHL.

1. The Parti communiste français would not, in any case, have been an inviting prospect for Jarrico. Under its longtime leader Maurice Thorez (d. 1964), the party acted more dogmatically and rigidly pro-Soviet than the CPUSA, strictly condemning all "deviations" (Titoist, Trotskyist, and opportunist) and remaining mostly isolated politically.

2. Dalton Trumbo to Albert Maltz, January 9, 1959, in Trumbo, *Additional Dialogue*, 470–71. Trumbo believed that the producers were ready to stop using the blacklist but that they would never publicly disavow it. If, he argued, blacklisted artists publicly and constantly stated that the blacklist was over, studio executives would come to accept that it was. Lawsuits would only embarrass and anger studio executives and resuscitate the "idiot right." Dalton Trumbo to Frank King, March 4, 1959, King Brothers Collection, AMPAS; Dalton Trumbo to Michael Wilson, February 24, 1959, in Trumbo, *Additional Dialogue*, 480–81.

3. Arnaud d'Usseau to Paul Jarrico, February 16, 1959, PJP-MHL; Tiba Willner to Paul Jarrico, February 11, April 9, 1959, PJP-MHL; Arnaud d'Usseau to Paul Jarrico, May 20, June 27, 1959, PJP-MHL; Paul Jarrico to Arnaud d'Usseau, July 18, 1959, PJP-MHL.

4. See Murray Schumach, "Hollywood Blues," *New York Times*, September 6, 1959, section 2, p. 7.

5. That and a smaller tract, *Red Stars*—No. 3, were issued by the Cinema Educational Guild in June 1959. General AMPAS file, box 6, Communist charges—1959, AMPAS.

6. *New York Times*, January 20, 1960, 1, 8; *Los Angeles Times*, January 20, 1960, 2; *Hollywood Reporter*, January 20, 1960, 1. Kirk Douglas, the producer

and star of *Spartacus*, later claimed that he broke the blacklist a few days before Preminger's announcement when he telephoned the gate attendant at Universal-International Films, where *Spartacus* was being filmed, to leave a pass there for Dalton Trumbo. Kirk Douglas, *The Ragman's Son: An Autobiography* (New York: Simon and Schuster, 1988), 323. See also Jeffery P. Smith, "'A Good Business Proposition': Dalton Trumbo, *Spartacus*, and the End of the Blacklist," *Velvet Light Trap* 23 (Spring 1989): 85.

7. *New York Times*, February 8, 1960, 1, 35.

8. Ibid., January 21, 1960, 26. Universal and Bryna waited until August 7 to announce that Trumbo would receive screen credit for *Spartacus*. Ibid., August 8, 1960, 25.

9. Ibid., February 9, 1960, 28, February 10, 1960, 43; *Weekly Variety*, March 21, 1960, 24, April 9, 1960, 1; Sidney Buchman to Paul Jarrico, April 6, 1960, PJP-MHL; Paul Jarrico to Bill Jarrico, April 27, 1960, PJP-MHL; *New York Times*, October 16, 1960, section 2, p. 9; Adrian Scott to Paul Jarrico, February 9, 1961, PJP-MHL; *New York Times*, September 5, 1960, 11.

10. Paul Jarrico to Bill Jarrico, February 5, 19, 1961, PJP-MHL; Paul Jarrico to Nel King, February 16, 1961, PJP-MHL; Paul Jarrico to Ben Margolis, June 14, 1962, PJP-MHL. Buchman left the project in early March.

11. Herbert Biberman to Paul Jarrico, March 28, 1961, PJP-MHL.

12. Paul Jarrico to George Brussel Jr., May 1, 1961, PJP-MHL; Ben Margolis to George Brussel Jr., May 3, 1961, PJP-MHL; Ben Margolis to Paul Jarrico, May 4, 1961, PJP-MHL; Edward Labaton to Ben Margolis, May 5, 1961, PJP-MHL; Paul Jarrico to Sylvia Jarrico, January 15, 1961, PJP-LBJ.

13. Jarrico deposition, *Independent Productions Corp. and I.P.C. Distributors, Inc. v. Loew's, Inc., et al.*, December 20, 1961, 1257–59.

14. Paul Jarrico to Ben Margolis and Herbert Biberman, August 26, 1964, PJP-MHL.

15. Ibid.

16. *New York Times*, November 14, 1964, 20. The verdict received very little coverage, and the comments of the plaintiffs none at all.

17. Harrison Salisbury, *New York Times*, September 8–15; Paul Jarrico to Chaim Shapiro, October 8, 1959, PJP-MHL; Paul Jarrico to Esther and Abram Shapiro, September 12, 1959, PJP-MHL.

18. Paul Jarrico to Dorothy Healey, August 23, 1960, PJP-MHL.

19. Jarrico had begun using Christmas as the occasion to make a political statement in 1953. That year, he and Sylvia and Bill sent out as a Christmas card a photograph of themselves carrying signs that read "PEACEFUL CO-EXISTENCE." Every year thereafter, he composed a poem or song (what he called his "Parodies Lost") and sent it to hundreds of people. The cards are in PJP-MHL.

20. Paul Jarrico to Bill Jarrico, March 11, 1962, PJP-LBJ; Paul Jarrico, "From the Credo to the Grave (A Revisionist Manifesto): Toward a Fundamental Revision of Marxist Theory as the Basis of a New Left Socialist Movement in the U.S.A.," n.d., PJP-MHL.

21. Paul Jarrico, "A Thought for Today . . . ," February 3, 1963, PJP-MHL.

22. Paul Jarrico to William and Christina Blake, February 2, 1964, PJP-MHL. There is no further correspondence on this project in Jarrico's papers.

23. Jarrico, agenda book entry, May 1, 1965, PJP-LBJ.

24. Healey and Isserman, *Dorothy Healey Remembers*, 224–26.

25. Paul Jarrico to Dorothy Healey, May 26, 1968, PJP-MHL.

26. For a good overview of the 1968 events, see Mark Kurlansky, *1968: The Year That Shook the World* (New York: Ballantine, 2004). For an analysis of the ensuing events, see Kieran Williams, *The Prague Spring and Its Aftermath: Czechoslovak Politics, 1968–1970* (Cambridge: Cambridge University Press, 1997).

27. Paul Jarrico to Abram and Esther Shapiro, November 10, 1968, PJP-MHL; Paul Jarrico to Vivienne Nearing, August 23, 1968, PJP-MHL.

28. Sigal, interview.

29. Paul Jarrico to Jules Dassin, June 26, 1970, PJP-MHL; Paul Jarrico to James Jones, June 28, PJP-MHL.

30. Paul Jarrico to Dorothy Healey, December 6, 1969, January 6, 1972, PJP-MHL.

31. Paul Jarrico to Michael Wilson, September 1, 1969, enclosing clipping of Ernst Fischer, "A Veteran Communist Warns the New Left," *Times* (London), August 20, 1969, 9, PJP-MHL.

32. Paul Jarrico and John Berry, confidential memorandum, July 28, 1972, PJP-MHL.

33. Henrik Stangerup to Paul Jarrico, February 8, 1974, PJP-MHL; Paul Jarrico to Henrik Stangerup, February 9, 1974, PJP-MHL; Paul Jarrico to Michael Wilson, February 26, 1974, PJP-MHL; Paul Jarrico to Henrik Stangerup, February 6, 1975, PJP-MHL; Henrik Stangerup to Paul Jarrico, February 10, 1975, PJP-MHL.

34. The MPLA (Popular Movement for the Liberation of Angola), formed in 1956, was the largest. It was originally supported by countries in western Europe and Africa, with some aid from the Soviet Union. By the time of the Jarricos' involvement, MPLA was receiving support from the USSR and Cuba. The FNLA (National Front for the Liberation of Angola) was formed in 1962, and it received funds from the United States, Zaire, and the People's Republic of China. I have not been able to discover how

Yvette became involved with UNITA, but Jarrico's involvement must seem incredible to those who know the path of its leader, Jonas Savimbi, in the years after Jarrico tried to assist him. For a balanced assessment of Savimbi, see James Ciment, *Angola and Mozambique: Postcolonial Wars in Southern Africa* (New York: Facts on File, 1997). For a pro-Savimbi perspective, see Fred Bridgland, *Jonas Savimbi: A Key to Africa* (Edinburgh: Mainstream, 1986).

35. Paul Jarrico to UNITA leaders, January 29, 1975, PJP-MHL; Paul Jarrico to Sylvia and Bill Jarrico, January 17, 1975, PJP-LBJ. In April, Yvette attended a press conference in Paris with Savimbi, and Jarrico recorded the following in his agenda book: "Home very late, shaken—Savimbi says they don't really know her." Jarrico, agenda book entry, April 14, 1975, PJP-LBJ. In the ensuing civil war, the USSR and Cuba supported the MPLA, and the United States funded an alliance of the FNLA, UNITA, Zaire, and Zambia. The MPLA defeated its opponents and established a people's republic in July 1976. UNITA continued to fight for more than two decades, with support from the Union of South Africa and the United States. In 1978, UNITA and the FNLA sponsored, in Lisbon, a conference against the Russian threat. Yvette wrote the historical introduction to the published speeches: *Angola, l'UNITA et le FNLA prennent le parole* (Paris: Mouvement pour l'indépendance et la liberté, 1978).

36. Paul Jarrico, interview by Haudiquet, revised ending, PJP-MHL.

11. Back in the USA, 1975–97

Epigraph: Paul Jarrico, quoted in Joseph McBride, "New Hollywood Freedom Elates Blacklist Exile Paul Jarrico," *Variety*, January 28, 1977, 1, 45.

1. Rosenfelt, *Salt of the Earth*; Barbara Zheutlin and David Talbot, *Creative Differences: Profiles of Hollywood Dissidents* (Boston: South End Press, 1978). Talbot, Zheutlin, Rosenfelt, and other members of the media group of the New American Movement organized an event they titled "The Hollywood Blacklist" at Oakwood School on September 6, 1975. It was one of the first postblacklist evenings. After a screening of *Hollywood on Trial*, Will Geer, John Randolph, Karen Morley, and Jarrico spoke.

2. Schwartz, *Hollywood Writers' Wars*; Ceplair and Englund, *Inquisition in Hollywood*; Navasky, *Naming Names*.

3. Paul Jarrico to Yvette Le Floc'h, April 9, 1976, PJP-LBJ; Paul Jarrico to Ed Kraus, August 14, 1976, PJP-MHL.

4. Lia Benedetti Jarrico, interview by the author, June 20, 2005.

5. Yvette was working on a novel and writing regularly for *Topafrica*. She later coauthored, with Elizabeth Kerby, an article on third world and cold war politics in Madeira, "A Taste of Madeira," *San Diego Magazine*, February 1980. Sylvia was working regularly with Elena Boder, with whom

she coauthored *The Boder Test of Reading-Spelling Patterns: A Diagnostic Test for Subtypes of Reading Disability* (New York: Grune and Stratton, 1982). She also worked with William Marshall on his one-person Frederick Douglass performance and the scripts for his *Blacula* movies.

6. Heidi Wall, e-mail message to the author, July 9, 2004; Don Newman, interview by the author, September 8, 2004; Melinda Jason (Phil Gersh Agency) to Paul Jarrico, February 12, 1980, PJP-MHL.

7. Paul Jarrico, *The Ghosts of Paha Sapa* (treatment), May 12, 1978, PJP-MHL; Paul Jarrico to John Beck, July 15, 1978, PJP-MHL; Paul Jarrico, notes on conversations with John Beck, [ca. late July 1978], PJP-MHL.

8. See Michael Leahy, "Gunned Down in a Cross Fire of Egos and Conflicting Demands," *TV Guide*, June 1–7, 1985, 36–39.

9. Paul Jarrico to Mark Carliner, October 17, 1991, PJP-MHL. Jarrico did not receive a cocredit because, in television, a cocredit required a 50 percent contribution. Jarrico calculated that he had altered about one-third of Monash's original script. That same year, Jarrico wrote a movie script about Richard Sorge, the Soviet spy who had warned Stalin about the pending German invasion. Two years later, he wrote a television script about Mikhail Gorbachev. Neither was produced.

10. Pancho Kohner, interview by the author, July 7, August 16, 2004; *Variety*, September 21, 1988, 3.

11. Paul Jarrico, "Leonardo, Genghis Khan and I: Problems in Dramatizing History," October 2, 25, 1982, PJP-MHL. The play was performed November 11–13 and 17–20.

12. Paul Jarrico to Matti Salo, June 30, 1988, PJP-MHL.

13. Paul Jarrico, note, October 4, 1994, PJP-MHL.

14. Paul Jarrico, proposal, 1994, PJP-MHL; Paul Jarrico to Pierre Rissient, [ca. November 1995], PJP-MHL; Paul Jarrico, "Genghis Khan as a Mega-Musical" (preliminary outline), June 1996, PJP-MHL; Paul Jarrico, "A Possible Structure of Genghis Khan as a Musical" (first draft), December 13, 1996, PJP-MHL.

15. Paul Jarrico, letter to the editor, *Los Angeles Times*, January 3, 1977.

16. Paul Jarrico, "An Open Letter to Gustav Husak," *Los Angeles Times*, March 2, 1977, section 2, p. 6. At the insistence of the Russians, Husak had in April 1969 replaced Dubček as head of the Czech Communist Party. For an account of the opposition to him, see Vladimir V. Kusin, *From Dubček to Charter 77: A Study of Normalisation in Czechoslovakia, 1968–1978* (Edinburgh: Q. Press, 1978).

17. Paul Jarrico, notes for KCET interview, December 29, 1981, PJP-MHL.

18. Paul Jarrico, "Some Remarks by Paul Jarrico at a WGAw Forum on the Blacklist," January 19, 1989 (typescript), PJP-MHL.

19. Jarrico, *Hollywood Blacklist*, 169–71.

20. Paul Jarrico, "What's Playing at Plato's Cave?" speech, European Film College, Ebeltoft, Denmark, September 5, 1996, PJP-MHL.

21. Stephanie Jenz, interview by the author, June 4, 2004.

22. His effort to control the rights to *Salt of the Earth* was hampered when, in 1982, a representative of the copyright office gave him the wrong information about the copyright renewal date. As a result, his application for renewal was rejected. Such a decision cannot be appealed.

23. Paul Jarrico to Richard Smith and Tony Grutman, August 30, 1978, PJP-MHL. When they rewrote it and sent it to him nineteen years later, he told them, "It's a good, well-written script, but I'm far too close to the subject to be an objective critic." For the most part, he added, it "rings true." Paul Jarrico to Tony Grutman, July 25, 1997, PJP-MHL.

24. Paul Jarrico to Marine Dominguez, July 13, 1985, PJP-MHL. Dominguez then contracted with Sylvia Morales to write a script. Morales said that Jarrico was supportive of her effort and generous with his time. Sylvia Morales, interview by the author, August 1, 2004. Two fund-raising benefits were held in 1987 and 1988, but Jarrico was not a sponsor of either. The film has not been made.

25. Frank Gruber, interview by the author, August 19, 2004.

26. Jarrico, agenda book entry, February 17, 1994, PJP-LBJ; Moctezuma and Esparza are currently working on a remake of the original with another company, headed by David Riker, in association with Michael Wilson's daughters.

27. Paul Jarrico to Karl Francis, March 22, 1995, May 5, 15, 1997, PJP-MHL; see Ceplair, "Many Fiftieth Anniversaries," 8–10.

28. *Esperanza*, music by David Bishop, libretto by Carlos Morton, directed by Karlos Moser. It was mentioned in the *Nation*, October 2, 2000, 9.

29. The First Amendment/Blacklist Project commissioned Jenny Holzer to design an installation. It consists of benches, plaques, and walkways with names and quotations. Jarrico, Frank Tarloff, the Levitts, Abe Polonsky, Jean Butler, and Joan Scott were among those on the committee.

30. Judy Chaikin, interview by the author, August 28, 2004. Jarrico had assisted Chaikin with her documentary *Legacy of the Hollywood Blacklist* (Direct Cinema Limited, 1987).

31. *Los Angeles Times*, November 3, 1997, F3; *LA Weekly*, November 7–13, 1997, 28.

32. Chaikin, interview. Meltzer, who had written scripts for Charlie Chaplin and Orson Welles, was killed in France in 1944. Jarrico and Meltzer were friends, and when Jarrico learned that Meltzer was missing in action, he devoted three pages of his journal to him and contemplated writing a

novel based on his life. Jarrico, journal entry, September 19, 1944, PJP-LBJ. Four years after Meltzer's death, the SWG initiated an award in his name, to be given to the script that most ably depicted American social problems. According to Dalton Trumbo, someone told the House Committee on Un-American Activities that Meltzer had been a Communist. Trumbo, *Additional Dialogue*, 570. Though Meltzer was not publicly named by any witness, FBI documents indicate that he was a party member. In any event, the SWG ceased giving the Meltzer award after 1951. It was reestablished in 1991, and Kirk Douglas was its first recipient.

Epilogue

Epigraph: Paul Jarrico, quoted in Larry Ceplair, "Who Wrote What? A Tale of a Blacklisted Writer and His Front," *Cineaste* 18, no. 2 (1991), 21.

1. Ibid.

2. Larry Ceplair, "Screenwriter Albert Maltz's Best-Kept Movie Secret," *Los Angeles Herald-Examiner*, June 2, 1985, F1, F4.

3. Matti Salo, *Hiljaiset Sankerit* (Helsinki: Painatuskekus/Suomen Elekuva-Arkisto, 1992). Salo translated it as *The Brave Ones: Hollywood's Blacklisted Screenwriters*. It covers the careers of fifty-three screenwriters. Salo first contacted Jarrico in August 1984, and an extensive correspondence ensued. Salo provided the blacklist credits committee with blacklisted writers' contact information, and Jarrico tried to get Salo's book translated and published in the United States. A translation of the section on Michael Wilson is in PJP-MHL.

4. WGAw board meeting, October 30, 1989, supplement to *WGAw Journal*, December–January 1990, n.p. Wilson had written two drafts of the *Lawrence of Arabia* script before leaving the project. Robert Bolt had then been assigned to rewrite Wilson. When the movie was released (by a British company), Wilson petitioned the British Screenwriters Guild for a cocredit. He was successful, but Columbia Pictures, the U.S. distributor of the film, refused to put Wilson's name on its prints. Jarrico believed that director David Lean was the main obstacle. Paul Jarrico, conversation with the author, January 1991.

5. Del Reisman, interview by the author, June 18, 2002.

6. *WGAw Journal*, August 1991, 16–19.

7. Barr had previously helped restore a composer credit for the blacklisted composer Larry Adler. Larry Adler, *It Ain't Necessarily So: An Autobiography* (New York: Grove Press, 1987), 181–85.

8. Joel Hodson, "Who Wrote 'Lawrence of Arabia'? Sam Spiegel and David Lean's Denial of Credit to a Blacklisted Writer," *Cineaste* 20, no. 4 (1994): 12–18; WGAw Journal, March 1995, 20.

9. WGAw blacklist credits committee, meeting notes, March 27, 1996, PJP-MHL.

10. Reisman, interview; Cathy Reed, interview by the author, July 15, 2002; Jenz, interview.

11. Reed, interview; Reisman, interview.

12. Paul Jarrico, "Some Observations," memorandum to WGAw blacklist credits committee, July 11, 1997, PJP-MHL.

13. Christopher Trumbo, e-mail messages to the author, May 27, 2004, October 17, 2005. Christopher Trumbo claimed that Dalton Trumbo had written an original script for *Roman Holiday* but admitted that the Trumbo family did not have a copy of that script. However, Christopher Trumbo had earlier told an interviewer that he had no knowledge of how much of his father's work had been incorporated in the final shooting script. Christopher Trumbo to Paul Jarrico, July 12, 1997, PJP-MHL; *Hollywood Reporter*, August 12, 1991, 1, 21. Hunter, however, had been telling interviewers that Trumbo had written only a very long treatment (seventy pages). Therefore, the committee members could not, according to their rules, give Trumbo a co–screenplay credit. For more details, see Dick, *Radical Innocence*, 203–4; Howard Suber, "Dalton Trumbo's Real Role in 'Roman Holiday,'" *Los Angeles Times*, August 19, 1991, F3; Ian Hunter, interview by Jan Herman, "Dalton Trumbo Asked Me to Front for Him," *Los Angeles Times*, August 25, 1991, 19, 85.

14. John Berry, eulogy of Paul Jarrico, in the possession of Lia Benedetti Jarrico. Norma Barzman read the eulogy at Jarrico's memorial.

INDEX